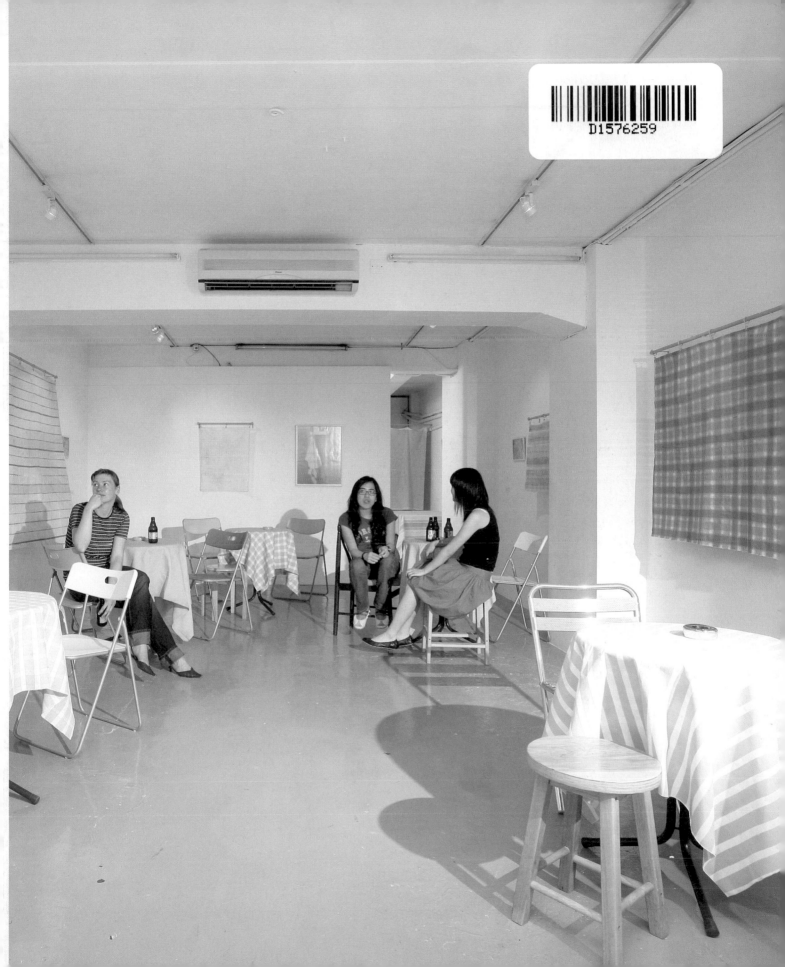

DIE PARKETT-REIHE MIT GEGENWARTSKÜNSTLERN / THE PARKETT SERIES WITH CONTEMPORARY ARTISTS

Book Series with contemporary artists in English and German, published two times a year. Each volume is created in collaboration with artists, who contribute an original work specially made for the readers of Parkett. The works are reproduced in the regular edition and available in a limited and signed Special Edition.

Buchreihe mit Gegenwartskünstlern in deutscher und englischer Sprache, erscheint zweimal im Jahr. Jeder Band entsteht mit Künstlern oder Künstlerinnen, die eigens für die Leser von Parkett einen Originalbeitrag gestalten. Diese Werke sind in der gesamten Auflage abgebildet und zusätzlich in einer limitierten und signierten Vorzugsausgabe erhältlich.

PARKETT 99 ERSCHEINT IN COLLABORATION MIT • OMER FAST, CAO FEI, ADRIAN GHENIE, LYNETTE YIADOM-BOAKYE • WILL BE COLLABORATING ON PARKETT NO. 99

JAHRESABONNEMENT (ZWEI NUMMERN) / ANNUAL SUBSCRIPTION (TWO ISSUES) SFR. 95.– (SCHWEIZ), 72 (EUROPA), US$ 78 (USA AND CANADA ONLY)

ZWEI- UND DREIJAHRESABONNEMENTPREISE SIEHE BESTELLKARTE IM HEFT / FOR TWO & THREE YEAR RATES, PLEASE CONSULT ORDER FORM. (S./P.227)

FO - Zürisee AG (Stäfa) Satz, Litho, Druck / Copy, Printing, Color Separations

PARKETT-VERLAG AG   ZÜRICH   JUNE 2016   PRINTED IN SWITZERLAND   ISBN 978-3-907582-58-9   ISSN 0256-0917

HEFTRÜCKEN / SPINE 96–99: CHUAN LUN

Cover: ED ATKINS, RIBBONS, 2014, 3-channel HD video / BÄNDER, 3-Kanal-HD-Video.

Back Cover: THEASTER GATES, GROUND RULES (FREE THROW POSSIBILITY), 2014, detail, wood flooring / GRUNDREGELN (FREI-WURF-MÖGLICHKEIT), Detail, Holzboden.

Cover Flap: LEE KIT, SUNDAY AFTERNOON: PICNIC WITH FRIENDS AND HAND-PAINTED CLOTH AT YUNG SHU O, SAI KUNG, 2003, acrylic on fabric, photo document / SONNTAGNACHMITTAG, PICKNICK MIT FREUNDEN UND HANDBEMALTEM TUCH, Acryl auf Stoff, Photodokument.

Inside cover flap: MIKA ROTTENBERG, NONOSEKNOWS, 2015, video with sound, sculptural installation / KEINENASEWEISS, Video mit Ton, skulpturale Installation.

Page 1: LEE KIT, "3/4 Suggestions for a better living," 2007, Para Site Art Space, Hong Kong, exhibition view / Ausstellungsansicht.

(All images slightly cropped / Alle Bilder leicht beschnitten.)

PARKETT Zürich New York

Bice Curiger Chefredaktorin / Editor-in-Chief; **Jacqueline Burckhardt** Redaktorin / Senior Editor; **Nikki Columbus** Redaktorin USA / Executive Editor US; **Mark Welzel** Redaktor / Editor; **Hanna Willamson · Simone Eggstein** Graphik / Design, **Trix Wetter** Graphisches Konzept / Founding Designer (–2001); **Catherine Schelbert** Englisches Lektorat / Editorial Assistant for English; **Claudia Meneghini Nevzadi & Richard Hall** Korrektorat / Proofreading

Beatrice Fässler Vorzugsausgaben, Inserate / Special Editions, Advertising; **Nicole Stotzer** Buchvertrieb, Administration / Distribution, Administration; **Božena Civic & Mathias Arnold** Abonnemente / Subscriptions; **Melissa Burgos** Vorzugsausgaben, Inserate und Abonnemente USA / Special Editions, Advertising, and Subscriptions US.

Jacqueline Burckhardt – Bice Curiger – Dieter von Graffenried Herausgeber / Parkett Board;
Jacqueline Burckhardt – Bice Curiger – Dieter von Graffenried – Walter Keller – Peter Blum Gründer / Founders

Dieter von Graffenried Verleger / Publisher

www.parkettart.com

PARKETT-VERLAG AG, QUELLENSTRASSE 27, CH-8031 ZÜRICH, TEL. 41-44-271 81 40, FAX 41-44-272 43 01
PARKETT, NEW YORK, 145 AV. OF THE AMERICAS, N.Y. 10013, PHONE (212) 673-2660, FAX (212) 271-0704

EDITORIAL 98

Issues of materiality, embodiment, and subjectivity are explored in this volume of *Parkett*. Our four artist-collaborators tackle the vast questions of who we are as individuals, how we interact with others, and what we create with our labor.

The videos of Ed Atkins feature solitary avatars whose prolix and euphuistic monologues—written and voiced by the artist—plumb the sorrily sentimental and the sordidly somatic. Always white and male, these hyperreal, high-definition, digitally animated talking heads seem to be suffering, or are "perhaps just insufferable" (Leslie Jamison, p. 36).

Theaster Gates's practice spans sculpture and ceramics, architecture and urban planning, operating within a "circular economy" that connects "underserved black communities on the South Side of Chicago with the institutional art world" (Andrew Herscher, p. 66). Materials from disused buildings are transformed into gallery-ready art objects, the sales of which fund the structures' renovation and repurposing as neighborhood archives and meeting spaces.

Long concerned with the privatization of public space in Hong Kong, Lee Kit has sought both to occupy and to withdraw, alternating between interaction and interiority. He salvages the imprints of our bodies—stains, shadows, scrawled words—with simple materials like cotton or cardboard, creating works that overlap multiple genres, at once domestic still lifes and landscapes, self-portraits and history paintings (Doryun Chong, p. 110).

Finally, human traces are packaged as commercial products in Mika Rottenberg's colorfully abject allegories of global capitalism. Splicing together fictional scenarios performed by actors and documentary footage of factory workers, her videos depict elaborate assembly lines of women interlinked across time and space. The resulting works are "more realistic than most Realism" as they lay bare the "strange imperatives imposed on life and labor by the exigencies of universal commodification" (Jonathan Beller, p. 155).

Inspired by museum objects and displays, the Insert (p. 193) by Iman Issa offers a photographic collection imagining the various forms that materials can take.

Nikki Columbus and Bice Curiger

EDITORIAL 98

Materialität, Verkörperung und Subjektivität sind die Themenkreise, die in diesem *Parkett*-Band untersucht werden. Unsere vier Collaboration-Künstler greifen so gewaltige Fragen auf wie: «Wer sind wir als Individuen?», «Wie interagieren wir mit anderen?» und «Was schaffen wir durch unsere Arbeit?»

Die Videos von Ed Atkins zeigen einsame Avatare, deren weitschweifige und gespreizte – vom Künstler verfasste und gesprochene – Monologe das traurig Sentimentale und erbärmlich Somatische ausloten. Die stets männlichen und weissen, animierten sprechenden Köpfe scheinen zu leiden oder sind «vielleicht nur unerträglich» (Leslie Jamison, S. 42).

Theaster Gates' Kunst umfasst Skulptur und Keramik, Architektur und Städtebau, und sie funktioniert in Form einer «Kreislaufwirtschaft», welche «die benachteiligten schwarzen Gemeinden auf Chicagos Südseite mit der institutionellen Kunstwelt (...) verbindet» (Andrew Herscher, S. 76). Materialien aus stillgelegten Gebäuden werden in ausstellungsfertige Kunstobjekte verwandelt, aus deren Verkauf die Sanierung und der Umbau des Gebäudes finanziert werden: zu Archivräumen und Treffpunkten für die Einwohner des jeweiligen Stadtviertels.

Die Privatisierung des öffentlichen Raums in Hongkong beschäftigt Lee Kit schon längere Zeit. Hin und her gerissen zwischen Besetzung und Rückzug, Interaktion und Innerlichkeit, birgt er die Spuren unserer Körper – Flecken, Schatten, hingekritzelte Worte – mithilfe einfacher Materialien wie Baumwolle oder Karton und schafft Werke, in denen sich die Gattungen überlagern, zugleich häusliche Stillleben und Landschaften, Selbstporträts und Historienbilder (Doryun Chong, S. 117).

In Mika Rottenbergs grellbunten Allegorien des globalen Kapitalismus schliesslich sind die menschlichen Spuren als Handelsprodukt verpackt. Ihre Videos verquicken von Schauspielern gespielte fiktive Szenarien mit Dokumentarfilmmaterial von echter Fabrikarbeit. Wir sehen die anspruchsvolle Fliessbandarbeit von Frauen, die über Zeit und Raum hinweg miteinander vernetzt sind. Die so entstandenen Werke sind «realistischer als fast der gesamte Realismus» und entlarven «die seltsamen Lebens- und Arbeitszwänge, die mit der allumfassenden Kommerzialisierung einhergehen» (Jonathan Beller, S. 164).

Das *Insert* von Iman Issa (S. 193) ist von Museumsobjekten und -auslagen inspiriert und präsentiert eine photographische Sammlung möglicher Formen, die Materialien annehmen können.

Nikki Columbus und Bice Curiger

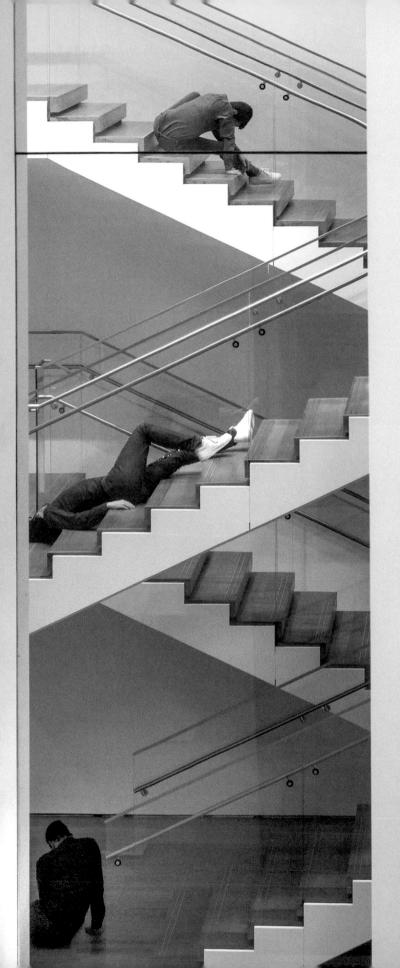

MARIA HASSABI, PLASTIC, 2015, Museum of Modern Art, New York, 2016, performers: Michael Helland, Niall Jones, Tara Lorenzen. (PHOTO: THOMAS PORAVAS)

DEATH BECOMES HER:

MARIA HASSABI AT THE MUSEUM

CLAIRE BISHOP

For almost as long as museums have existed, they have been criticized as mausoleal: the place that art goes to die. A whole slew of notable thinkers—from Quatremère de Quincey to Nietzsche to Adorno to Douglas Crimp—have argued that these institutions sever the work of art from its own time and a direct connection to life; in the museum, art is no longer something to be lived with, but something to be stared at by a passive, alienated viewer.[1] Strangely, the recent incursion of dance and performance into museum institutions, which has gathered such momentum over the last decade, has occasioned a new iteration of this familiar narrative, but reframed as a positive assessment. Consider, for example, Hal Foster's recent piece in the *Art Newspaper*, "In Praise of Dead Art": Skeptical of the institutional rehabilitation of performance art as a strategy to "activate" the museum, he argues that the work of art was never alive in the first place.[2]

CLAIRE BISHOP is professor in the PhD Program in Art History at the Graduate Center, City University of New York.

Walking into New York's Museum of Modern Art earlier this year, where Greek Cypriot choreographer Maria Hassabi and a team of sixteen dancers were performing her work *PLASTIC*, one would be forgiven for thinking that the museum was not only a repository of dead art but also of dead performance. The dancers resembled lifeless bodies strewn on the Atrium floor and two staircases, as if recently shot or felled by hazardous radiation. This impression was particularly striking when viewed from above, a perspective that rendered the dancers' prone and sprawled bodies more visible—not least Hassabi herself, contorted on the main staircase beneath the permanent installation of a green Bell-47D1 helicopter. The abject horizontality contrasted with the tribes of vertical visitors who either stared at, walked past, or stepped over the dancers as if nothing were happening. This was performance as the antithesis of activation: Rather than animating the space, *PLASTIC* formed a counterpoint composition of still bodies that underscored the sepulchral quality of the museum. If the audience was animated by this necrospectacle, it was only to the extent of taking photographs: the zombie automatism of reaching for an iPhone and seizing the perfect shot.

Of course, the dancers in PLASTIC—which was presented last year on a smaller scale at the Hammer Museum in Los Angeles and the Stedelijk Museum in Amsterdam—are not entirely still. Movements are incremental to the point of only just being visible; it took two hours, for example, for Hassabi to descend the twenty-four steps of MoMA's main staircase. In the meantime, streams of visitors trudged past her, herded by a solicitous gallery guard. Like most performance in the museum, this was disarmingly low-tech: no stage, no seating, no special lighting to demarcate the performance area, and no props or special effects. Nor was there an official beginning or end to the work, just a continual performance during opening hours. Unusually, however, music was deployed (an ambient soundscape by Morten Norbye Halvorsen and Marina Rosenfeld), and the performers wore costumes, albeit ones that only subtly differentiated them from the crowd: a uniform gray denim (styled by threeASFOUR) matching the color of MoMA's floor, with flashes of crystals on the inseams of the legs.

The risk, of course, was that such artful soundscape and styling, combined with the pseudocatastrophic poses, might resemble a fashion shoot—but PLASTIC willingly consorted with the photographic and the sculptural, the two modes to which contemporary performance in the museum is most readily compared. Tim Griffin discusses the former in his essay on MoMA's website: All performance today, he writes, has an "imagistic quality . . . either modeled after photographic documentation of performances from the past—obtaining, in effect, the virtual sensibility of a picture rendered in space, or anticipating their own photographic reproduction and circulation as so many images in turn."[3] PLASTIC was certainly Instagram fodder: It was hard to watch the performance without being aware of multiple visitors photographing the dancers. And yet most of these images uploaded to social media attempt to "purify" the performance by cropping out the audience. PLASTIC created a social situation but was recoded as living sculpture.

All of which is not surprising, as the sculptural has become the go-to analogy for live art in the museum. Curiously, there is a reluctance among a certain sector of the art world to use the word performance to describe performance in the gallery; instead, the work is said to approach the condition of sculpture.[4] Dorothea von Hantelmann describes Tino Sehgal's KISS (2004) as a sculpture because "one can move around this 'freestanding' work and view it from all sides," while Klaus Biesenbach observed that the performers re-enacting Marina Abramović's works in her 2010 retrospective "will be present as if they were sculpture."[5] Performance historian Rebecca Schneider has suggested that the insistence on aligning performance with sculpture is a way of validating this work against "the messy, impure, and historically feminized performance-based arts of theatre and dance."[6] She suggests that, for the art world, live art needs to be affiliated with sculpture in order to reassert a privileged (i.e., financialized) relationship to aura, exclusivity, and reproduction.[7]

Yet even though PLASTIC tarries with the sculptural[8]—the very word evokes the shaping or modeling of form—I would argue that the more accurate paradigm for Hassabi's PLASTIC derives from digital technology. The core structure of this work, as with many performances in the gallery space, is the automated loop, a mechanism synonymous with the compact disc and the DVD, respectively introduced in the 1980s and 1990s.[9] For example, during the 2013 Venice Biennale, Hassabi presented INTERMISSION inside a Brutalist gymnasium dating from the 1970s.[10] The choreographer and two other dancers moved diagonally down the bleachers at a glacial pace, falling in perfectly poised slow-motion over the steeply raked seating. INTERMISSION was performed for seven hours a day for seven days, and relied upon the structure of the loop not just in the overall structure of top-to-bottom descent but in the sequence of movements within each trajectory. When one of the dancers reached the bottom, having deftly avoided the sculptures that were also installed on the bleachers, she disappeared briefly before returning to the back of the stadium to recommence her barely perceptible diagonal descent. The dancers' actions were both quotidian and inexplicable, and the atmo-

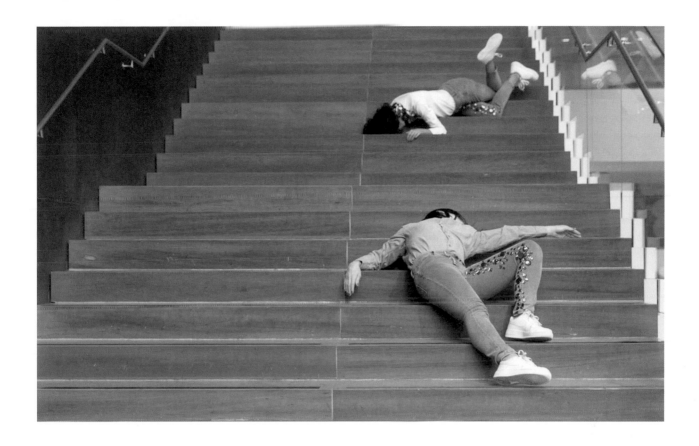

MARIA HASSABI, PLASTIC, 2015, Museum of Modern Art, New York, 2016. (PHOTO: THOMAS PORAVAS)

sphere was otherworldly. INTERMISSION introduced a temporality entirely remote from the frenetic pace with which one normally consumes the Biennial. Slouched on the bleachers, rapt in the performers' quiet intensity, one entered a different time zone, a suspended deceleration of body and mind.

The same logic of the loop governs PLASTIC: "Stillness here is held much longer than in my theater works," Hassabi explains, "[and] because we need to sustain the 'loop,' which is essentially the structure of the work, counting becomes very important." Each of the movements is performed according to counts, "and we synchronize our rhythm of counting with the iPhone timer in the morning—like little machines."[11] It seems telling that despite the stripped-

down character of dance in the museum, in which the theatrical apparatus is rejected in order to expose the "degree zero" of choreography—bodies in space and time—technology re-enters the frame as a method of organizing duration. This digital logic is what decisively separates this work from the art-historical paradigm of sculpture. At the same time, PLASTIC also foregrounds the non-mediated and non-technological: a confrontation with physical materiality as the dancers press themselves against and into the building's floors and steps. This gravitational pull into the (nominally) dirty ground beneath our feet, rather than identifying with the elevated sterile whiteness of the museum's vertical walls, could not be less virtual in its physicality.

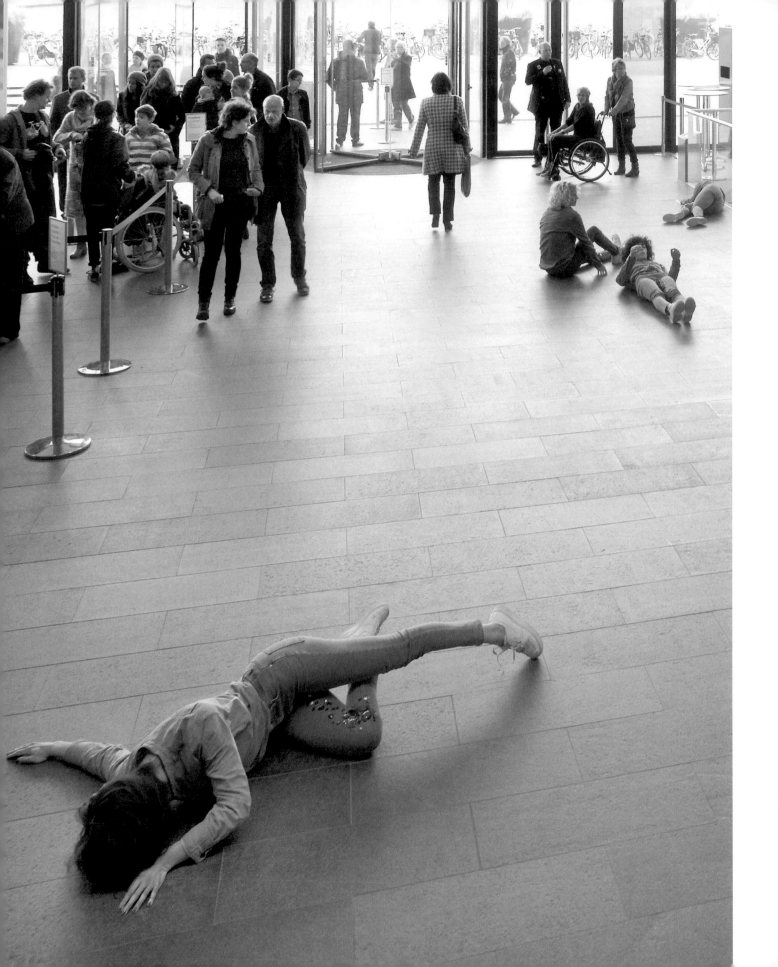

The adaptability implicit in the word *PLASTIC* could even be stretched to encompass the social choreography of the museum and its behavioral codes, flows of traffic, patterns of movement, and habits of attention. Hassabi and her dancers were alternately rushed past, ignored, tiptoed around, stepped over, intrusively photographed, or watched for long durations of time. Performing on the crowded main staircase, Hassabi was precariously close to being trampled by the daily traffic of MoMA's tourists. The performers in the Atrium, meanwhile, slumped on or off sofas and lay elegantly motionless on the floor; occasionally, visitors sat close by, more interested in their phones than in observing the dance taking place within inches of their bodies. The scale of the Atrium, whose lower walls were painted gray to match the floor and costumes, also contributed to the relative invisibility of the dancers. The most effective performance area was the staircase connecting the fourth and fifth floors of the painting and sculpture collection. In this tightly contained frame, one or two performers gradually inched down the stairs; their eyes, if they met ours at all, were glazed and inscrutable. Occasionally, a visitor would step over them, which produced an awkward tension verging on violation.

That the public's own choreography was exposed through *PLASTIC*'s stillness also underscores the crucial difference between the art object (photography, sculpture) and the performing body. Performance in the gallery stages the public as much as it stages itself—although any claim to publicness needs to take into account the enormous restructuring of the boundary between public and private that has taken place in the last decades under the pressure of a neoliberal economic project, on the one hand, and digital technologies and social media, on the other. Both formations have troubled the existence of "public space" and both have an intimate relationship to temporality and attention. But the collective presence of the public—in however fraught and compromised a form—is arguably the core of what animates the museum, not performance (or photography, sculpture, painting, or any other medium). This is not to essentialize the ineffable humanism of live performance (a claim already problematized by Hassabi's necrospectacular aesthetics) but to note that the migration of dance into the museum occasions both a social choreography and photographic remediation. These responses enable us to grasp the way in which, today, collective presence is as important as selective semi-absence: a syncopated time in which we fall in and out of step with our surroundings.

1) For a good summary of these positions, see Didier Maleuvre, *Museum Memories* (Stanford, CA: Stanford University Press, 1999).
2) Hal Foster, "In Praise of Dead Art," *Art Newspaper*, September 18, 2015, www.theartnewspaper.com/comment/reviews/books/hal-foster-in-praise-of-dead-art. The article is an excerpt from the final chapter of Foster's *Bad New Days* (London: Verso, 2015).
3) Tim Griffin, "Living Contradiction," www.moma.org/momaorg/shared/pdfs/docs/calendar/MariaHassabi_FINAL_V5.pdf, 1.
4) Throughout the 2000s, Tino Sehgal argued that his "situations" were best thought of as sculpture, present in the gallery during the entire working day: "[I] was trying to fulfill all conventions to make my work comparable to a traditional sculpture." Sehgal, quoted in Elizabeth Carpenter, "Be the Work: Intersubjectivity in Tino Sehgal's *This Objective of that Object*," Walker Art Center blog, 2014, www.walkerart.org/collections/publications/performativity/be-the-work.
5) Dorothea von Hantelmann, *How to Do Things with Art* (Zurich: JRP Ringier, 2010), 137; Klaus Biesenbach, quoted in Rebecca Schneider, *Performing Remains: Art and War in Times of Theatrical Reenactment* (New York: Routledge, 2011), 130.
6) Schneider, *Performing Remains*, 130.
7) Such a position also reinforces the art world's wariness of spectacle and entertainment, summed up in visual art's long-standing "anti-theatrical prejudice." See Jonas Barish, *The Antitheatrical Prejudice* (Berkeley: University of California Press, 1981).
8) However, it is notable that Hassabi doesn't refer to her work as sculpture but as "live installation," since it occupies a longer duration and invites a different attention span from her theatrical productions.
9) Even though film began to be shown in art galleries as early as the late 1960s, this was in a theatrical mode (i.e., screened from beginning to end). Displaying film on a loop only arose in the wake of the precedent set by the continuous loop of the CD and DVD.
10) INTERMISSION was performed as part of the Cyprus and Lithuania pavilion, curated by Raimundas Malašauskas.
11) Maria Hassabi, e-mail to the author, November 7, 2015.

DER TOD STEHT IHR GUT:

MARIA HASSABI IM MUSEUM

CLAIRE BISHOP

Seit es Museen gibt, wurden sie wiederholt als Mausoleen beschimpft: Orte, wo die Kunst nur hinkommt, um zu sterben. Eine ganze Reihe namhafter Denker – von Quatremère de Quincey über Nietzsche und Adorno bis zu Douglas Crimp – vertraten die Ansicht, dass diese Institutionen das Kunstwerk aus seiner Zeit und seinem direkten Lebenszusammenhang herausreissen; im Museum ist die Kunst nichts mehr, mit dem man zusammenlebt, sondern etwas, das von einem passiven, entfremdeten Betrachter angestarrt wird.[1] Seltsamerweise gab jedoch die Tatsache, dass neuerdings auch Tanz und Performance in den Museen Einzug halten – eine Tendenz, die sich in den letzten zehn Jahren noch verstärkt hat –, Anlass zur Wiederholung dieser alten Argumentation, diesmal jedoch ins Positive gewendet. Schauen wir etwa Hal Fosters jüngsten Beitrag in *Art Newspaper* an, «In Praise of Dead Art» (Lob der toten Kunst): Gegen-

über der institutionellen Rehabilitation der Performance als «Aktivierungsstrategie» für das Museum hegt er seine Zweifel und behauptet schlicht, dass das Kunstwerk *per se* noch nie lebendig gewesen sei.[2]

Jedem, der seinen Fuss dieses Frühjahr ins New Yorker Museum of Modern Art gesetzt hat, als die griechisch-zypriotische Choreographin Maria Hassabi mit einer Truppe von 15 Tänzerinnen das Stück *PLASTIC* inszenierte, hätte man den Gedanken verziehen, dass das Museum nicht nur die Ruhestätte toter Kunst, sondern auch toter Performance sei. Die Tänzerinnen glichen leblosen, über den Boden des Atriums und zwei Treppen verstreuten Leibern, als wären sie soeben erschossen oder von einer gefährlichen Strahlung dahingerafft worden. Besonders eklatant war dieser Eindruck von oben betrachtet, einem Blickwinkel, aus dem die hingestreckten und -gespreizten Körper der Tänzerinnen besonders gut zu sehen waren – nicht zuletzt Hassabi selbst, die seltsam verdreht auf der Haupttreppe unter der permanenten Installation eines grünen Bell-47D1-Heli-

CLAIRE BISHOP ist Professorin für Kunstgeschichte am Graduate Center der City University of New York.

MARIA HASSABI, PLASTIC, 2015, Museum of Modern Art, New York, 2016, performer: Maria Hassabi. (PHOTO: THOMAS PORAVAS)

MARIA HASSABI, INTERMISSION, 2013, installation view, Cyprus and Lithuanian Pavilion, 55ᵗʰ Venice Biennale, performers: Hristoula Harakas, Maria Hassabi; artwork by PHANOS KYRIACOU, ELEVEN HOSTS, TWENTY-ONE GUESTS, NINE GHOSTS, 2013, mixed media / UNTERBRECHUNG, Installationsansicht; ELF GASTGEBER, EINUNDZWANZIG GÄSTE, NEUN GEISTER, verschiedene Materialien. (PHOTO: ROBERTAS NARKUS)

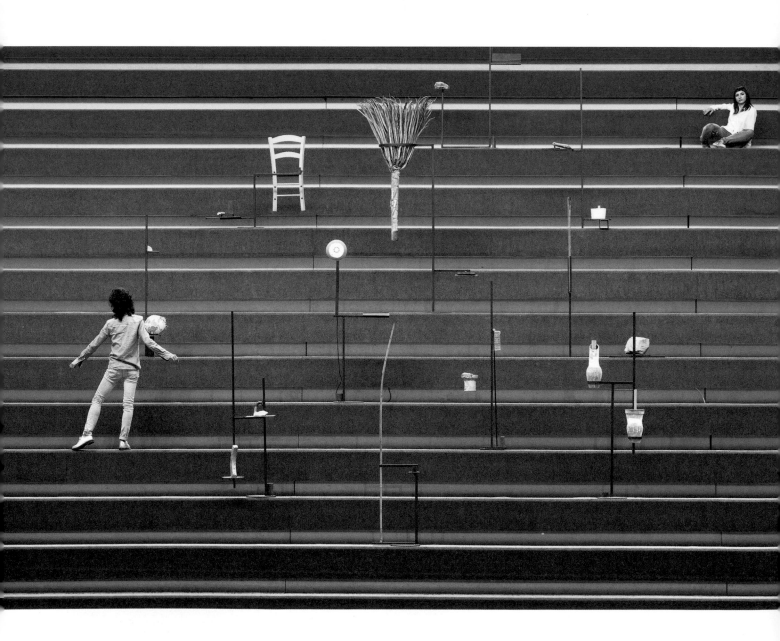

köpfeis lag. Ihre elenden horizontalen Stellungen standen in starkem Kontrast zur aufrechten Haltung der Horde von Besuchern, die aufrecht daherkamen und die Tänzerinnen entweder anstarrten, an ihnen vorbeigingen oder über sie hinwegschritten, als wären sie gar nicht da. Diese Performance war die Antithese jeglicher Aktivierung: Statt den Raum zu beleben, war *PLASTIC* eine kontrapunktische Komposition aus reglosen Leibern, die den sepulkralen Charakter des Museums hervorhob. Die belebende Wirkung dieses Nekrospektakels auf das Publikum beschränkte sich auf eifriges Photographieren: auf den zombiehaften Reflex, sein iPhone zu zücken und einen gelungenen Schnappschuss zu schiessen.

Natürlich sind die Tänzerinnen in *PLASTIC* – das letztes Jahr in etwas bescheidenerem Rahmen auch im Hammer Museum in Los Angeles und im Stedelijk Museum in Amsterdam zu sehen war – nicht völlig reglos. Doch ihre Bewegungen erfolgen in kleinen, kaum sichtbaren Schritten; es dauerte beispielsweise zwei Stunden, bis es Hassabi über die 24 Stufen der grossen Treppe im MoMA hinuntergeschafft hatte. Inzwischen waren ganze Ströme von Besuchern an ihr vorbeigetrottet, angetrieben von einer beflissenen Museumsaufsicht. Wie die meisten

Performanceauftritte in Museen war auch dieser mit entwaffnend wenig technischem Aufwand verbunden: keine Bühne, keine Sitzplätze, keine spezielle Beleuchtung zur Abgrenzung des Auftrittsbereichs und keinerlei Requisiten oder Spezialeffekte. Das Werk war ohne offiziellen Anfang oder Ende, es war einfach eine kontinuierliche Performance im Rahmen der üblichen Öffnungszeiten. Ungewöhnlich war jedoch, dass Musik zum Einsatz kam (eine Umgebungsklangkulisse von Morten Norbye Halvorsen und Marina Rosenfeld), und die Tänzerinnen trugen Kostüme, allerdings solche, die sie kaum vom Publikum abhoben: einheitlich graue, auf die Farbe des Bodens im MoMA abgestimmte Shirts und Jeans (von threeASFOUR) mit blitzenden Glaskristallen entlang der Jeans-Innennähte.

Es bestand natürlich die Gefahr, dass eine so kunstvolle Klanglandschaft und Ausstattung in Kombination mit den pseudokatastrophischen Posen wie eine Modeaufnahme wirken konnte – *PLASTIC* flirtete jedoch ganz bewusst mit Photographie und Skulptur, jenen beiden Gattungen, mit denen die zeitgenössische Performance in Museen am ehesten verglichen wird. Hinsichtlich der Photographie äussert sich Tim Griffin in seinem Essay auf der MoMA-Website: Heute

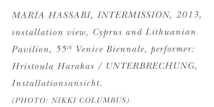

MARIA HASSABI, INTERMISSION, 2013, installation view, Cyprus and Lithuanian Pavilion, 55th Venice Biennale, performer: Hristoula Harakas / UNTERBRECHUNG, Installationsansicht.
(PHOTO: NIKKI COLUMBUS)

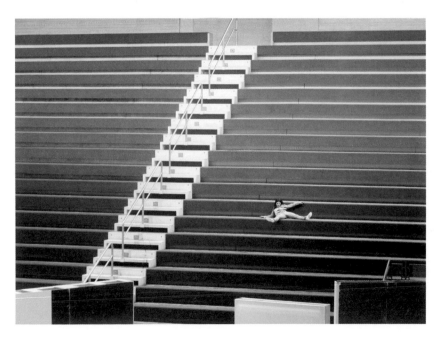

besitzt jede Performance, schreibt er, eine «bildhafte Qualität …, die sich entweder an photographischen Dokumentationen früherer Performances orientiert – und dadurch die virtuelle Sinnlichkeit eines im Raum dargestellten Bildes erhält –, oder aber ihre eigene photographische Reproduktion und Verbreitung in weiteren Bildern vorwegnimmt».[3] *PLASTIC* war natürlich ein gefundenes Fressen für Instagram: Es war fast unmöglich, sich die Performance anzuschauen, ohne zugleich die vielen photographierenden Besucher wahrzunehmen. Dennoch wurde in den meisten der in den Social Media hochgeladenen Aufnahmen versucht, das Publikum auszublenden. *PLASTIC* schuf zwar eine soziale Situation, wurde jedoch zur lebenden Skulptur umgedeutet.

Das ist durchaus nicht überraschend, denn die Skulptur wird inzwischen gern als naheliegende Analogie zur Live-Kunst im Museum bemüht. Seltsamerweise verwendet man in einem gewissen Bereich der

Kunstwelt das Wort Performance nur widerstrebend, sobald es um Performance im Ausstellungsraum geht, und sagt stattdessen lieber, das Werk weise weitgehend die Züge einer Skulptur auf.[4] Dorothea von Hantelmann bezeichnet Tino Sehgals KISS (Kuss, 2004) als Skulptur, denn «man kann sich um dieses ‹frei stehende› Werk herumbewegen und es von allen Seiten betrachten», während Klaus Biesenbach bemerkte, dass die Darsteller, die Marina Abramovićs Werke in deren Retrospektive 2010 nachvollziehen sollten, «so präsent sein werden, als wären sie Teil einer Skulptur».[5] Die Performance-Historikerin Rebecca Schneider gab der Vermutung Ausdruck, dass es bei dem beharrlichen Vergleich von Performance und Skulptur vor allem darum gehe, diese Kunst von «den chaotischen, unreinen und historisch vorwiegend weiblich konnotierten Darstellungskünsten in Tanz und Theater» abzugrenzen.[6] Sie nimmt an, dass Live-Kunst für die Kunstwelt mit der plastischen Kunst in Verbindung gebracht werden muss, um ihr dieselben privilegierten (das heisst finanziell verwertbaren) Umstände der Ausstrahlung, Exklusivität und Reproduktion zu sichern.[7]

Doch obwohl *PLASTIC* mit dem Skulpturalen flirtet[8] – allein schon der Titel evoziert das Gestalten und Modellieren einer Form –, möchte ich behaupten, dass das eigentliche Paradigma für Hassabis *PLASTIC* der Digitaltechnik entliehen ist. Die zentrale Struktur des Werks ist – wie bei vielen Performancearbeiten im Ausstellungsraum – die automatisierte Endlosschleife, der Loop, das heisst derselbe Mechanismus wie bei den CDs oder DVDs, die in den 1980er beziehungsweise 1990er Jahren aufkamen.[9]

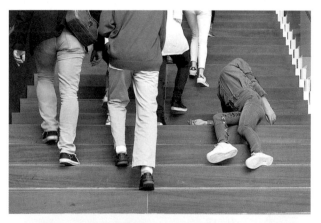

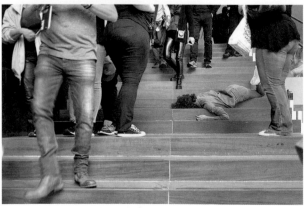

MARIA HASSABI, PLASTIC, 2015,
Museum of Modern Art, New York, 2016,
performer: Maria Hassabi.
(PHOTO: THOMAS PORAVAS)

16

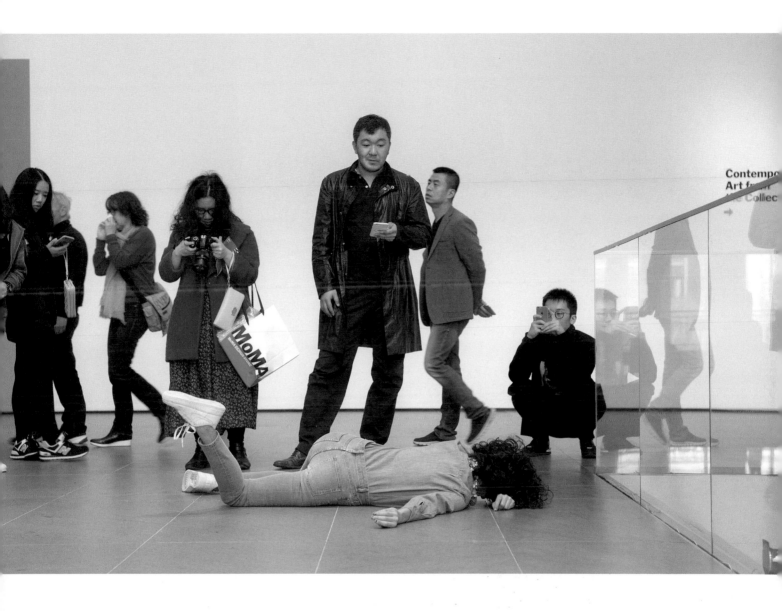

MARIA HASSABI, PLASTIC, 2015, Museum of Modern Art, New York, 2016, performer: Maria Hassabi. (PHOTO: THOMAS PORAVAS)

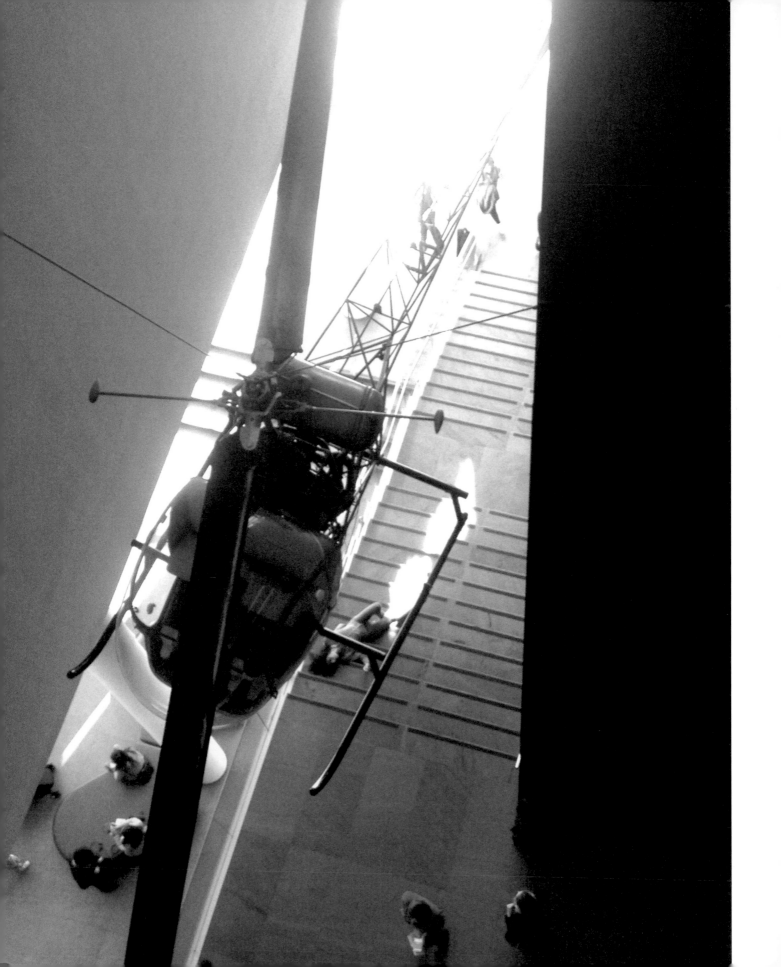

So präsentierte Hassabi beispielsweise an der Biennale Venedig 2013 das Werk INTERMISSION in einer brutalistischen Beton-Turnhalle aus den 1970er-Jahren.[10] Die Choreographin und zwei weitere Tänzerinnen bewegten sich im Zeitlupentempo diagonal über die Tribünenstufen herunter, indem sie sich in perfekt ausbalancierter Slow Motion über die steil abfallenden Sitzreihen fallen liessen. INTERMISSION wurde sieben Tage lang täglich während sieben Stunden gezeigt und basierte auf der Struktur der Endlosschleife, nicht nur hinsichtlich des Gesamtablaufs von oben nach unten, sondern auch in der Abfolge der einzelnen Bewegungsschritte innerhalb jedes Bewegungsablaufs. Wenn eine der Tänzerinnen unten ankam, nachdem sie den ebenfalls auf den Tribünen installierten Skulpturen geschickt ausgewichen war, verschwand sie kurz, bevor sie zur Rückseite der Tribüne zurückkehrte und ihren kaum wahrnehmbaren diagonalen Abstieg erneut in Angriff nahm. Die Handlungen der Tänzerinnen waren ebenso alltäglich wie unerklärlich, die Atmosphäre gespenstisch. INTERMISSION brachte eine Zeitlichkeit ins Spiel, die zu dem fieberhaften Tempo, mit dem man gewöhnlich an der Biennale unterwegs ist, in krassem Gegensatz stand. Man fläzte sich auf der Tribüne hin, verlor sich in der stillen Intensität der Tänzerinnen und betrat eine andere Zeitzone – eine schwebende Entschleunigung von Körper und Geist.

Dieselbe Logik der Endlosschleife bestimmt auch PLASTIC: «Die Reglosigkeit wird hier viel länger beibehalten als in meinen Theaterarbeiten», erläutert Hassabi, «[und] weil wir den ‹Loop›, der im Wesentlichen die Struktur des Werks ausmacht, aufrechterhalten müssen, wird das Zählen extrem wichtig. Jede Darstellerin zählt alles, was wir machen, und wir synchronisieren unseren Zählrhythmus jeden Morgen mit dem iPhone-Timer – wie kleine Maschinen.»[11] Es ist aufschlussreich, dass die Digitaltechnik hier erneut als Methode der Zeitorganisation ins Spiel

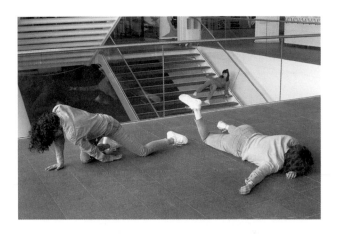

MARIA HASSABI, PLASTIC, 2015, Stedelijk Museum, Amsterdam, 2015. (PHOTO: ERNST VAN DEURSEN)

kommt, trotz der demontierten Form des Tanzes im Museum und dem Verzicht auf jegliche Bühnenmaschinerie, um zum Nullpunkt der Choreographie zu gelangen: Körper in Raum und Zeit. Die digitale Logik hebt dieses Werk entscheidend vom kunsthistorischen Paradigma der Skulptur ab. Gleichzeitig betont PLASTIC auch das Nicht-Vermittelte und Nicht-Technologische: in der Konfrontation mit der physischen Materialität, wenn die Tänzerinnen sich gegen und in die Stufen und Böden des Gebäudes pressen. Nichts ist weniger virtuell als die physische Realität der Erdanziehungskraft, die uns an den (sprichwörtlich) dreckigen Boden unter unseren Füssen bindet und uns die Identifikation mit der erhaben sterilen Weisse der vertikalen Museumswände verwehrt.

Die Anpassungsfähigkeit, die im Wort *Plastic* (Plastik oder plastisch) steckt, liesse sich sogar so weit strapazieren, dass sie die soziale Choreographie des Museums mit seinen Verhaltensregeln, Zirkulationsflüssen, Bewegungsmustern und Sehgewohnheiten umfasst. Hassabi und ihre Tänzerinnen wurden abwechselnd hastig passiert, ignoriert, auf Zehenspitzen umgangen, man schritt einfach über sie hinweg, hat sie aufdringlich photographiert oder über längere Zeit beobachtet. Bei ihrem Einsatz auf

MARIA HASSABI, PLASTIC, 2015,
Museum of Modern Art, New York, 2016,
performer: Maria Hassabi.
(PHOTO: NIKKI COLUMBUS)

der zentralen Treppe lief Hassabi buchstäblich Gefahr, vom täglichen Strom der MoMA-Touristen mit Füssen getreten zu werden. Die Darstellerinnen im Atrium fielen derweil auf oder von Sofas und lagen elegant bewegungslos auf dem Boden; hin und wieder sassen Besucher in der Nähe und waren mehr an ihren Mobiltelefonen interessiert als daran, den Tanz zu beobachten, der sich unmittelbar um ihre eigenen Körper herum abspielte. Die Grösse des Atriums, dessen weniger hohe Wände passend zum Boden grau gestrichen waren, trug zusätzlich zur relativen Unauffälligkeit der Tänzer bei. Der wirkungsvollste Performancebereich war die Treppe zwischen dem vierten und fünften Stockwerk der Malerei- und Skulpturensammlung: In diesem eng begrenzten Rahmen bewegten sich ein bis zwei Tänzerinnen Zentimeter um Zentimeter die Treppe hinunter; ihre Augen, wenn sie unserem Blick überhaupt begegneten, waren glasig und unergründlich. Hin und wieder schritt ein Besucher über sie hinweg, was eine seltsame Spannung erzeugte und einer gewaltsamen Grenzüberschreitung nahekam.

Dass *PLASTIC* mit seiner scheinbaren Reglosigkeit die dem Publikum eigene Choreographie offenlegte, unterstreicht auch den entscheidenden Unterschied zwischen Kunstobjekt (Photographie, Skulptur) und körperlicher Darstellung. Eine Performance im Museum stellt das Publikum genauso aus wie sich selbst, obwohl jeder Anspruch auf Öffentlichkeit der enormen Umstrukturierung der Grenze zwischen Öffentlichem und Privatem Rechnung tragen muss, die in den letzten Jahrzehnten – unter dem Druck einer neoliberalen Wirtschaft einerseits und dem Einfluss digitaler Technologien und sozialer Medien andrerseits – stattgefunden hat. Beide Entwicklungen haben die Existenz des «öffentlichen Raumes» empfindlich gestört und beide stehen in engem Zusammenhang mit Zeit und Aufmerksamkeit. Doch die kollektive Präsenz des Publikums – egal in welch angespannter und beeinträchtigter Form – ist nachweislich das Herzstück eines lebendigen Museums und nicht die Performance (oder Photographie, Skulptur, Malerei oder gleich welches Medium). Damit will ich nicht das unglaublich Menschliche einer Live-Performance in den Vordergrund rücken (ein Anspruch, den Hassabi schon durch ihre nekrospektakuläre Äs-

thetik in Frage stellt), sondern vielmehr festhalten, dass die Verlagerung des Tanzes ins Museum sowohl eine soziale Choreographie als auch eine photographische Überarbeitung nach sich zieht. Diese Reaktionen machen deutlich, dass die kollektive Präsenz heute genauso bedeutsam ist wie die selektive partielle Abwesenheit: in einer synkopischen Zeit, in der wir uns abwechselnd auf unsere Umgebung einlassen und ihr wieder entgleiten.

(Übersetzung: Suzanne Schmidt)

1) Eine gute Zusammenfassung dieser Positionen findet sich bei Didier Maleuvre, *Museum Memories*, Stanford University Press, Stanford, Kalifornien, 1999.
2) Hal Foster, «In Praise of Dead Art», *Art Newspaper*, 18. September 2015, www.theartnewspaper.com/comment/reviews/books/hal-foster-in-praise-of-dead-art
Der Artikel ist ein Auszug des letzten Kapitels von Fosters *Bad New Days*, Verso, London 2015.
3) Tim Griffin, «Living Contradiction», Publikation zur Ausstellung im Museum of Modern Art, New York 2016, S. 1, siehe www.moma.org/momaorg/shared/pdfs/docs/calendar/MariaHassabi_FINAL_V5.pdf
4) Ab 2000 vertrat Tino Sehgal zehn Jahre lang die Ansicht, dass seine «Situationen» am besten als Skulpturen betrachtet werden sollten, die sich während des ganzen Arbeitstages im Ausstellungsraum befänden: «[Ich] versuchte allen herkömmlichen Regeln gerecht zu werden, damit mein Werk einer traditionellen Skulptur gleichkäme.» Sehgal, zit. in: Elizabeth Carpenter, «Be the Work: Intersubjectivity in Tino Sehgal's *This Objective of that Object*», Walker Art Center-Blog, 2014, www.walkerart.org/collections/publications/performativity/be-the-work
5) Dorothea von Hantelmann, How to Do Things with Art, JRP Ringier, Zürich 2010, S. 137. Klaus Biesenbach, zit. in: Rebecca Schneider, *Performing Remains: Art and War in Times of Theatrical Reenactment*, Routledge, New York 2011, S. 130.
6) Schneider, *Performing Remains*, S. 130.
7) Diese Haltung trug mit zu den Vorbehalten der Kunstwelt gegenüber Schauspiel und Unterhaltung bei, wie sich in der jahrelangen «Voreingenommenheit der bildenden Kunst gegen das Theater» gezeigt hat. Siehe Jonas Barish, *The Antitheatrical Prejudice*, University of California Press, Berkeley, Kalifornien, 1981.
8) Bemerkenswert ist jedoch, dass Hassabi ihre Arbeit nicht als Skulptur bezeichnet, sondern als «Live-Installation», da sie im Vergleich zu ihren Bühnenproduktionen mehr Zeit in Anspruch nimmt und eine andere Aufmerksamkeitsspanne erfordert.
9) Obschon Filme bereits in den späten 1960er-Jahren in Kunstgalerien und Museen Einzug hielten, geschah dies damals nach Art einer Kinovorstellung (d.h. sie wurden von Anfang bis Ende abgespielt). Der Film als Endlosschlaufe trat erst in Erscheinung nach der Einführung dieser Technik auf CD und DVD.
10) INTERMISSION (2013) war Teil der Darbietung im Biennale-Pavillon von Zypern und Litauen, kuratiert von Raimundas Malasaukas.
11) Maria Hassabi, E-Mail an die Autorin, 7. November 2015.

Ed Atkins

Born 1982 in Oxford UK, lives and works in London.

Geboren 1982 in Oxford, lebt und arbeitet in London.

Theaster Gates

Born 1973 in Chicago, where he lives and works.

Geboren 1973 in Chicago, wo er lebt und arbeitet

Lee Kit

Born 1978 in Hong Kong, lives and works in Taipei, Taiwan.

Geboren 1978 in Hongkong, lebt und arbeitet in Taipeh, Taiwan.

Mika Rottenberg

Born 1976 in Buenos Aires, lives and works in New York.

Geboren 1976 in Buenos Aires, lebt und arbeitet in New York.

Ed
Atkins

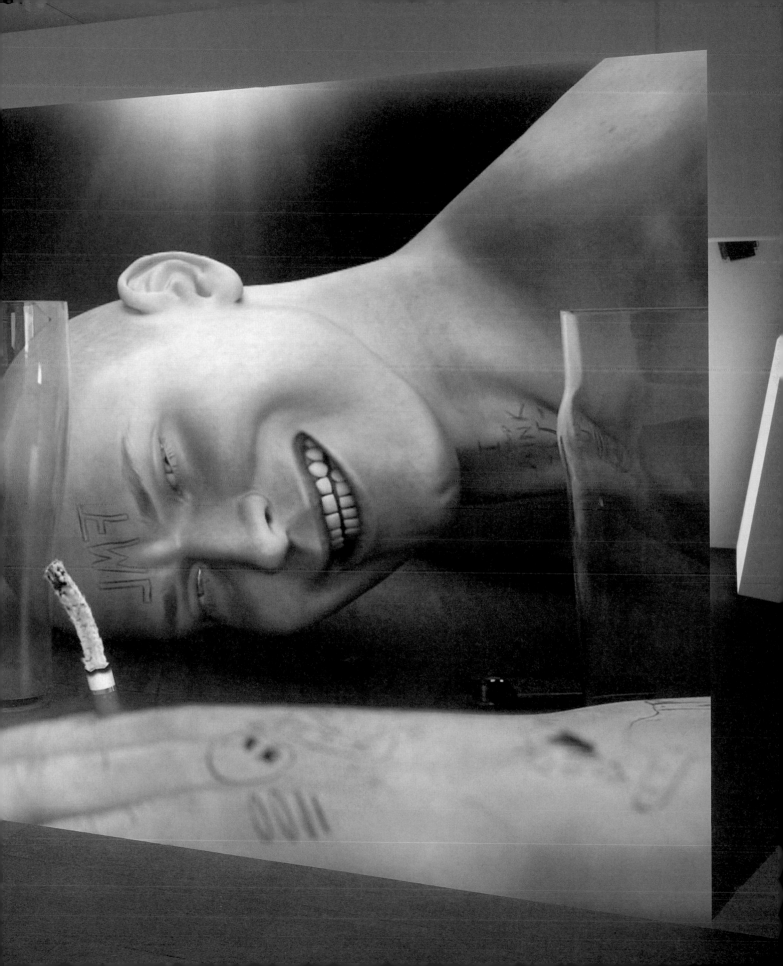

*At first sight, the image does not
resemble a cadaver, but it could
be that the strangeness of a cadaver
is also the strangeness of the image.*
—Maurice Blanchot[1]

ANDREW DURBIN

Missing Persons

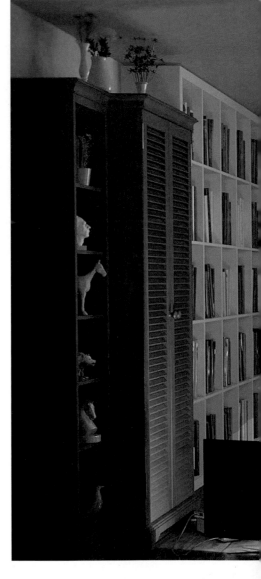

Halfway through Ed Atkins's HISSER (2015), a twenty-two-minute CGI-animated video, a man wakes up in a small bed in a dimly lit suburban bedroom. Staring out at us, his head against his pillow, he sings along to a moody piano track: "I didn't know I was asleep." Nor did we. When we first encountered him, he was wandering naked in the glowing white space of a flatscreen on the bedroom floor, whistling "Stranger in Paradise"—a pre-animated digital heaven, or dream. "I'm not sure what to say," he murmurs, but Atkins's avatars have never been short of things to talk about, and the assertion doesn't turn out to be entirely true of this guy either: "Sorry, I'm sorry," he repeats, but he doesn't seem to know why. Perhaps he's apologizing for his non-existence?

HISSER marks the second appearance of this particular avatar in Atkins's work, after HAPPY BIRTHDAY!! (2014). The artist's avatars have become progressively more realistic over time, but also less articulate. The florid monologues and recitations of poetry are gone, and all that remains are stutters, sad songs, and abject apologies, cued to wounded expressions directed straight at the camera. Perhaps this is why his face is bruised and purple, all black eyes and burst capillaries. His wrinkles and pores are so well rendered as to be "lifelike," to be so uncannily *like flesh*, and yet far from it—as made clear by eerily pearlescent teeth that

---

ANDREW DURBIN is the author of *Mature Themes* (Nightboat Books, 2014) and lives in New York.

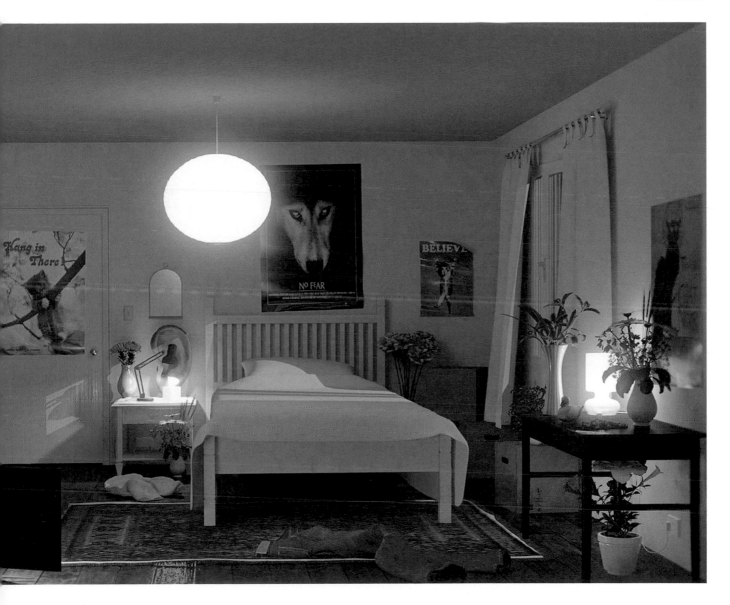

ED ATKINS, HISSER, 2015, video projection with 5.1 surround sound, 21 min. 51 sec. /
ZISCHER, Videoprojektion mit 5.1-Raumklang.

shine between cracked lips and the lack of weight perceptible in his movements and his pillow, barely dented by his head; his feet dangle off the end of the bed as if he were levitating.

This bedroom is the first complete environment Atkins has created for an avatar, but there seems to be little relationship between the two. Classic inspirational posters wall the room: BELIEVE, reads one with a kitten clinging to nothing but air; another kitten is encouraged to HANG IN THERE! as it dangles from the branch of a tree; NO FEAR announces a third above a quote from Helen Keller. On a bookshelf: *Find the Love of Your Life After 50!, High Percentage Golf, Classic Worship.* The only interaction the figure has with the space around him is with the one object that appears most out of place: the large screen, glowing brightly, on the floor

ED ATKINS, HISSER, 2015, video projection with 5.1 surround sound, 21 min. 51 sec. /
ZISCHER, Videoprojektion mit 5.1-Raumklang.

facing the bed. He sits in front of it in his underwear, shuffling through blank notecards. Later, he masturbates to those same cards, only they now picture Rorschach blots—does the idea of the unconscious turn on an avatar without consciousness? The scene is "shot" from his point of view, but as our eyes replace his, our own subjectivity stands in for his lack as we gaze at one ink splotch after another: two clowns in red hats; a bat with its wings spread. Nothing seems to get him off, and he moves on to an image of the Barberini Faun eternally poised in frozen bliss—his antithesis.

Atkins's avatars are obsessed with the sex they will never experience. As the decapitated head in US DEAD TALK LOVE (2012) explains:

Sex, death. Intimacy and its melancholy impossibility. REPRESENTATION—exhumed, upended turned over in hand—either to discover that, IN ACTUAL FACT, it's not a representation at all but the real thing: a curlicue of eyelash disguised as *the pronominal self*
—as I, as 'I'—[2]

Atkins cuts the comma and collapses "sex, death" into a single inquiry into the troubled sexiness of that pronominal self's subjectivity. A sense of this *sexdeath* percolates throughout his work as his avatars struggle to get off in those places where they might shove their "I." In RIBBONS (2014), for example, it's a glory hole with a shaved, flaccid penis placed before it. Later, the hole is a glass set on a table, variously filling with piss, blood, and whiskey, forming a gravitational center for the film that the protagonist resists but from which he cannot break free. He sits at the table; he sits under the table; he leaves the table. Ultimately, he circles back to it, gripped by these holes that might otherwise be formulated as tears in the room's internal logic, escape hatches for the cognitive blowout of booze or the forward motion and release of ejaculation, Shakespeare's "expense of spirit in a waste of shame."

Nothing real is found in Atkins's videos, no *I* except in "I," clipped by the scare quotes of representation. HISSER repeatedly strikes out against its own imperatives to more closely align the form with its content. Midway through the film, the room begins to roll down the screen, appearing again at the top, like an analog television that's lost its vertical hold. Or are there multiple identical rooms? The movement gains momentum, a nausea-inducing pinwheel suburbia. We cut to the figure in bed: "It took me so long to get my feet up off the ground," he sings. He didn't know he was asleep, but does he know he was never alive?

"The comparison I've rehearsed for several years now," Atkins writes, "is that of my videos to cadavers; that, really, I wanted to make cadavers. Literally, dead men."[3] He has further said that these dreamers of the big sleep embody Maurice Blanchot's "two versions of the imaginary": the dead body as both "spiritual and immaterial—in remembering and emotional affect" and "the most physically present thing you can imagine: a slumped pile of flesh."[4] Life*less* but near enough to life to be like us—a Mors of a digital underworld. Susan Sontag described photography as "a material vestige of its subject"—"a trace . . . like a footprint or a death mask."[5] The death mask is a final imprint of an individual, molded from the body at the moment it has ceased to live and kept for the living to hold off memory's slow degradation of what the dead once looked like, how the person's head occupied space; it preserves the face while reinforcing the absence of the rest. But the indexical relationship that Sontag points to is lost in digital imagery; in lieu of the trace, Atkins's avatars are metaphors for representation. Yet the idea of the death mask returns via the animation process: The avatar's face is three-dimensionally mapped onto the artist's as he performs the lines—in other words, then, the avatar serves as Atkins's own death mask.[6] He pushes this idea further in his most recent

ED ATKINS, HISSER, 2015, video projection with 5.1 surround sound, 21 min. 51 sec. /
ZISCHER, Videoprojektion mit 5.1-Raumklang.

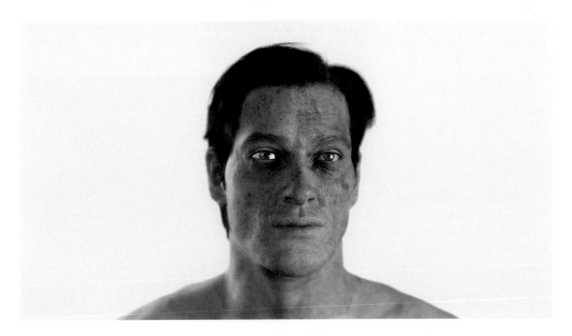

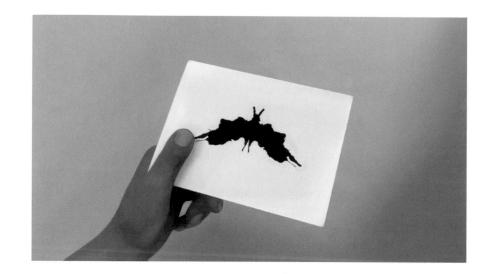

ED ATKINS, HISSER, 2015,
video projection with 5.1
surround sound, 21 min. 51 sec. /
ZISCHER, Videoprojektion
mit 5.1-Raumklang.

film, SAFE CONDUCT (2016), in which the same avatar—still beaten and bruised—pulls off his face only to reveal another, then another, ad nauseam, like the repeating bedroom.

Atkins wanted to create a dead body that could exist without ever having to die, and in so doing, he has created a digital netherworld for deathless protagonists who struggle to understand the place of their immaterial bodies. Their struggle is made more confusing by the fact that the body these death masks represent is not dead. And while it isn't materially present, its voice certainly is: We hear Atkins breathing, smacking his lips, cracking as he sings; amplified in surround sound, and unaltered by digital effects, he seems to speak directly into our ears. The result is that the artist feels remarkably present. As a kind of death mask, tuned to the unfiltered sound of a living person, his avatars adopt the role of a vexed *memento mori*—literally, "remember that you must die"—but their injunction to the living is now not so clear. Without any past, they become a different kind of memento, one that seems to urge us to "remember to *remember*"—but if the avatar doesn't have a past, what does he want us to remember? Remember to hang in there?

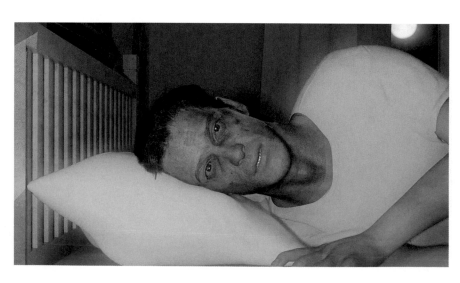

ED ATKINS, HISSER, 2015,
video projection with 5.1
surround sound, 21 min. 51 sec. /
ZISCHER, Videoprojektion
mit 5.1-Raumklang.

Near the end of HISSER, the room starts to shake. At first the bed appears empty, but then the perspective shifts to a bird's-eye view, and we see the figure once again asleep. Suddenly, a sinkhole forms in the floor, and the bed and the entire contents of the room disappear downward; the screen turns to black. It is as if the weightless avatar has been sucked in by the overwhelming gravitational pull of a black hole. But we emerge from the darkness into clouds and plummet into the sea, accompanied by the squawk of seagulls. The paradox inherent in this undead surrogate of reality is solved: The cadaver is buried without a trace.

1) Maurice Blanchot, "Two Versions of the Imaginary," in *The Gaze of Orpheus and Other Literary Essays*, ed. P. Adams Sitney, trans. Lydia Davis (Barrytown, New York: Station Hill Press, 1981), 81.
2) Ed Atkins, *Us Dead Talk Love script,* published in —*For the happy man!: Collected writing* (London: Whitechapel Gallery, 2013), n. p., www.whitechapelgallery.org/downloads/For_the_happy_man_collected_writings_ed_atkins.pdf (accessed March 21, 2016).
3) Ed Atkins, "Digital Reflex: Avery Singer and Ed Atkins Respond to Texte Zur Kunst," *Texte Zur Kunst*, no. 95 (September 2014), 76.
4) Ed Atkins, in Katie Guggenheim, "Interview with Ed Atkins," Chisenhale Gallery, London, September 2012, www.chisenhale.org.uk/archive/exhibitions/images/EAtkins_Interview.pdf.
5) Susan Sontag, "The Image-World," in *On Photography* (New York: Picador, 1990), 154.
6) It is interesting to note that in 2010, before he started working with avatars, Atkins titled a trilogy of works DEATH MASK I, II, and III; the first of these is a screenplay about Madame Tussaud.

ED ATKINS, HISSER, 2015, video projection with
5.1 surround sound, 21 min. 51 sec. /
ZISCHER, Videoprojektion mit 5.1-Raumklang.

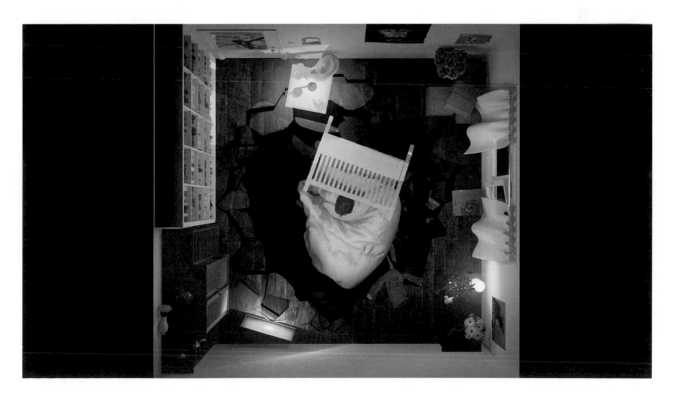

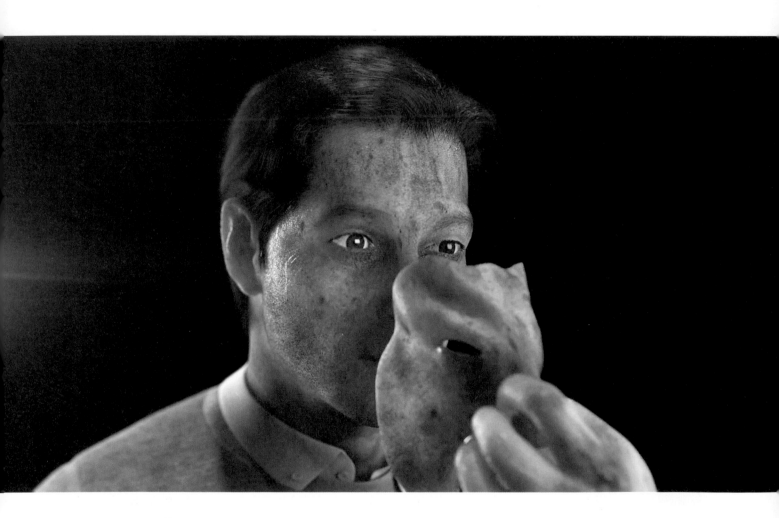

ED ATKINS, SAFE CONDUCT, 2016, 3-channel HD film with 5.1 surround sound /
FREIES GELEIT, 3-Kanal-HD-Film mit 5.1-Raumklang.

*Auf den ersten Blick ähnelt das Bild
nicht dem Leichnam, doch es könnte
sein, dass die Befremdlichkeit des
Leichnams auch die des Bildes ist.*
—Maurice Blanchot[1]

ANDREW DURBIN

Die Vermissten

Auf halber Strecke des computeranimierten 22-Minuten-Videos HISSER (Zischer, 2015) von Ed Atkins erwacht in einem schwach beleuchteten Vorstadtschlafzimmer ein Mann in einem kleinen Bett. Den Kopf gegen das Kissen gelehnt, starrt er uns an und singt zu einem stimmungsvollen Klavierstück vor sich hin: «Ich wusste nicht, dass ich geschlafen habe.» Wir auch nicht. Als wir ihm das erste Mal begegneten, spazierte er nackt und «Stranger in Paradise» pfeifend über den leuchtend weissen Bildschirm eines Flachbildfernsehers auf dem Zimmerfussboden – wie in einem vorab animierten Himmel, oder Traum. «Ich weiss nicht recht, was ich sagen soll», murmelt er, dabei hat es Atkins' Avataren noch nie an Dingen gefehlt, über die sie reden können, und auch bei diesem Kerl hier erweist sich die Beteuerung als nicht ganz zutreffend: «Entschuldigung, tut mir leid», wiederholt er, anscheinend ohne zu wissen, warum. Entschuldigt er sich vielleicht für seine Nichtexistenz?

In Atkins' Gesamtwerk hat dieser spezielle Avatar nach HAPPY BIRTHDAY!! (Alles Gute zum Geburtstag!!, 2014) in HISSER seinen zweiten Auftritt. Die Avatare des Künstlers sind mit der Zeit zwar zunehmend realistischer geworden, aber auch immer weniger wortgewandt. Die blumigen Monologe und Gedichtrezitationen sind verschwunden, alles, was bleibt, sind Gestotter, traurige Lieder und jämmerliche Entschuldigungen, abgestimmt auf ein weidwundes, direkt in die Kamera gerichtetes Mienenspiel. Vielleicht ist deshalb sein Gesicht blutunterlaufen und lila, eine Landschaft aus blau geschwollenen Augen und geplatzten Äderchen. Seine Falten und Poren sind so gut gemacht, dass sie «lebensecht» wirken, so verblüffend *wie Fleisch.* Und doch sind sie weit davon entfernt, wie die gespenstisch perlmuttartigen Zähne deutlich machen, die zwischen aufgesprungenen Lippen strahlen, und auch der Mangel an

---

ANDREW DURBIN ist der Autor der Textsammlung *Mature Themes* (Nightboat, 2014) und lebt in New York.

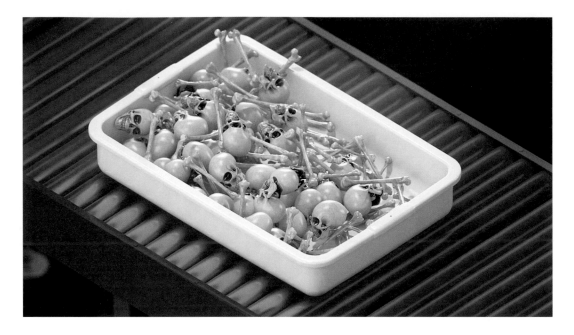

ED ATKINS, SAFE CONDUCT, 2016, 3-channel HD film with 5.1 surround sound /
FREIES GELEIT, 3-Kanal HD-Film mit 5.1-Raumklang.

Körpergewicht zeigt, der sich in den Bewegungen des Avatars äussert – und in dem Kissen, das von seinem Kopf kaum eingedrückt wird; seine Füsse baumeln über das Fussende des Bettes, als würde er schweben.

Dieses Schlafzimmer ist die erste komplette Umgebung, die Atkins für einen Avatar geschaffen hat, doch scheint es zwischen Figur und Raum kaum eine Verbindung zu geben. Klassische Motivationsplakate pflastern die Wände: GLAUBE, heisst es da über dem Bild eines Katzenbabys, das sich ausschliesslich an Luft klammert; HALTE DURCH!, wird ein anderes Kätzchen angefeuert, das am Ast eines Baums hängt; KEINE ANGST, verkündet ein dritter Leitspruch über einem Zitat der Schriftstellerin Helen Keller. Auf einem Bücherregal: *Find the Love of Your Life After 50!*, *High Percentage Golf*, *Classic Worship*. Das einzige Objekt in seiner Umgebung, mit dem der Avatar interagiert, ist ausgerechnet das scheinbar deplatzierteste von allen: der grosse, hell leuchtende, dem Bett zugewandte Bildschirm auf dem Boden. In Unterwäsche sitzt er davor und mischt leere Karteikarten. Später masturbiert er zu denselben Karten, nur dass sie jetzt Rorschachbilder zeigen. Turnt die Vorstellung des Unbewussten einen Avatar ohne Bewusstsein an? Die Szene ist aus seiner Sicht «gedreht», doch da unser Blick den seinen ersetzt, springt unsere eigene Subjektivität für seinen Mangel ein, während wir einen Tintenklecks nach dem anderen betrachten: zwei Clowns mit roten Hüten, eine Fledermaus mit ausgebreiteten Flügeln. Nichts scheint ihn zum Höhepunkt zu bringen, also geht er zu einem Bild des Barberinischen Fauns über, dem Inbegriff der in ewigem Gleichgewicht erstarrten Glückseligkeit – seinem Gegenbild.

Atkins' Avatare sind besessen von dem Sex, den sie niemals erleben werden. Wie der abgetrennte Kopf in US DEAD TALK LOVE (Wir Toten sprechen von Liebe, 2012) erklärt: *Sex, Tod. Intimität und ihre schwermütige Unmöglichkeit.*

DARSTELLUNG – exhumiert, hochkant in der Hand herumgedreht – beides, um festzustellen, dass die Darstellung FAKTISCH überhaupt keine ist, sondern Wirklichkeit: der Schnörkel einer Wimper getarnt als das pronominale Ich
– als Ich, als «Ich» –[2)]

Atkins streicht das Komma und verschmilzt «Sex, Tod» zu einer Untersuchung des gestörten Sex-Appeals, unter dem die Subjektivität dieses pronominalen Ichs leidet. Ein Gefühl für diesen *Sextod* durchdringt sein gesamtes Werk, wenn seine Avatare sich mühen, an allen Orten, in die sie womöglich ihr «Ich» schieben, zum Orgasmus zu kommen. In RIBBONS (Bänder, 2014) zum Beispiel ist ein rasierter, schlaffer Penis vor einem *Glory Hole* platziert. Später ist das Loch ein Glas auf einem Tisch, das sich abwechselnd mit Urin, Blut oder Whisky füllt und für den Film ein Gravitationszentrum bildet, dem der Protagonist widersteht, ohne sich jedoch von ihm losreissen zu können. Er sitzt an dem Tisch; er sitzt unter dem Tisch; er verlässt den Tisch. Am Ende bewegt er sich im Kreis zu ihm zurück, ergriffen von diesen Löchern, die andernfalls als Tränen in der inneren Logik des Raums formuliert sein könnten, als Notausstiege für den kognitiven Alkohol-Blow-out oder den Vorwärtsdrall der erlösenden Ejakulation, die Shakespeare als «der Seelen Tod in schimpflicher Zerstörung» bezeichnete.

Nichts Echtes findet sich in Atkins' Videos, kein *Ich* ausser im «Ich», das er in die modalisierenden Anführungszeichen der Darstellung setzt. HISSER teilt wiederholt gegen seine eigenen Imperative aus, um die Form stärker auf ihren Inhalt auszurichten. Mitten im Film beginnt der Raum die Leinwand hinabzurollen und oben wieder aufzutauchen, wie bei einem analogen Fernseher, dessen vertikaler Bildfang gestört ist. Oder gibt es mehrere identische Räume? Der Bilddurchlauf wird schneller, ein rotierendes Vorstadtszenario, das Übelkeit verursacht. Wir schneiden zu dem Kerl im Bett: «Ich habe so lange gebraucht, um meine Füsse in Bewegung zu setzen», singt er. Er wusste nicht, dass er geschlafen hat, aber weiss er, dass er nie gelebt hat?

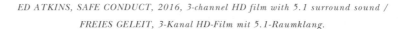

ED ATKINS, SAFE CONDUCT, 2016, 3-channel HD film with 5.1 surround sound /
FREIES GELEIT, 3-Kanal HD-Film mit 5.1-Raumklang.

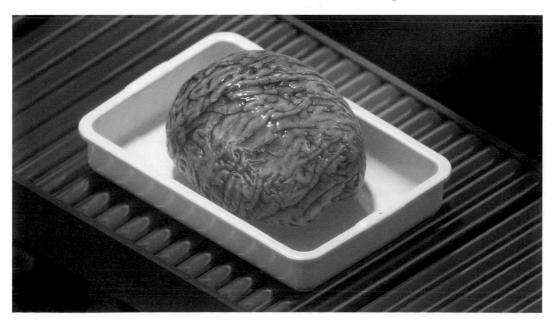

«Seit einigen Jahren mittlerweile erprobe ich den Vergleich zwischen meinen Videos und Kadavern», schreibt Atkins, «in dem Sinne, dass ich eigentlich vorhatte, Kadaver herzustellen. Tote Menschen. Selbstverständlich im Wortsinne.»[3] In diesen Träumern des grossen Schlafs sieht Atkins zudem Maurice Blanchots «zwei Fassungen des Bildlichen» verkörpert: den Leichnam, der sowohl «auf geistige und immaterielle Weise – in der Erinnerung und emotionalen Erregung» agiert als auch «die leibhaftigste Präsenz» darstellt, «die man sich vorstellen kann: einen zusammengesackten Haufen Fleisch.»[4] Leb*los*, aber lebensnah genug, um wie wir zu sein – ein Mors einer digitalen Unterwelt. Susan Sontag beschrieb die Photographie als «eine materielle Spur ihres Gegenstands» – «eine Spur [...] wie ein Fussabdruck oder eine Totenmaske».[5] Die Totenmaske ist der letzte Abdruck einer Person. In dem Moment vom Körper abgeformt, da das Leben aus ihm gewichen ist, und für die Lebenden bewahrt, um das langsame Schwinden der Erinnerung daran aufzuhalten, wie der Tote einmal aussah, wie sein Kopf den Raum einnahm, konserviert sie das Gesicht und verstärkt die Abwesenheit des restlichen Teils. Die indexikalische Beziehung aber, auf die Sontag verweist, geht in digitalen Bildern verloren; anstelle der Spur sind Atkins' Avatare Metaphern der Darstellung. Und doch kehrt die Idee der Totenmaske über den Umweg des Animationsprozesses wieder zurück: Das Gesicht des Avatars wird dreidimensional auf dem Gesicht des Künstlers abgebildet, während dieser die Texte vorträgt – mit anderen Worten fungiert also der Avatar als Atkins' eigene Totenmaske.[6] In seinem neuesten Film, SAFE CONDUCT (Freies Geleit, 2016), baut Atkins diese Idee weiter aus. Derselbe Avatar – noch immer geschlagen und blutunterlaufen – streift sein Gesicht ab, nur um ein anderes zu offenbaren, dann noch eins, bis zum Abwinken, wie das sich wiederholende Schlafzimmer.

Atkins wollte einen Leichnam erschaffen, der existieren kann, ohne jemals sterben zu müssen, und hat dabei ein digitales Totenreich für unsterbliche Protagonisten kreiert, die darum ringen, den Platz ihrer immateriellen Körper zu begreifen. Die Tatsache, dass der Körper, den diese Totenmasken repräsentieren, nicht tot ist, macht ihr Ringen noch verwirrender. Und während er stofflich nicht anwesend ist, ist seine Stimme es sehr wohl: Wir hören Atkins atmen, mit den Lippen schmatzen, sich beim Singen überschlagen; in Surround-Sound verstärkt und nicht durch Digitaleffekte verfälscht, scheint er uns direkt in die Ohren zu sprechen – mit dem Ergebnis, dass der Künstler sich bemerkenswert präsent anfühlt. Als eine Art Totenmaske, die auf den ungefilterten Klang einer lebenden Person eingestellt ist, nehmen seine Avatare die Rolle eines verärgerten Memento mori, eines buchstäblichen «Bedenke, dass du sterben musst» an, doch ihre Mahnung an die Lebenden ist jetzt nicht mehr so eindeutig. Ohne jede Vergangenheit werden sie zu einer anderen Art von Memento, das uns zu drängen scheint: «Bedenke, dass du *dich erinnern* musst.» Wenn aber der Avatar gar keine Vergangenheit hat, woran sollen wir uns nach seinem Willen dann erinnern? Etwa daran, durchzuhalten?

Gegen Ende von HISSER beginnt der Raum zu beben. Zuerst erscheint das Bett leer, doch dann schwenkt der Blick in die Vogelperspektive, und wir sehen die Figur erneut im Schlaf. Plötzlich bildet sich im Fussboden ein Krater, in dem das Bett und der gesamte Rauminhalt nach unten verschwinden; die Leinwand wird schwarz. Es ist, als wäre der Avatar von der überwältigenden Gravitationskraft eines schwarzen Lochs eingesogen worden. Doch dann geht die Dunkelheit in Wolken über, und wir stürzen von Möwengekreische begleitet ins Meer. Das Paradox, das in dieser untoten Ersatzrealität angelegt war, ist aufgelöst: Der Kadaver wurde ohne eine Spur begraben.

(Übersetzung: Kurt Rehkopf)

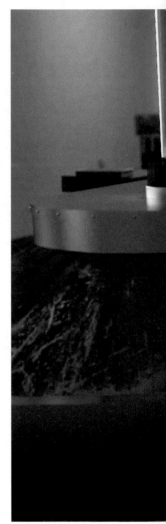

ED ATKINS, SAFE CONDUCT, 2016, 3-channel
HD film with 5.1 surround sound /
FREIES GELEIT, 3-Kanal HD-Film mit 5.1-Raumklang.

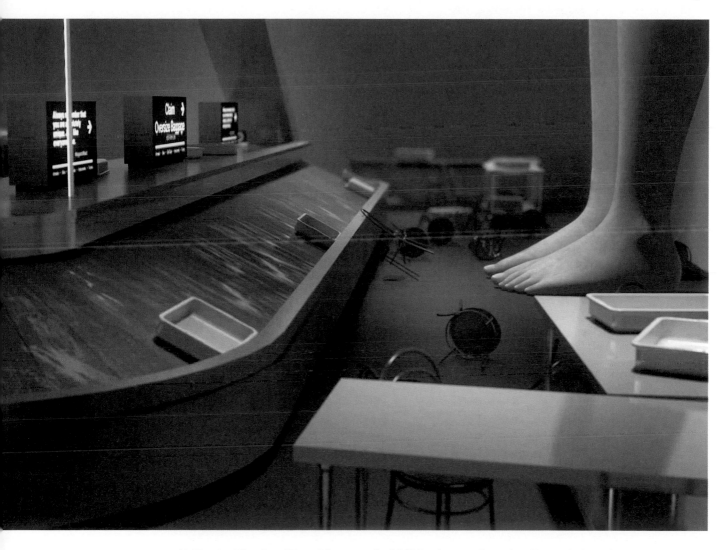

1) Maurice Blanchot, *Die zwei Fassungen des Bildlichen*, hrsg. und aus dem Französischen übersetzt von Hinrich Weidemann, [Berlin]: Potlatch Books, 2007, S. 11.
2) Ed Atkins, «Us dead talk love, 2012», Skript, veröffentlicht in ders., —*For the happy man! Collected writing*, London: Whitechapel Gallery, 2013, o. S., www.whitechapelgallery.org/downloads/For_the_happy_man_collected_writings_ed_atkins.pdf (letzter Zugriff 4. April 2016).
3) Ed Atkins, «Digitale Reflexe: Texte zur Kunst befragt Avery Singer und Ed Atkins», in *Texte Zur Kunst*, Nr. 95 (September 2014), S. 77, https://www.textezurkunst.de/95/digitale-reflexe-ed-atkins-avery-singer/ (letzter Zugriff 4. April 2016).
4) Ed Atkins zit. n. Katie Guggenheim, «Interview with Ed Atkins», Chisenhale Gallery, London, September 2012, www.chisenhale.org.uk/archive/exhibitions/images/EAtkins_Interview.pdf (letzter Zugriff 4. April 2016).
5) Susan Sontag, «Die Bilderwelt», *Über Fotografie*, Frankfurt am Main: Fischer, 2016, S. 147.
6) Interessanterweise gab Atkins, noch bevor er mit Avataren zu arbeiten begann, einer Werktrilogie aus den Jahren 2010/11 den Titel DEATH MASK (Totenmaske) I, II und III; dcr erste Teil ist ein Drehbuch über Madame Tussaud.

ED ATKINS, RIBBONS, 2014, 3-channel HD video (4:3 in 16:9) with 3 4.1 channel surround soundtracks, 13 min. / BÄNDER, 3-Kanal HD-Video (4:3 als 16:9) mit 3 4.1 Raumklang-Tonspuren.

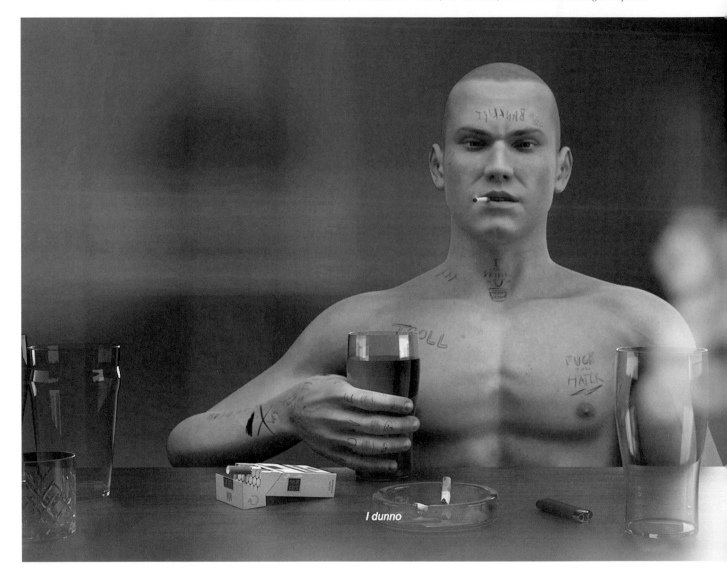

LESLIE JAMISON

He's a digital man, computer-generated. He seems to be suffering, or perhaps just insufferable. He sits with a cigarette in one hand and a beer in the other, croaking along to a Randy Newman song about lone-

LESLIE JAMISON is the author of *The Gin Closet*, a novel, and *The Empathy Exams*, a collection of essays.

liness. He crouches beneath a white tablecloth, offering an inane monologue about human existence. He lays his face against a wooden table, surrounded by empty glasses, as the chords of an operatic audio track let loose.

Scribbles cover his naked body like tattoos—I COULD DRINK U, reads one on his throat, with a glass

I'm Not Too Sad to Tell You

notes: DON'T DIE. WOUND BOUND. TRUE BROKEN WOUNDED BLUE.

Entering Ed Atkins's three-screen installation RIBBONS (2014) is something like walking into a debased confessional. Each video begins with a door opening to a bright light beyond, with gold block letters hovering among the clouds, like the cover of a mass-market paperback novel about the Rapture. The first screen announces: A DEMAND FOR LOVE. The second: MUTELY DEMAND. The third: HELP ME HOLD. What might it mean to ask someone for love with such bald intention? To ask someone to listen? To ask someone to pay a fucking *moment* of attention?

Our digital man feels the shame of it. "Help me communicate without debasement, darling," he says. We hear fart noises and bar chatter, whining drones like a mosquito in the ear. This guy *is* a mosquito in our ear. That's his project and his plight. He finishes with an apology: "Adam, sorry for that one particularly histrionic horrible mess." And then—with a pffft and a hiss—his head deflates. This digital man was having a moment, but apparently—unless your name is Adam—he wasn't having this moment with *you.*

This is the ham-fisted tyranny that sentimentality gets accused of: *Here is someone's sadness—feel sad for him.* As Jennifer Doyle writes, "The sentimental stands in opposition to the codes of conduct that regulate the social spaces of art consumption, in its messiness, its direct assertion of the world of feeling, and its hopeless association with the low and the popular." She wonders about the terms of this war: "How many times have you seen an artist's . . . lack of sentimentality cited as praise, as if the value of this were self-evident?"[1] The spectacle of someone else's emotional unraveling can be unappealing. In Marina Abramović's video THE ONION (1995), the artist eats an entire onion raw—the mess of it spreading across her face, smearing her lipstick—while her voiceover loops through the same list of complaints about her life:

I'm tired of changing planes so often, waiting in the waiting rooms, bus stations, train stations, airports. I am tired of . . . standing around with a glass of plain water, pretending that I am interested in conversation. I am tired of my migraine attacks. Lonely hotel room, room service, long distance telephone calls, bad TV movies. I am tired of always falling in love with the wrong man. I am tired of

drawn beneath it—and he's surrounded by the tropes of a sentimental set piece: a tumbler that keeps getting filled with various shades of booze (the prophecy on his throat come to life); a cigarette ghosting itself to ash; mournful British folk rock that warbles, "I've only sad stories to tell this town / My dreams have withered and died." Sentiment lives on sticky

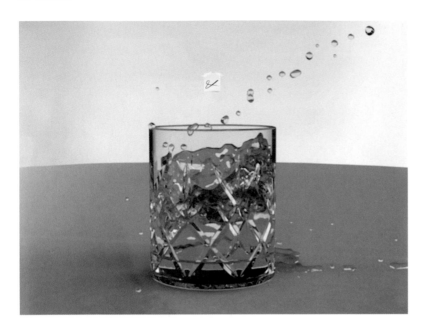

ED ATKINS, RIBBONS, 2014, 3-channel
HD video (4:3 in 16:9) with 3 4.1
channel surround soundtracks, 13 min. /
BÄNDER, 3-Kanal HD-Video (4:3 als 16:9)
mit 3 4.1 Raumklang-Tonspuren.

being ashamed of my nose being too big, of my ass being too
large, ashamed about the war in Yugoslavia.

Abramović's presentation is odd, challenging, pathetic, ugly. It feels self-indulgent. *Stop eating that fucking onion, then. Stop looping through those complaints.* As Doyle points out, however, emotion functions differently in work made by men, who are less frequently accused of sentimentality and allowed, instead, to follow in the "tradition of sad, melancholy white male artists."[2] She cites Bas Jan Ader's ironic engagement with this tradition in his three-minute short I'M TOO SAD TO TELL YOU (1971). Atkins offers a messier alternative to the deliberate withholding of Ader's piece—a man crying but too sad or discreet to narrate the occasion for his tears—by delivering, instead, his nonsensical verbal abundance: his monologues and shitty cover songs. These don't explain why he's sad, but they show him caught in the abject posture of *trying* to explain, or wanting to be understood. Atkins makes his avatar embarrassingly expressive, as if to push at the limits of what Doyle describes as our socialized willingness "to accept his tears as real" when the artist is male.

We're not always willing to accept them as anything. A concern troll posted about her experience of Atkins's irritating avatar in US DEAD TALK LOVE (2012):

I'm left wondering if this is what it's like to be the girlfriend of a young, emotionally fragile, yet egotistical, male artist. There are brief choirs of (digitally produced?) voices that repeat certain words as this whinger regales us with his inner monologue about relationships and "intimacy" without much content or thoughtfulness beyond the solipsistic enjoyment of the sound of his own voice, which is so carefully edited in all of its insipidity.

Part of me says, Amen. Another part says, *Yes, but.* The content of the monologues isn't the point. The avatar talks about someone "defrauding families up and down the coast"; "resuscitating long-dead treasured pets." He says, "I could never simply conflate hiding with cowardice." His words aren't offering profundity but a cheap prefab reproduction of profundity. The point isn't their intelligence but the fact that they want it, just like the visual metaphors that float across the screen, rusted chains in a deep sea of whiskey brown *something*. The feeling is not the feeling of metaphor offered or accomplished—the chains of loneliness or alcoholism—it's more desperate than that. It's a desperate *reaching* for metaphor, clutching at its possibility.

The language is unsettling—even irritating—because it gestures at meaning without delivering it, just as the avatar is unsettling because his face gestures at humanity but isn't human. His features move, but they are clearly *made*, his voice summons the specter of a sophisticated robot who has managed to feel despite his programming. Everything here lives in the uncanny valley, that strange space of revulsion that holds the almost human—what's us, but not quite.

In these videos, emotion itself has been banished to the uncanny valley: Emotion is almost human but not quite; it attracts and repels at once. Here is all the ridiculous pageantry of emotional expression—the sad cowboy songs and the absurdly caricatured tropes of youthful angst—but we have no stable sense of what is actually being expressed. It's just an uncomfortable emotional field that's getting generated—everything is off, disjointed, interrupted. I feel unsettled and betrayed and disappointed. All the things I want are withheld: insight, narrative, humanity. I'm forced into the non-progressive, non-narrative, non-redemptive; the space of *almost*.

Eve Kosofsky Sedgwick argues that the modern critique of sentimentality faults the "tacitness and non-accountability of the identification between sufferer

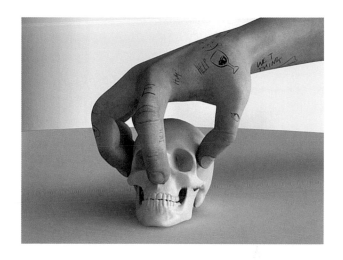

ED ATKINS, RIBBONS, 2014, 3-channel HD video (4:3 in 16:9) with 3 4.1 channel surround soundtracks, 13 min. / BÄNDER, 3-Kanal HD-Video (4:3 als 16:9) mit 3 4.1 Raumklang-Tonspuren.

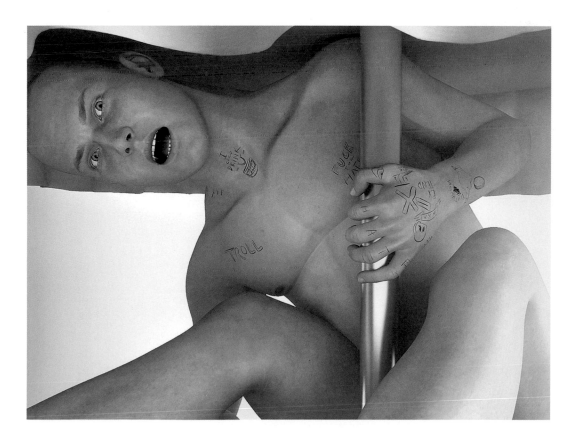

and sentimental spectator."[3] But these videos are playing with that process of identification rather than peddling it. Instead of constructing a false premise of absolute identification—between artist and viewer, or viewer and suffering subject—they explode and challenge the premise of identification entirely, expose its absurdity, show the gauche strain of reaching for it. How can we identify with this unlikable avatar? We constantly want to get away from him. But there are always *three* of him emoting at once.

We are not in the presence of pain so much as the idea of expressing it. *Help me communicate without debasement, darling.* But this work is all about debasement—the debasement of communication itself.

The vapid monologues dramatize the spectacle of speaking feeling, and the shame of it—the ponderous tones of our feeble attempt to get melancholy with each other just because we can't stand to stay alone in it, and the embarrassment of that transaction. *Sorry for that one particularly histrionic horrible mess.* At one point, we hear heavy breathing: a voice exhausted by all its monologuing. Then suddenly, he deflates; there was nothing inside all along.

This isn't art about intimacy in the digital era; it's using the digital form to illuminate something much closer to the core of intimacy itself—how we seek it from each other and from art; how we can experience simultaneous attraction and revulsion to ex-

ED ATKINS, RIBBONS, 2014, 3-channel HD video (4:3 in 16:9) with 3 4.1 channel surround soundtracks, 13 min. /
BÄNDER, 3-Kanal HD-Video (4:3 als 16:9) mit 3 4.1 Raumklang-Tonspuren.

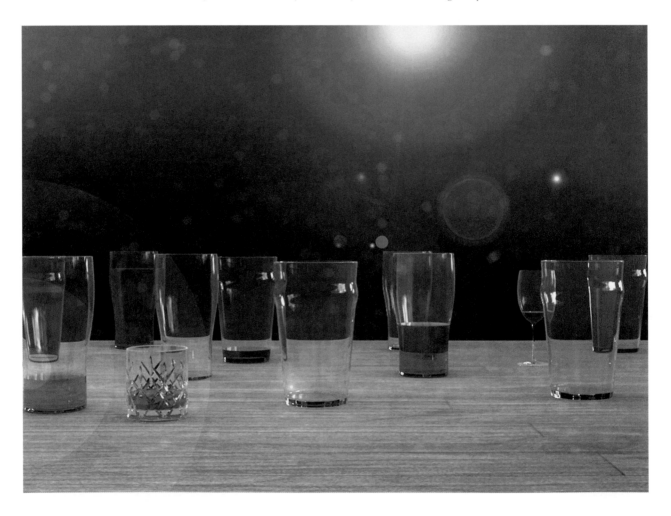

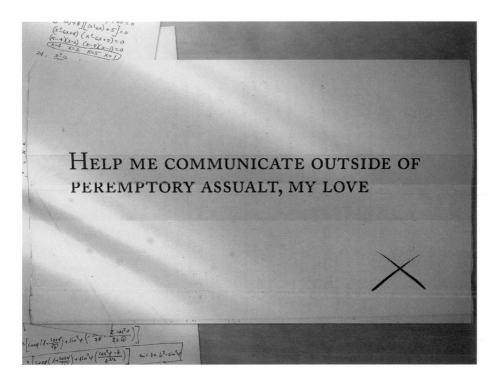

HELP ME COMMUNICATE OUTSIDE OF PEREMPTORY ASSUALT, MY LOVE

ED ATKINS, RIBBONS, 2014,
3-channel HD video (4:3 in 16:9)
with 3 4.1 channel surround
soundtracks, 13 min. /
BÄNDER, 3-Kanal HD-Video
(4:3 als 16:9) mit 3 4.1
Raumklang-Tonspuren.

pressions of feeling. This pathetic avatar is a chance to reckon with how violently we flee the possibility of the sentimental—its specter lurking on the horizon, rising like a full, glowing moon over the tumblers on the table, rising like a bald head regarding a skull.

Is all this just poking fun at the tropes of angst and melodrama? Or is it a critique of a critique—a rejection of the knee-jerk rejection of the sentimental? For me, the weirdest moments in these videos are when they stop being a negation; those moments when identification sets up shop in the most inhospitable climate and happens *anyway*. I feel for this digital avatar not when he says that he's sad, but when he apologizes for saying so; he's an avatar who knows how unappealing his sad-sack persona is. I don't feel for him because DON'T DIE is written on his forehead, but because it's written backward: The message is meant for him—looking in the mirror, telling himself not to die—not for me. Maybe he *does* die at the end: my egotistical boyfriend, my run-on heart, my deflated balloon.

Part of me feels foolish and ashamed because early on in one of the videos, there's a brief moment when his face crumples. I know he'll deflate, and I listen anyway. I know he's not real, and I listen anyway. I want to believe not in what he's saying, but in the moment I'm having with him. I'm not Adam, but I'm here, just across the screen. *Art* doesn't satisfy desire or dull it; it's simply another way it manifests, and the question of performing pain isn't just a question of making art: Genuine hurt—in order to get expressed—always requires its own performance. Atkins recognizes the simultaneous shame and the necessity of this act: We try to build something real enough to say what we want to say, an animation or a sentence or a bald head covered with chicken scratch. It isn't real enough; it can't say anything; and we listen anyway.

1) Jennifer Doyle, *Hold It Against Me: Difficulty and Emotion in Contemporary Art* (Durham, NC: Duke University Press, 2013), 77, 80.
2) Ibid., 88.
3) Eve Kosofsky Sedgwick, *Epistemology of the Closet* (Berkeley, CA: University of California Press, 1990), 151.

Ich bin nicht zu traurig, um es dir zu sagen

LESLIE JAMISON

Er ist ein digitaler Mann, computergeneriert. Er scheint zu leiden oder ist vielleicht nur unerträglich. Mit einer Zigarette in der einen und einem Bier in der anderen Hand sitzt er da und quakt zu einem Randy-Newman-Song über Einsamkeit vor sich hin. Er kauert unter einer weissen Tischdecke und offeriert uns einen geistlosen Monolog über das menschliche Dasein. Er legt sein Gesicht auf einen Holztisch voller leerer Gläser, während die Tonspur opernhafte Akkorde von sich gibt.

Wie Tattoos übersäen Kritzeleien seinen nackten Oberkörper – auf seinem Hals etwa steht, mit einem Glas darunter: ICH KÖNNTE DICH TRINKEN –, während die klassischen Zutaten für ein sentimentales Rührstück ihn umgeben: ein Glas, das laufend mit verschiedenen Sorten Alkohol gefüllt wird (und die Vorhersage auf seinem Hals zum Leben erweckt); eine Zigarette, die sich wie von Geisterhand zu Asche zersetzt; schwermütige Lieder, die trällern: «Ich habe dieser Stadt nur traurige Geschichten zu erzählen ... Meine Träume sind verkümmert und sterben.» Empfindung lebt auf Klebezetteln: STIRB NICHT. AUF KRÄNKUNG FIXIERT. WAHR GEBROCHEN VERWUNDET TRAURIG.

Die 3-Kanal-Installation RIBBONS (Bänder, 2014) von Ed Atkins zu betreten, ähnelt dem Gang in einen entwürdigten Beichtstuhl. Jedes Video beginnt mit einer Tür, hinter der im grellen Licht goldene Blockbuchstaben zwischen Wolken schweben wie auf dem Cover eines billigen Taschenbuchromans über die Entrückung. Die erste Leinwand verkündet: EIN VERLANGEN NACH LIEBE. Die zweite: STUMMES VERLANGEN. DIE DRITTE: HILF MIR FESTHALTEN. Was

LESLIE JAMISON ist die Autorin von *The Gin Closet*, einem Roman, und dem Essayband *Die Empathie-Tests*.

könnte es bedeuten, jemanden mit so unverhüllter Absicht um Liebe zu bitten? Jemanden zu bitten zuzuhören? Jemanden zu bitten, einen verfickten *Moment* lang achtzugeben?

Unser digitaler Mann fühlt die Schande. «Hilf mir ohne Entwürdigung zu kommunizieren, Darling», sagt er. Wir hören Furzgeräusche und Kneipengespräche, Gejammer dröhnt wie eine Mücke im Ohr. Dieser Typ *ist* eine Mücke in unserem Ohr. Das ist

ED ATKINS, RIBBONS, 2014, 3-channel HD video (4:3 in 16:9) with 3 4.1 channel surround soundtracks, 13 min. / BÄNDER, 3-Kanal HD-Video (4:3 als 16:9) mit 3 4.1 Raumklang-Tonspuren.

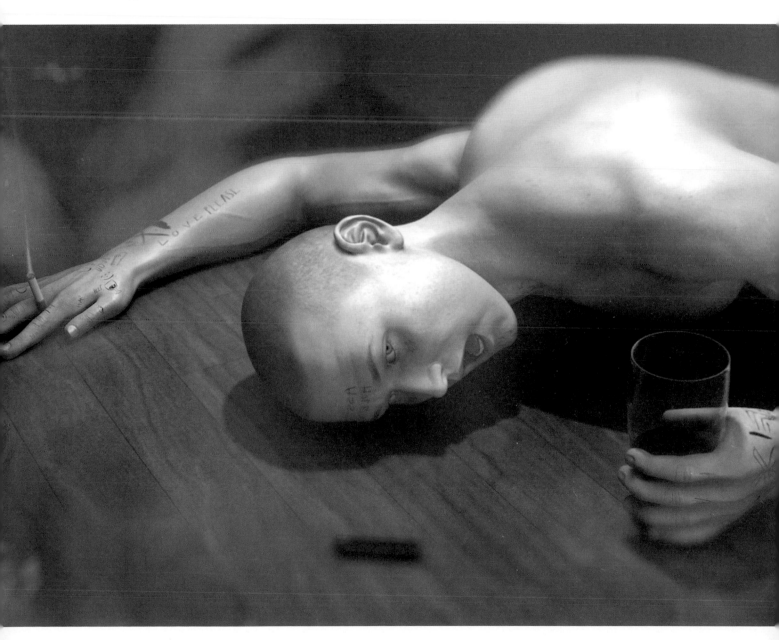

ED ATKINS, RIBBONS, 2014, 3-channel HD video (4:3 in 16:9) with 3 4.1 channel surround soundtracks, 13 min. /
BÄNDER, 3-Kanal HD-Video (4:3 als 16:9) mit 3 4.1 Raumklang-Tonspuren.

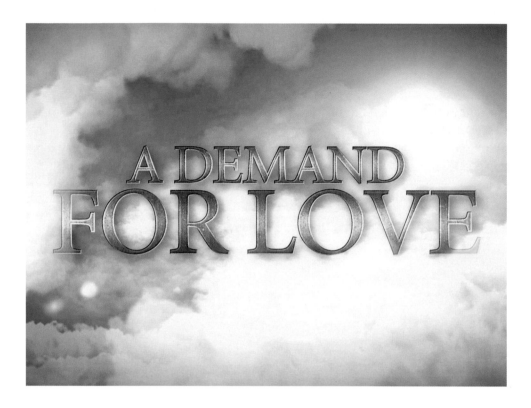

sein Projekt und seine Misere. Er schliesst mit einer Abbitte: «Adam, es tut mir leid wegen dieser einen besonders theatralischen entsetzlichen Schweinerei.» Und dann – mit einem Pfft und einem Zischen – entweicht die Luft aus seinem Kopf. Dieser digitale Mann hatte seinen Moment, aber anscheinend – es sei denn, Sie heissen Adam – hatte er ihn nicht mit *Ihnen.*

Das ist die ungeschickte Tyrannei, die man der Empfindsamkeit vorwirft: *Hier ist jemandes Traurigkeit – bedauern Sie ihn.* Wie Jennifer Doyle schreibt: «Das Sentimentale steht in Opposition zu den Verhaltensnormen, die die sozialen Räume des Kunstkonsums regeln – es ist chaotisch, verschafft der Gefühlswelt unmittelbare Geltung und ist hoffnungslos mit dem Niederen und dem Populären verknüpft.» Doyle macht sich Gedanken über die Bedingungen dieses Krieges: «Wie oft schon hat man erlebt, dass ein Künstler ... für seine mangelnde Empfindsamkeit gelobt wurde, als wäre sie ein selbstverständlicher

Wert?»[1] Jemandem dabei zuzusehen, wie er oder sie sich emotional auszieht, kann ein unappetitliches Spektakel sein. In ihrem Video THE ONION (Die Zwiebel, 1995) verspeist die Künstlerin Marina Abramović eine ganze rohe Zwiebel – die sich über ihr Gesicht verteilt und ihren Lippenstift verschmiert –, während ihre Stimme aus dem Off die immer gleiche Liste von Beschwerden über ihr Leben abspult:

Ich habe es satt, so oft umzusteigen, in den Wartesälen, Busbahnhöfen, Bahnhöfen und Flughäfen zu warten. Ich habe es satt ... mit einem Glas Wasser herumzustehen und so zu tun, als würde mich Konversation interessieren. Ich habe meine Migräneanfälle satt. Einsames Hotelzimmer, Zimmerservice, Ferngespräche, schlechte Fernsehfilme. Ich habe es satt, mich immer in den falschen Mann zu verlieben. Ich habe es satt, mich für meine zu grosse Nase zu schämen, für meinen zu grossen Hintern, für den Krieg in Jugoslawien.

Abramovićs Vorführung ist merkwürdig, herausfordernd, mitleiderregend, hässlich. Sie fühlt sich masslos an. *Dann hör doch auf, diese verdammte Zwiebel zu essen. Hör auf, dich ununterbrochen zu beschweren.* Wie Doyle indes betont, funktioniert Emotion anders, wenn die Kunst von Männern stammt, die weniger oft der Sentimentalität bezichtigt werden und stattdessen in der «Tradition trauriger, melancholischer weisser männlicher Künstler» agieren dürfen.[2] Dazu zitiert sie Bas Aders ironische Auseinandersetzung mit dieser Tradition in seinem dreiminütigen Kurzfilm I'M TOO SAD TO TELL YOU (Ich bin zu traurig, um es dir zu sagen, 1971). Atkins setzt der bewussten Enthaltung in Aders Werk – einem Weinenden, der jedoch zu traurig oder diskret ist, um den Grund für seine Tränen zu nennen – eine schmutzigere Alternative entgegen, indem er stattdessen seine sinnfreie Wortfülle abliefert: seine Monologe und beschissenen Coversongs. Die erklären zwar nicht, warum er traurig ist, aber sie zeigen ihn gefangen in der erbärmlichen Pose, eine Erklärung zu *versuchen* oder verstanden werden zu wollen. Atkins verleiht seinem Avatar eine beschämende Ausdruckskraft, so als lote er die Grenzen eines Phänomens aus, das Doyle als unsere sozialisierte Bereitschaft bezeichnet, «seine Tränen als echt zu akzeptieren», wenn der Künstler männlich ist.

Nicht immer sind wir bereit, sie als irgendetwas zu akzeptieren. Ein weiblicher Bedenkentroll postete über ihr Erleben des irritierenden Avatars in Atkins' US DEAD TALK LOVE (Wir Toten sprechen von Liebe, 2012):

Ich frage mich, ob es sich wohl so anfühlt, die Freundin eines jungen, emotional anfälligen, aber geltungsbedürftigen männlichen Künstlers zu sein. Man hört kurze Chöre von (digital erzeugten?) Stimmen, die bestimmte Wörter wiederholen, während dieser Jammerlappen uns mit seinem inneren Monolog über Beziehungen und «Intimität» ohne viel Inhalt oder Tiefgang jenseits der solipsistischen Freude am Klang seiner eigenen Stimme unterhält, die in all ihrer Geistlosigkeit so sorgfältig bearbeitet ist.

Ein Teil von mir sagt: *Amen*, ein anderer sagt: *Ja, aber.* Auf den Inhalt der Monologe kommt es nicht an. Der Avatar redet über jemanden, der «die Küste rauf und runter Familien betrügt» und «seit Langem verstorbene, geliebte Haustiere wiederbelebt». Er sagt: «Ich konnte Verstecken nie bloss mit Feigheit verbinden.» Seine Worte bieten keine Tiefe, sondern eine billige, vorgefertigte Nachbildung von Tiefe. Es geht nicht um die Intelligenz der Worte, sondern um die Tatsache, dass sie intelligent sein *wollen*, so wie die Bildmetaphern, die über die Leinwand gleiten, rostige Ketten in einem tiefen Meer von whiskybraunem *Etwas*. Das Gefühl ist nicht das Gefühl von dargebotenen oder vollendeten Metaphern – den *Ketten* der Einsamkeit oder des Alkoholismus –, es ist verzweifelter als das. Es ist ein verzweifeltes *Greifen* nach Metaphern, ein sich an ihre Möglichkeit Klammern.

Die Sprache ist verstörend, ja ärgerlich, weil sie Bedeutung vorspielt, ohne sie zu liefern, genauso wie der Avatar verstört, weil sein Gesicht Menschlichkeit vorspielt, aber nicht menschlich ist. Seine Züge bewegen sich, sind aber eindeutig *hergestellt*, seine Stimme beschwört den Geist eines kultivierten Roboters herauf, der es trotz seiner Programmierung geschafft hat zu fühlen. Alles hier lebt im unheimlichen Tal, diesem seltsamen Raum der Abscheu, der das beinahe Menschliche birgt – das so ist wie wir, aber nicht ganz.

In diesen Videos wurde die Emotion selbst ins unheimliche Tal verbannt: Gefühle sind beinahe menschlich, aber nicht ganz; sie wirken anziehend und stossen gleichzeitig ab. Wir sehen das ganze lächerliche Gepränge der Gefühlsausdrücke – die traurigen Cowboylieder und die bis ins Absurde karikierten bildlichen Ausdrücke jugendlicher Angst –, doch uns fehlt ein solides Gefühl für das wirklich Ausgedrückte. Was erzeugt wird, ist nichts weiter als ein unbehagliches emotionales Feld – alles ist aus, zerrissen, unterbrochen. Ich fühle mich verunsichert und verraten und enttäuscht. Alles, was ich will, wird mir vorenthalten: Einsicht, Erzählung, Menschlichkeit. Ich werde ins Nichtfortschreitende, Nichterzählerische, Nichterlösende gezwungen – in den Raum des *Beinahe*.

Eve Kosofsky Sedgwick argumentiert, dass die moderne Kritik der Empfindsamkeit das «Implizite und Nichterklärliche der Identifikation zwischen dem Leidenden und dem sentimentalen Zuschauer» beanstandet.[3] Atkins' Videos dagegen spielen eher mit diesem Prozess der Identifikation, als ihn feilzubieten. Anstatt eine falsche Prämisse von absoluter Identifikation aufzustellen – zwischen Künstler und Betrachter oder Betrachter und leidendem Subjekt –, sprengen und hinterfragen sie die Prämisse der Identifikation komplett, entlarven ihre Absurdität und führen den unbeholfenen Kraftakt vor, nach ihr zu greifen. Wie können wir uns mit diesem unsympathischen Avatar identifizieren? Wir wollen ihm unentwegt entkommen. Doch ständig sind da *drei* von ihm, die ihren Gefühlen gleichzeitig freien Lauf lassen.

Wir befinden uns weniger in der Gegenwart des Schmerzes als vielmehr in der Gegenwart der *Idee*, ihn zu äussern. *Hilf mir ohne Entwürdigung zu kommunizieren, Darling.* Dabei handelt dieses Werk von nichts anderem als von Entwürdigung – der Entwürdigung der Kommunikation selbst. Die leeren Monologe dramatisieren das Schauspiel, über Gefühle zu sprechen, und dessen Schande: die gewichtigen Töne unseres kraftlosen Versuchs, miteinander in Melancholie zu verfallen, nur weil wir es nicht aushalten, mit ihr allein zu bleiben, und die Peinlichkeit dieser Transaktion. *Es tut mir leid wegen dieser einen besonders theatralischen entsetzlichen Schweinerei.* An einem Punkt hören wir schweres Atmen. Eine vom ganzen Monologisieren erschöpfte Stimme. Dann, plötzlich, entweicht aus ihm die Luft – sein Inneres war die ganze Zeit über leer.

Dies ist keine Kunst über Intimität im Digitalzeitalter; sie benutzt nur die digitale Form, um auszuleuchten, was dem Kern der Intimität wesentlich näher ist, nämlich wie wir sie beieinander und bei der Kunst suchen, wie wir uns von Gefühlsäusserungen zugleich angezogen und abgestossen fühlen können. Dieser jämmerliche Avatar ist eine Chance, mit der Frage abzurechnen, wie stürmisch wir vor der Möglichkeit des Sentimentalen fliehen – deren Schemen am Horizont lauert und wie ein voller, leuchtender Mond über den Gläsern auf dem Tisch aufgeht, sich erhebt wie ein Kahlkopf beim Betrachten eines Totenschädels.

Ist all dies nur ein Sichlustigmachen über die Tropen von Angst und Melodrama? Oder ist es eine Kritik einer Kritik – eine Absage an die reflexhafte Ablehnung des Sentimentalen? Für mich sind diese Videos in den Momenten am bizarrsten, wenn sie aufhören,

eine Verneinung zu sein; jenen Momenten, wenn die Identifikation im unwirtlichsten Klima ihre Zelte aufschlägt und *so oder so* geschieht. Ich fühle mit diesem digitalen Avatar – nicht wenn er sagt, dass er traurig ist, sondern wenn er sich dafür entschuldigt, dass er es sagt; er ist ein Avatar, der weiss, wie unattraktiv seine trottelige Persona ist. Ich fühle nicht mit ihm, weil auf seiner Stirn STIRB NICHT geschrieben steht, sondern weil es rückwärts geschrieben ist: Die Botschaft gilt ihm – wenn er in den Spiegel sieht und sich selbst ermahnt, nicht zu sterben –, nicht mir. Vielleicht stirbt er am Ende *wirklich*: mein selbstgefälliger Freund, mein übersprudelndes Herz, mein entleerter Ballon.

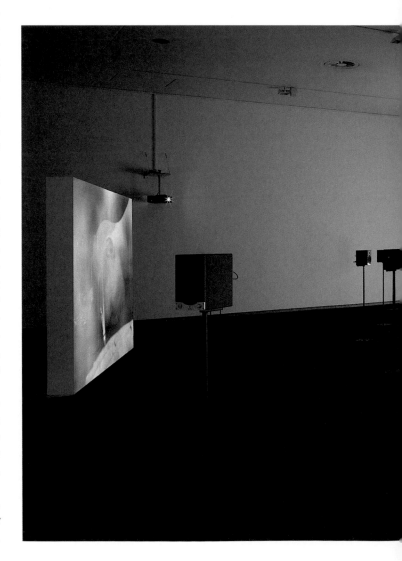

ED ATKINS, RIBBONS, 2014,
installation view Stedelijk Museum, 2015 /
BÄNDER, Installationsansicht.

Ein Teil von mir fühlt sich dumm und beschämt, weil es schon früh in einem der Videos einen kurzen Moment gibt, in dem sein Gesicht einfällt. Ich weiss, ihm wird die Luft ausgehen, und höre trotzdem zu. Ich weiss, er ist nicht echt, und höre trotzdem zu. Ich möchte nicht an das glauben, was er sagt, sondern an den Moment, den ich mit ihm habe. Ich bin nicht Adam, aber ich bin hier, direkt gegenüber der Leinwand. *Kunst* befriedigt kein Verlangen oder schwächt es ab; sie ist bloss ein anderer Zustand, in dem es sich offenbart, und die Frage der Schmerzperformance ist nicht nur eine Frage der Kunstproduktion: Wahrer Schmerz braucht – um ausgedrückt zu werden – immer seine eigene Performance. Atkins erkennt die simultan auftretende Scham und die Notwendigkeit dieses Handelns: Wir versuchen etwas zu konstruieren, das echt genug ist, um das zu sagen, was wir sagen wollen, eine Animation oder einen Satz oder einen mit Krickelkrakel überzogenen Kahlkopf. Es ist nicht echt genug, es kann nichts sagen, und trotzdem hören wir zu.

(Übersetzung: Kurt Rehkopf)

1) Jennifer Doyle, *Hold It Against Me: Difficulty and Emotion in Contemporary Art*, Durham: Duke University Press, 2013, S. 77, 80.
2) Ebd., S. 88.
3) Eve Kosofsky Sedgwick, *Epistemology of the Closet*, Berkeley: University of California Press, 1990, S. 151.

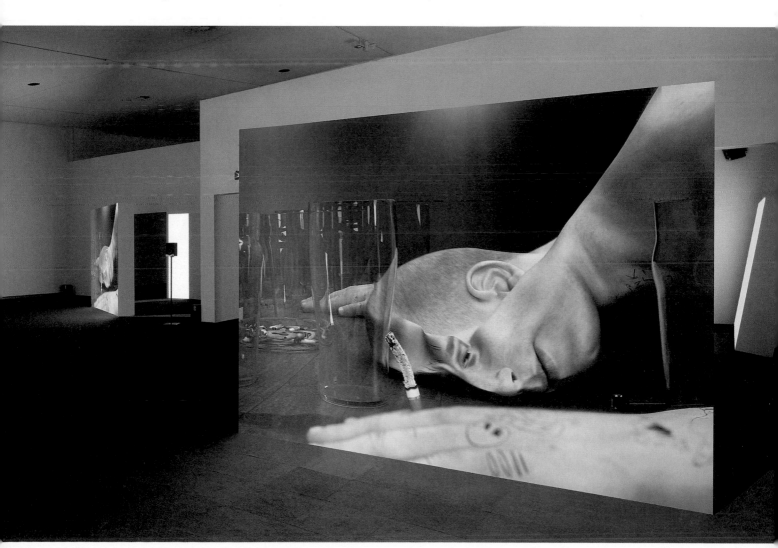

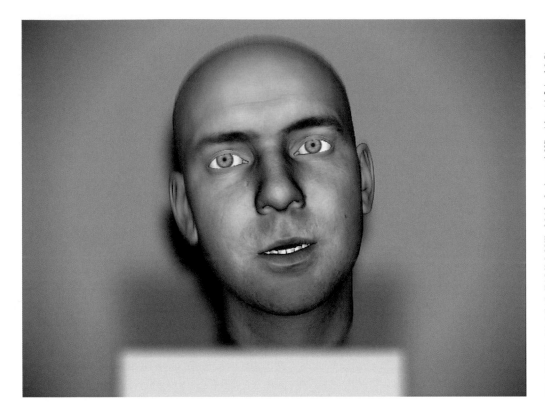

ED ATKINS, US DEAD TALK LOVE, 2012, 2-channel HD video (4:3 in 16:9) with 5.1 surround sound, 37 min. 24 sec. / WIR TOTEN SPRECHEN VON LIEBE, 2-Kanal HD-Video (4:3 in 16:9) mit 5.1-Raumklang.

Mary Shelley App

BRUCE HAINLEY

Mary Shelley: Sorry. (*She clears her throat.*) You were saying?

Monster: That I want to shove my extra cocks down their throats just to shut them the fuck up.

MS: I didn't know you had more than one.

Monster: As many as there are holes in the world. They're detachable. I press a button and off they go without me. Solar-powered, just like desire.

MS: You don't want to listen to what they're telling you, these Max Headroom 2.0s?

Monster: I'm not sure I'd put it quite like that, but neither is it a question of approval or disapproval. Assent or dissent's redundant, haven't you heard? My progeny require only a hit, their genomic coding soothed by any kind of attention, "positive" or "negative."

BRUCE HAINLEY is the author of *Under the Sign of [sic]: Sturtevant's Volte-Face* and ~~*Art & Culture*~~, both published by Semiotext(e). He teaches in the Graduate Art program at Art Center College of Design, Pasadena, California.

MS: What kind of involvement is "liking" something? What does an IG posting confirm or communicate?

Monster: *Wish you were here.* But then, more times than not, *sotto voce*, insinuating, *but you're not, are you, darling?* What are scare quotes is more like it. What is the difference between irony and "irony"? Would you like another drink?

MS: "Please"? By progeny you mean . . . ?

Monster: Various avatars, trolls, amalgamations—*animations*, really—the artist has given life to, made to speak. Human likenesses, filled to the rim with poignance, filled fuller than any cut-glass tumbler is with booze, blood, paint, or piss, what's your poison, poignancies via mumbled language, talking to oneself, and lonely singing, hums and glottal pops, bodily crunches, farts, sonics standing in, gropingly, for the lyric.

MS: And by *lyric*, I assume you mean, well, I could quote Percy on that, but let's make things a bit more spiked. Hmmm . . . T. J. Clark writes something about the "illusion in an artwork of a singular voice or viewpoint, uninterrupted, absolute, laying claim to a world of its own," but, pardon me, fuck him. The man seems never to have had a critical moment for artists or writers who are women.

Monster: Yes, indeed. Nevertheless, however named, these HD *Caprichos* end up mirroring their creator, not because they necessarily all look like him, no, but rather because images supersede their objects, in their excruciating hi-def realization—eyelash delicacy, hirsute softness, and de-

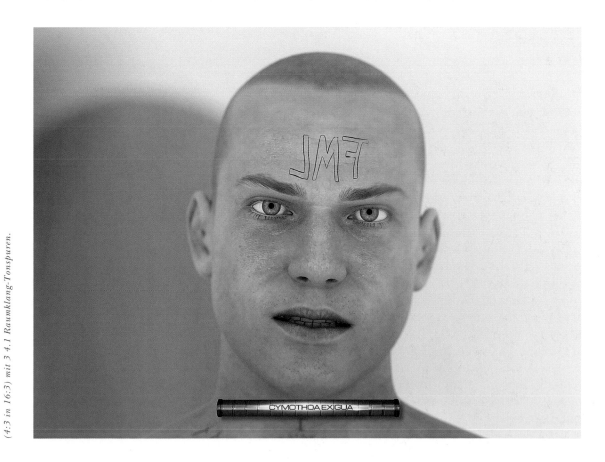

ED ATKINS, RIBBONS, 2014, 3-channel HD video (4:3 in 16:3) with 3 4.1 channel surround soundtracks, 13 min. / BÄNDER, 3-Kanal HD-Video (4:3 in 16:3) mit 3 4.1 Raumklang-Tonspuren.

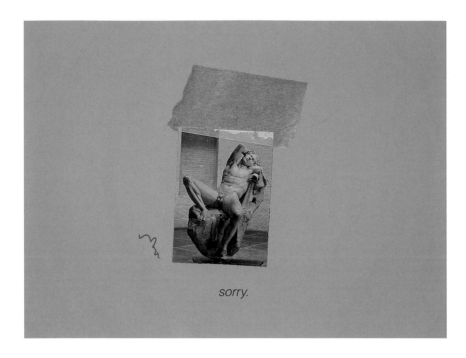

sorry.

*ED ATKINS, US DEAD TALK
LOVE, 2012, 2-channel HD
video (4:3 in 16:9) with 5.1
surround sound, 37 min. 24 sec. /
WIR TOTEN SPRECHEN
VON LIEBE, 2-Kanal HD-Video
(4:3 in 16:9) mit 5.1-Raumklang.*

flations, powdery explosions, streams of smoke, and eyes, eyes, imploring, why, oh, why, master, have you forsaken me to this void . . .

MS: Which some of us call existence. (*She sighs.*) By which you mean the screen's deathly perfection. It's as much resemblance as we can bear.

Monster: Which is what makes them monstrous.

MS: Or him monstrous.

Monster: It takes one to no one, and he's no monster. Or no more a monster than you or I. His métier's heartbreak.

MS: So that we might feel *something.* Imagine an artist wanting us to feel something! (*She laughs.*) Some of what he finds heartbreaking remains the fact that, like moths attracted to flickering light, in our fascinations we begin—brighter than us they glow—to ape these avatars that surpass us. Do all technologies, representational or otherwise, end up cruel tools? When I looked in the still mirror of Lake Geneva did I see myself or Victor Frankenstein or you? I don't remember.

Monster: You saw habitués of that old dive bar, Romanticism. More clearly than anyone else, except for maybe Dorothy Wordsworth. She looked away from man, in her otherkin apartness, nevertheless tracing his effect in movements of the clouds, meteorological disturbances, creatures quivering, flora; you looked down into the murk of human desire and saw something horrifying, relentless.

MS: Now, who's the earnest dear one in *Eat Pray Love* . . .

Monster: US DEAD TALK LOVE . . .

MS: Right. That yearning one, am I wrong in believing he looks something like the artist? "His" eyes always start from his sockets, sweetly programmed tic of human affect. Always with these young guns, something with the eyes. The artist's wanker monologuists, gurglers, are the 2D version—kissing cousins once removed, better by far—of that robot stripper, in whom/which any empathy, ersatz entirely, is manipulated by "its" ("her"?) eyes. The female figure *seeks viewers out with her eyes*, and gleefully, viewers kvell, like toddlers who become perplexed if you don't acknowledge them. Insidious that we want our being ratified by a tawdry inanimate object, that now art must perform a return of our monstrously needy gaze. A search for human kindness leading us to seek it, overflowing, from animatronics and CGI stand-ins rather than from one another.

Monster: As if we'd get a bad case of the sads if every fucking atom or pixel didn't return our gaze. Our programming would be disappointed. Why's Dead Talker the one who gets to sing the song from *Sweeney Todd*? Some reason connected to Johanna's witnessing and blood relation to the tonsorial goings-on? Why does the entire thing begin with sorry, and why is that sentiment associated with the picture of the Barberini Faun, spread out like Jeff Aquilon for Bruce Weber in the *Soho Weekly News*, circa, what, 1980? Apology that what we're seeing doesn't equal the cold perfection of its bodily offering or that DT, whatever his tremblings or *tremens*, will never equal what precedes him?

MS: The Faun was eventually sold to Ludwig, prince of Bavaria, who planned a special room in the Glyptothek for the flagrant treasure, even before the final bill of sale was inked. Edmé Bourchardon's homage in the Louvre remains more salacious than the original, by which I mean more accurate, louche, the way secondhand climaxes often are.

Monster: Pygmalion is only another version of "our" tale, no? Stephen Sondheim knows a thing or two about S/M, bondage scenes with musical accompaniment, man caves, sex closets, the inanimate coming to life and life itself snuffed out.

MS: Sweeney Todd, or, seeing how the sausage is made. Why do the artist's chatty dudes speak in rhythms that recall Yaz's "I Before E Except After C"?

Monster: Inside you can feel th- / Outside you can see the difference

MS: Inside, stop, inside, difference / Outside, out stop, inside you can feel the difference. . . . Self-reflection's a bitch. I should know.

Monster: It's why many outsource selfics, so nothing remains to be reflected . . . reflected upon?

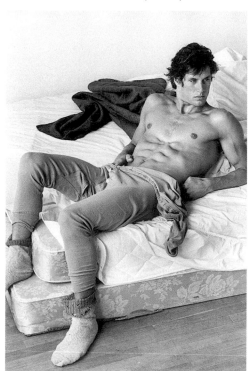

MS: An HD mirror on which to dwell.

Monster: A lot of tech talk and highfalutin discursivity—Blanchot, Malabou, etc.—when maybe someone should sit down and rewatch *Blade Runner*.

MS: Sean Young . . . (*she sighs*) . . . played the Johanna of that tale, exquisitely in the flick, and then, brutally, the playing subsumed her life.

Monster: What does the human owe to the inhuman? What does it owe to the animal? Why, why is a perfect representation so cold? Who created whom? Did you create me or did my infamy retroactively make you known? Would you, could you, exist without me?

MS: Careful, or I'll paper cut you a thousand times with this photocopy of *Le Rire de la Méduse*.

Monster: Ah, 凌遲. Better than death by "The Cyborg Manifesto."

MS: Who's the one in the sensory deprivation tank?

BRUCE WEBER, JEFF AQUILON, NEW YORK, NEW YORK, 1982, silver gelatin print, 11 x 14" / Silbergelatine-Abzug, 28 x 35,5 cm. (COPYRIGHT: BRUCE WEBER)

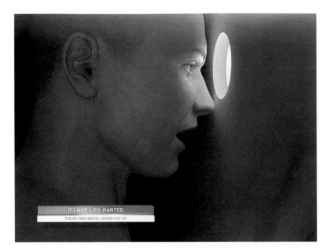

ITS NOT LIPS, PARTED

TWO OR THREE BEATS, EXHALE AND LIP

ED ATKINS, RIBBONS, 2014, 3-channel HD
video (4:3 in 16:9) with 3 4.1 channel surround
soundtracks, 13 min. / BÄNDER, 3-Kanal HD-Video
(4:3 als 16:9) mit 3 4.1 Raumklang-Tonspuren.

Monster: Warmworm? We'll nickname "him," almost eponymously.

MS: Or Locks. Because of how close it is to Looks.

Monster: I'm pretty sure that's the masculine of Goldilocks. He's into watersports.

MS: Locksy's an inch away from some old-school butch queen teaching him a thing or two about identity theft, cultural appropriation, putting him through an erotic asphyxiation session avec deprivation the likes of which he knows absolutely *nada.*

Monster: Locksy will end up so fucking out of it, one breath away from dead, and some dude unwrapping his long mane from around his neck, cutting it off, wadding it into the man bun it's just dying to be, and then wiping up his load, shoving the sticky bundle . . .

MS: . . . into his mouth. (*She pauses.*) You survived longer than any of my other children. Is it because I loved you more, or is it because of some vital hate?

Monster: Will Dave outlive Ed?

MS: Nothing will save any of us from extreme data rot.

Monster: Ed insists Dave is "straight."

MS: Aren't we all? #nohomo. By "straight," he means generic and privileged. "Art world," to put its, um, class specificity another way.

Monster: #webromo

MS: #bestr8acting. Or as flexible and death adjacent as a boy falling out of the pages of a Dennis Cooper novel. Maybe, *The Sluts.*

Monster: I don't know what "straight" identity confirms anymore. The idea that a certain kind of mainstreamed, coupled, children-rearing, *instrumentalized* gayness isn't *more or,* at the very least, as privileged as any kind of globalized privilege goes, I find specious. Many (most?) of the top (whatever that means) gay (whatever that means) porn stars (talk about aren't we all?) are "straight" (whatever . . . ditto).

MS: The "guys" on Flirt4Free, too.

Monster: ?

MS: Mother does her "research." Does *anything* about "identity" cohere now? Despite this Caitlyn-ish moment—I hear Ryan Seacrest's production team's at work on yet another remake in which Jenner stars as both Victor Frankenstein *and,* well, something like you—in which we're becoming oh so tender and politic about variegated ways of being, hasn't what used to be subsumed under "identity" been algorithmically fractured, sorted into niche markets targeting the "personal" or "individual" in ways that remain anything but transparent?

Monster: According to the artist, Dave's supposedly young, dumb . . . and full of brotein.

MS: He's the somewhat James Richards-y one?

Monster: Which might make some ask why's he the one with FML marked on his forehead, looking like a pass-around cumdump after an all-night kegger ready for another toss?

MS: A sluttishness mother admires but which might make one inquire about the glory holes—"mis-used" (for comic effect?) by fingers, nose, flaccid member—and "super-communicative anal sacs," why any of it/them should be secured under the category of a straightness which no longer exists, if it ever did. And, yet, look around you, seems to be, paradoxically, still winning. The only thing more obsolete than heterosexuals are faggots. Faggotry—*sheesh*—I don't have to tell you, isn't and has never been the same thing as homosexuality or gayness.

Monster: Winning in the Charlie Sheen sense or actually succeeding sense?

MS: Well, you're the one who claimed any positive or negative valence to such difference redundant.

Monster: And you're the one who wrote that "in a solitary chamber, or rather cell, at the top of the house, and separated from all the other apartments by a gallery and staircase, I kept my work-shop of filthy creation, my eyeballs were starting from their sockets in attending to the details of my employment." Portrait of the artist. Any artist. Alone. Aloner than many.

MS: As in, what would it mean merely to adore this work? However often that's done, it wouldn't confront the solitude at its core. So many technologies for us not to be by ourselves anymore. (*Mumbling*) ". . . The visitor replies . . . why not be alone together?" (*She sighs.*) Laughable. The workshop's now lit by ubiquitous LED, as "problematic" as the element spelled out by that funny acronym, abracadabra-like, but still filthy. Filthier. And I wonder, these figures, not unlike my monster/my self, which or who, in Barbara Johnson's words, can "be seen as a figure for autobiography as such," with all their articulations, bankrupt speechifying settling into lonesome, murmuring—"whatever"—recitatives . . .

Monster: What's actually being said?

MS: And what's being shown? Queries to be set in some blockbuster-size *Harry Potter*-ish or *Star Wars*-esque font.

Monster: The world's a mess it's in my kiss? Abreactions to the sleep of reason produce . . .

MS: (*Interrupting*) . . . the jukebox at the dive bar has many answers, a better Magic 8-Ball for a blackballed existence.

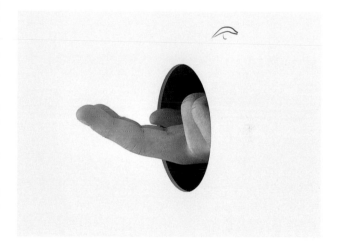

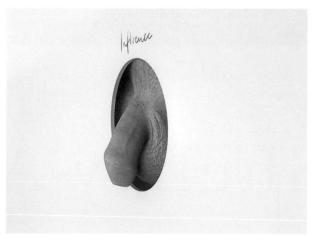

ED ATKINS, RIBBONS, 2014, 3-channel
HD video (4:3 in 16:9) with 3 4.1 channel
surround soundtracks, 13 min. /
BÄNDER, 3-Kanal HD-Video (4:3 als 16:9)
mit 3 4.1 Raumklang-Tonspuren.

ED ATKINS, WARM, WARM, WARM SPRING MOUTHS, 2013,
HD film with with 5.1 surround sound, 12 min. 50 sec. /
WARM, WARM, WARMER FRÜHLINGSMUND, HD-Film mit 5.1-Raumklang.

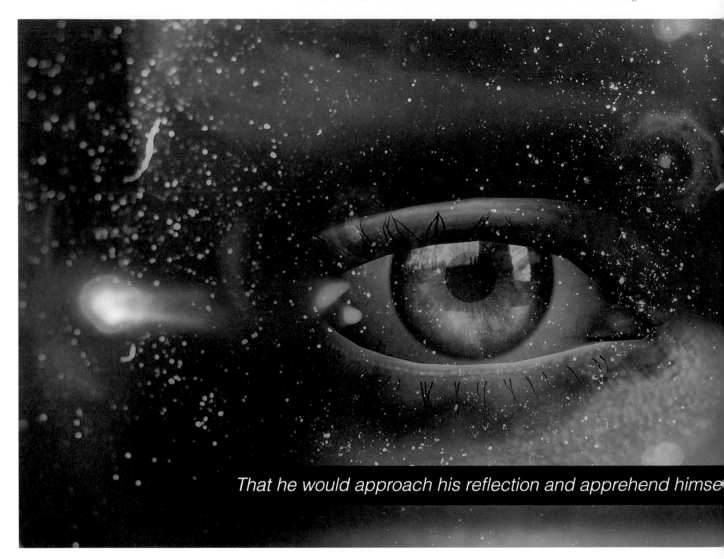

That he would approach his reflection and apprehend himse[lf]

Die
Mary-Shelley-App

54

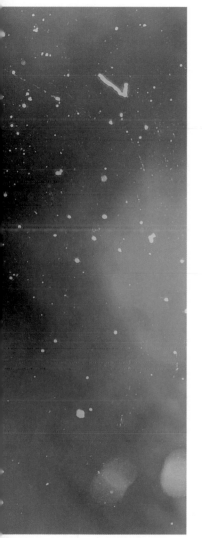

BRUCE HAINLEY

Mary Shelley: Tut mir leid. (*Sie räuspert sich.*) Was hast du eben gesagt?

Monster: Dass ich ihnen meine Extraschwänze in den Rachen rammen will, um ihnen endlich das Maul zu stopfen.

MS: Ich wusste gar nicht, dass du mehr als einen hast.

Monster: So viele, wie es Löcher auf der Welt gibt. Sie sind abnehmbar. Ich drücke auf den Knopf und los geht's. Mit Sonnenenergie, genau wie die Lust.

MS: Du willst nicht hören, was sie dir zu sagen haben, diese Max Headroom 2.0s?

Monster: So würde ich das wohl nicht formulieren, aber es geht weder um Zustimmung noch um Ablehnung. Hast du noch nie gehört, dass Einigkeit und Widerspruch redundant sind? Meine Nachkommen brauchen nur einen Treffer, jede Art von Aufmerksamkeit, «positiv» oder «negativ», lindert ihre Genomkodierung.

MS: Was für eine Beteiligung ist das denn, etwas zu «liken»? Was bestätigt oder besagt eine Mitteilung auf Instagram?

Monster: *Wärst du doch hier.* Aber auch öfter als nicht, *sotto voce*, bloss angedeutet, *Aber du bist es nicht, oder, mein Schatz?* Mehr so was, wie warnende Anführungszeichen. Was *ist* der Unterschied zwischen Ironie und «Ironie»? Möchtest du noch einen Drink?

MS: «Bitte»? Mit Nachkommen meinst du …?

Monster: Diverse Avatare, Trolle, Mischwesen – eigentlich *Animationen* –, die der Künstler ins Leben gerufen, zum Sprechen gebracht hat. Menschenähnliche Gestalten, bis obenhin voller Biss, randvoll, voller, als je ein geschliffenes Glas mit Alk, Blut, Farbe oder Pisse gefüllt war, oder was immer dein bevorzugtes Gift ist, bissige Sprüche, nur vor sich hin gemunkelt, vor sich hin gesungen, gesummt, gerotzt, körperliche Knackgeräusche, Fürze, ein ganzes Spektrum tapsiger Laute anstelle von Text.

MS: Und mit Text meinst du wohl, nun, ich könnte dazu Percy zitieren, aber lass uns die Sache etwas dornenreicher gestalten. Hmmm … T. J. Clark schreibt etwas wie, «die Illusion in einem Kunstwerk, das mit einer Stimme oder aus einem bestimmten Blickwinkel spricht, ungebrochen, absolut, erhebt Anspruch auf eine eigene Welt», aber – pardon – scheiss drauf! Der Typ scheint nie auch nur einen kritischen Augenblick für weibliche Kunstschaffende oder Autoren übriggehabt zu haben.

BRUCE HAINLEY ist der Autor von *Under the Sign of [sic]: Sturtevant's Volte-Face* und ~~*Art & Culture*~~, beide bei Semiotext(e) erschienen. Er unterrichtet im Rahmen des Graduate Art Program am Art Center College of Design, Pasadena, Kalifornien.

Monster: So ist es. Trotzdem, egal wie ihre Titel lauten, all diese HD-*Caprichos* widerspiegeln letztlich ihren Schöpfer, nicht weil unbedingt alle so aussehen wie er, sondern weil die Bilder in dieser unerträglichen HD-Wiedergabe ihren Gegenstand verdrängen – mit ihren feinen Wimpern, ihrer haarigen Weichheit und ihrem Jammer, mit ihren pulverigen Explosionen, Rauchschwaden und Augen, inständig flehenden Augen, warum, oh, warum, Herr, hast du mich in diese Leere verstossen …

MS: Manche nennen das *Existenz*. (*Sie seufzt.*) Du meinst damit die tödliche Perfektion des Bildschirms. Eine kaum noch zu ertragende Ähnlichkeit.

Monster: Deshalb wirken sie so monströs.

MS: Oder er.

Monster: Es braucht eins, um eins zu verteufeln, und er ist kein Monster. Oder jedenfalls nicht mehr als du oder ich. Die Seelenqual ist sein Metier.

MS: Damit wir etwas empfinden. Stell dir vor, ein Künstler will, dass wir etwas empfinden! (*Sie lacht.*) Von all dem, was er herzzerreissend findet, bleibt uns die Tatsache, dass wir, wie die Motten angezogen vom flackernden Licht, in unserer Begeisterung beginnen, die uns überflügelnden Avatare – denn sie strahlen heller als wir – nachzuäffen. Werden alle technischen Darstellungs- und sonstigen Techniken am Ende zu Folterwerkzeugen? Habe ich, als ich in den stillen Spiegel des Genfersees schaute, mich selbst gesehen oder Victor Frankenstein oder dich? Ich weiss es nicht mehr.

Monster: Du hast die Stammgäste der alten Spelunke namens Romantik gesehn. Und zwar deutlicher als sonst jemand, vielleicht mit Ausnahme von Dorothy Wordsworth. Die schaute in ihrem fremdartigen Anderssein vom Menschen weg und verfolgte dennoch seine Spuren in Wolkenzügen, meteorologischen Störungen, zitternden Kreaturen und der Pflanzenwelt; du hast in das Dunkel der menschlichen Sehnsucht hinabgeblickt und etwas Grauenerregendes, Unerbittliches gesehen.

MS: Hm, wer ist dieser ernste Typ in *Eat Pray Love* …

Monster: US DEAD TALK LOVE …

MS: Genau, dieser Sehnsüchtige. Irre ich mich, oder gleicht er ein bisschen dem Künstler? «Seine» Augen treten immer leicht aus den Höhlen, ein nett programmierter, emotionaler menschlicher Tick. Bei diesen Jungspunden ist immer etwas mit den Augen. Die monologisierend gurgelnden Wichser des Künstlers sind die 2-D-Version – viel besser ohne die knutschenden Cousins – dieses strippenden Roboters, bei dem jede Empathie, reines, durch «seine» («ihre»?) Augen gesteuertes Surrogat bleibt. Die weibliche Figur, *deren Augen die Betrachter suchen*, worauf diese freudig zu strahlen beginnen wie kleine Kinder, die beleidigt sind, wenn man sie nicht beachtet. Peinlich, dass wir die Bestätigung eines billigen unbelebten Objekts erheischen und nun schon die Kunst unseren geradezu monströs bedürftigen Blick erwidern muss; und dass wir dabei nach menschlicher Freundlichkeit suchen, übervoll von animatronischen und computergenerierten Bildwelten statt voneinander.

Monster: Als ob es uns in tiefste Depression stürzen würde, wenn nicht jedes verdammte Körnchen oder jeder Pixel unseren Blick erwidert. Unsere Software wäre frustriert. Warum darf gerade dieser tote Sprecher den Song aus *Sweeney Todd* singen? Hängt dies vielleicht mit Johannas Blutsverwandtschaft und ihrem Wissen um die Vorgänge im Barbierladen zusammen? Weshalb beginnt das Ganze mit dem Wort «Sorry» und weshalb wird dieses Gefühl mit dem Bild des Barberini-Fauns verknüpft, der so gespreizt hingestreckt posiert wie Jeff Aquilon für Bruce Weber in den *Soho Weekly News*, so um 1980 herum? Verzeihung, dass das, was wir sehen, nicht der kalten Perfektion der körperlichen Opfergabe entspricht, oder dass ein Delirium tremens allem Beben und Zittern zum Trotz nie an das herankommt, was ihm vorausging.

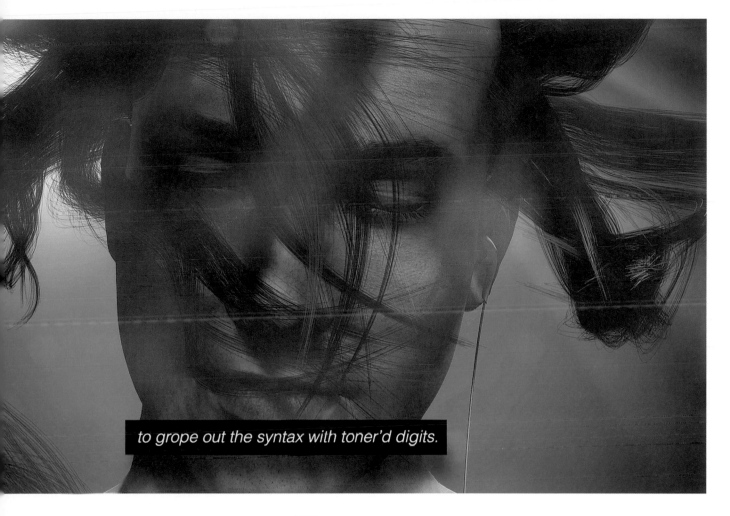

to grope out the syntax with toner'd digits.

ED ATKINS, WARM, WARM, WARM SPRING MOUTHS, 2013, HD film with with 5.1 surround sound, 12 min. 50 sec. /
WARM, WARM, WARMER FRÜHLINGSMUND, HD-Film mit 5.1-Raumklang.

MS: Der Faun wurde schliesslich an Ludwig, den Bayernkönig, verkauft, der in der Glyptothek einen besonderen Raum für diesen schamlosen Schatz vorgesehen hatte, noch bevor
der definitive Kaufvertrag unterzeichnet war. Edmé Burchardons Hommage im Louvre
bleibt schlüpfriger als das Original, damit meine ich: präziser, anrüchiger, wie es Orgasmen
aus zweiter Hand so an sich haben.
Monster: *Pygmalion* ist nur eine andere Variante «unserer» Geschichte, nicht? Stephen
Sondheim weiss ein, zwei Dinge über S/M, musikalisch untermalte Bondage-Szenen, Män-
nerrefugien, Sexkabinette sowie über das zum Leben Erwachen des Leblosen und das Auslö-
schen wahren Lebens.
MS: Sweeney Todd oder sehen, wie die Wurst gemacht wird. Weshalb reden die geschwät-
zigen Typen dieses Künstlers in Rhythmen, die an Yazoos *I Before E Except After C* erinnern?
Monster: «Inside you can feel th- / Outside you can see the difference»
MS: «Inside, stop, inside, difference / Outside, out stop, inside you can feel the difference ... » Selbstreflexion ist knifflig. Ich sollte das ja wissen.

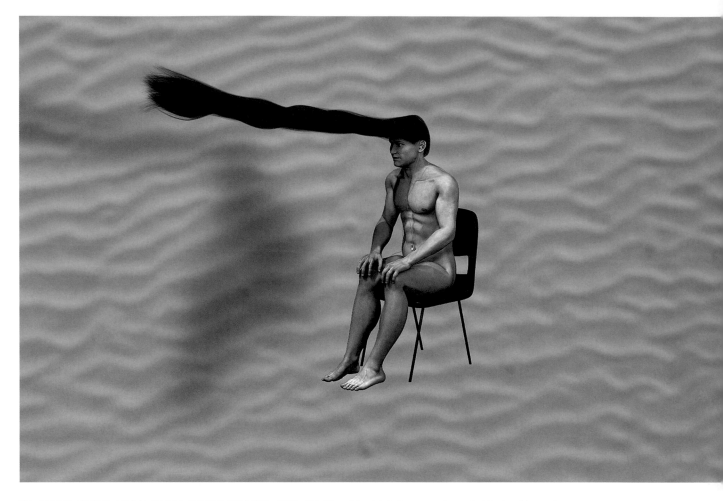

ED ATKINS, WARM, WARM, WARM SPRING MOUTHS, 2013, HD film with with 5.1 surround sound, 12 min. 50 sec. /
WARM, WARM, WARMER FRÜHLINGSMUND, HD-Film mit 5.1-Raumklang.

Monster: Deshalb lassen viele ihre Selfies von andern machen, damit nichts mehr reflektiert wird ... über nichts mehr reflektiert werden muss?

MS: Ein HD-Spiegel, vor dem man verweilen kann.

Monster: Eine Menge Technogeschwätz und hochtrabendes Geschwafel – Blanchot, Malabou usw. – , statt dass sich endlich mal jemand hinsetzt und sich *Blade Runner* wieder anschaut.

MS: Sean Young ... (*sie seufzt*) ... spielte die Johanna in dieser Geschichte, herrlich in diesem Streifen, danach sollte sich diese Rolle als erbarmungslose Zusammenfassung ihres Lebens entpuppen.

Monster: Was schuldet der Mensch dem Nichtmenschen? Was schuldet er dem Tier? Warum, warum ist eine perfekte Darstellung so kalt? Wer erschuf wen? Hast du mich erschaffen, oder hat mein schlechter Ruf dich rückwirkend berühmt gemacht? Würdest du, könntest du ohne mich existieren?

MS: Vorsicht, oder ich zerschneide dich 1000-mal mit dieser Photokopie von *Le Rire de la Méduse.*

Monster: Ah, 凌遲. Immer noch besser, als durch das *Cyborg Manifesto* zu sterben.

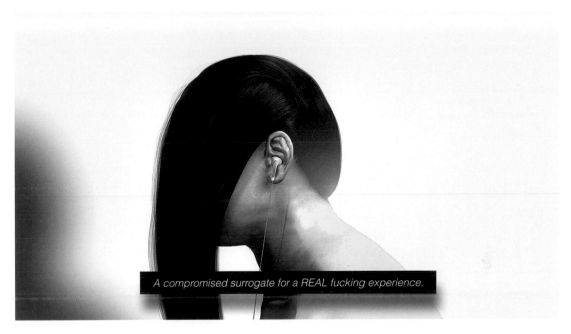

A compromised surrogate for a REAL fucking experience.

ED ATKINS, WARM, WARM, WARM SPRING MOUTHS, 2013, HD film with with 5.1 surround sound, 12 min. 50 sec. /
WARM, WARM, WARMER FRÜHLINGSMUND, HD-Film mit 5.1-Raumklang.

MS: Wer steckt schon wieder im sensorischen Deprivationstank?

Monster: Warmwurm? Wir geben «ihm» diesen quasi gleichlautenden Spitznamen.

MS: Oder Locks. Weil es so nah bei Looks liegt.

Monster: Ich bin mir ziemlich sicher, das ist das männliche Pendant zu Goldilocks. Und er treibt Wassersport.

MS: Locksy ist nur wenige Zentimeter entfernt von einer maskulinen Lesbe alter Schule, die ihm ein, zwei Dinge über Identitätsklau und kulturelle Appropriation beibringt und ihm eine Lektion in erotischer Atemkontrolle *avec* diversen Deprivationspraktiken erteilt, von denen er noch nie was gehört hat, *nada*.

Monster: Locksy wird danach total weggetreten sein, ein Atemzug vom Tod entfernt, und ein Typ wird die Schlinge seiner lange Mähne von seinem Hals wickeln, sie abschneiden und zu dem Männerdutt verknoten, der sie schon immer gern gewesen wäre, seine Wichse damit aufwischen und ihm das klebrige Paket …

MS: ins Maul stopfen. (*Sie hält inne.*) Du hast länger überlebt als meine anderen Kinder. Ist das, weil ich dich mehr geliebt habe, oder steckt ein vitaler Hass dahinter?

Monster: Wird Dave Ed überleben?

MS: Der extreme Datenverfall wird uns alle nicht verschonen.

Monster: Ed beharrt darauf, dass Dave «straight» sei.

MS: Sind wir das nicht alle? #nohomo. Mit «straight» meint er arttypisch und privilegiert. Oder «zur Kunstwelt gehörig», um seine, ähm, spezifische Klasse anders zu umschreiben.

Monster: #webromo

MS: #bestr8acting. Oder so flexibel und dem Tode nah wie ein aus den Seiten eines Dennis-Cooper-Romans entsprungener Knabe. Vielleicht aus *The Sluts* (Die Nutten).

Monster: Ich weiss nicht, was dieses «Straight»-Sein noch aussagen soll. Die Vorstellung, dass eine bestimmte verbreitete Form des paarweisen, Kinder grossziehenden, *instrumentalisierten* Schwulseins nicht stärker oder zumindest ebenso privilegiert sein soll wie jedes andere, global gesehen privilegierte Leben, finde ich läppisch.

Viele (die meisten?) der Top-(was immer das heisst)-Schwulen-(was immer das heisst)-Porno-stars (von wegen, sind wir das nicht alle?) sind «straight» (was immer … dito).

MS: Die «Kerle» von *Flirt4Free* auch.

Monster: ?

MS: Mama macht auch ihre «Recherchen». Ergibt *überhaupt noch etwas* an der «Identität» einen Sinn? Abgesehen von diesem Caitlyn'schen Moment – wie ich höre, arbeitet Ryan Seacrests Produktionsteam an einem weiteren Remake, in dem Caitlyn Jenner sowohl Victor Frankenstein als

ED ATKINS, WARM, WARM, WARM SPRING MOUTHS, 2013, HD film with with 5.1 surround sound, 12 min. 50 sec. / WARM, WARM, WARMER FRÜHLINGSMUND, HD-Film mit 5.1-Raumklang.

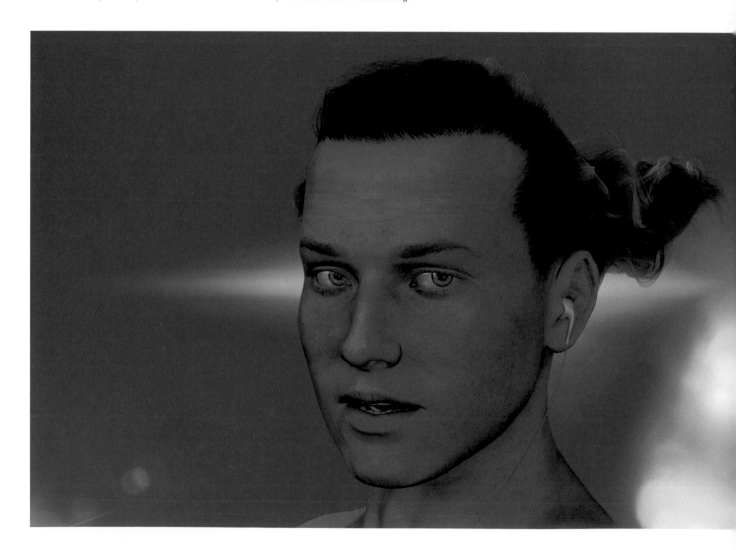

auch, nun ja, jemanden wie dich spielen soll, und in dem wir uns ach so zartfühlend und politisch über die vielfältigen Weisen des Seins auslassen werden. Wurde das, was bisher unter den Begriff «Identität» fiel, nicht algorithmisch aufgebrochen und auf Nischenmärkte verteilt, die auf vielfältige Weisen auf das Persönliche oder Individuelle abzielen, die ihrerseits alles andere als transparent sind?

Monster: Laut dem Künstler soll Dave angeblich jung, dumm … und mit *Brotein* vollgepumpt sein.

MS: Ist das dieser James-Richards-artige Typ?

Monster: Was einige dazu veranlassen könnte, zu fragen, warum ausgerechnet ihm FML (Fuck My Life) auf der Stirn geschrieben steht und warum er aussieht wie ein rumgereichter Wichskübel, der nach durchzechter Nacht auf den nächsten Einwurf wartet.

MS: Eine Verderbtheit, die Mama zwar bewundert, die aber durchaus Fragen aufwerfen konnte zu diesen Prachtlöchern – die (um der Komik willen?) mit Fingern, Nase, schlaffem Glied «missbraucht» werden – und diesen «superkommunikativen Analsäcken», warum so etwas in einer Kategorie *Straightness* untergebracht werden sollte, die es nicht mehr gibt, falls es sie überhaupt je gab, und die, man braucht sich bloss umzuschauen, seltsamerweise trotzdem noch die Oberhand zu behalten scheint. Das Einzige, was noch obsoleter ist als Heterosexuelle, sind Schwuchteln. Schwuchteltum – *ogottogott*, das muss ich dir nicht erläutern – ist und war nie dasselbe wie Homosexualität oder Schwulsein.

Monster: Die Oberhand behalten – wie Charlie Sheen oder im Sinn eines echten Sieges?

MS: Du bist es doch, der behauptet hat, jede positive oder negative Wertigkeit einer solchen Unterscheidung sei redundant.

Monster: Und du bist es doch, die schrieb: «In einem stillen, abgelegenen Zimmer, oder besser gesagt einer Kammer unter dem Dache, von allen übrigen Räumen durch eine Galerie und eine Treppe getrennt, vollbrachte ich mein ekelerregendes Werk. Die Augen traten mir aus den Höhlen vor Erregung und Anspannung.» Ein Porträt des Künstlers. Jedes Künstlers. Allein. Einsamer als viele.

MS: Wie in, was hiesse es, einfach sein Werk zu bewundern? Egal wie häufig das geschieht, der Einsamkeit in seinem Innersten begegnet man dabei nicht. So viele Mittel und Techniken, um nicht mehr allein zu sein. (*Murmelnd*) «… der Gast entgegnet, (…) könnten wir's nicht miteinander sein?» (*Sie seufzt.*) Lächerlich. Heute wird die Kammer von allgegenwärtigen LEDs erleuchtet, nicht minder «problematisch» als das Teil, das sich hinter diesem schrägen Akronym versteckt, abrakadabramässig, aber dennoch schmuddelig. Schmuddeliger. Und ich frage mich, diese Gestalten, nicht unähnlich meinem Monster / meinem Selbst, das, wie Barbara Johnson meint, «als Figur für die Autobiographie als solche angesehen werden» kann, mit all ihren Artikulationen, ihren windigen Wortschwällen, die in einsam gemunkelten – «trotz allem» – Rezitativen enden …

Monster: Was wird wirklich gesagt?

MS: Und was wird gezeigt? Fragen, die in einer gigantischen kassenschlagermässigen, *Harry Potter* oder *Star Wars* würdigen Schrift gesetzt werden müssen.

Monster: The world's a mess it's in my kiss? Überreaktionen auf den Schlaf der Vernunft gebären …

MS: (fällt ihm ins Wort) … die Jukebox in der Kneipe hält viele Antworten bereit, ein besserer *Magic 8 Ball* für eine verworfene Existenz.

(Übersetzung: Suzanne Schmidt, WunderWelt GmbH, Zürich)

EDITION FOR PARKETT 98

ED ATKINS

SAFE CONDUCT EPIDERMAL, 2016

Archival pigment print on rubber,
23 ⁵/₈ x 20 x ¹/₈", two grommets, printed by Laumont, New York.
Ed. 35 / XX, signed and numbered certificate.

Alterungsbeständiger Pigmentdruck auf Gummi,
60 x 51 x 0,1 cm, zwei Ösen, gedruckt von Laumont, New York.
Auflage 35 / XX, signiertes und nummeriertes Zertifikat.

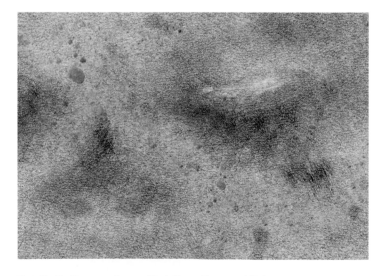

Detail of left eye and nose / Detail von Nase und linkem Auge.

The Epidermis of the head and neck of the artist's most recent digital surrogate—made real and human-scaled. Used in his video, *Safe Conduct*, this epidermis of Ed Atkins' surrogate has been carefully bespoke-bruised, battered—flecked and streaked with grime, tears, exposure. Printed on rubber, the surrogacy of the artist's digital figure becomes that of a mask.

Die Kopf- und Nackenhaut des neusten digitalen Künstler-Stellvertreters – realitätsnah und massstabsgetreu. Diese Stellvertreter-Epidermis wurde im Video *Safe Conduct* verwendet, sie wurde zu diesem Zweck sorgfältig gekratzt, geschlagen, gesprenkelt, geädert – mit Schmutz, Tränen, Strapazen. Auf Gummi gedruckt wird aus dem digitalen Stellvertreterbildnis eine Maske.

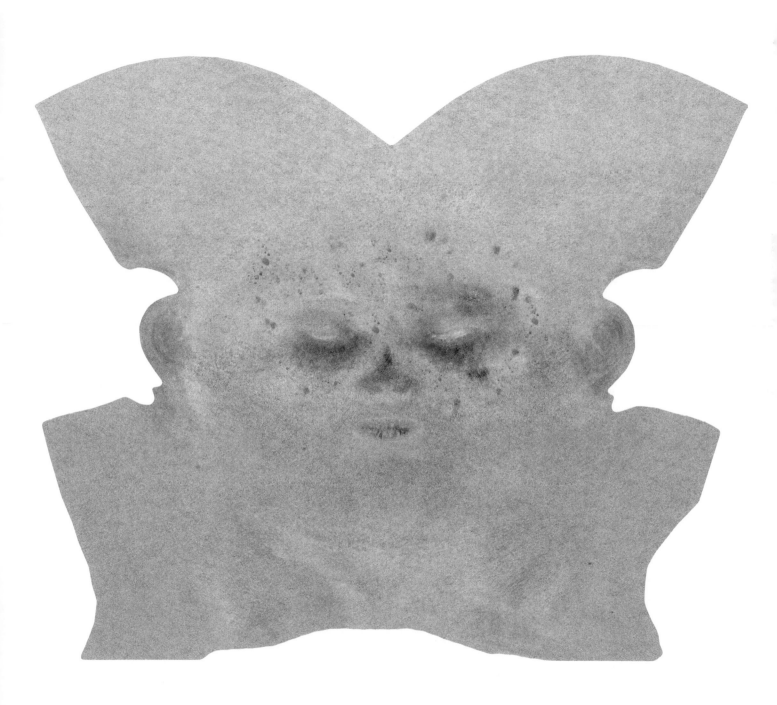

THEASTER GATES

THEASTER GATES and the Black Monks of Mississippi perform at St. Laurence Church during the building's demolition, South Side of Chicago, 2014 / Theaster Gates und die Black Monks of Mississippi bei einer Aufführung während des Abbruchs der St.-Laurence-Kirche.

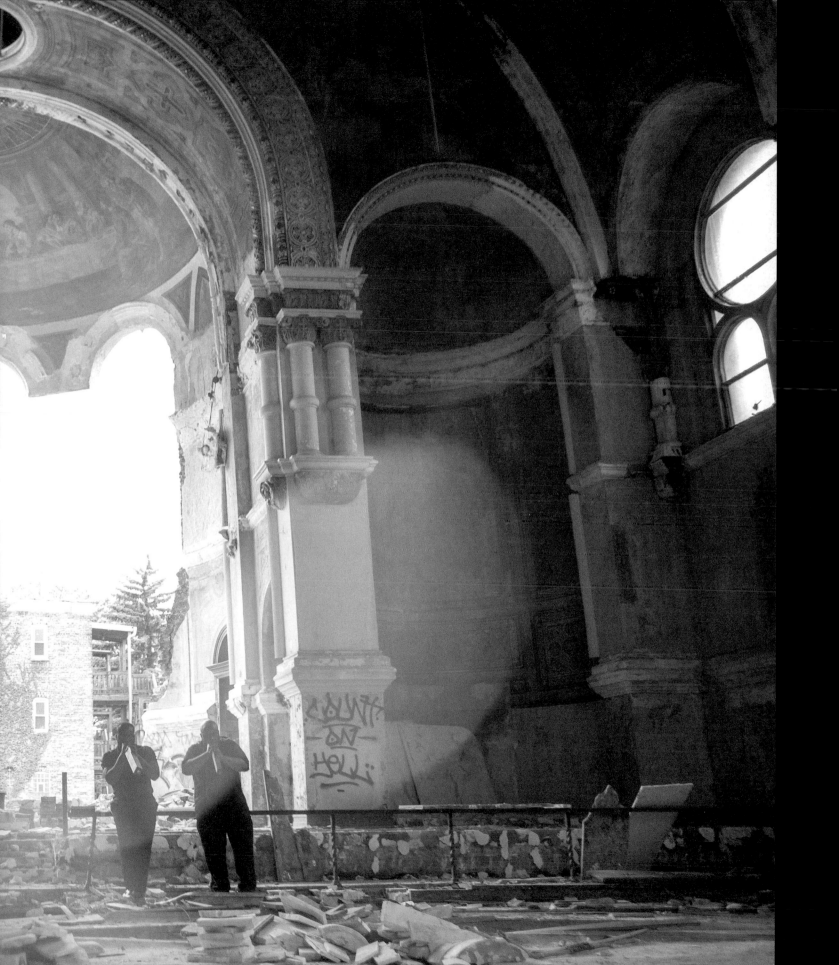

JUST WHAT IS IT THAT MAKES TODAY'S ARTIST-LED URBAN DEVELOPMENT SO DIFFERENT, SO APPEALING?

ANDREW HERSCHER

In the wake of the state violence perpetrated in American cities throughout the twentieth century and continuing into the twenty-first—variously billed as "slum eradication," "urban redevelopment," "urban renewal," and "blight removal"—the current attention to artist-led urban development is easy to understand. In scale, intent, procedure, and effect, artist-led development provides alternatives to racially inflected urban displacement—the functional equivalent, in James Baldwin's famous words, of "Negro removal."[1] Contemporary efforts to define and animate what Theaster Gates has termed "black space," then, have particular resonance in the contexts of histories and lived experiences of that space as a site of precarity, exclusion, and dispossession.

But violence in black space was also part of a process of capital accumulation. The practices of urban renewal allowed white elites, business interests, and their governmental patrons to raise property values, expand tax bases, and accumulate capital in the guise of fighting slums, blight, and other pathologizations of urban difference.[2] Black space, in this sense, was one of the sacrifice zones necessary to the operation of modern industrial capitalism: Black space housed populations of reserve labor that could be displaced and replaced according to the rhythms of business, and it was made up of property whose ownership could be smoothly transferred according to the imperatives of the real-estate market. Black space, then, was where the social costs of the uneven development inherent in capitalist economies could be sequestered and supposedly removed from the spaces produced by and for those who benefited from that development.

Gates has described his work connecting underserved black communities on the South Side of Chicago with the institutional art world as a "circular economy." Attention to the urban dimensions of capitalism's uneven development suggests that this circular economy reconnects realms that are en-

ANDREW HERSCHER is a member of the We the People of Detroit Community Research Collective and associate professor of architecture at the University of Michigan, in Ann Arbor.

THEASTER GATES, Dorchester Art + Housing Collaborative, Chicago, 2012. (PHOTO: SARA POOLEY / COURTESY OF REBUILD FOUNDATION)

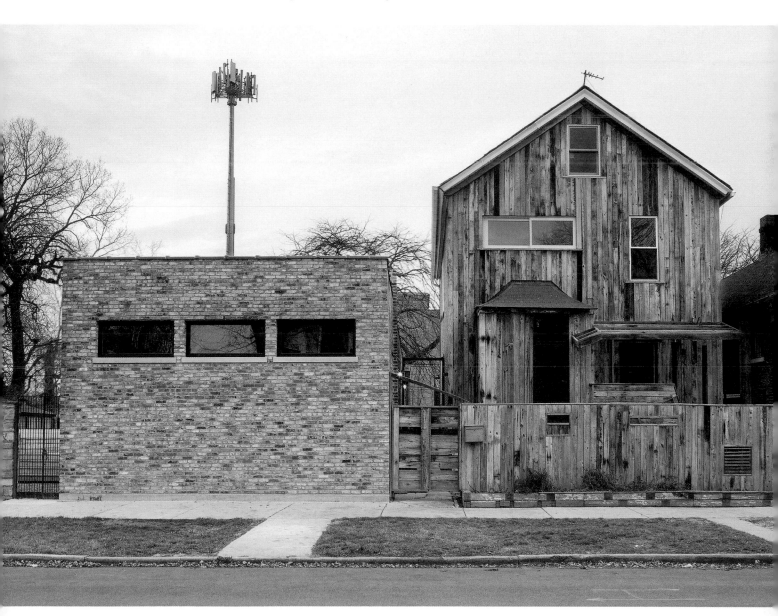

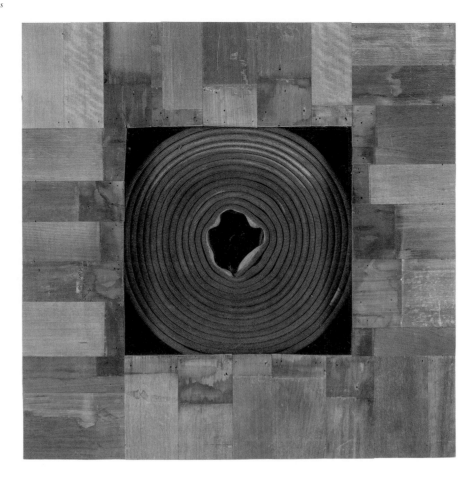

*THEASTER GATES, EXECUTIVE SUITE, 2013, wood, decomissioned fire hose, 31 x 31 x 7" / CHEFETAGE, Holz, ausgemusterter
Feuerwehrschlauch, 78,7 x 78,7 x 17,8 cm. (PHOTO: SARA POOLEY)*

meshed with one another, albeit in often disavowed ways: black urban neighborhoods defined by capital extraction, on the one hand, and art collections, art institutions, and cultural foundations built upon capital accumulation, on the other. So how does Gates's circular economy relate to the larger economy, an economy in which no exchange is equal and all exchange must yield an excess? And how does that relationship inform what makes today's artist-led urban development so different and so appealing?

Gates narrates his circular economy like this: *Here is an abandoned and fire-damaged building. We gut it and try to capture as much of it as we can and put those materials to their highest possible use, to make them more special than they were. They go into a gallery, a museum, and be-* *cause somebody sees them in that context, they become even more special, and because of that, I get a check, the gallery gets a check and that check helps me finance something on the block. To me that process feels like one work of art over two years, over 10 years.*[3]

The abandoned buildings whose pieces become artworks are located in the sacrifice zones that are created by just the processes of capital extraction and accumulation that yield the galleries and museums in which those works are displayed and sold. What Gates's circular economy does, then, is provide material and seemingly ameliorative connections between two worlds whose social and economic relations are typically occulted or even denied. Leave it to *Bloomberg Business News* to at once edit out the art and

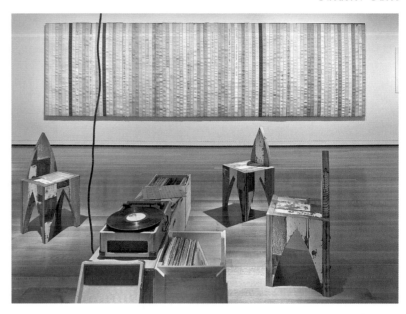

discover a new form of urban philanthrocapitalism: "Theater Gates Sells Fire Hoses to Rebuild Chicago Slums."[4]

Yet it is precisely as philanthrocapitalism that artist-led urban development may be acquiring at least some of its appeal. In the era of the American welfare state, government assumed responsibility for underserved and disadvantaged citizens and neighborhoods; but today, when government has shrunk to the provision of basic services under neoliberal austerity doctrines, it is nonprofits, community groups, foundations, and, most recently, visionary artists who assume this responsibility.[5] In other words, the call for artistic involvement in urban development is to some degree based upon the premise that the state no longer bears responsibility for underserved communities. The artist-developer is called upon as a moral actor able to defy, exceed, hack, or queer the imperatives of surplus-value accumulation in market-driven development and thereby work on behalf of a greater good. In this sense, artist-led urban development may at once be symptom of, response to, and

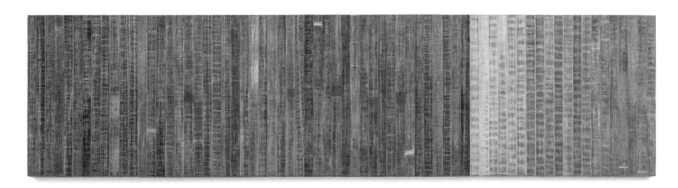

THEASTER GATES, MAMA RED, 2013, wood, decomissioned fire hose, 10 x 40' /
MAMA ROT, Holz, ausgemusterter Feuerwehrschlauch, 3 x 12,1 m.

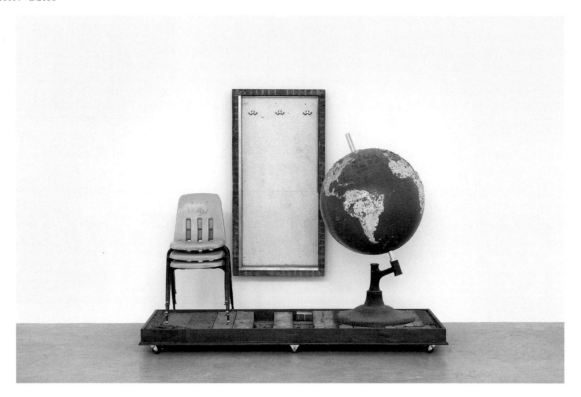

THEASTER GATES, CLASSROOM, 2013, wood, plastic, metal, dimensions variable /
KLASSENZIMMER, Holz, Kunststoff, Metall, Masse variabel.

critique of the neoliberal privatization of social welfare that is one of its conditions of possibility.[6]

In Gates's version of this project, however, still more of the appeal seems to rest specifically in the art that provides capital for reinvestment in underserved communities. Many of the accounts of his project include descriptions of the felt experience of purchasing his artwork. "Collectors and museums are eager to get their hands on manifestations of what [Gates] calls his 'shine' and the larger social interventions that they represent," writes Huey Copeland, pointing toward the affective experiences of race and class alterity mediated by Gates's artwork.[7] Or consider the depiction of the following scene in which notable members of the Chicago art gentry are ushered by Gates's gallerist to Dorchester Projects, the collection of buildings on the city's South Side that the artist is transforming into cultural institutions:

Kavi Gupta, whose gallery continues to represent Gates, brought some of the city's wealthiest art collectors to Dorchester, where they fell under Gates's spell. Not only did they buy his work, but they also asked how their foundations could support his larger enterprise. Well, Gates told them, this building does need a new heating-and-cooling system. Gupta says a check was written, the HVAC purchased soon thereafter.[8]

What I'm interested in here is the *spell*—a term that registers a surplus of affect that redirects not only the agency of the art collector, in this case toward the purchase of art, but also shifts subject position itself, in this case from the art collector to the foundation director, who ostensibly whips out a different checkbook with which to make a donation to the "larger enterprise." What this scene documents, that is, is the way in which Gates's alchemic transmutations of detritus into art and into cultural institutions for underserved communities promotes affects; the circular economy is also an affective economy, a system in which emotions are produced, processed, and discharged.

Copeland describes Gates's production of art as a process in which "works, which may be derived from floors, sinks, or walls, are squared off and positioned in the gallery as Afro-modernist ripostes to the white past masters of abstract art and civil society"—a formal reformatting that inscribes architectural detritus into art history.[9] But this formal reformatting is complemented by a semantic formatting, enacted through titling, that inscribes the resulting artwork in histories of American racial injustice. Two series of pieces composed of fire hoses from a decommissioned firehouse (the sales of which are "rebuilding Chicago slums"), for example, are IN CASE OF A RACE RIOT (2011–) and IN THE EVENT OF A RACE RIOT (2011–).

Describing the sale of one of these pieces at a charity auction at the Anderson Ranch Arts Center in Aspen, Colorado, Matthew Jesse Jackson provides a mini-ethnography of the liberal white experience of Gates's work. Jackson concludes that the fire hoses, titled to evoke the white supremacist response to civil rights activism, "summon the Ghost of Bull Connor onto an upper-middle-class stage, so it's a psychological twofer: potency and pain in one package. Or to

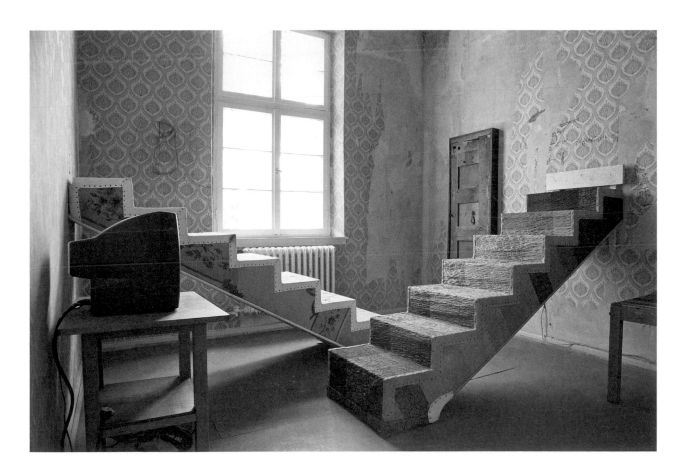

THEASTER GATES, 12 BALLADS FOR HUGUENOT HOUSE, 2012, installation view, Documenta 13, Kassel /
12 BALLADEN FÜR DAS HUGENOTTENHAUS, Installationsansicht.

paraphrase James Baldwin, white liberals tend to get an erotic charge from their fantasies of black rage. That is, it gives them a little shiver."[10]

By channeling capital from art sales to Dorchester Projects, Gates's circular economy also provides a mechanism that allows this erotic charge to be discharged and replaced by a catharsis of virtuousness, pride, and perhaps also relief: affects attendant upon philanthrocapitalist engagement in a site of black exclusion and suffering. This engagement has funded the renovation of buildings to house a series of cultural institutions, several of which accommodate displaced collections of cultural artifacts. At Dorchester Projects, a single-family house and candy store were converted into an Archive House and Listening House holding 14,000 architecture books purchased from Chicago's renowned Prairie Avenue Bookshop, closed in 2009; a 60,000-piece glass lantern slide collection from the University of Chicago's art history department, made obsolete in the era of digital projection; 8,000 LPs purchased from Dr. Wax Records, a popular music store in Chicago that closed in 2010; and the editors' library of the Chicago-based Johnson Publishing Corporation, the largest black-owned publishers in the United States. A former Anheuser-Busch distribution facility has been converted into the Black Cinema House. A former public housing project has been converted into a housing collaborative providing accommodations for artists and members of the community, along with an arts center, public meeting space, and community garden. And, most recently, a building that once housed a community savings and loan company has been converted into the Stony Island Arts Bank, where spaces have been provided for exhibitions, residencies, and the collections formerly held in the Archive and Listening Houses.

The building renovations carried out in Dorchester Projects use "repurposed materials from all over Chicago."[11] Unlike the artwork that supported these renovations, however, the actual or symbolic provenance of this material is not called out; contemporary displacement yields resources for renovations more than traces of violence.[12] The same may be true for some of the archival material collected in Dorchester Projects; for example, the closing of Dr. Wax Records was, according to its owners, driven by the University of Chicago's purchase of the Harper Court shopping center in which it was located.[13] The neoliberal present may not only be a condition of possibility for Gates's circular economy; it may also tacitly function as a discursive filter organizing the representation of politics, on the level of content, in the work that circulates through that economy.

But perhaps this, too, is appealing. The Rebuild Foundation, which Gates founded to manage Dorchester Projects, describes itself as "a nonprofit organization that endeavors to rebuild the cultural foundations of underinvested neighborhoods and incite movements of community revitalization that are culture based, artist led, and neighborhood driven."[14] And the products of the circular economy in which Dorchester Projects is included have undeniably served to revitalize the communities of the art world, from Chicago to far beyond. On some level, Gates is offering the collectors of his work, and the entire ecology of foundations and institutions that these collectors sponsor, manage, and inhabit, a way to feel good—or maybe just *feel*—both through and about the extraction and circulation of surplus value.

In so doing, though, Gates is also able to offer new spaces and resources to the communities in which this surplus value is reinvested. The fact that these communities are appealed to by many who find Gates's project so appealing does not mean that those communities do not find this project so appealing, too. And yet, questions remain as to whether and how his various interventions are indeed revitalizing these communities—a crucial issue to the extent that his project is approached as urban development, but is one about which I cannot find any sustained investigation. These questions are irrelevant to the profitable operation of the circular economy; just for this reason, however, we might appeal for answers.

1) James Baldwin spoke about urban renewal in "The Negro and the American Promise," a television program that was broadcast on PBS in 1963.

2) It was the presumably social functions of urban renewal, in excess of its function as property development, that allowed it to be funded by the state and enabled by eminent domain; see, for example, Samuel Zipp, *Manhattan Projects: The Rise and Fall of Urban Renewal in Cold War New York* (Oxford: Oxford University Press, 2012); Christopher Klemek, *The Transatlantic Collapse of*

Urban Renewal: Postwar Urbanism from New York to Berlin (Chicago: University of Chicago Press, 2012); and Patrick Sharkey, *Stuck in Place: Urban Neighborhoods and the End of Progress toward Racial Equality* (Chicago: University of Chicago Press, 2013).

3) Theaster Gates, in Lilly Wei, "Theaster Gates," *Art in America*, December 1, 2011, www.artinamericamagazine.com/news-features/magazine/theaster-gates (accessed February 9, 2016).

4) James S. Russell, "Theaster Gates Sells Fire Hoses to Rebuild Chicago Slums," *Bloomberg Business*, December 18, 2012, www.bloomberg.com/news/articles/2012-12-18/theaster-gates-sells-fire-hoses-to-rebuild-chicago-slums (accessed February 9, 2016).

5) Claire Bishop narrates this relationship in the European context in *Artificial Hells: Participatory Art and the Politics of Spectatorship* (Verso: London, 2012).

6) On the separation of neoliberal tactics from neoliberal politics, see James Ferguson, "Uses of Neoliberalism," *Antipode 41* (2009).

7) Huey Copeland, "Dark Mirrors," *Artforum*, October 2013, 229.

8) Ben Austen, "Chicago's Opportunity Artist," *New York Times*, December 20, 2013.

9) Copeland, "Dark Mirrors," 227.

10) Matthew Jesse Jackson, "The Emperor of the Post-Medium Condition," in *Theaster Gates: 12 Ballads for Huguenot House* (Cologne: Walther König, 2012), 19.

11) "Dorchester Projects," www.theastergates.com/section/117693_Dorchester_Projects.html (accessed February 9, 2016).

12) At the Huguenot House, a project at Documenta 13, in Kassel, Germany, Gates used material from, among other places, the Crispus Attucks Elementary School on Chicago's South Side. At Crispus Attucks, one of fifty schools controversially shut down under Chicago Mayor Rahm Emanuel, 97% of the students were from low-income families and 48% were homeless, and the closing of the school was passionately protested by families and neighborhood groups. Gates also used material from Crispus Attucks in *Holding Court*, his project at the 2012 Armory Show in New York, and in "My Back, My Wheel, and My Will," his 2013 exhibition at the White Cube galleries in Hong Kong and São Paulo. On the closing of Crispus Attucks, see www.everyschoolismyschool.org/2013/05/05/attucks (accessed February 9, 2016).

13) Ben Sigrist, "Swan Song: Dr. Wax Closes its Doors," *Chicago Maroon*, February 9, 2010, www.chicagomaroon.com/2010/02/09/swan-song-dr-wax-closes-its-doors (accessed February 9, 2016).

14) "Rebuild's Story," www.rebuild-foundation.org/about/our-story (accessed February 9, 2016).

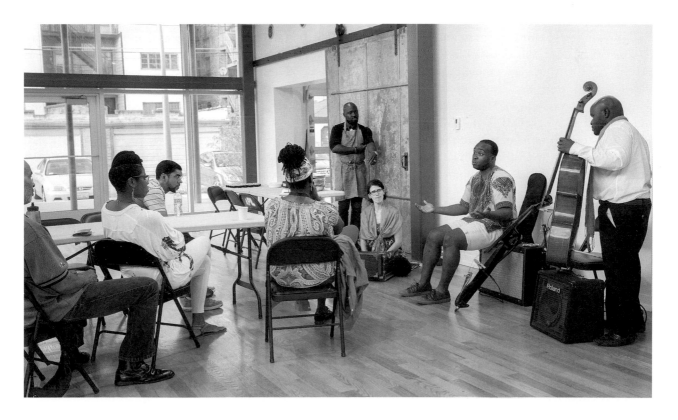

THEASTER GATES, Dorchester Art + Housing, Chicago, collaborative event / Gemeinschaftliche Veranstaltung. (PHOTO: SARA POOLEY / COURTESY OF REBUILD FOUNDATION)

WAS MACHT HEUTIGE STADT- ENTWICKLUNGSPROJEKTE VON KÜNSTLERN SO ATTRAKTIV?

ANDREW HERSCHER

Nach der staatlichen Gewalt, die in amerikanischen Städten im Lauf des 20. und 21. Jahrhunderts regelmässig ausgeübt wurde – ob im Namen der «Slumbeseitigung», der «Stadtsanierung», der «allgemeinen Erneuerung» oder der «Ausmerzung von Schandflecken» –, ist die Aufmerksamkeit, die heute der Stadtentwicklung unter der Leitung von Künstlern zuteil wird, gut zu verstehen. Hinsichtlich Grössenordnung, Absicht, Vorgehen und Wirkung bietet eine von Künstlern betriebene Stadtentwicklung eine echte Alternative zu ethnisch bedingten Verdrängungsprozessen, die dem entsprechen, was James Baldwin einst als «Negro removal», das Entfernen der Schwarzen, bezeichnet hat.[1] Den aktuellen Versuchen, den von Theaster Gates genannten «schwarzen Raum» zu definieren und zu beleben, kommt angesichts einer Vergangenheit, in der dieser Raum als prekärer, von Ausschluss und Enteignung bedrohter Ort erlebt wurde, besondere Bedeutung zu.

Doch die Gewalt in diesem schwarzen Raum war auch Teil eines Prozesses der Kapitalvermehrung.

ANDREW HERSCHER ist Mitglied des We the People of Detroit Community Research Collective und Associate Professor für Architektur an der University of Michigan in Ann Arbor.

Die urbanen Sanierungsmassnahmen erlaubten es den weissen Eliten, Wirtschaftsunternehmen und ihren Schirmherren innerhalb der Regierung, den Wert der Grundstücke zu steigern, die Steuersätze zu erhöhen und Kapital anzuhäufen unter dem Vorwand, Slums, Schandflecken und andere Entwicklungen innerhalb des wirtschaftlichen Gefälles der Stadt zu bekämpfen.[2] So gesehen, war der schwarze Raum eine jener Zonen, die dem modernen industriellen Kapitalismus geopfert wurden. Der schwarze Raum beherbergte mit seiner Bevölkerung einen Vorrat an Arbeitskräften, die entsprechend der wirtschaftlichen Konjunktur verschoben und ersetzt wurden, und er bestand aus Grundstücken, deren Besitz je nach den Erfordernissen des Immobilienmarktes problemlos auf andere übertragen werden konnte. Der schwarze Raum war also der Ort, wo sich die gesellschaftlichen Kosten der ungleichen Entwicklung, die notwendigerweise mit dem Kapitalismus einhergehen, abkapseln und vermeintlich von den Räumen fernhalten liessen, welche für die von dieser Entwicklung Profitierenden erbaut wurden.

Gates hat sein Projekt, die benachteiligten schwarzen Gemeinden auf Chicagos Südseite mit der institutionellen Kunstwelt zu verbinden, als «Kreislauf-

THEASTER GATES, Theaster Gates Studio, Chicago, 2014. (PHOTO: SARA POOLEY)

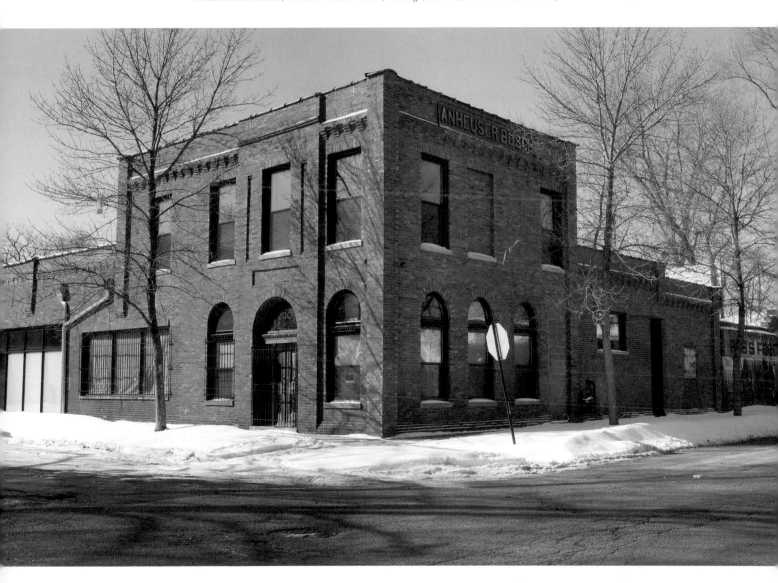

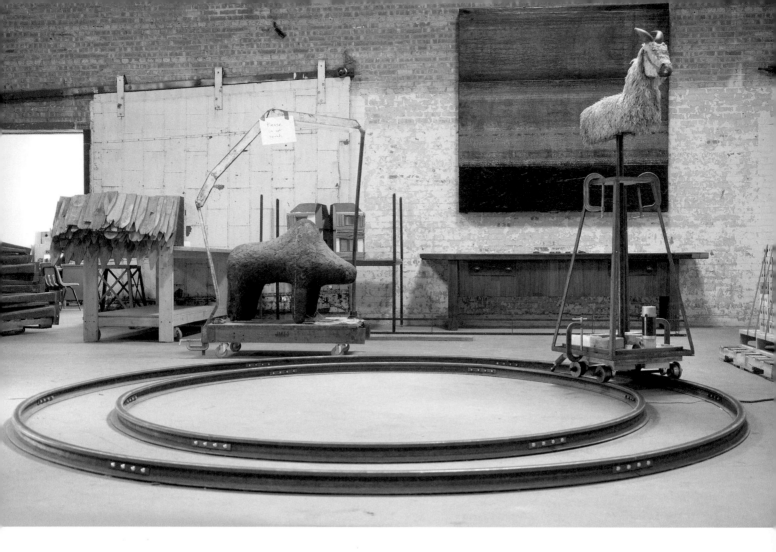

wirtschaft» bezeichnet. Betrachtet man die Folgen der ungleichen Entwicklung im Kapitalismus im urbanen Kontext, so zeigt sich, dass diese Kreislaufwirtschaft Bereiche miteinander verbindet, die bereits miteinander verflochten sind, obschon dies gern verdrängt wird: vom Kapitalschwund gekennzeichnete schwarze Stadtviertel auf der einen Seite und durch die Anhäufung von Kapital möglich gewordene Kunstsammlungen, Kunstinstitutionen und Kulturstiftungen auf der anderen Seite. Wie verhält sich demnach Gates' Kreislaufwirtschaft zur Wirtschaft im Allgemeinen, einer Wirtschaft, in der kein Austausch gleichwertig ist und jeder Handel einen

Überschuss erzielen muss? Und welchen Einfluss hat dieses Verhältnis auf die Andersartigkeit und Attraktivität der heutigen von Künstlern geförderten Stadtentwicklung?

Gates beschreibt seine Kreislaufwirtschaft wie folgt: *Hier steht ein verlassenes Gebäude mit Brandschäden. Wir kernen es aus, versuchen so viel wie möglich davon zu erhalten und verwenden die daraus gewonnenen Materialien so hochwertig wie möglich, um sie zu etwas Spezifischem zu machen, als sie es ursprünglich waren. Sie kommen in eine Galerie, ein Museum, und weil jemand sie in diesem Kontext sieht, wirken sie noch ausserordentlicher, also bekomme ich einen Scheck, die Galerie bekommt einen Scheck, und dieser Scheck erlaubt mir, Mittel für den Häuserblock bereitzustellen. Dieser Prozess fühlt sich an wie ein Kunstwerk, das sich über zwei Jahre, über zehn Jahre hinzieht.*[3]

Die verlassenen Gebäude, deren Bestandteile zu Kunstwerken werden, liegen in den Zonen, die den Prozessen des Kapitalabzugs und der Kapitalanhäufung zum Opfer fallen, die ebenjene Galerien und Museen speisen, in denen diese Werke ausgestellt und verkauft werden. Gates' Kreislaufwirtschaft liefert Materialien und verbessert scheinbar die Anknüpfungspunkte zwischen den beiden Welten, deren gesellschaftliche und wirtschaftliche Beziehungen gewöhnlich verschleiert oder gar geleugnet werden.

Überlassen wir es den *Bloomberg Business News*, mit einem Schlag die Kunst auszublenden und eine neue Form des urbanen Philanthrokapitalismus zu entdecken: «Theaster Gates verkauft Feuerwehrschläuche zugunsten des Wiederaufbaus von Slums in Chicago.»[4]

Andrerseits ist es genau diese philanthropisch kapitalistische Geste, die zumindest einen Teil des Charmes der von Künstlern initiierten Stadtentwicklung ausmacht. Zu Zeiten des amerikanischen Wohlfahrtsstaates übernahm die Regierung die Verantwortung für unterversorgte und benachteiligte Bürger und Stadtbezirke; doch heute, wo die Regierung einen neoliberalen Sparkurs verfolgt und ihre Leistungen bis auf die Grundversorgung reduziert hat, sind es Non-Profit-Organisationen, Gemeinschaftsinitiativen, Stiftungen und neuerdings visionäre Künstler, die diese Verantwortung wahrnehmen.[5] Mit anderen Worten, der Ruf nach künstlerischer Mitwirkung bei der Stadtentwicklung ist bis zu einem gewissen Grad eine Folge der Tatsache, dass der Staat für benachteiligte Stadtteile keine Verantwortung mehr übernimmt. Der Künstler-Entwickler wird als moralischer Akteur angerufen, der in der Lage ist, den Geboten der Mehrwertschöpfung im marktabhängigen Bau- und Entwicklungswesen zu trotzen und sie um eines höheren Nutzen willen zu überbieten, zu hacken oder gegen den Strich zu bürsten. In diesem Sinne ist die von Künstlern initiierte Stadtentwicklung zugleich Symptom und Kritik der neoliberalen Privatisierung eines Sozialwesens und gleichzeitig liefert

sie eine Antwort auf die Bedingungen, die sie hervorgerufen haben.[6]

Bei Gates' Projekt scheint der Reiz jedoch immer noch vorwiegend in der Kunst zu liegen, die das Kapital für die Neuinvestitionen in den unterversorgten Gemeinden liefert. Viele Berichte über sein Projekt enthalten Schilderungen über die Emotionen der Käufer beim Erwerb seiner Kunst. «Sammler und Museen sind ganz versessen darauf, Ausdrucksformen dessen in die Hände zu bekommen, was Gates seinen ‹Glanz› nennt, einschliesslich der dazugehörigen gesellschaftlichen Interventionen, für die sie stehen», schreibt Huey Copeland und verweist auf die affektiven Erfahrungen der rassen- und klassenspezifischen Andersartigkeit, die Gates' Werke vermitteln.[7] Man halte sich das Bild vor Augen, wie bedeutende Mitglieder des Chicagoer Kunstadels von Gates' Galerist zu den Dorchester Projects geführt werden, einer Gruppe von Gebäuden im Süden der Stadt, die der Künstler zurzeit in kulturelle Institutionen umwandelt:

Kavi Gupta, dessen Galerie Gates weiterhin vertritt, brachte einige der betuchtesten Kunstsammler nach Dorchester, wo sie Gates' Charme erlagen. Sie kauften nicht nur seine Kunst, sondern fragten ihn, wie ihre Stiftungen sein Gesamtunternehmen unterstützen könnten. Nun ja, meinte Gates, dieses Gebäude braucht ein neues Heizungs- und Kühlsystem. Gupta sagt, ein Scheck sei ausgefüllt worden und bald darauf wurde die neue Gebäude-Klimaanlage gekauft.[8]

Mich interessiert hier der *Zauber* – ein Begriff, der einen Affektüberschuss anzeigt, der nicht nur die Tätigkeit des Kunstsammlers beeinflusst, in diesem Fall zum Kauf von Kunst, sondern in ihm auch den Stiftungsdirektor weckt, der anscheinend ein anderes Scheckbuch zückt, um eine Spende an das «Gesamtunternehmen» auszustellen. Diese Szene dokumentiert, wie Gates' alchemistische Transmutationen – von Bauschutt zu Kunst zu kulturellen Institutionen für unterversorgte Stadtgemeinden – Gefühle wecken; die Kreislaufwirtschaft ist auch eine affektive Ökonomie, ein System, in dem Affekte produziert, aufbereitet und freigesetzt werden.[9]

Copeland beschreibt Gates' Kunstproduktion als Prozess: «Werke, die aus Böden, Waschbecken oder Wänden stammen können, werden in Stellung ge-

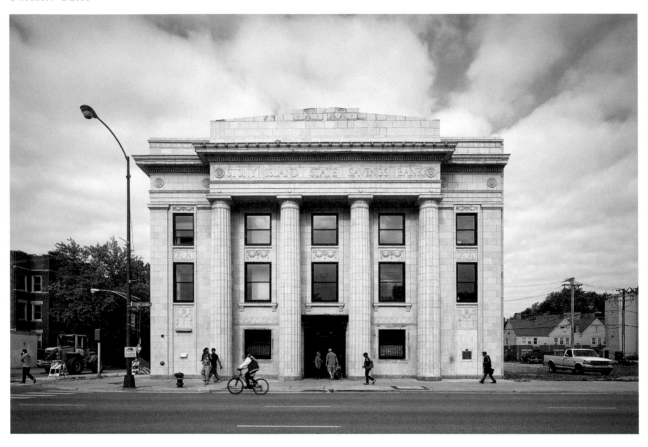

THEASTER GATES, Stony Island Arts Bank, 2012.

bracht und in der Galerie als afro-modernistische Entgegnung auf die einstmaligen weissen Meister der abstrakten Kunst und der Zivilgesellschaft präsentiert» – eine formale Umformatierung, die Architekturschutt zu Kunstgeschichte erklärt.[10] Diese Umformatierung wird jedoch durch eine semantische Formatierung ergänzt, die im Titel zum Ausdruck kommt, der das entstandene Kunstwerk in die Geschichte der amerikanischen Rassendiskriminierung einreiht. Zwei Serien von Werken, die aus Feuerwehrschläuchen einer stillgelegten Feuerwache bestehen (und deren Verkauf den «Wiederaufbau von Slums in Chicago» finanziert), heissen beispielsweise IN CASE OF A RACE RIOT (Im Falle eines Rassenkrawalls, 2011–) und IN THE EVENT OF A RACE RIOT (Bei etwaigem Rassenkrawall, 2011–).

In seiner Schilderung des Verkaufs eines dieser Werke an einer Benefizauktion im Anderson Ranch Arts Center in Aspen, Colorado, liefert Matthew Jesse Jackson eine Mini-Ethnographie der liberalen weissen Rezeption von Gates' Kunst. Jackson kommt zu folgendem Schluss: Die Feuerwehrschläuche, deren Titel an die dominante weisse Reaktion auf die Bürgerrechtsbewegung erinnern, «beschwören den Geist von Bull Connor auf einer Bühne des gehobenen Mittelstandes und damit ein psychologisches Doppelpack: Macht und Leid in einem. Oder in einer Paraphrase auf James Baldwin; ihre Phantasien über den ‹Schwarzen Zorn› versetzen liberale Weisse häufig in erotische Spannung. Das heisst, ein leises Schaudern durchfährt sie.»[11]

Durch das Umlenken von Kapital aus Kunstverkäufen für/in seine Dorchester Projects bietet Gates' Kreislaufwirtschaft auch einen Ansatz zur Entladung dieser erotischen Spannung, sodass stattdessen eine

Katharsis einsetzt, die auf Rechtschaffenheit, Stolz und wohl auch auf Erleichterung beruht: Gefühle, die das philanthrokapitalistische Engagement für ein Gelände begleiten, das bisher ein Ort der Ausgrenzung und des Leidens der schwarzen Bevölkerung war. Dieses Engagement finanzierte die Renovation von Gebäuden, in denen eine Reihe kultureller Institutionen einen neuen Ort gefunden haben, darunter einige, die Sammlungen kultureller Artefakte beherbergten. Bei Dorchester Projects wurden ein Einfamilienhaus und ein Süsswarenladen zu einem Archive House und einem Listening House umgebaut, einem Archiv und einer Anlaufstelle für Sorgen aller Art. Hier gibt es 14000 Architekturbücher, die aus dem berühmten, 2009 geschlossenen Prairie Avenue Bookshop in Chicago stammen; eine Glasdiasammlung der kunsthistorischen Fakultät der University of Chicago, die 60000, im Zeitalter der digitalen Projektion technisch überholte Dias umfasst; 8000 LPs, die dem beliebten, 2010 geschlossenen Chicagoer Musikgeschäft Dr. Wax Records abgekauft wurden; auch die Verlagsbuchhandlung der in Chicago an-

sässigen Johnson Publishing Corporation ist hier untergebracht, der grösste US-amerikanische Verlag in schwarzem Besitz. Eine ehemalige Vertriebsstelle für Anheuser-Busch-Bier wurde zum Black Cinema House umfunktioniert und ein ehemaliges Sozialwohnungsprojekt in eine Wohngenossenschaft; sie bietet nun Wohnraum für Künstler und Genossenschafter, beherbergt aber auch ein Kulturzentrum, einen öffentlichen Treffpunkt und einen Gemeinschaftsgarten. Und erst jüngst wurde ein Gebäude, in dem eine Gemeindesparkasse und -kreditanstalt untergebracht war, zur Stony Island Arts Bank umgebaut, wo es Räume für Ausstellungen, Stipendienaufenthalte und für jene Sammlungen gibt, die sich zuvor im Archive House und im Listening House befanden.

Bei den Gebäuderenovationen im Rahmen der Dorchester Projects wurden «umfunktionierte Materialien aus ganz Chicago» verwendet.[12] Im Gegensatz zu den Kunstwerken, die diese Renovationen unterstützten, wird die tatsächliche oder symbolische Herkunft dieser Materialien jedoch nicht genannt;

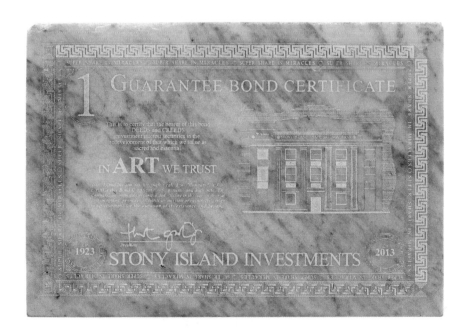

THEASTER GATES, BANK BOND, 2013, marble, 6 $^{1}/_{8}$ x 8 $^{5}/_{8}$ x $^{13}/_{16}$" / BANKOBLIGATION, Marmor, 15,5 x 21,9 x 2,1 cm.

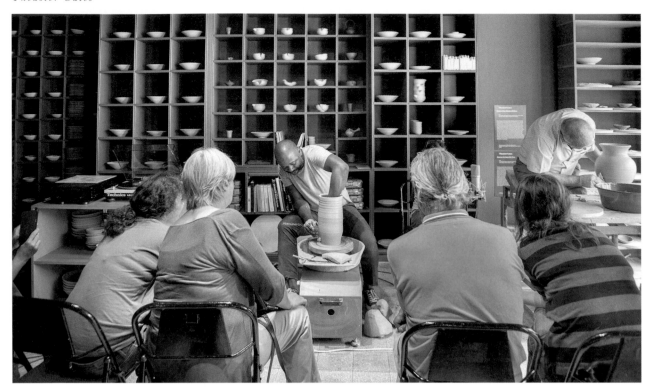

THEASTER GATES, THREE OR FOUR SHADES OF BLUES, 2015, Theaster Gates throws pottery in the installation, Istanbul Biennial /
DREI ODER VIER BLUESTÖNE, Theaster Gates an der Töpferscheibe in der Installation. (PHOTO: KORHAN KARAOYSAL)

wichtiger als die Spuren von Gewalt ist die heutige Umlagerung von Ressourcen für die Renovationen.[13] Dasselbe mag auf einen Teil des Archivmaterials zutreffen, das in den Dorchester Projects versammelt ist; so erfolgte beispielsweise die Schliessung von Dr. Wax Records laut Auskunft der Besitzer, weil das Harper Court Shoppingcenter, in dem der Laden untergebracht war, von der University of Chicago gekauft wurde.[14] Die neoliberale Gegenwart ist vielleicht mehr als nur eine Bedingung für Gates' Kreislaufwirtschaft; womöglich regelt sie auf inhaltlicher Ebene die politischen Bedingungen, die in der innerhalb dieser Wirtschaft zirkulierenden Kunst zum Ausdruck kommen.

Doch vielleicht hat auch dies seinen Charme. Die Rebuild Foundation, eine Stiftung für den Wiederaufbau, die Gates für die Realisierung der Dorchester Projects ins Leben rief, charakterisiert sich selbst als «eine Non-Profit-Organisation für den Wiederaufbau der kulturellen Grundlagen vernachlässigter Stadtviertel und als Anreiz für kulturell basierte Aktivitäten zur Wiederbelebung städtischer Gemeinden unter der Leitung von Künstlern und unter Mitarbeit der örtlichen Bevölkerung».[15] Ausserdem brachten die Produkte der Kreislaufwirtschaft, zu der auch die Dorchester Projects gehören, frischen Wind in die Kreise der Kunstszene in Chicago und weit darüber hinaus. In gewissem Sinn bietet Gates den Sammlern seiner Werke und dem gesamten Stiftungs- und Institutionsumfeld, das von diesen Sammlern gesponsert, geführt und bewohnt wird, eine Möglichkeit, sich wohlzufühlen – oder vielleicht überhaupt etwas zu *fühlen*: dank und angesichts des Erzielens und In-Umlauf-Bringens eines Mehrwerts.

Dieses Vorgehen versetzt Gates auch in die Lage, den Gemeinden neue Räume und Ressourcen anzubieten, in die dieser Mehrwert wieder investiert wird. Die Tatsache, dass die Gemeinden den Zuspruch von vielen erfahren, die von Gates' Projekt begeistert sind, bedeutet nicht, dass die Gemeinden selbst von diesem Projekt nicht genauso angetan wären. Dennoch bleibt es fraglich, ob und inwiefern seine diversen Interventionen diese tatsächlich neu beleben – die Frage ist insofern von Bedeutung, da sein Projekt als städtebauliches Entwicklungsprojekt betrachtet wird, zu dem es jedoch keine nachhaltige Untersuchung zu geben scheint. Zwar sind diese Fragen für das profitable Funktionieren der Kreislaufwirtschaft irrelevant; vielleicht sollten wir aber genau aus diesem Grund nach Antworten suchen.

(Übersetzung: Suzanne Schmidt)

1) In «The Negro and the American Promise», einer Fernsehsendung, die 1963 auf PBS ausgestrahlt wurde, äusserte sich James Baldwin zu solchen Sanierungsmassnahmen.
2) Neben der Funktion, den Immobilienstandard zu verbessern, war es die angeblich gesellschaftliche Funktion der Stadtsanierungsmassnahmen, die entsprechende staatliche Finanzierungshilfen und Enteignungsverfahren ermöglichte; siehe beispielsweise Samuel Zipp, *Manhattan Projects: The Rise and Fall of Urban*

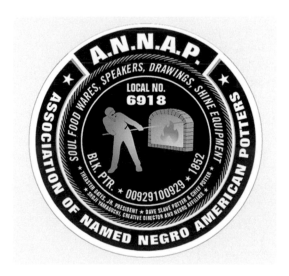

THEASTER GATES, *Association of Named Negro American Potters (ANNAP), 2010, logo / Verband Schwarz amerikanischer Töpfer, Logo.*

Renewal in Cold War New York, Oxford University Press, Oxford 2012; Christopher Klemek, *The Transatlantic Collapse of Urban Renewal: Postwar Urbanism from New York to Berlin*, University of Chicago Press, Chicago 2012; sowie Patrick Sharkey, *Stuck in Place: Urban Neighborhoods and the End of Progress toward Racial Equality*, University of Chicago Press, Chicago 2013.
3) Theaster Gates in Lilly Wei, «Theaster Gates», *Art in America*, 1. Dezember 2011, www.artinamericamagazine.com/news-features/magazine/theaster-gates (abgerufen am 9. Februar 2016). (Zitat aus dem Engl. übers.)
4) James S. Russell, «Theaster Gates Sells Fire Hoses to Rebuild Chicago Slums», *Bloomberg Business*, 18. Dezember 2012, www.bloomberg.com/news/articles/2012-12-18/theaster-gates-sells-fire-hoses-to-rebuild-chicago-slums (abgerufen am 9. Februar 2016). (Zitat aus dem Engl. übers.)
5) Claire Bishop erläutert diese Beziehung im europäischen Kontext in *Artificial Hells: Participatory Art and the Politics of Spectatorship*, Verso, London 2012.
6) Zur Unterscheidung von neoliberalen Strategien und neoliberaler Politik, siehe James Ferguson, «Uses of Neoliberalism», *Antipode 41*, 2009.
7) Huey Copeland, «Dark Mirrors», Artforum, Oktober 2013, S. 229.
8) Ben Austen, «Chicago's Opportunity Artist», *The New York Times*, 20. Dezember 2013.
9) Den Begriff «affektive Ökonomie» (affective economy) entlehne ich aus Vincanne Adams, *Markets of Sorrow, Labors of Faith: New Orleans in the Wake of Katrina*, Duke University Press, Durham, North Carolina, 2013.
10) Copeland, «Dark Mirrors», op. cit. (Anm. 7), S. 227.
11) Matthew Jesse Jackson, «The Emperor of the Post-Medium Condition», in *Theaster Gates: 12 Ballads for Huguenot House*, Verlag der Buchhandlung Walther König, Köln 2012, S. 19.
12) «Dorchester Projects», www.theastergates.com/section/117693_Dorchester_Projects.html (abgerufen am 9. Februar 2016).
13) Im Hugenottenhaus in Kassel, einem Projekt für die Documenta 13, verwendete Gates unter anderem Materialien aus der Crispus Attucks Elementary School im südlichen Teil Chicagos. Die Schliessung dieser Grundschule ist nur eine von fünfzig umstrittenen Schulschliessungen, die unter dem Chicagoer Bürgermeister Rahm Emanuel erfolgten. 97 Prozent der Schülerinnen und Schüler stammten aus Familien mit niederem Einkommen und 48 Prozent waren obdachlos; Familien und Gemeindegruppierungen protestierten vehement gegen die Schliessung. Auch bei Holding Court, seinem Projekt für die Armory Show 2012 in New York, verwendete Gates Material aus der Crispus Attucks Elementary School und ebenso in «My Back, My Wheel, and My Will», seiner Ausstellung bei White Cube Hongkong und White Cube São Paulo 2013. Zur Schliessung von Crispus Attucks siehe www.everyschoolismyschool.org/2013/05/05/attucks (abgerufen am 9. Februar 2016).
14) Ben Sigrist, «Swan Song: Dr. Wax Closes its Doors», *Chicago Maroon*, 9. Februar 2010, www.chicagomaroon.com/2010/02/09/swan-song-dr-wax-closes-its-doors (abgerufen am 9. Februar 2016).
15) «Rebuild's Story», www.rebuild-foundation.org/about/our-story (abgerufen am 9. Februar 2016).

Rebuilding the Future

CHRISTINE MEHRING & SEAN KELLER

Although typically considered alongside other artists working in social practice, Theaster Gates is notable for his refusal to emphasize relations at the expense of materiality: Real-estate agreements, governmental deals, and cultural partnerships form an important part of his practice, but they do not replace more traditional interests in aesthetics. Not only does he exhibit objects—the sales of which famously fund his renovations—but the actual physical stuff of the buildings themselves remains central. Take his signature undertaking, Dorchester Projects, in which an assortment of rescued structures presents a unified vision, one immediately recognizable as Gates's own: facades striped in multicolored planks of wood, punctured by unusually shaped windows; and interiors made from rough lumber reined in by clean lines, prominent patterns, and generous open space.

A Chicago native, Gates only moved to the city's South Side in 2006, but he has quickly acquired a sizeable collection of buildings. Remade and reprogrammed, these properties have attracted an art-world audience far beyond their immediate setting. In this, Gates might recall another artist who reshaped his adopted home: Donald Judd. Beginning in the early 1970s, Judd spent increasingly less time in New York and gradually moved to the small west Texas town of Marfa, where, over the course of two decades, he bought buildings, ranches, and a former fort to serve as homes, studios, offices, and exhibition spaces for his own work and that of others he admired. The Minimalist artist was highly attentive to his interventions,

CHRISTINE MEHRING is professor and chair of the department of Art History at the University of Chicago. / SEAN KELLER is associate professor and director of History and Theory at the IIT College of Architecture, Chicago.

THEASTER GATES, „HOUSE ARMOIRE, 2012, wood, 76 x 27 ¹/₂ x 25" / HUGENOTTENHAUS-SCHRANK, Holz, 193 x 69,9 x 66 cm.

selectively stripping existing buildings and thereby paying tribute to their original, often anonymous, makers and to vernacular design details, such as ornamental tiles and tin and stucco ceilings; he also preserved the scars of previous modifications and the quotidian passage of time, holding on to peeling plaster layers, missing bricks, and gouged floorboards. Judd then mobilized this interior architecture to set up a bold dialogue with his sculpture and furniture, as well as with his extensive collections of art and design objects—a dialogue that both challenged and strengthened his work.

Gates too works across art, architecture, and design. Excavated materials might be reused in buildings or installations; furniture made from recycled wood planks is exhibited as sculpture. His entire practice is guided by variations on the theme of "re-": rebuild, recirculate, reuse, recover, reconnect, re-present, redeem. More than a tinge of nostalgia is inevitable in the almost-soothing assemblages of objects, environments, images, words, and sounds that result—especially in his collections of collections, the most significant of which is the recently opened Stony Island Arts Bank, which brings together pre-existing collections of glass slides and records, among others. There is an undeniable continuity between his works and the popular turn to a local, craft aesthetic in product design and cuisine. However, this apparent similarity should not mask crucial distinctions: One must always look through the style to see the traumatic histories of Gates's material—the racism, discrimination, predatory economics, and political disenfranchisement that are frequently the underlying context of the materials themselves and the reason for their discarded condition.[1]

The Grand Crossing neighborhood on the South Side of Chicago, where Gates lives and works, has been made—and unmade—by a tumult of global forces: slavery and the Great Migration, the boom of Chicago as a world center of industry and trade, racial discrimination, urban renewal schemes, the 2008 real-estate crash. Gates's own genealogy and practice connect directly with these forces. His parents came to Chicago from Yazoo City, Mississippi, during the Great Migration, and, as a roofer, his father helped build the city. Gates worked in the University of Chicago provost's office as that institution was simultaneously imagining new ways of civic engagement with its South Side neighbors and establishing a series of Global Centers. His first houses-cum-artworks were purchased around the burst of the real-estate bubble, and his studio is now located in a former Anheuser-Busch distribution facility—all are located within steps of the train tracks on which beer, steel, and other commodities moved through the neighborhood on their way to and from downtown Chicago.

The notion of redemption is key to Gates's works. Their pleasing sensuality, and the ceremonial performances that often accompany them—frequently featuring Gates himself and his group the Black Monks of Mississippi—are intended to raise up objects, histories, and people that have been cast off; to restore dignity and meaning to what global culture has cast aside. Chicago, with its vast accumulations of discarded urban and architectural artifacts,

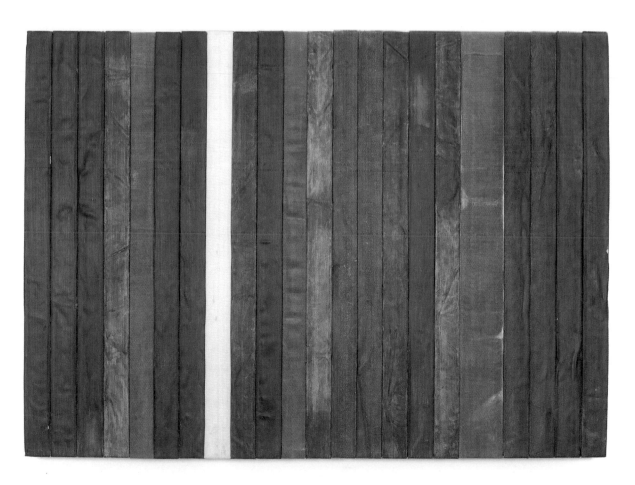

THEASTER GATES, MOSTLY STRAIGHT AMERICAN, 2013, wood, decommissioned fire hose, 66 x 92 x 5" /
MEISTENS DIREKTER AMERIKANER, Holz, ausgemusterter Feuerwehrschlauch, 167,6 x 233,7 x 12,7 cm.

85

provides fertile ground that Gates can mine: a shuttered architectural bookstore; the storage depot of the Chicago Park District; a failed hardware store; and the vast storerooms of Architectural Artifacts, the reseller of many fragments of the city's material history. Here Gates joins the company of contemporary Chicagoans such as artist Dan Peterman, who works with salvaged materials and who took a young Gates under his wing; architect John Vinci, who famously saved the original interior of the Chicago Stock Exchange; and Tim Samuelson, the city's official cultural historian and pioneering preservationist.

Unlike many others who turn to the local past, however, Gates's interest is not a retreat—after all, much of that past was far from laudatory—nor an attempt to isolate the local from the global. Instead, Gates hopes to restitch the local into a global fabric from which it has nearly been detached. Thus, in his more recent, larger projects, such as the Stony Island Arts Bank and the Dorchester Art + Housing Collaborative, the markers of professionalized architecture—engineered steel, commercial glazing, catalogue furniture and lighting—come to take their place alongside the more idiosyncratic, self-built character of his earlier projects. It has become increasingly clear that this intricately modulated exchange between the local and global is the central theme of Gates's ever-expanding portfolio of projects. He is, in sociologist Ulrich Beck's sense, a "cosmopolitan," working to multiply and deepen the exchanges between a specific locality and the worldwide networks of art, architecture, money, and politics.

Of course, Gates's buildings, ceramics, sculptures, performances, events, and finances are executed by many hands, minds, eyes, and voices. This too is a sign of his cosmopolitanism—his willingness to be constantly in exchange with others, and to encourage exchanges among these individuals. Indeed, another way of describing the overarching aim of Gates's efforts is to say that he wants to be a catalyst, multiplying the number and quality of exchanges between the people and materials of Grand Crossing and those of everywhere else. These exchanges are central to his objects and environments, however beautiful they may be.

Yet with Gates shopping at Restoration Hardware and Marfa now a hipster outpost of Chelsea, how are we to interpret the trajectory of these practices? Do they demonstrate the seemingly inescapable entwinement of rigorous artistic practice with the global market for design? Not entirely. For the architectural ventures of both artists are entirely strategic. The histories, func-

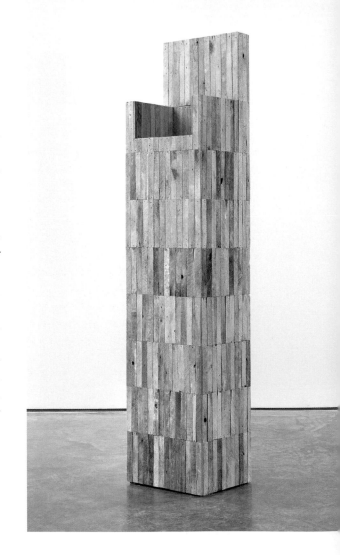

THEASTER GATES, STANDING THRONE 1, 2012, wood lathe, plywood, 96 ¹/₂ x 20 ¹/₂ x 17" / STEHENDER THRON 1, gedrechseltes Holz, Sperrholz, 245,1 x 52 x 43,2 cm.

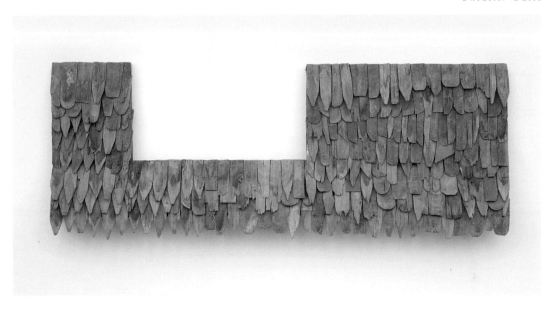

*THEASTER GATES, TIKI TEAK, 2014, wood, roofing paper, 169 x 63 $^1/_2$ x 12" /
Holz, Dachpappe, 429,2 x 161,3 x 30,5 cm.*

tions, materials, and forms of their buildings resonate deeply with—and become extensions of—their artistic outlooks.

Ultimately, however, the two artists deploy these architectural materials for different ends. In New York in the '60s, Judd was committed to the antiwar effort and engaged in community activism, but he always insisted on a strict division between his art and his politics.[2] His strong individualist, libertarian streak as well as an intense dislike of consumer culture ultimately led him to retreat to Marfa. But if Judd moved to the west Texan desert to save his art, Gates went to the South Side to test his. The contrast is neatly captured by the artists' two banks: Judd's Marfa National Bank building houses a historic collection of modern furniture with which the artist worked through, in isolation, the value and limitations of design for his sculptural practice; Gates's Stony Island Savings Bank, on the other hand, stages cultural events and opens archives and collections for a diverse public, expressing that convergence of social, economic, and aesthetic forces that is his medium. Where one artist bought a town to house his (specific) objects, the other is selling objects to save a (specific) neighborhood. Judd wanted to escape a world that he ultimately considered inalterable. Gates seeks to let in a world that he fiercely, stubbornly believes he can change, one building at a time.

1) Similarly, Gates's art objects often contain formal echoes of Minimalism and post-Minimalism, but their materials—e.g., fire hoses—refer to the civil rights movement, which was concurrent with but hardly reflected in those practices.
2) It is worth noting, however, that Judd took great care to preserve inscriptions for, and murals by, the German prisoners of war who had been housed in Fort D. A. Russell during World War II. As the frame for his most ambitious sculptural installation—one hundred untitled works in mill aluminum (1982–86)—this resonant content complicates the strict division he insisted on between his "specific objects" and his political activism.

Die Zukunft erneuern

CHRISTINE MEHRING & SEAN KELLER

Theaster Gates wird häufig mit anderen Künstlern in Zusammenhang gebracht, die im sozialen Raum arbeiten. Was seine Position indessen so einzigartig macht, ist die Weigerung, Beziehungsnetze auf Kosten der Materialität zu privilegieren. Immobilienverträge, Amtsgeschäfte und Kulturallianzen bilden wichtige Komponenten seiner Praxis, doch das bedeutet nicht, dass er deswegen traditionelle ästhetische Interessen hintanstellt. Abgesehen davon, dass er Objekte in den Ausstellungsraum bringt – mit deren Verkaufserlös er bekanntermassen seine Revitalisierungsprojekte finanziert –, schreibt Gates der physischen Bausubstanz selbst zentrale Bedeutung zu. Man nehme zum Beispiel eine seiner berühmtesten Realisierungen, Dorchester Projects, die ein Ensemble baufälliger Strukturen zu einer einheitlichen Vision zusammenfasst, die man sofort als Gates' persönliche Vision erkennt: gestreifte Fassaden aus vielfarbigen Holzlatten, hier und dort von ungewöhnlichen Fensterformaten durchbrochen, Innenräume aus rohen, klarlinig ausgelegten Bohlen, dazu auffallende Muster und der allgemeine Eindruck einer grosszügigen Offenheit.

Der in Chicago geborene Künstler wohnt erst seit 2006 an der South Side, wo er binnen kurzer Zeit eine Reihe von Gebäuden erwarb. Die renovierten und umgewidmeten Objekte sind seither weit über die Grenzen des Stadtteils hinaus zu einer Attraktion für das internationale Kunstpublikum geworden. Die völlige Umwertung eines neu gewählten Aufenthaltsorts erinnert an einen anderen Künstler: Donald Judd, der Anfang der 1970er-Jahre New York mit dem kleinen westtexanischen Ort Marfa vertauschte. Dort kaufte Judd im Lauf

CHRISTINE MEHRING ist Professorin an der Universität von Chicago. / *SEAN KELLER* ist Privatdozent und Leiter von History and Theory am IIT College of Architecture, Chicago.

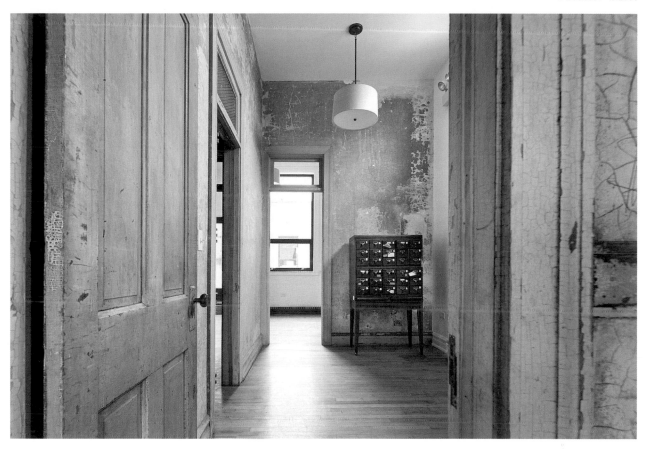

THEASTER GATES, Stony Island Arts Bank, 2015. (PHOTO: STEVE HALL)

der nächsten zwanzig Jahre Häuser, Ranches und sogar ein ehemaliges Fort auf, um sie als Wohnungen, Ateliers, Büros und Ausstellungsräume für eigene Werke wie auch für Werke geschätzter Künstlerkollegen zu nutzen. Der Pionier der Minimal Art ging bei seinen Eingriffen höchst bedacht vor. Gebäude wurden aller unnötigen Details entledigt, um die bodenständigen Entwürfe der oft anonymen Baumeister klar hervortreten zu lassen, mit Details wie gemusterten Fliesen und Zinn- und Stuckdecken. Die Narben, die frühere Umbauten sowie der Zahn der Zeit hinterlassen hatten – abblätternde Putzschichten, fehlende Ziegel, abgenutzte Dielen –, wurden nicht kaschiert.

Auch Gates ist ein Grenzgänger zwischen Kunst, Architektur und Design. Restmaterialien, die bei Renovierungen abfallen, finden Wiederverwertung in anderen Bauprojekten oder in Installationen; Möbel aus Altholz werden als Skulpturen ausgestellt. Gates' gesamte Kunstpraxis ist von Variationen derartiger Kreisläufe gekennzeichnet: Umbau, Rückführung, Wiederverwendung, Rückgewinnung, Neuverknüpfung, Wiedergabe, Rehabilitierung. Den fast beruhigend wirkenden Assemblagen aus Objekten, Environments, Bildern, Wörtern und Tönen haftet mehr als eine Spur Nostalgie an. Dies gilt besonders für die Sammlungen von Sammlungen, deren bedeutendste, die jüngst eröffnete Stony Island Arts Bank, ältere Kollek-

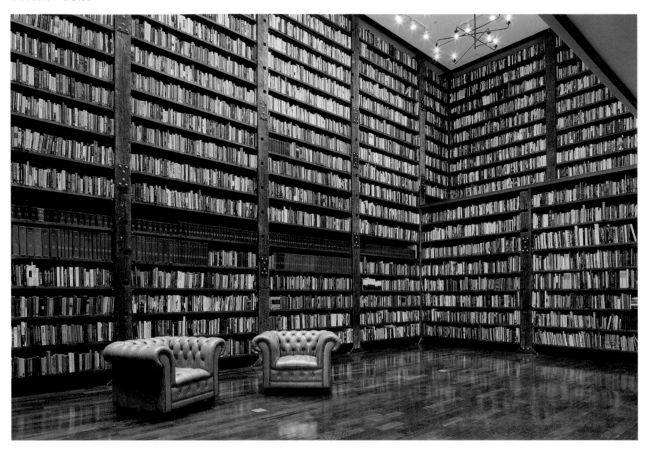

THEASTER GATES, *Johnson Publishing Library, Stony Island Arts Bank, 2015.* (PHOTO: TOM HARRIS)

tionen von Glasdias und Schallplatten unter einem Dach vereint. Dass zwischen Gates' Ansatz und dem Trend zu einer lokalen, handwerklich orientierten Ästhetik im Produktdesign und in der Gastronomie gewisse Gemeinsamkeiten bestehen, lässt sich nicht bestreiten, aber man darf dabei nicht die Unterschiede übersehen. Erst wer durch die Stil-Fassade hindurchblickt, wird erkennen, welch traumatische Geschichten in Gates' Materialien eingeschrieben sind – Rassismus, Diskriminierung, rücksichtslose Geschäftemacherei und Rechtsentzug sind der Kontext, dem sie entnommen sind und häufig auch der Grund dafür, dass sie vernachlässigt und weggeworfen wurden.[1)]

Das Viertel Grand Crossing an der South Side von Chicago, wo Gates heute lebt und arbeitet, verdankt seinen Aufstieg – und Abstieg – einer Verflechtung globaler Kräfte: Sklaverei, Great Migration, das Aufblühen Chicagos zum internationalen Industrie- und Handelszentrum, Rassendiskriminierung, Stadterneuerung, die US-Immobilienkrise von 2008. Gates' Herkunft und Praxis sind direkt mit diesen Kräften verbunden. Seine Eltern übersiedelten während der Great Migration (der Abwanderung von Afroamerikanern aus den Südstaaten in die Nordstaaten) von Yazoo City, Mississippi, nach Chicago. Der Vater war als Dachdecker am Aufbau der Stadt beteiligt. Gates jr. arbeitete im Büro des Rektors der University of Chicago, als die Institution sich bemühte, engere Kontakte zu ihren Nachbarn an der South Side zu knüpfen, und Studienzentren in aller Welt einrichtete. Die ersten Gebäude-Kunstwerke erwarb Gates zur Zeit der Immobilienblase. Sein gegenwärtiges Atelier ist in den ehemaligen Lagerhallen einer Brauerei untergebracht – wenige Schritte von den Gleisen, auf denen Bier, Stahl und andere Erzeugnisse durch die Wohnsiedlungen hindurch zum und vom Stadtzentrum transportiert wurden.

Erlösung ist ein Leitmotiv in der Kunst von Theaster Gates: Die ansprechende Sinnlichkeit seiner Werke sowie die zeremoniellen Performances, die sie häufig begleiten – zumeist mit Musik von Gates und seiner Band The Black Monks of Mississippi –, sollen erniedrigte Objekte, Geschichten und Menschen wieder erheben und die Würde und Bedeutung dessen wiederherstellen, was von der globalen Kultur übergangen wurde. Chicago, mit seinem schier endlosen Reichtum an Relikten urbaner und architektonischer Aktivität, bietet einen fruchtbaren Boden für Gates' Suchexpeditionen: ein Architekturbuchladen mit geschlossenen Fensterläden, ein Lagerhaus des Chicago Park District, eine aufgelassene Eisenhandlung sowie nicht zuletzt die riesigen Schauräume von Architectural Artifacts, wo so manches Über-

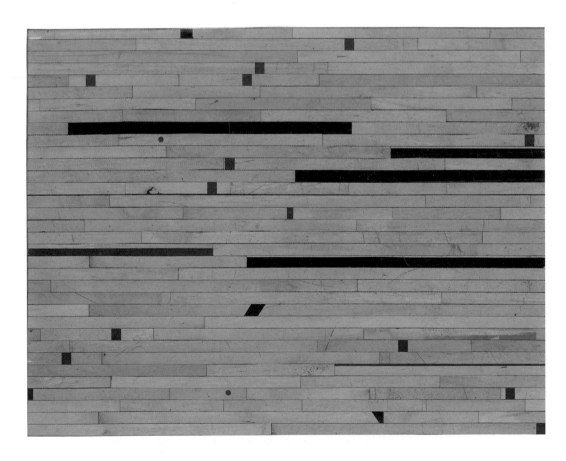

THEASTER GATES, GROUND RULES (ARCHITECURE FOR ATHLETIC FUTURES), 2015,
wood flooring, 78 $^1/_4$ x 100 $^3/_{16}$ x 2 $^9/_{16}$" / GRUNDREGELN (ARCHITEKTUR FÜR ATHLETISCHE
TERMINGESCHÄFTE), Holzboden, 198,8 x 254,5 x 6,4 cm.

bleibsel der materiellen Geschichte der Stadt ein zweites Mal verkauft wird. Gates trifft dort gleich gesinnte Mitbürger wie den Künstler Dan Peterman, der mit Altmaterialien arbeitet und den jungen Gates unter seine Fittiche nahm, den Architekten John Vinci, der als Retter der Original-Innenausstattung der Chicago Stock Exchange zum Lokalhelden aufstieg, oder Tim Samuelson, den offiziellen Kulturhistoriker und querdenkenden Denkmalschützer der Stadt.

Anders als viele andere Künstler, die sich der Geschichte eines spezifischen Orts zuwenden, sucht Gates darin weder eine Zuflucht von der Welt – schliesslich war die von ihm aufgearbeitete Geschichte nie eine «gute alte Zeit» –, noch nutzt er sie als Vorwand, um das Lokale vom Globalen abzusondern. Im Gegenteil, Gates setzt sich mit aller Energie dafür ein, dass das Lokale wieder Anschluss an die Welt findet, von der es fast völlig abgeschnitten ist. In neueren, grösseren Projekten wie der Stony Island Arts Bank und dem Dorchester Art + Housing Collaborative mischen sich Anzeichen professioneller Baugestaltung – Stahlelemente, Verglasungen, Designermöbel und -leuchten – in den unkonventionellen Do-it-

THEASTER GATES, Dorchester Art + Housing Collaborative. (PHOTO: SARA POOLEY / COURTESY OF REBUILD FOUNDATION)

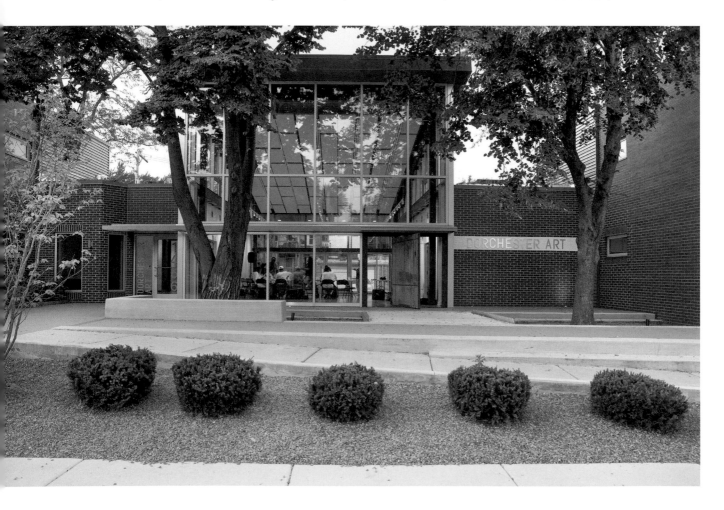

-Charakter früherer Vorhaben. Genau dieser komplex modulierte Austausch zwischen dem Lokalen und dem Globalen ist, wie sich mit immer grösserer Deutlichkeit herausstellt, das Kernanliegen von Gates' laufend erweitertem Werkportfolio. Er ist im Sinne des Soziologen Ulrich Beck ein «Kosmopolit», der sich dafür einsetzt, die Wechselwirkungen zwischen einem spezifischen Ort und den weltumspannenden Netzen von Kunst, Architektur, Geld und Politik zu multiplizieren und zu vertiefen.

Selbstverständlich bedürfen Gates' Bauten, Keramiken, Skulpturen, Performances, Events und Finanzen des Zusammenspiels vieler Hände, Köpfe, Augen und Stimmen. Auch das ist ein Zeichen seines Kosmopolitismus: die Bereitschaft, ständig im Austausch mit anderen zu stehen und ständig den Austausch unter anderen anzuregen. Man könnte auch sagen, es wäre Gates' Ziel, ein Katalysator zu sein, der die Quantität und Qualität der Wechselbeziehungen zwischen den Menschen und den Materialien in Grand Crossing und weit darüber hinaus erhöhen will. Die genannten Wechselbeziehungen sind das Herzstück seiner Objekte und Environments, wie «schön» diese auch immer sein mögen.

Doch wie sieht jetzt, wo Gates bei Möbelketten einkauft und Marfa zum Mekka der Kunstschickeria geworden ist, die Zukunft derartiger Positionen aus? Dienen sie einzig als Beweis dafür, dass rigorose Kunstpraktiken unentwirrbar mit dem globalen Designmarkt verknüpft sind? Ich halte einen solchen Schluss für übertrieben, denn man darf nicht vergessen, dass die architektonischen Exkurse beider Künstler rein strategischer Natur sind. Die Geschichten, Funktionen, Materialien und Formen ihrer Gebäude stehen in vollkommenem Einklang mit ihren künstlerischen Absichten – die sie konstruktiv erweitern.

Am Ende verfolgen Judd und Gates mit ihren Bauprojekten verschiedene Ziele. Judd engagierte sich im New York der 1960er-Jahre für die Friedens- und Bürgerrechtsbewegung, bestand jedoch darauf, dass Kunst und Politik säuberlich getrennt bleiben.[2] Sein Individualismus, seine Freiheitsliebe und seine Abneigung gegen die Konsumkultur veranlassten ihn zum Ortswechsel nach Marfa. Während Judd in die westtexanische Wüste zog, um seine Kunst zu retten, zog Gates an die South Side Chicagos, um seine Kunst zu testen. Der Unterschied zwischen den zwei Künstlern lässt sich gut an ihren Banken ermessen: Judds Marfa National Bank beherbergt eine Sammlung moderner Möbel, anhand derer er privat den Wert und die Grenzen seiner skulpturalen Praxis zu bestimmen suchte. Die von Gates initiierte Stony Island Arts Bank organisiert Kulturveranstaltungen und präsentiert ihre Sammlungen und Archive einem vielfältigen Publikum. Genau dieser Schnittpunkt sozialer, ökonomischer und ästhetischer Ströme bildet das Medium, in und mit dem Gates arbeitet. Der eine Künstler kaufte eine ganze Gemeinde als Standort für seine (spezifischen) Objekte, der andere verkauft Objekte, um ein (spezifisches) Stadtviertel zu retten. Donald Judd wollte einer Welt entrinnen, die er im Innersten für unveränderlich hielt. Theaster Gates öffnet sich einer Welt, von der er nie aufhören wird zu glauben, dass er sie verändern kann – ein Haus nach dem anderen.

(Übersetzung: Bernhard Geyer)

1) In Gates' Kunstobjekten hallen oft formelle Elemente des Minimalismus und Post-Minimalismus nach, aber deren Materialien – unter anderem Feuerwehrschläuche – nehmen Bezug auf die Bürgerrechtsbewegung, die, obwohl zeitgleich, in den Praktiken des Minimalismus kaum je reflektiert wurde.
2) Interessant erscheint uns in diesem Zusammenhang, dass Judd grossen Wert auf die Erhaltung der Inschriften und Wandbilder von deutschen Gefangenen legte, die während des Zweiten Weltkriegs im Fort D. A. Russell untergebracht waren. Sie bilden einen geschichtsträchtigen Rahmen für Judds ehrgeizigste Skulptureninstallation, der die scharfe Trennung zwischen seinen «spezifischen Objekten» und seinem politischen Aktivismus erschwert.

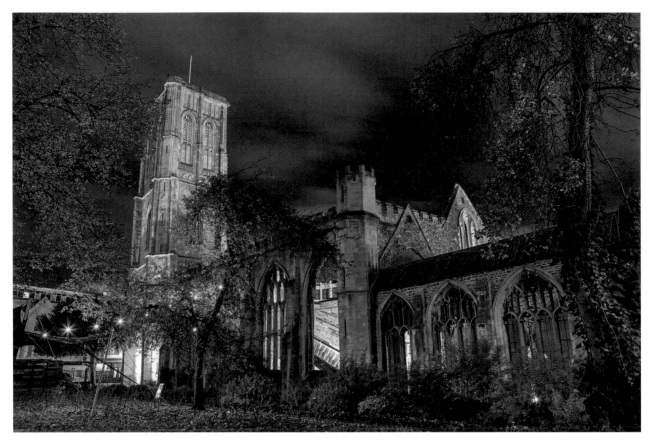

THEASTER GATES, SANCTUM, 2015, produced by Situations, installation view, Bristol / HEILIGTUM, produziert von Situations, Installationsansicht. (PHOTO: MAX MACCLURE)

Raise High the Roof Beam:

[I]n a Gothic building, the roof both within and without . . . is the crown of its beauties, the abiding place of its brain.
—William Morris

In 1985, Kunsthalle Basel hosted a two-part round-table discussion featuring four major figures from the European neo-avant-garde and its so-called "trans-avantgarde" offspring—namely, Joseph Beuys, Enzo Cucchi, Anselm Kiefer, and Jannis Kounellis. Somewhat incongruously, one overarching image dominated much of the conversation's concluding exchanges:

DIETER ROELSTRAETE is a member of the curatorial team for Documenta 14.

Kounellis: A monument like the Cologne Cathedral indicates a centralization, encompasses a culture, and points the way for future development. Without signs like this we would run the risk of becoming nomads.
Beuys: The Cologne Cathedral is a bad sculpture. It would make a good train station. Chartres is better. But what Kounellis says about the cathedral is a nice image. The old cathedrals were built in a world that was still round, but that in the meantime has been constricted by materialism. There was an internal necessity to narrow it like that, since in that way human consciousness became sharpened, espe-

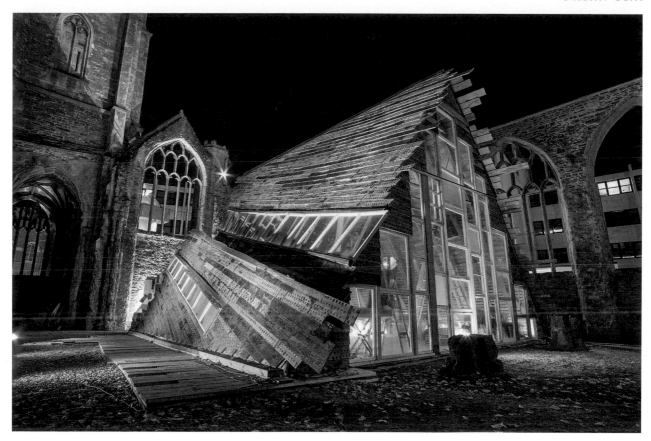

THEASTER GATES, SANCTUM, 2015, produced by Situations, installation view, Bristol / HEILIGTUM, produziert von Situations, Installationsansicht. (PHOTO: MAX MACCLURE)

Theaster Gates and Cathedrals

DIETER ROELSTRAETE

cially in its analytic functions. Now we have to carry out a synthesis with all our powers, and build a new cathedral.[1]

As the debate drifts on, with Beuys (unsurprisingly) talking more than the rest, references to cathedral-building keep recurring: "The esthetic sense is disturbed nowadays like never before in history. So let's build the cathedral!" Or: "We're not here talking together to improve our relationship, which is good anyway. We're here to build the cathedral." And: "Regarding art as the only way to build the cathedral, I really do need the spoken language." Beuys, of course,

is the founding father and foremost theorist of *Soziale Plastik*, or "social sculpture," and thus an obvious point of reference for any discussion of Theaster Gates's own (in many ways arch-American) brand of "social sculpture" and its (predominantly European) art-historical antecedents. My primary reason for recalling the above round table, however, relates not so much to Beuys's ambiguous stature as an avatar of twenty-first-century "social practice"—as the post-political afterlife of *Soziale Plastik* is now infelicitously named—as it does to the forceful image of the cathe-

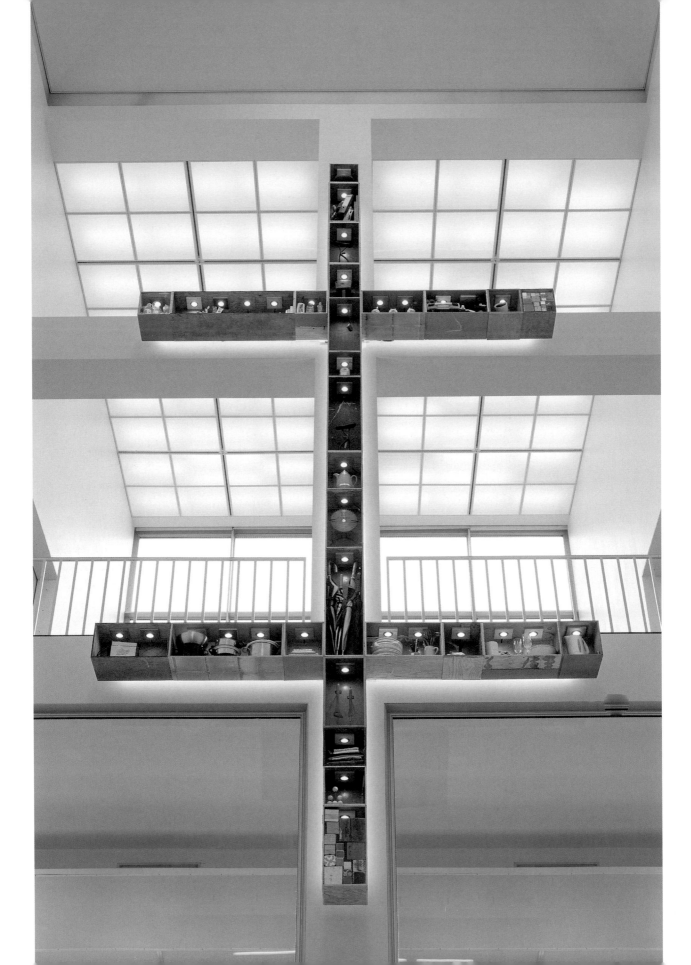

dral (and, inevitably, its anonymous community of builders) to which Beuys and company continuously return.[2] It is this image of the cathedral and the culture of cathedral-building that I want to explore here to shed more light on a specifically European dimension, so to speak, of Gates's work.

In 1967, the French historian Georges Duby, one of the leading thinkers in the French *Annales* school of sociologically inflected historiography, published his tripartite magnum opus chronicling the ascent of medieval Europe. Duby's history hinges on what he terms the "age of the cathedrals," spanning a century and a half between the middle of the twelfth century and the end of the thirteenth century, during which time Western Europe saw its greatest cathedrals rise from the nondescript flatlands north of and surrounding Paris—Amiens, Beauvais, Chartres, Laon, Reims, Troyes, and finally, Paris's own Notre Dame. Duby observes, "Cathedral art was urban art": The medieval building boom heralded the "rebirth of the cities," and each "new cathedral was a eulogy to the entire urban settlement," embodying "the townspeople's pride, as its plenitude of spires, gables, and pinnacles thrust up toward the heavens a dream city, an idealization of the city of God which magnified the urban landscape."[3] It served not only as a place of worship but as a meeting point where guilds could assemble and townspeople could gather. Cathedrals functioned as beacons of light in the rural desolation of Europe, driving urban development and attracting the region's best artisans—"artists" as protean and talented as Michelangelo or Tilman Riemenschneider to be sure, though belonging to an older, pre-individual (indeed, *pre-artistic*) era, one of guilds and crafts. It was this pre-modern ethos of anonymous, truly communal authorship and individual sacrifice

THEASTER GATES, 13TH BALLAD, 2013, wood, steel, neon, paper, Huguenot House remnants, dimensions variable / 13. BALLADE, Holz, Stahl, Neonlampe, Papier, Hinterlassenschaften Hugenottenhaus, Masse variabel.

which much later led the nineteenth-century British art critic John Ruskin to write so rhapsodically about the Gothic "style" in art—an *ethic*, in short, as much as, if not more than, an *aesthetic*. (William Morris was another hugely influential sympathizer whose name may indeed seem too glaringly obvious, in the current art-historical context.)

Civic pride, economic *nous*, and urban development; craft, collectivity, and community; the creative tension between group and individual, between art(s) and craft(s)—these have become well-worn tropes in the discussion of Theaster Gates's work. "The city is my medium," he has said, and indeed, over the past five years, he has steadily transformed the psychogeography of Chicago's South Side—renovating abandoned buildings for reuse as meeting spaces and arts centers.[4] And most importantly, of course—literally, *above all*—there is the matter of *faith,* and the very real castles it enables us/him to build in the air. Mapping out the many instances where Gates's upbringing in African-American religious traditions intersects with his evolving, ever-expanding artistic practice would lead us much too far for the current essay's rather modest purposes, although it is worth pausing here—with an eye on our reading of Duby's chronicle of medieval cathedral-building cultures—to reflect on one of Gates's recent projects, the video installation GONE ARE THE DAYS OF SHELTER AND MARTYR (2014). Included in the exhibition "All the World's Futures," curated by Okwui Enwezor, at the 2015 Venice Biennale, this work features a bronze bell, a slanting wall of slate roof tiles, and the melancholy statue of a saint, presumably depicting Saint Laurence. A large-scale projection presents a scene set inside the wrecked interior from which these objects were salvaged, namely the neo-gothic St. Laurence Church that once stood a block away from Gates's studio on the South Side. Built in 1911, the Roman Catholic sanctuary closed its doors in 2002, a victim of decades of demographic and denominational change; the building was demolished in 2014, meeting the same sorry fate as innumerable neighborhood churches in impoverished black urban areas across America. (How fitting, incidentally, that this church should have been dedicated to the patron saint of *archivists and librarians*, for a true archi-

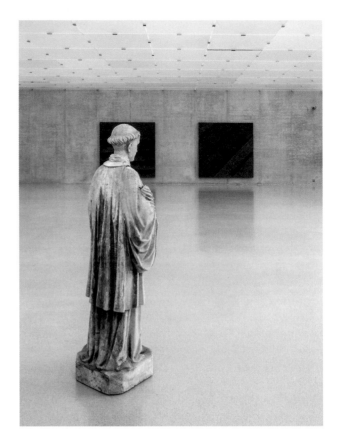

val impulse deeply colors Gates's art of conversion, conservation, and preservation—so much so that one could think of St. Laurence as the primary protector of Gates himself. Think, for instance, of the once-doomed contents of Chicago's legendary Prairie Avenue Bookshop, of the Johnson Publishing Library, of Dr. Wax Records, or the University of Chicago glass lantern slide collection—all have found their way, thankfully, into the widening protective embrace of Gates's various building schemes.)

The video shows members of the Black Monks of Mississippi, Gates's long-running music ensemble, dressed in sorrowful black: One performer plays a cello while others improvise in song; two men continually lift and drop tall wooden doors to a limping beat to better hammer the point of pity home. It seems strangely fitting, somehow, that Gates's most emphatic engagement with ecclesiastical architecture to date mourns the destruction of an existing church rather than celebrate the *construction* of a new one—fitting, that is, for an otherwise upbeat entrepreneurial practice grounded in belief (in general) and faith in art (in particular), reminding us that it's one thing to build an art center, say, or web of business opportunities, but another thing altogether to build a church, let alone a *cathedral.*[5]

Let's briefly return to Duby's *Age of the Cathedrals.* In a chapter titled "God is Light, 1130–1190," the historian describes the engineering ingenuity that made possible the construction of the great cathedrals. The Gothic style was conceived as a theology of light cast in stone, in contrast to the cavernous darkness of earlier Romanesque churches. To achieve more light, the cathedrals needed additional height, which required new window designs as well as novel roofing techniques. Not only did these improbable new structures tower over every other building around them, their naves were often the only covered gathering

place in the center of town—giving newly embodied meaning to the notion of "divine shelter." As it happens, references to roofs are scattered throughout Gates's art, including paintings created collaboratively with his father, Theaster Senior, who worked as a roofer. While this autobiographical element might have provided a point of departure, Gates's concerns have since expanded outward: "I'm looking at roofs and the sublime. I'm looking at Shinto structures and how these old Japanese Buddhist temples were made so that the roof actually held up the walls. I'm learning all this stuff about fourteenth-century cathedrals. I'm just kind of interested in roofing."[6] Roofs, of all things, those selfsame "castles in the air"[7]— and by way of rounding off this train of thought, it is worth referring to Gates's SANCTUM project last year, for which he erected a shelter within the bombed-out, roofless shell of the Temple Church in Bristol, England.[8] Theaster Gates is looking at roofs and the sublime: upward.

1) Joseph Beuys, Jannis Kounellis, Anselm Kiefer, and Enzo Cucchi, "The Cultural-Historical Tragedy of the European Continent," in Charles Harrison and Paul Wood, eds., *Art in Theory 1900–1990: An Anthology of Changing Ideas* (Oxford, UK: Blackwell Publishers, 1992), 1032–36. The complete transcript was originally published by *Parkett* in 1986 as *Ein Gespräch / Una Discussione.*

2) Note, as well, that another Euro-aesthetic paradigm sporadically associated with Gates's work, namely, the Bauhaus, touches upon some of these notions: The opening sentence of Walter Gropius's "Bauhaus Manifesto and Program" from 1919 dramatically states that "the ultimate aim of all visual arts is the complete building!" The image that adorns this seminal document is a drawing, by Lyonel Feininger, of a church.

3) Georges Duby, *The Age of the Cathedrals: Art and Society, 980–1420*, trans. Eleanor Levieux and Barbara Thompson (Chicago: University of Chicago Press, 1981), 93. I owe thanks to Abigail Winograd for helping me develop this specifically "medievalist" analysis of Theaster Gates's work.

4) Theaster Gates, in "Carol Becker in conversation with Theaster Gates," in *Theaster Gates* (London: Phaidon, 2015), 17.

5) Much more can be said, of course, about the asymptotic relation between entrepreneurship and religiosity, between money and faith, the conjoining of which drove the urban revolution of early medieval Europe, and continues to determine the face and shape of American politics—but that too would doubtless lead us too far astray. Suffice it to observe, for now, how the closure of countless small businesses has had a profound impact on Gates's South Side surroundings—and how many of the resulting empty storefronts have been taken over, in the course of the years, by DIY churches. . . .

6) Theaster Gates, in "Carol Becker in conversation with Theaster Gates," 19.

7) In the aforementioned interview, Becker remarks: "A roof holding up the walls is a pretty interesting idea, because we always say we don't build the house from the roof down, but maybe you do? And that's a good metaphor for you." Ibid. This is precisely where the utopian spirit of Beuysian cathedral-building survives in Gates's work—an old-fashioned art of the seemingly impossible.

8) Built from reclaimed wood and windows, Gates's teepee-like structure hosted a series of performances over a twenty-four-day period.

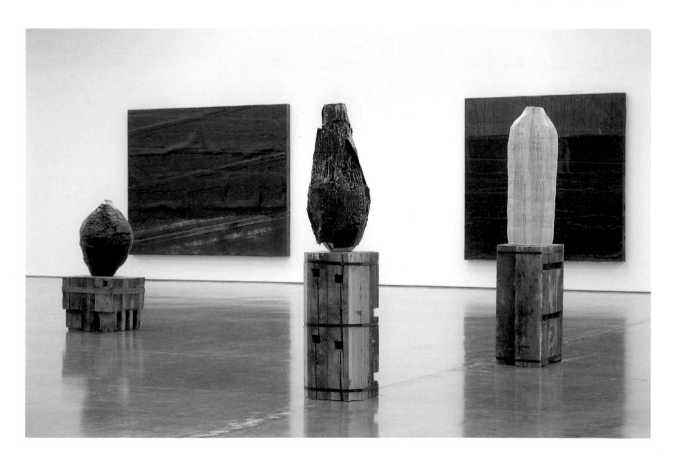

THEASTER GATES, "Freedom of Assembly," 2015, exhibition view / Ausstellungsansicht, White Cube London. (PHOTO: GEORGE DARRELL)

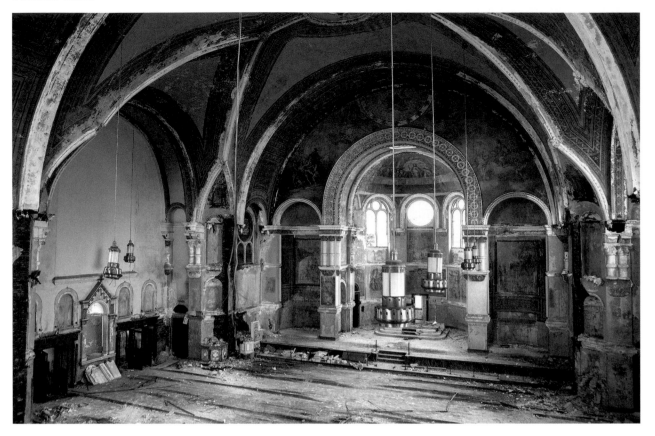

THEASTER GATES, GONE ARE THE DAYS OF SHELTER AND MARTYR, 2014, video, 6 min. 31 sec. / VORBEI DIE ZEIT DER ZUFLUCHT UND DES MÄRTYRERS, Video.

Hebt den Dachbalken hoch:

[I]n einem gotischen Bau befindet sich das Dach sowohl innen als auch aussen ... die Krone seiner Schönheit, die Schale seines Gehirns.
– William Morris

Jean-Christophe Ammann, der damalige Leiter der Kunsthalle Basel, organisierte 1985 ein zweiteiliges Gespräch mit vier Leitfiguren der europäischen Neoavantgarde und ihres Ablegers, der sogenannten Transavantgarde: Joseph Beuys, Enzo Cucchi, Anselm Kiefer und Jannis Kounellis. Vielleicht etwas

DIETER ROELSTRAETE ist Mitglied des Kuratorenteams der documenta 14.

ausserhalb des Kontexts trat im Schlussteil ein verbindendes Motiv in den Vordergrund:

Kounellis: Ja, aber die Kathedrale von Köln weist auf eine Zentralität hin, umfasst eine Kultur und weist auf die Zukunft. Sonst würden wir riskieren, Nomaden zu werden.
Beuys: Die Kathedrale von Köln ist eine schlechte Skulptur. Sie wäre gut als Bahnhof. Chartes ist besser. Aber was Kounellis von der Kathedrale sagt, ist ein schönes Bild. Die alten Kathedralen stehen irgendwo in einer Welt, die

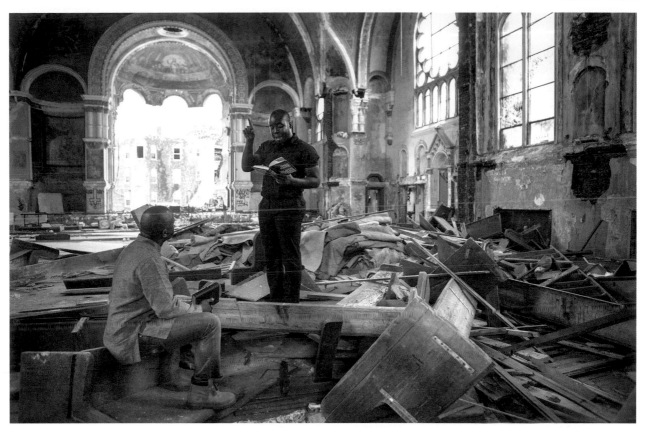

THEASTER GATES, GONE ARE THE DAYS OF SHELTER AND MARTYR, 2014, *video,* 6 min. 31 sec. / VORBEI DIE ZEIT DER ZUFLUCHT UND DES MÄRTYRERS, *Video.*

Theaster Gates
und die Kathedrale

DIETER ROELSTRAETE

noch rund war. Aber dann wurde die Welt durch den Materialismus reduziert. Es war eine innere Notwendigkeit, sie so zu verengen, denn dadurch wurde das menschliche Bewusstsein geschärft, ganz besonders in seiner analytischen Tätigkeit. Jetzt müssen wir eine Synthese vollziehen mit all unseren Kräften, und das ist die Kathedrale.[1]

Im weiteren Verlauf der Diskussion, wobei Beuys (wohl kaum überraschend) sich am häufigsten äusserte, ertönte mehrfach der Aufruf zum Bau von

Kathedralen: «Der ästhetische Sinn ist heute, wie nie in der Geschichte, gestört. Also bauen wir die Kathedrale!» Oder: «Wir sprechen hier doch nicht zusammen, um unser Verhältnis, das sowieso gut ist, zu verbessern. Wir sind hier, um die Kathedrale zu bauen.» Und: «In Bezug auf die Kunst als dem alleinigen Mittel, um die Kathedrale zu bauen, brauche ich doch die gesprochene Sprache.» Als Begründer und Haupttheoretiker der «sozialen Plastik» eignet sich Beuys ideal als Anknüpfungspunkt für eine Besprechung von Theaster Gates' eigener (in vieler Hinsicht ur-amerikanischen) Version der sozialen Skulptur und deren (überwiegend europäischen) kunsthistorischer Vorläufer. Der eigentliche Grund, warum ich mich an das fragliche Gespräch erinnerte, war indessen weniger die vage Position, die Beuys als Gallionsfigur der «sozialen Praxis» des 20. Jahrhunderts einnimmt (wie das postpolitische Nachleben der sozialen Skulptur heutzutage etwas unglücklich genannt wird), als vielmehr das eindringliche Bild der Kathedrale (und der anonymen Gemeinschaft der Bauhütte), zu dem Beuys & Co. wiederholt zurückkehrten.[2] Dieses Bild und die gesamte Kultur des gotischen Kirchenbaus möchte ich hier etwas näher betrachten, um einen, wie mir scheint, spezifisch europäischen Aspekt in der Kunst von Theaster Gates zu beleuchten.

Der französische Historiker Georges Duby, ein führender Vertreter der soziologisch orientierten Annales-Schule der Geschichtswissenschaft, veröffentlichte 1967 sein dreibändiges Hauptwerk, das den Aufstieg Europas im Mittelalter nachzeichnet. Bereits im Titel verwendet Duby den Zentralbegriff «Zeit der Kathedralen», der jene 150 Jahre zwischen der Mitte des 12. und dem Ende des 13. Jahrhunderts bezeichnet, in denen Westeuropa die Errichtung seiner grössten Kathedralen im flachen Pariser Vorland erlebte: Amiens, Beauvais, Chartres, Laon, Reims, Troyes und schliesslich in der Hauptstadt selbst Notre-Dame. Die Kunst der Kathedrale war eine städtische, urteilt Duby. Der Bauboom des Mittelalters führte zu einer Widergeburt der Städt und jede Kathedrale feiert den Wohlstand der gesamten Siedlung, «Wie eine Traumstadt erheben sich die zahllosen Turmspitzen, Giebel und Zimmen als Krönung des Bauwerks gen Himmel, und diese ideale Gottesstadt verklärt die städtische Landschaft».[3] Die Kathedralen dienten

THEASTER GATES, GONE ARE THE DAYS OF SHELTER AND MARTYR, 2014, video, 6 min. 31 sec. / VORBEI DIE ZEIT DER ZUFLUCHT UND DES MÄRTYRERS, Video.

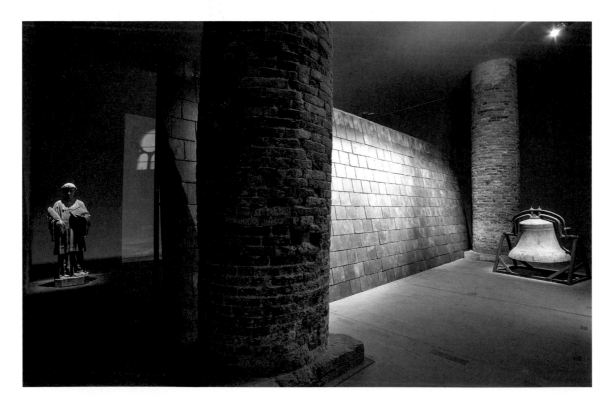

nicht nur als Ort der Gottesverehrung, sondern darüber hinaus als Sammelpunkt der Handwerkszünfte und der Stadtbürger schlechthin. Aufragend wie Leuchttürme in den Ebenen Europas bildeten sie Kristallisationskerne für das Wachstum der Städte. Die besten Handwerker der Umgebung fühlten sich von ihrem Fanal angezogen – «Künstler», die fraglos ebenso universal begabt waren wie ein Michelangelo Buonarroti oder ein Tilman Riemenschneider, auch wenn sie einem früheren, vorindividuellen (ja vor-*künstlerischen*) Zeitalter angehörten, bestimmt von Handwerk und Zunft. Das vormoderne Ethos der namenlosen, wahrhaft gemeinschaftlichen Kunstproduktion ohne Privilegierung des Individuums inspirierte im 19. Jahrhundert den englischen Kunsthistoriker John Ruskin zu Lobeshymnen auf den gotischen Stil in der Kunst – den er offenbar ebenso sehr, wenn nicht mehr, als *Ethik* auffasste denn als *Ästhetik*. (Ein weiterer, immens einflussreicher Anhänger der Gotik war William Morris, dessen Name in der heutigen Kunstgeschichte so geläufig ist, dass es überflüssig scheint, ihn zu erwähnen.)

Bürgerstolz, Geschäftssinn und Stadtentwicklung; Handwerk, Gemeinsamkeit und Gemeinschaft; die kreative Spannung zwischen Gruppe und Individuum, zwischen Kunst und Kunsthandwerk – alles Schlagwörter, die man häufig in Rezensionen von Gates' Werk findet. «Die Stadt ist mein Medium», sagt der Künstler, der im Lauf der letzten fünf Jahre die Psychogeographie der South Side von Chicago nachhaltig verändert hat – unter anderem durch die Renovierung leer stehender Gebäude als Versammlungsräume und Kulturzentren.[4] Von – buchstäblich – *höchster* Wichtigkeit für Gates ist allerdings die Frage des *Glaubens*, denn dieser ermöglicht es ihm und uns, Schlösser in die Luft zu bauen. Jeden einzelnen Punkt zu verzeichnen, an dem die afroamerikanischen religiösen Traditionen, mit denen Gates aufwuchs, sich mit seiner kontinuierlich fortschreitenden Kunstpraxis überschneiden, würde weit über den Rahmen dieses Aufsatzes hinausführen. Dennoch empfiehlt es sich – mit einem Auge auf Dubys Geschichte des gotischen Kirchenbaus –, kurz einen Blick auf eines der neueren Projekte des Künstlers zu werfen. Die Videoinstallation GONE ARE THE DAYS OF SHELTER AND MARTYR (Vorbei die Zeit

der Zuflucht und des Märtyrers, 2014), Teil der Ausstellung «All the World's Futures» auf der Biennale von Venedig 2015, umfasste eine Bronzeglocke, eine schräge Dachschieferwand und eine melancholische Heiligenstatue, die vermutlich den heiligen Laurentius verkörperte. Eine wandgrosse Videoprojektion führte in den verfallenen Innenraum, in dem all diese Objekte einst untergebracht waren: das Schiff der neogotischen St. Laurence Church. 1911 nur eine Strasse von Gates' Atelier entfernt in der South Side Chicagos errichtet, schloss das katholische Gotteshaus im Jahr 2002 seine Tore, ein Opfer des demographischen und konfessionellen Wandels. Der Bau wurde 2014 abgerissen, wie so viele andere Kirchen in verarmten afroamerikanischen Stadtvierteln in ganz Amerika. (Wie passend also, dass die St. Laurence Church dem Schutzheiligen der *Archivare* und *Bibliothekare* geweiht war, denn Gates' Kunst der Konvertierung, Konservierung und Präservierung treibt ein wahrhaft archivarischer Impuls – so sehr, dass man sagen könnte, er selbst stände unter dem Schutz des heiligen Laurentius. Man denke nur an den Inhalt solch ehemaliger Wahrzeichen des Chicagoer Stadtlebens wie den Prairie Avenue Bookshop, die Johnson Publishing Library und den Plattenladen Dr. Wax Records oder an die Glasdiasammlung der University of Chicago, die alle, Gott sei Dank, Zuflucht unter den schützenden Dächern von Gates' ständig erweiterten Bauvorhaben gefunden haben.)

Das Video zu GONE ARE THE DAYS zeigt Mitglieder der Band Black Monks of Mississippi, mit der Gates seit längerer Zeit zusammenarbeitet. Alle Akteure sind in Schwarz gekleidet. Ein Cellist spielt zu improvisiertem Gesang. Zwei Männer heben im Takt des holpernden Beats hohe Holztüren und lassen sie wieder fallen – ein schlagendes Bild des Mitlebens mit dem urbanen Zerfall. Dass die am tiefsten empfundene aller bisherigen Auseinandersetzungen des Künstlers mit der Sakralarchitektur die *Zerstörung* einer alten Kirche betrauert, anstatt die *Errichtung* einer neuen zu feiern, scheint passend im Kontext einer generell optimistischen, engagierten Praxis, die im Glauben (im Allgemeinen) und im Glauben an die Kunst (im Besonderen) verwurzelt ist. Dem Betrachter ruft die Installation in Erinnerung, dass es eine Sache ist, ein Kulturzentrum oder ein Netz

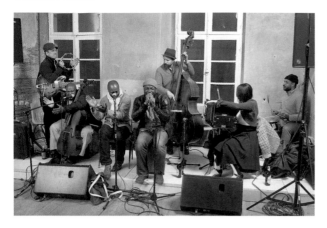

THEASTER GATES, 12 BALLADS FOR HUGENOT HOUSE, 2012,
installation view Documenta 13, Kassel / 12 BALLADEN FÜR
DAS HUGENOTTENHAUS, Installationsansicht.

von Geschäftsinitiativen auf die Beine zu stellen, und dass es eine völlig andere Sache ist, eine Kirche zu bauen, nicht zu reden von einer *Kathedrale*.[5]

Kehren wir kurz zu Dubys *Zeit der Kathedralen* zurück. Im Kapitel «God is Light, 1130–1190» beschreibt der Historiker den Erfindergeist, der den Bau der grossen Kathedralen überhaupt erst möglich machte. Die gotische Baukunst verstand sich als in Stein gemeisselte Theologie des Lichts – eines Lichts, das die höhlenartige Finsternis des romanischen Kirchenraums überflutete. Um mehr Licht einzulassen, musste die Decke der Kirchen erhöht werden, und dies erforderte wiederum neue architektonische Lösungen für die Fensteröffnungen und den Dachstuhl. Die Wagestücke des gotischen Kirchenbaus ragten nicht nur weit über die Giebel aller umstehenden Gebäude hinaus, ihr Schiff war nicht selten der einzige überdachte Versammlungsort einer Gemeinde – sie bildeten somit eine neue Form der «heiligen Zufluchtsstätte». Wie es Gott oder der Zufall will, taucht das Motiv des Dachs in mehreren Werken von Gates auf. Etwa in den Gemälden, die er gemeinsam mit seinem Vater Theaster senior, einem gelernten Dachdecker, schuf. Dieses autobiographische Faktum hätte als Ansatzpunkt für weitere Recherchen dienen können, doch der Künstler wandte sich einem ausgedehnteren Horizont zu: «Ich interessiere mich

für Dächer und für das Erhabene. Ich interessiere mich für Shinto-Bauten. Die alten buddhistischen Tempel Japans sind so konstruiert, dass die Wände vom Dach aufrecht gehalten werden. Ich habe eine Menge über die Kathedralen des 14. Jahrhunderts gelernt. Es interessiert mich einfach, wie Dächer gemacht werden.»[6] Dächer, die auf ihre Art nichts als Luftschlösser sind.[7] Um diesen Gedanken zu Ende zu denken, möchte ich abschliessend das letztjährige SANCTUM-Projekt erwähnen, für das Gates in der ausgebombten, dachlosen Ruine der Temple Church in Bristol einen überdachten Holzverschlag errichtete.[8] Theaster Gates richtet seinen Blick auf Dächer und auf das Erhabene: himmelwärts.

(Übersetzung: Bernhard Geyer)

1) Joseph Beuys, Jannis Kounellis, Anselm Kiefer, and Enzo Cucchi, *Ein Gespräch / Una Discussione*, Parkett-Verlag, 1988, Zürich, S. 158.
2) Eine andere europäische Kunstströmung, die gelegentlich mit Gates in Verbindung gebracht wird, das Bauhaus, beschäftigte sich gleichfalls mit diesem Problemkreis. Das Bauhaus-Manifest (1919) von Walter Gropius verkündete im ersten Satz: «Das Endziel aller bildnerischen Tätigkeit ist der Bau!» Das Titelblatt des berühmten Dokuments ist mit einem Holzschnitt von Lyonel Feininger versehen, der eine Kathedrale wiedergibt.
3) Georges Duby, *Die Zeit der Kathedralen. Kunst und Gesellschaft 980–1420*, Suhrkamp, Frankfurt/M. 2002, S. 193. Ich danke Abigail Winograd für ihre Unterstützung bei dieser «mediävistischen» Analyse von Gates' Werk.
4) Theaster Gates, zitiert nach «Carol Becker in conversation with Theaster Gates», in *Theaster Gates*, Phaidon, London 2015, S. 17.
5) Die asymptotische Beziehung zwischen Unternehmertum und Religiosität, zwischen Geld und Glauben, wäre natürlich ein Thema für sich. Das Zusammenwirken dieser beiden Kräfte löste die urbane Revolution des frühmittelalterlichen Europa aus und prägt noch heute das Gesicht der amerikanischen Politik. Wir beschränken uns hier darauf zu erwähnen, dass die Schliessung zahlloser kleingewerblicher Betriebe die South Side Chicagos schwer beeinträchtigt hat. Viele der leeren Geschäfte wurden übrigens von Do-it-yourself-Kirchen revitalisiert.
6) Theaster Gates, zitiert nach «Carol Becker in conversation with Theaster Gates», S. 19.
7) Im erwähnten Interview kommentiert Becker: «Ein Dach, das die Wände aufrecht hält – eine faszinierende Idee. Wir sagen immer, ‹wer ein gutes Haus bauen will, beginnt nicht mit dem Dach›, aber vielleicht stimmt das gar nicht. Auf jeden Fall hast du da eine gute Metapher gefunden.» Ebd. Genau in dieser Idee lebt der utopische Geist des Beuys'schen Kathedralenbaus in Gates' Werk fort – eine altmodische Kunst des angeblich Unmöglichen.
8) Unter dem zeltartigen Dach der Konstruktion aus Altholz und Altfenstern lief eine 24-stündige Veranstaltungsserie.

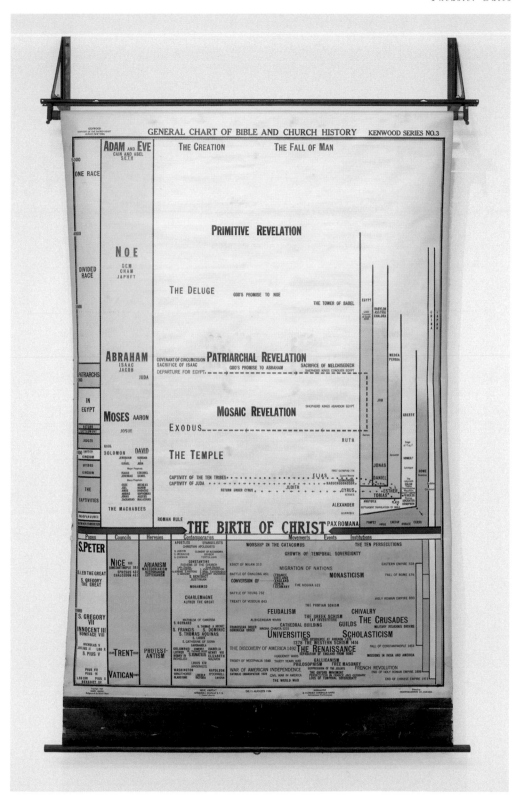

THEASTER GATES, A
COMPLICATED RELATIONSHIP
BETWEEN HEAVEN AND EARTH,
OR, WHEN WE BELIEVE, 2015,
Artes Mundi, Cardiff, Wales /
EINE KOMPLIZIERTE BEZIEHUNG
ZWISCHEN HIMMEL UND ERDE,
ODER, WENN WIR GLAUBEN.
(PHOTO: SARA POOLEY)

EDITION FOR PARKETT 98

THEASTER GATES

SOUL BOWL, 2016

Stoneware with glaze, two bowls, one in black and
one in white, each unique, diameter 4–5", height 3–3 $^1/_2$",
weight each ca. 1,2 lbs.
Packed in box with Association of Named Negro
American Potters (A.N.N.A.P.) Logo.
Ed. 15 / X, signed and numbered certificate.

Zwei Tonschalen, glasiert, je eine in schwarz und weiss,
Einzelstücke, Durchmesser 10–13 cm, Höhe 7–9 cm,
Gewicht je ca. 550 g.
Verpackt in Schachtel mit dem Logo der Association of Named
Negro American Potters (A.N.N.A.P.).
Auflage 15 / X, signiertes und nummeriertes Zertifikat.

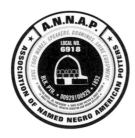

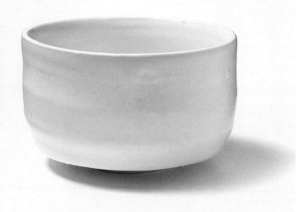

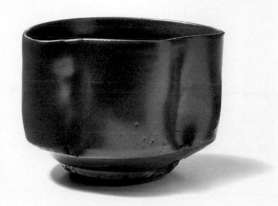

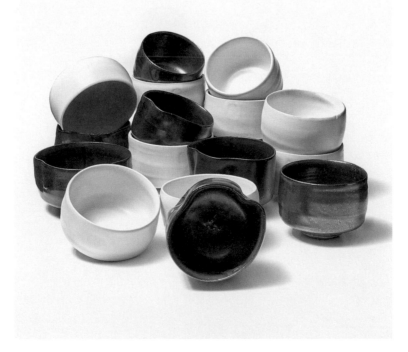

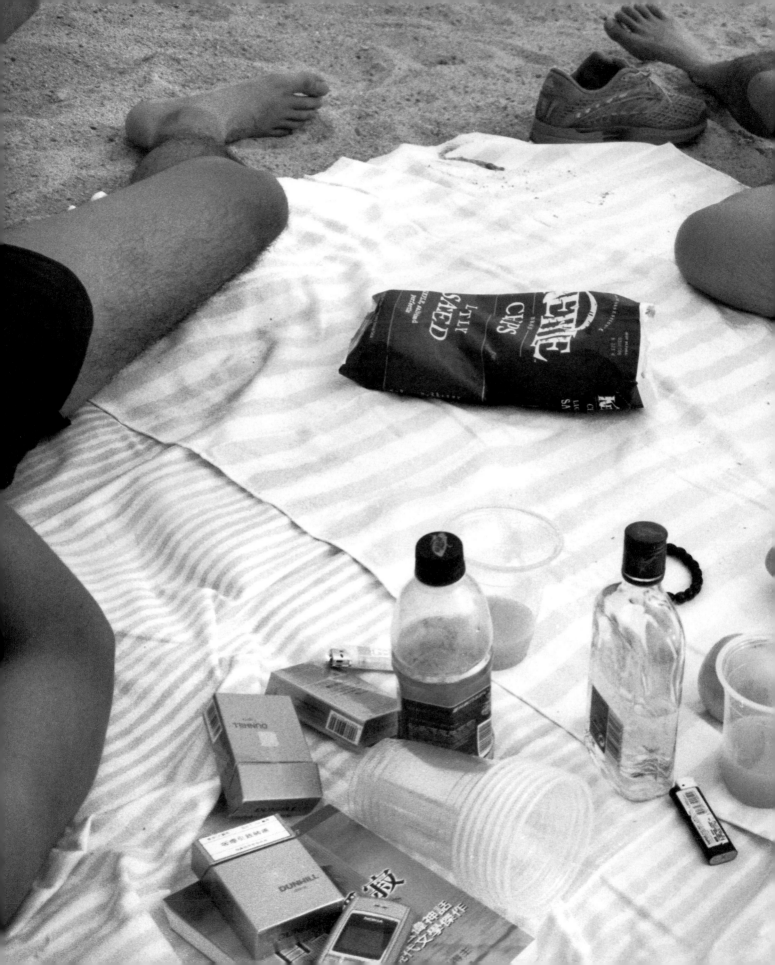

LEE KIT, *HOW LONG?: PICNIC WITH FRIENDS AND HAND-PAINTED CLOTH AT REPULSE BAY, HONG KONG*, 2006, *photo document, 8 $\frac{1}{4}$ x 10 $\frac{1}{2}$" / WIE LANGE?: PICKNICK MIT FREUN-DEN UND HANDBEMALTEM TUCH AN DER REPULSE BAY, HONGKONG, Photodokument, 182,9 × 110,5 cm. (ALL IMAGES COURTESY OF THE ARTIST, JANE LOMBARD GALLERY, NEW YORK; AIKE-DELLARCO, SHANGHAI; M+, WKCDA AND HKADC, HONG KONG; VITAMIN CREATIVE SPACE, GUANGZHOU; SHUGO ARTS, TOKYO.)*

Lee Kit

Scenes of *Everyday Life*

DORYUN CHONG

Toward the end of the Golden Age of Dutch painting in the seventeenth century, Johannes Vermeer created an extraordinary group of pictures. No more than three dozen paintings are attributed to him, most of them less than a meter in height and width. While Dutch paintings of the Baroque period are distinct from other European counterparts for their relative lack of religious topics, dramatic compositions, and physical splendor, they evolved remarkably in their representation of the vagaries and realities of human life, ushering in, one might say, modernity in Western painting. Almost exclusively concentrating on genre painting, specifically middle-class interior domestic scenes, Vermeer was perhaps the most modern of them all. The master of Delft is believed to have worked alone in a room on the second floor of his house, slowly and methodically producing just

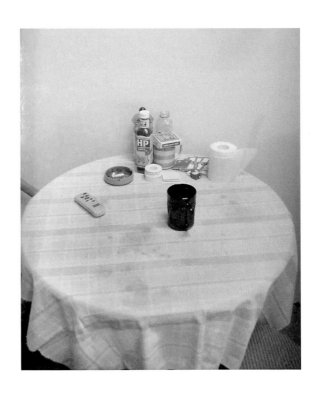

*LEE KIT, HAND-PAINTED CLOTH USED AS TABLECLOTH,
2010–2011, acrylic on fabric, photo document, dimensions variable, cloth: 40 ³/₄ x 42 ³/₄" / HANDBEMALTES
TUCH VERWENDET ALS TISCHTUCH, Acryl auf Textil,
Photodokument, Masse variabel, Tuch: 103,5 x 108,5 cm.*

DORYUNG CHONG is deputy director and chief curator of
M+, Hong Kong.

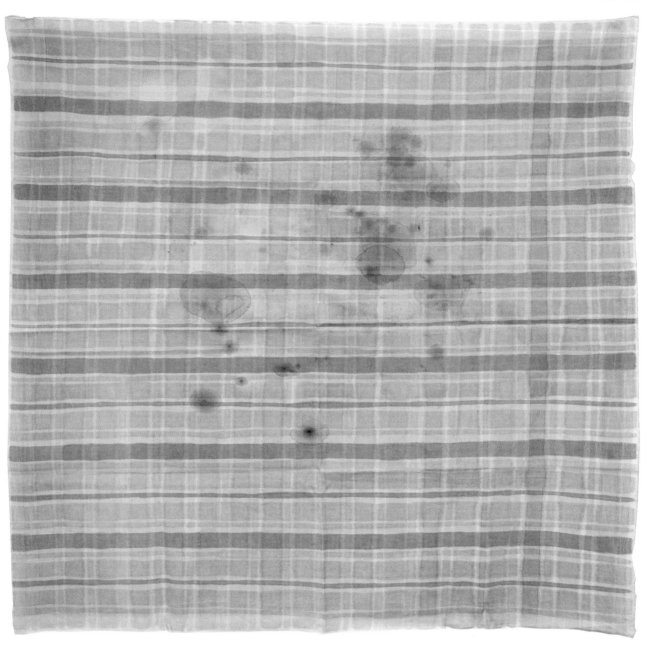

LEE KIT, HAND-PAINTED CLOTH USED AS A TABLE CLOTH, 2010, detail /
HANDBEMALTES TUCH VERWENDET ALS TISCHTUCH, Detail.

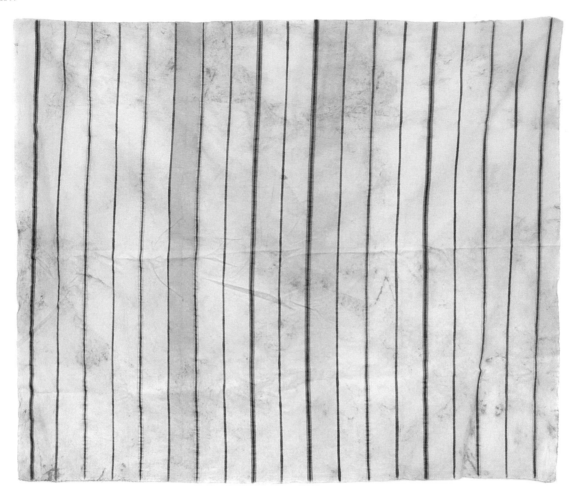

a handful of paintings a year. The black-and-white checkerboard floor, the timber ceiling, and soft northern light pouring in from the windows often seen on the left side of his compositions are the features of this room where he painted for a decade or so.

In one recent conversation over many glasses of wine, Lee Kit proclaimed without hesitation that Vermeer is his favorite artist—in fact, the only artist he likes—a declaration he has made previously in other contexts. This realization came upon his encounter with the first Vermeer painting he saw in real life: A LADY SEATED AT A VIRGINAL (c. 1670–75) at the National Gallery in London. The rendezvous with one of the last paintings by the Dutch master preceded

two others: THE LOVE LETTER (c. 1667–70, Rijksmuseum, Amsterdam) and THE ART OF PAINTING (c. 1662–68, Kunsthistorisches Museum, Vienna). All three examples possess elements of the classic Vermeer picture: The ladies are surrounded by paintings and rich textiles, signs of bourgeois life; music is also prominently present, as all three women are pictured with musical instruments—the viola da gamba, the cittern, the trumpet, and the virginal.

When prompted to explain why he loves Vermeer, Lee has ready answers, which reveal his desire to be at once typical and personal. He appreciates the refined sense of light and space as well as the social messages embedded in Vermeer's pictures. They capture humanity and are sincere. The longing for quietude also resonates with him—the old master "liked to stay at home," just as Lee does. Lee has made no secret that his art is inextricably connected to that penchant, that longing. (It is also well known that he is a prodigious consumer of music in his private space.) In many respects, Lee is fundamentally a classical, studio-based artist, who holds onto the romance of solitude in alternately insouciant and melancholy ways.

Solitude, for Lee, is not an asocial attitude, however. His well-known critical stance, even rage, vis-à-vis the state of things in the strange microcosm that is Hong Kong suggests that his art may not have been possible without the weariness arising from both a wholehearted acceptance of the present and a need to shut it out. In that sense, it is far from surprising that windows frequently appear or are intimated by raking light in photographs of his paintings at home or in the studio (which he then frequently exhibits alongside the paintings in the exhibition space). Lee's windows exist not as a source of light and air, as in Vermeer's paintings, or as a logical frame on an unruly world, in the Renaissance sense, so much as an imperfect safeguard against and even a risky exposure to the outside. Lee realized this simple, obvious fact some years ago when he was away from Hong Kong in Wellington, New Zealand, for a residency. In order to protect himself from the curious

gazes of passersby, he hung his hand-painted cloths over the windows. Not only did he realize that "opening or closing it can completely determine the circumstances of my environment," but this act also led to him to tend to the windows and understand that "housekeeping inexplicably becomes my internal language . . . a fine and important behavior."[1] The utter ordinariness, or banality, of the particular artistic production of hand-painted cloth as painting, in which he had been engaged for several years and for which he had gained recognition, could be crystallized only when the layers of social relevance, overdetermined in Hong Kong, were stripped away. The necessity of housekeeping reestablished, perhaps paradoxically, the *fine*-ness of the "fine art"—art for art's sake—of Lee's labor.

It might seem counterintuitive that he understood this at such a far distance from Hong Kong, as Hong Kong is very possibly the city of windows, far more so than any other. The city's notorious density of dizzyingly vertical residential and commercial buildings, in which the vast majority of its inhabitants live and work, means that what people see out their windows are more windows. In residential districts, glimpses of private spaces are almost always unavoidable, and people are inured to living with the fact of mindlessly seeing others as much as being seen by them. And if private space is a practically nonexistent concept for

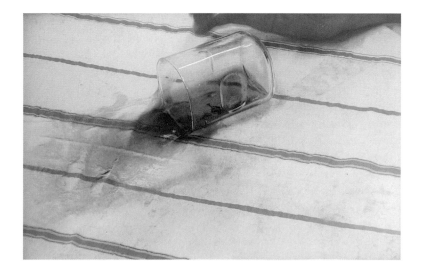

LEE KIT, I AM ABLE TO DIP A CUP OF TEA: HAND-PAINTED CLOTH USED AS TABLE CLOTH, 2007, photo document, acrylic on fabric, 48 x 59", 8 ¹/₂ x 12 ¹/₂" / ICH KANN EINE TASSE TEE EINTAUCHEN: HANDBEMALTES TUCH VERWENDET ALS TISCHTUCH, Acryl auf Stoff, Photodokument, 122 x 150 cm, 22 x 31,8 cm.

most, the lack of public space in Hong Kong is a matter of constant complaint. The increasingly raucous politics around the contested notion of the body politic—between the tiny Special Administrative Region and the behemoth "motherland" of the People's Republic of China—often dovetail with the politics of space in this increasingly crowded and unaffordable city. All of these are usually cited as reasons for the small scale, conceptual bent, and edginess of the work of Hong Kong artists. Lee's practice is often framed in relation to these peculiarities, and is seen as the archetype. The artist's own description of what he tries to accomplish refers to constructing his life by closing the door—but perhaps not the windows—and the difficulty of doing so.

Arguably, the most striking aspect of Lee's handpainted cloth work, for which he may still be best known, is its palette dominated by soft pastel tones of pinks, sky blues, and creams, rarely associated with and even irreconcilable with the kind of intellectual rigor expected of contemporary art-making. If the tonality of Lee's work has distinguished itself with insistent gentleness from the torrents of ever intensifying visual impact in the work of his contemporaries internationally, it may carry a particular resonance in

LEE KIT, BATHED WITH HANDPAINTED CLOTH, 2003, acrylic on fabric, photo document, dimensions variable / GEBADET MIT HANDBEMALTEM TUCH, Acryl auf Stoff, Photo-dokument, Masse variabel.

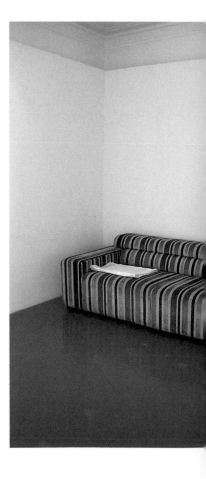

the city where it began. A vast majority of buildings in Hong Kong are daubed in faded pastel tones of grays and beiges and pinks, allegedly for cost effectiveness and easy maintenance, and possibly as a tactic of psychological pacification of the densely cohabiting populace. To say that the palette of Lee's paintings is a reflection of the architectural semiotics of his home would be, if simplistic, not off the mark. Lee's cloth paintings stick to material and formal basics as well. He uses no precious fabrics—no velvet or silk, not even canvas or linen, but simplest cotton. The forms or compositions of his paintings, which may be assumed to be modernist or minimalist, or inspired by those movements, are mostly tartan or stripes.

What makes the determined ordinariness of his hand-painted, unstretched paintings so notable is how they have been transformed into domestic, utilitarian objects, displaying the classical artist's touch while also thumbing their noses at notions of the sin-

gularity and sanctity of the artwork. Of course, this gesture is not revolutionary per se. The matter-of-fact commonness of Lee's paintings—which have been curtains, handkerchiefs, picnic blankets, and tablecloths—renders the description of his work as "performative" or "blurring the boundaries between life and art" not only too formulaic but also too grand. Lee's early work gained much of its mythic aura through outdoor interventions in the city at times

LEE KIT, BATHED WITH
HANDPAINTED CLOTH, 2003,
acrylic on fabric, photo
document, dimensions variable /
GEBADET MIT
HANDBEMALTEM TUCH,
Acryl auf Stoff, Photo-
dokument, Masse variabel.

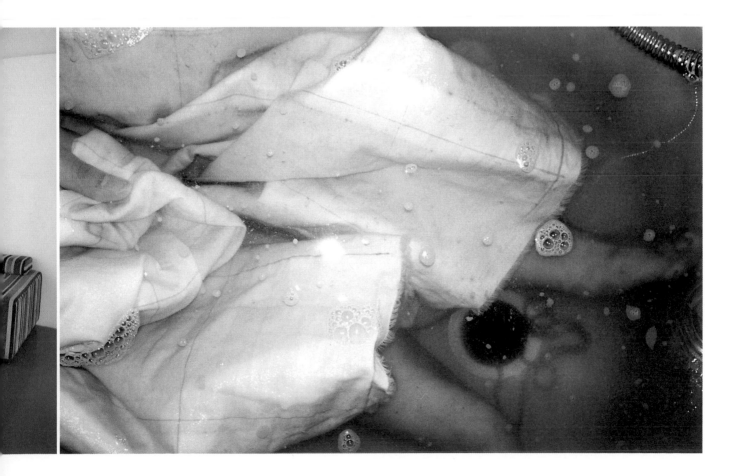

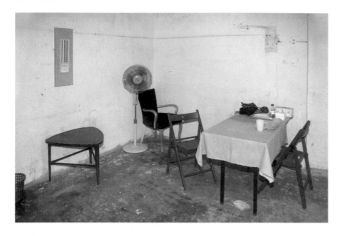

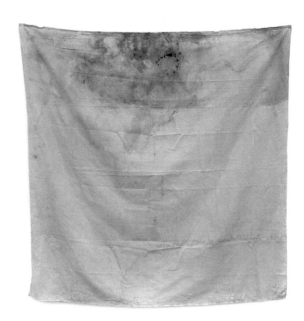

LEE KIT, A PERFECT DAY FOR A QUIET FRIEND, 2008,
acrylic on fabric, coffee, dimensions variable /
EIN PERFEKTER TAG FÜR EINEN RUHIGEN FREUND,
Acryl auf Stoff, Kaffee, Masse variabel.

of political upheaval and a public health emergency, but strictly speaking, its ideological core lies in the fact that it has always been domestic and superfluous.[2] In real life, none of what Lee's paintings are or represent is a real necessity; they are merely the signs and niceties of petit-bourgeois life, comportment, and leisure.

As gemlike as they are now, Vermeer's genre paintings occupied a clearly middling position in the hierarchy of paintings that was firmly in place at the time, an art-historical phenomenon that should be seen in relation to the onset of modern capitalism and the formation of the middle class. Still life, landscape, and portraiture were redefined according to a newly anthropocentric set of rules and values that placed the human subject at the center and in relation to other social beings and material objects in the progressively colonized natural environment; history painting, however, still belonged to the realm of allegories and mythologies. Similarly, the deliberately average tenor of Lee's paintings may well be understood in relation to the increasingly explicit and violent manifestations of capital and class in Hong Kong. And yet, his work could be seen to function in multiple categories within the hierarchy simultaneously. As reflected in the mysteriously lyrical and

heartbreakingly fragmentary photographic evidence of their usage, they are at once domestic still lifes and landscapes—shutting out but inevitably evoking the only landscapes possible in such a dense urban setting, namely, those that are thoroughly engineered and controlled. Touched and handled, and at times stained, they are also records of past moments in the artist's life, and are thus self-portraits. How, then, might history be represented now, by an artist hailing from the forest of the built environment and the pressure-cooker politics of early twenty-first-century Hong Kong, where history is felt to be immensely intimidating and unpredictably directionless? Perhaps by sustaining adamant privacy and interiority, and by drawing and staining cheap cotton fabrics with one straight pastel line at a time.

1) Lee Kit, "Ready Made (Everyday)," in *"You (you)."—Lee Kit, Hong Kong,* ed. Yung Ma, 55th Venice Biennale, exh. cat. (Hong Kong: M+, West Kowloon Cultural District Authority, 2012), 30.
2) Lee's painting was first used outside as a picnic blanket in 2003, when his then girlfriend impulsively suggested an outing while Hong Kong was shut down by an outbreak of SARS. A year later, the artist and his friends carried another painting in place of a banner or a flag during the annual July 1 protest march. And for his solo show at Para Site, the most important nonprofit contemporary art space in the city, in 2007, he turned the entire gallery into a social space outfitted with his paintings to be touched and used.

Szenen
des Alltags

DORYUN CHONG

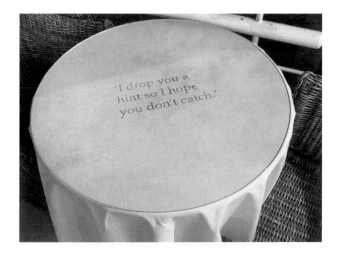

LEE KIT, POPPING UP, 2010, 20 pieces of hand-painted cloth
with text, used as a window curtain, tablecloth, installation view,
Hong Kong Arts Centre / AUFTAUCHEND, 20 handbemalte Tücher
mit Text, als Vorhang verwendet, Tischtuch, Installationsansicht.

Gegen Ende des Goldenen Zeitalters der niederländischen Malerei schuf Johannes Vermeer eine aussergewöhnliche Gruppe von Bildern. Lediglich drei Dutzend Gemälde werden ihm zugeschrieben und die meisten davon sind weniger als einen Meter breit und hoch. Die niederländische Malerei des Barock, die sich im Vergleich zum übrigen Europa weniger durch religiöse Themen, dramatische Kompositionen und materielle Pracht auszeichnete, vollzog in dieser Zeit eine bemerkenswerte Hinwendung zur Darstellung der Wechselfälle und Realitäten des menschlichen Lebens und leitete damit, wenn man so will, die Moderne in der abendländischen Malerei ein. Vermeer, der sich fast ausschliesslich auf Genremalerei und speziell auf häuslich-bürgerliche Interieurszenen konzentrierte, war vielleicht der Modernste von allen. Der Meister von Delft soll alleine in einem Zimmer im ersten Stock seines Hauses gearbeitet und langsam und methodisch lediglich eine Handvoll Gemälde im Jahr gemalt haben. Der schwarzweisse Schachbrettboden, die Holzdecke und das sanfte Nordlicht, das durch die häufig auf der linken Seite seiner Kompositionen zu sehende Fenster

DORYUN CHONG ist stellvertretender Direktor und Chefkurator am M+ in Hongkong.

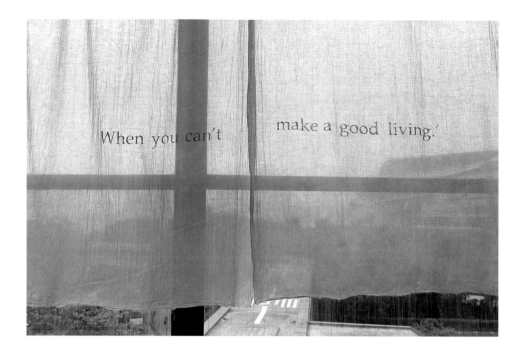

LEE KIT, POPPING UP, 2010, 20 pieces of hand-painted
cloth with text, used as a window curtain, tablecloth, in-
stallation view, Hong Kong Arts Centre / AUFTAUCHEND,
20 handbemalte Tücher mit Text, als Vorhang verwendet,
Tischtuch, Installationsansicht.

einströmt, sind Merkmale jenes Zimmers, in dem er etwa ein Jahrzehnt lang malte.

Neulich erklärte Lee Kit in einem Gespräch bei jeder Menge Wein, Vermeer sei sein Lieblingskünstler, ja, der einzige Künstler, den er gerne habe — eine Erklärung, die er bereits bei früheren Gelegenheiten von sich gegeben hat. Die Einsicht kam ihm bei seiner ersten leibhaftigen Begegnung mit einem Gemälde Vermeers: DAME AM VIRGINAL (um 1670–1675) in der National Gallery in London. Auf das Rendezvous mit einem der letzten Gemälde des niederländischen Meisters folgten zwei weitere, nämlich DER LIEBESBRIEF (um 1667–1670, Rijksmuseum, Amsterdam) und DIE MALKUNST (um 1662–1668, Kunsthistorisches Museum, Wien). Alle drei Beispiele weisen Elemente des klassischen Vermeer-Bildes auf: Die Damen sind umringt von Gemälden und prächtigen Textilien, Zeichen bürgerlichen Lebens. Die Musik ist ebenfalls auffallend präsent, da alle drei Frauen entweder ein Musikinstrument in der Hand halten (Cister, Trompete) oder an oder neben einem Instrument sitzen (Viola da Gamba, Virginal).

Nach einer Erklärung für seine Vermeer-Vorliebe befragt, hat Lee Antworten parat, die gleichzeitig das Typische und das Persönliche an seiner Bewunderung erkennen lassen. Er schätzt das feine Gespür für Licht und Raum ebenso wie die in den Bildern Vermeers eingebetteten sozialen Botschaften. Sie erfassen das Menschsein und sind aufrichtig. Auch die Sehnsucht nach Stille findet Widerhall bei ihm: Der alte Meister «blieb gerne zu Hause», ganz so wie Lee. Lee hat kein Hehl daraus gemacht, dass seine Kunst untrennbar mit dieser Vorliebe, diesem Verlangen verbunden ist. (Bekanntermassen ist er privat ein intensiver Konsument von Musik.) Lee ist in mancherlei Hinsicht ein zutiefst klassischer Atelierkünstler, der unbekümmert und melancholisch an der Romantik der Einsamkeit festhält.

Einsamkeit ist für Lee jedoch keine gesellschaftliche Haltung. Seine bekanntermassen kritische Einstellung zu, ja, seine Wut gegenüber dem Stand der Dinge im eigentümlichen Mikrokosmos namens

Hongkong lässt vermuten, dass seine Kunst ohne den Überdruss, der sich aus der Verbindung einer rückhaltlosen Hinnahme der Gegenwart und eines Bedürfnisses nach Abschottung von ihr ergibt, vielleicht nicht denkbar wäre. So gesehen, ist es keineswegs überraschend, dass in den Aufnahmen, die er von seinen Gemälden zu Hause oder im Atelier macht (und die dann häufig neben den Gemälden im Ausstellungsraum gezeigt werden), vielfach Fenster auftauchen oder durch Seitenlicht angedeutet werden. Lees Fenster sind weniger Licht- und Luftquelle wie in den Gemälden Vermeers oder ein der unbändigen Welt übergestülptes logisches Gerüst im Sinne der Renaissance, sondern eher ein unvollkommener Schutz oder gar eine gefährliche Exponierung gegenüber dem Draussen. Lee wurde sich dieser simplen, naheliegenden Tatsache vor einigen Jahren bewusst, als er sich als Artist-in-Residence fern von Hongkong in Wellington, Neuseeland, aufhielt. Um sich vor den neugierigen Blicken von Passanten zu schützen, hängte er seine handbemalten Tücher vor die Fenster. Er erkannte nicht nur, dass «Öffnen und Schliessen mein Umfeld komplett bestimmen kann», sondern diese Handlung bewog ihn auch, sich um die Fenster zu kümmern und einzusehen, dass «Haushaltsführung unerklärlicherweise zu meiner inneren Sprache wird – ein schönes und wichtiges Verhalten».[1] Die vollkommene Alltäglichkeit oder Banalität der künstlerischen Produktion handbemalter Tücher als Gemälde, mit der er sich über mehrere Jahre hinweg beschäftigt und die ihm Anerkennung eingebracht hatte, konnte sich nur dann kristallisieren, wenn die – in Hongkong überdeterminierten – Schichten der gesellschaftlichen Relevanz abgestreift worden waren. Die Unerlässlichkeit der Haushaltsführung führte dem Werk Lees – paradoxerweise vielleicht – wieder das «Schöne» der «schönen Kunst» – Kunst um der Kunst willen – zu.

Gleichzeitig mag es widersinnig erscheinen, dass ihm diese Einsicht in derart grosser Entfernung von Hongkong kam, da Hongkong die vielleicht weltweit unerreichte Stadt der Fenster ist. Die bekannte Dichte schwindelerregend hoher Wohn- und Geschäftsbauten in der Stadt, in denen die übergrosse Mehrzahl ihrer Einwohner wohnen und arbeiten, bedeutet, dass die Leute, wenn sie aus dem Fenster blicken, nur weitere Fenster sehen. In Wohngegenden sind Einblicke in Privaträume geradezu unvermeidbar und die Leute haben sich an den Umstand gewöhnt, gedankenlos andere Leute zu sehen und selbst ebenso von ihnen gesehen zu werden. Und da privater Raum für die meisten etwas ist, das praktisch nicht existiert, ist der Mangel an öffentlichem Raum in Hongkong Gegenstand andauernder Beschwerden. Die zunehmend raue Politik rund um den umstrittenen Begriff des Staatswesens – zwischen der winzigen Sonderverwaltungszone und dem riesigen «Mutterland» Volksrepublik China – ist in dieser immer überfüllteren und unbezahlbaren Stadt

LEE KIT, "YOU, (YOU).," 2013, installation view,
Venice Biennale / «DU, (DU)», Installationsansicht.
(PHOTO: DAVID LEVENE)

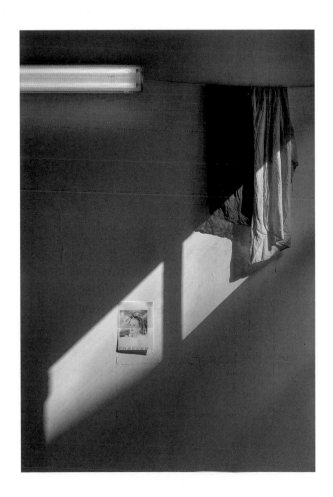

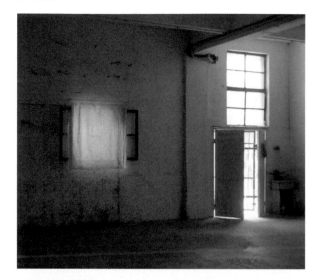

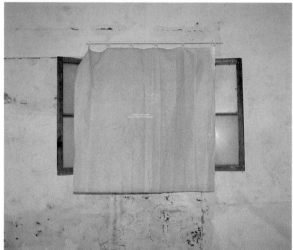

LEE KIT, AND IF YOU CLOSE THE DOOR, I'LL NEVER HAVE TO SEE THE DAY AGAIN, 2007, acrylic on fabric / UND WENN DU DIE TÜRE SCHLIESST, MUSS ICH DEN TAG NIE MEHR SEHEN, Acryl auf Stoff.

weiterhin am ehesten bekannt ist, ist die Farbpalette, in der sanfte rosa, himmelblaue und cremefarbene Pastelltöne dominieren und die selten mit der Art von intellektueller Strenge assoziiert wird, die man von zeitgenössischem Kunstschaffen erwartet, ja, mit dieser unvereinbar ist. Während sich die zarte Tonalität von Lees Werk gegen die Schwälle immer intensiverer optischer Wirkungen im Schaffen internationaler zeitgenössischer Künstler abhebt, mag ihr in der Stadt, in der die Kunst Lees ihren Anfang nahm, besondere Bedeutung zukommen. Bauten in Hongkong sind in überwiegender Mehrzahl in verblichenen grauen, beigen und rosa Pastelltönen gestrichen, angeblich zwecks Kosteneinsparung und wegen der Pflegeleichtigkeit und möglicherweise auch als Strategie der psychologischen Beruhigung der dicht aufeinanderwohnenden Bevölkerung. Zu behaupten, die Palette von Lees Gemälden sei ein Abbild der architektonischen Semiotik seiner Heimatstadt, wäre zwar grob vereinfachend, aber nicht falsch. Lees Tuchmalereien halten sich auch an materielle und formale Grundlagen. Er verwendet keine wertvollen Stoffe – keinen Samt, keine Seide, ja nicht einmal Leinen, sondern nur ganz schlichte Baumwolle. Die Formen oder Kompositionen seiner Gemälde, die als der Moderne oder der Minimal Art verpflichtet erscheinen mögen, sind zumeist Schottenkaro oder Streifen.

Was die entschlossene Alltäglichkeit dieser handbemalten und nicht auf Rahmen gespannten Gemälde beachtenswert macht, ist die Art, wie sie sich in häusliche Gebrauchsgegenstände verwandelt haben und sich mit der klassischen Handschrift des Künstlers brüsten, während sie gleichzeitig Vorstellungen der Seltenheit und Unantastbarkeit des Kunstwerks eine lange Nase drehen. An sich ist diese Geste natürlich nicht revolutionär. Angesichts der nüchternen Alltäglichkeit der Gemälde Lees, die als Vorhänge, Taschentücher, Picknick- und Tischdecken gedient haben, erscheint es nicht nur zu formelhaft, sondern

häufig mit der Raumpolitik verzahnt. All dies wird oft als Grund für die Kleinformatigkeit, die konzeptuelle Tendenz und die Trendigkeit des Schaffens von Künstlern aus Hongkong angeführt. Lees Praxis wird vielfach in Beziehung zu diesen Besonderheiten beschrieben und als archetypisch angesehen. Wenn der Künstler selbst seine Ziele beschreibt, spricht er davon, sein Leben dadurch zu gestalten, dass er die Tür schliesst – aber vielleicht nicht die Fenster –, und von der Schwierigkeit, die ihm dies bereitet.

Der wohl bemerkenswerteste Aspekt von Lees Arbeit mit handbemalten Tüchern, für die er wohl auch zu hochfliegend, sein Werk als «performativ» zu beschreiben oder zu behaupten, es «verwische die Grenzen zwischen Kunst und Leben». Lees Frühwerk erlangte seine mythische Aura vor allem durch seine «Auftritte» in Zeiten der politischen Bedrängnis der Stadt und des öffentlichen Gesundheitsnotstandes, sein idealer Kern aber liegt streng genommen in der Tatsache, dass es schon immer häuslich und entbehrlich war.[2] Im tatsächlichen Leben ist nicht eines der Dinge, als die Lees Gemälde fungiert haben, eine echte Notwendigkeit, sondern bloss fundamentale Zeichen und Feinheiten der kleinbürgerlichen Existenz, Haltung und Musse.

Die heute wie Prachtstücke anmutenden Genrebilder Vermeers nahmen als ein kunsthistorisches Phänomen, das in Zusammenhang mit dem Aufkommen des modernen Kapitalismus und der Entstehung des Bürgertums zu sehen ist, in der damals fest verankerten Hierarchie der Malerei fraglos einen mittleren Rang ein. In entsprechender Weise kann das Streben der Gemälde Lees nach gewollter Durchschnittlichkeit durchaus in Beziehung zu den immer deutlicheren und heftigeren Ausprägungen von Kapital und Klasse in dieser Stadt gesehen werden. Man kann sie aber auch so verstehen, dass sie eine solche Funktion erfüllen und obendrein weit mehr leisten. Obwohl bilderlos, aber voller Gefühl, agieren sie in allen übrigen Kategorien der Hierarchie gleichzeitig. Wie die geheimnisvoll lyrischen und herzzerbrechend bruchstückhaften photographischen Zeugnisse ihres Gebrauchs zeigen, sind sie zugleich häusliche Still-

leben und Landschaften, die die einzig möglichen – ganz und gar technisierten und kontrollierten – Landschaften im äusserst dichten grossstädtischen Umfeld ausschliessen, am Ende aber doch immer beschwören. Angefasst und hantiert und manchmal auch beschmutzt, sind sie auch Zeugnisse vergangener Momente im Leben des Künstlers und damit Selbstporträts. Diese Gattungen – Stillleben, Landschaft und Porträtmalerei – wurden in Vermeers Zeit neu definiert gemäss einem neuen anthropozentrischen, kapitalistischen Regel- und Wertekanon, der das menschliche Subjekt in den Mittelpunkt und in ein Verhältnis zu anderen sozialen Wesen und materiellen Objekten innerhalb einer zunehmend kolonisierten Natur stellte. Das Geschichtsgenre jedoch gehörte weiterhin zum Bereich der Allegorien und Mythologien. Wie aber liesse sich jetzt Geschichte darstellen – durch einen Künstler, der aus dem dichten Hochhauswald und dem politischen Dampfkessel des Hongkong des frühen 21. Jahrhunderts stammt, wo Geschichte als ungemein einschüchternd und unberechenbar richtungslos empfunden wird? Vielleicht durch die hartnäckige Wahrung von Privatsphäre und Innerlichkeit und durch das Bemalen und Beschmutzen von billigen Baumwollstoffen mit einer geraden Pastelllinie nach der anderen.

(Übersetzung: Bram Opstelten)

1) Lee Kit, «Ready Made (Everyday)», in *«You (you).»—Lee Kit, Hong Kong*, hrsg. v. Yung Ma, 55. Biennale von Venedig, Ausst.-Kat. M+, West Kowloon Cultural District Authority, Hongkong 2012, S. 30.
2) Lees Malerei fand zum ersten Mal draussen als Picknickdecke Verwendung, als seine Freundin in der Zeit, da Hongkong im Jahr 2003 wegen SARS (Schweres Akutes Atemwegssyndrom) abgeriegelt war, spontan einen Ausflug vorschlug. Ein Jahr später führten der Künstler und seine Freunde bei dem jährlichen Protestmarsch am 1. Juli statt eines Transparents oder einer Flagge ein anderes Gemälde mit sich. Und für seine Einzelausstellung 2007 im Para Site, dem bedeutendsten gemeinnützigen Zentrum für Gegenwartskunst in der Stadt, verwandelte er den ganzen Ausstellungsraum in einen sozialen Raum, wo seine Gemälde berührt und benutzt werden konnten.

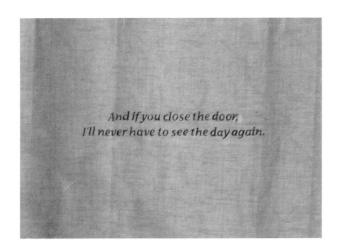

LEE KIT, AND IF YOU CLOSE THE DOOR, I'LL NEVER HAVE TO SEE THE DAY AGAIN, 2007, acrylic on fabric / UND WENN DU DIE TÜRE SCHLIESST, MUSS ICH DEN TAG NIE MEHR SEHEN, Acryl auf Stoff.

CHRISTINA LI

CLAIMING SPACE:

Trained as a painter, Lee Kit has spent the last decade and a half expanding and reframing the medium. His work often features common and humble supports, such as pillowcases and cardboard as well as cloth, painted with pastel stripes or checked lines, that could be found in a typical domestic setting. Lee has frequently turned his hand-painted fabrics into window curtains, tablecloths, and bed sheets, which he makes use of in his home before exhibiting the items—sometimes with stains and other markings—alongside photographs that document their routine employment. Merging artistic practice with everyday life, these efforts ultimately redefine both the function of painting and, in turn, the exhibition context.

Notably, however, many of Lee's explorations have occurred in public space—an increasing rarity in the artist's native city of Hong Kong, where high density and breathtaking verticality are the defining characteristics of the urban landscape. In 2003, Lee began organizing outdoor picnics, inviting friends to eat while sitting on his own hand-painted cloths. Hong Kong was then at the center of the SARS epidemic, during which time the local government asked residents to remain indoors and effectively shut down and quarantined areas of the city. Lee's picnic in a deserted park, then, was not only an occasion to shift his painting into social practice—or a chance to get fresh air—but an act of defiance.

CHRISTINA LI is director and curator of Spring Workshop, Hong Kong.

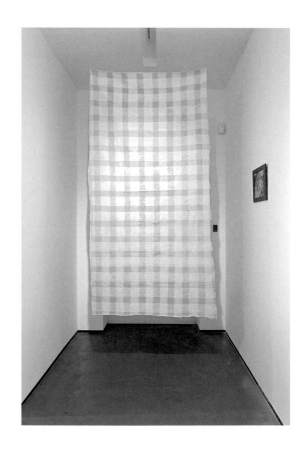

LEE KIT, HAND-PAINTED CLOTH USED FOR A PICNIC, 2009, acrylic on fabric, photograph, dimensions variable / HANDBEMALTES TUCH VERWENDET FÜR EIN PICKNICK, Acryl auf Stoff, Photographie, Masse variabel.

OCCUPATION AND WITHDRAWAL IN THE WORK OF LEE KIT

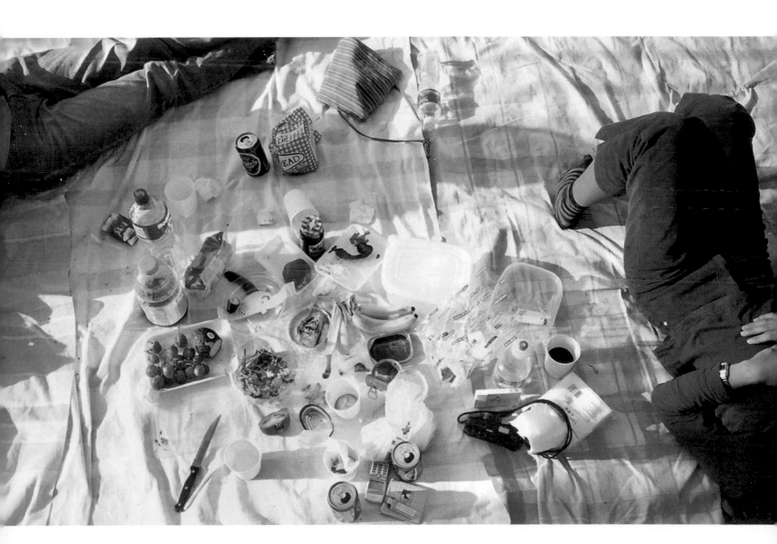

LEE KIT, ANOTHER SUNNY DAY, hand-painted cloth, 2003, detail / WIEDER EIN SONNIGER TAG, handbemaltes Tuch, Detail.

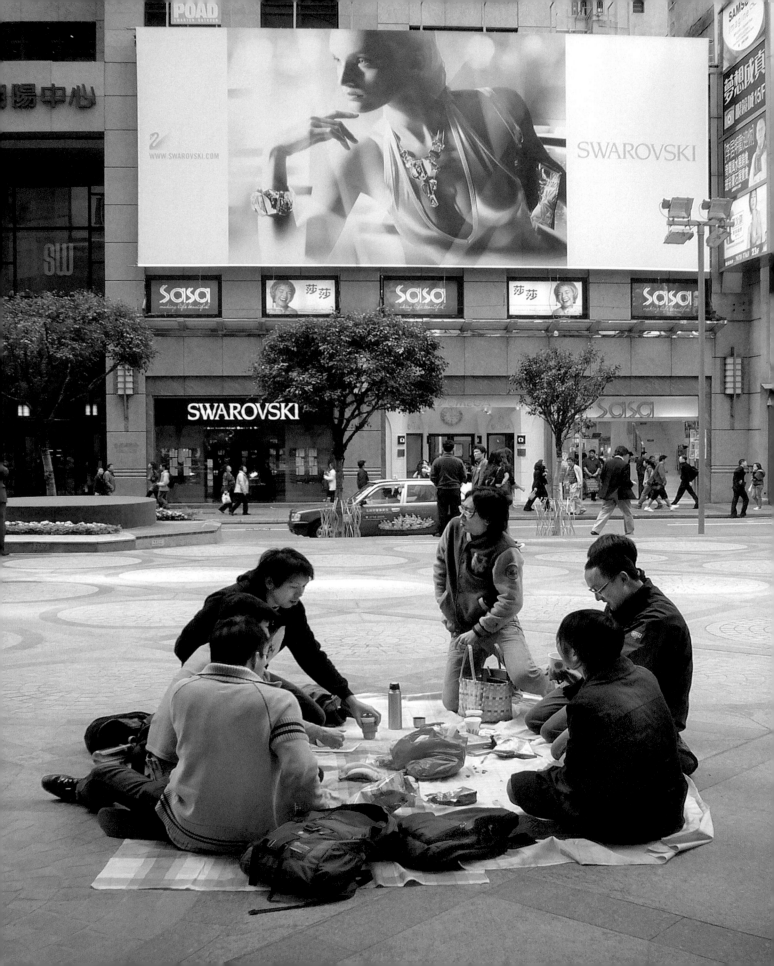

The following year, Lee brought his work into a more explicitly political context: the July 1 demonstration, which has taken place annually since Hong Kong's handover to China in 1997. Amid a sea of flags and placards calling for universal suffrage, freedom of speech, minority rights, and other demands, Lee and friends held aloft a blank banner—one of his typical painted fabrics. In this playful action, the artist silently protested against the pro-Chinese government, whose primary interest is in maintaining a superficial harmony.

The issue of privatization of Hong Kong's public spaces erupted in 2008 when it was revealed that Times Square, in Causeway Bay, was illegally leasing its open plaza. Lee joined the ensuing protests to "hijack" the plaza in a collaboration with artist Luke Ching Chin-wai.[1] The action was once again catalyzed by Lee's painting, as a group of artists gathered on his picnic cloth in the middle of Times Square. Despite numerous interruptions by security guards, the picnic lasted two hours.[2] A week later, Lee organized a picnic in front of the International Finance Center tower—another plot of land zoned for public use but fenced off by management.[3]

In 2007, Lee's private and public investigations came together in the space of the gallery. For his first solo exhibition, "3/4 suggestions for a better living," held at Hong Kong's Para Site, he transformed the nonprofit's storefront space into a café. Fabric hung on the walls (accompanied by photo documentation of previous uses) but also covered the tables, painted with patterns as well as familiar phrases pulled from films and pop lyrics. Encircled by the traces of former social occasions, the space was also activated in real time: Friends and Para Site staff (including myself)—clad in black T-shirts with white cursive script that read *MY FAVOURITE WASTE OF TIME*—served beer to gallery visitors, alongside a sporadic program of talks and musical performances.

LEE KIT, Picnic on Times Square,
Hong Kong, 2008 / Picknick am
Times Square.
(PHOTO: THOMPSON TONG)

LEE KIT, Picnic on Times Square,
Hong Kong, 2008 / Picknick am
Times Square.
(PHOTO: THOMPSON TONG)

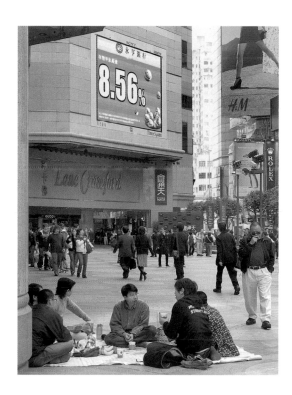

The artist himself was always present during these planned or improvised affairs, chatting and drinking beer. Yet if the exhibition revolved around sociality, promising exposure and inviting public participation, Lee adeptly constructed an intimate space within it: He was surrounded by friends, providing a buffer from visitors and allowing him to simply hang out as he usually would—his favorite waste of time.[4] Alongside this bid for privacy and amid his orchestration of collective experience, however, Lee once again gestured toward the city's increasingly stringent spatial politics. Despite a recent law that banned smoking in restaurants and bars, visitors were allowed to smoke inside the gallery—a flagrant retort that also tested the boundaries of permissiveness within an institutional framework.

Around this time, Lee's work shifted away from public actions and saw an increasing involvement with video. Works such as FILLING UP AN ASHTRAY (2008), in which the frame is focused tightly on a plastic dish as it fills with ashes over the course of an hour, document private performances in his studio, while a series of "pseudo-karaoke" video installations—featuring melancholic English pop songs accompanied by Lee's personal vignettes—provide no outlet for participation. This act of withdrawal in his art was matched in life when, in 2012, Lee moved to Taipei. His self-exile took place as a number of political decisions in Hong Kong appeared to erode the city's autonomy and accelerate integration with mainland China, including the approval of the Guangzhou–Hong Kong high-speed rail link in 2010[5] and the implementation of the "moral and national education" school curriculum in 2012.[6] Neighboring Taiwan, on the other hand, in the midst of a similar struggle with mainland China, remains more independent.

Since his relocation to the slower-paced city, away from the heated political debates in Hong Kong, Lee has continued to explore his interior world. This finds enigmatic expression in THERE'S A CUP ON THE PILLOW (2014). Presented on a wall-mounted flatscreen, the somewhat shaky video depicts the title objects, although the cup is concealed by a small towel draped over the screen. This hide-and-seek interplay between disclosure and concealment resonates with the artist's continuing quest for privacy as well as intimacy.

Recently, Lee has begun creating installations that combine paintings with projected images, often of interiors. For a group exhibition that I curated last year at Spring Workshop, in Hong Kong, Lee made a site-specific work. FLOWERS (2015) overlays three planes: A projection shows a window, viewed from inside the artist's old Taipei apartment, blown up to fill the wall; affixed to it, an inkjet-and-pencil work on paper depicts a hand; and a handwritten word, FLOWERS, is printed directly on the wall. The work interacts further with the gallery's ceiling pipe, its shadow cast alongside visitors' onto the unfocused image. From the pipe hangs an exit sign, with a green arrow pointing rightward beside a tiny fleeing figure. In this context, it is tempting to read the image as a portrait of the artist—but is he escaping the room through the window or leaving the world behind to slip back inside? The anonymous hand posted on the wall sits on the edge of the window, half within the rectangle of light, half in darkness. Caught on this threshold, it appears to wave good-bye.

1) The picnic was one in a series of actions performed under the umbrella title "Hijacking Public Space." See Lam Ka Man, "Visual Arts and Public Space Issue," *Hong Kong Visual Arts Yearbook 2008*, May 2009, www.hkvisualartsyearbook.org/2008/publicissues_items.php?post_id=10055 (accessed February 9, 2016).
2) As of 2008, 156 public spaces in the city were managed by private developers, adding up to an area larger than Hong Kong Park. See Luke Ching Chin-wai, "Lee Kit's Picnic, Outside Times Square Causeway Bay, Hong Kong, on 5 March, 2008," *Ming Pao Daily*, March 9, 2008; his full, unedited text (in Cantonese) can be found online at www.lukeching.blogspot.com/2008/03/blog-post_08.html (accessed February 9, 2016).
3) See www.peppeppep.wordpress.com/2008/03/17 (accessed February 9, 2016).
4) As Lee has explained: "If anyone asked me, 'Where is the artist?,' I would just say, 'The artist is not here.' I wanted to hide in that way, and the purpose of that kind of social event is to hide. There were also times when I arranged a space or an event just to create a reason for me to sit there and space out. I was just one of the people sitting there and spacing out or having a drink." Lee Kit, in Yung Ma and Lee Kit, "Conversation: That was life, not a social obligation," in *"You (you)."—Lee Kit, Hong Kong*, ed. Yung Ma, 55th Venice Biennale, exh. cat. (Hong Kong: M+, West Kowloon Cultural District Authority, 2012), 25.
5) The construction of a high-speed railway linking Hong Kong with mainland China is widely viewed as an enormous governmental expenditure that will benefit only a small economic elite. Activists have also pointed to environmental and structural issues at building sites.
6) Moral and national education, which replaced moral and civic education, has been criticized for praising China's government and denouncing democracy. After numerous protests in 2012, the implementation of the curriculum was temporarily put on hold.

LEE KIT, 7ᵀᴴ OF JUNE: DEMONSTRATION WITH FRIENDS AND HAND-PAINTED CLOTH, 2004, acrylic on fabric, photo document / 7. JUNI: DEMONSTRATION MIT FREUNDEN UND HAND-BEMALTEM TUCH, Acryl auf Tuch, Photodokument. (COURTESY THE ARTIST & VITAMIN CREATIVE SPACE)

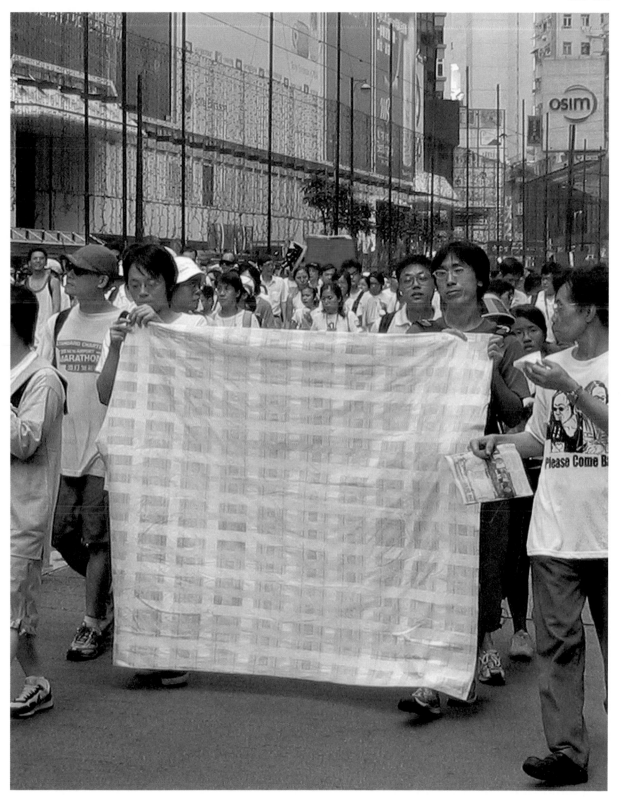

CHRISTINA LI

PLATZ BEHAUPTEN:

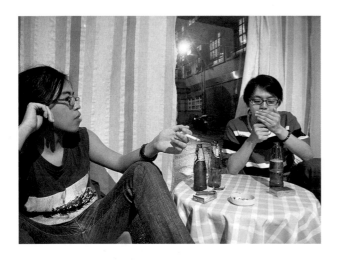

*LEE KIT, "3/4 Suggestions for a Better Living," 2007, exhibition
view, Para/site Art Space, Hong Kong / Ausstellungsansicht.*

Nach seinem Studium der Malerei hat Lee Kit die
letzten zehneinhalb Jahre damit verbracht, dieses
Medium zu erweitern und in neuen Kontexten zu er-
proben. Er verwendet gern einfache, ganz alltägliche
Trägermedien, wie Kissenbezüge und Karton oder
Stoff, die er mit Streifen oder Karomustern bemalt,
wie sie in jedem Haushalt zu finden sind. Lee hat
seine handbemalten Textilien häufig zu Vorhängen,

Tischtüchern und Bettzeug verarbeitet und zu Hause
auch als solche verwendet, bevor er sie – manchmal
mit Flecken und anderen Gebrauchsspuren – zusammen mit Photographien ausstellte, die ihre täg-
liche Verwendung dokumentierten. Durch diese
Verschmelzung von künstlerischer Tätigkeit und
Alltagsleben definiert der Künstler die Funktion der
Malerei und folglich auch den Ausstellungskontext
vollkommen neu.

Bemerkenswert ist jedoch, dass viele von Lees Er-
kundungen im öffentlichen Raum stattfanden – eine
zunehmende Seltenheit in Hongkong, der Heimatstadt des Künstlers, deren Stadtbild von der hohen
Dichte und schwindelerregenden Höhe ihrer Wolkenkratzer bestimmt wird. 2003 begann Lee, Pick-
nicks im Freien zu organisieren; er lud Freunde ein,
auf seinen handbemalten Tüchern Platz zu nehmen,
um gemeinsam zu essen. Etwas früher im selben Jahr
war in Hongkong eine gefährliche Erkrankung der
Atemwege ausgebrochen (severe acute respiratory
syndrom, SARS) und die lokalen Behörden hatten
die Einwohner aufgefordert, zu Hause zu bleiben.
Einige Stadtviertel waren tatsächlich stillgelegt worden und standen unter Quarantäne. Lees Picknick
im verlassenen Park war also nicht nur eine Gelegenheit, seine Malerei zu einer gesellschaftlichen Aktivität zu machen oder frische Luft zu schnappen, nein –
es war ein Protestakt.

Im folgenden Jahr praktizierte Lee seine Kunst in
einem noch eindeutiger politischen Kontext: inmitten der Protestkundgebungen, die seit 1997 an jedem

CHRISTINA LI ist Direktorin und Kuratorin des Spring
Workshop in Hongkong.

BESETZUNG UND RÜCKZUG IM WERK VON LEE KIT

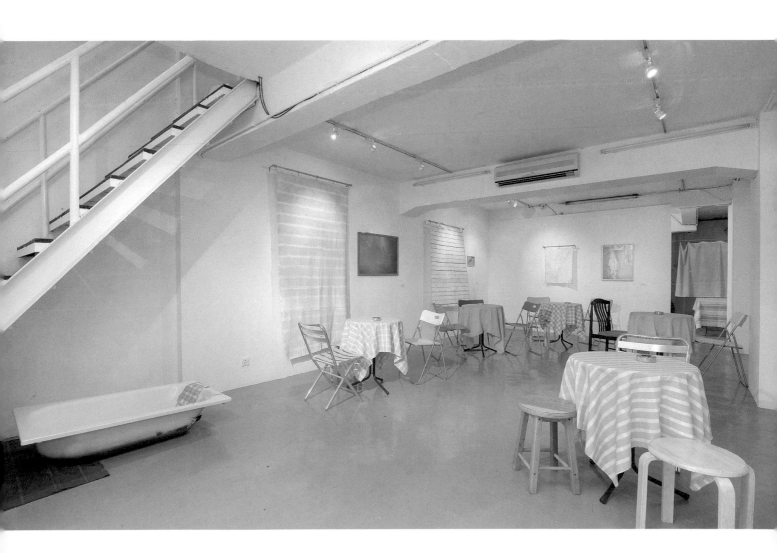

LEE KIT, "3/4 Suggestions for a Better Living," 2007, exhibition view, Para/site Art Space, Hong Kong / Ausstellungsansicht.

1. Juli stattfinden, dem Tag des Übergangs von Hongkong an China. In einem Meer von Spruchbändern und Plakaten, die das allgemeine Stimm- und Wahlrecht, freie Meinungsäusserung, Rechte für Minderheiten und anderes forderten, hielten Lee und seine Freunde ein unbeschriftetes Transparent in die Höhe: eines seiner typischen handbemalten Tücher. Mit dieser stummen Aktion demonstrierte der Künstler seinen stillen Protest gegen die prochinesische Regierung, der es in erster Linie darum geht, eine oberflächliche Harmonie aufrechtzuerhalten.

Die Diskussion um die Privatisierung des öffentlichen Raumes in Hongkong entbrannte erstmals 2008, als bekannt wurde, dass die öffentliche Fläche des Times Square, im Stadtteil Causeway Bay, illegal vermietet wurde. Lee schloss sich den Protesten an, indem er den Platz mit der Aktion PASSIVE RECREATION: PICNIC CREATION OF LEE KIT (Passive Freizeitgestaltung: eine Picknick-Kreation von Lee Kit, 2008) «besetzte». Als Katalysator dieser in Zusammenarbeit mit dem Künstler Luke Ching Chin-wai organisier-

ten Aktion diente wiederum Lees Malerei – eine Gruppe von Künstlern versammelte sich auf seiner mitten auf dem Times Square ausgebreiteten Picknickdecke. Trotz mehrmaliger Störungen durch Sicherheitsleute dauerte das Picknick zwei Stunden.[1] Eine Woche später veranstaltete Lee ein Picknick vor dem Wolkenkratzer des Two International Finance Centre (2 IFC) – ein weiteres Grundstück, das ursprünglich zur öffentlichen Nutzung bestimmt war, vom Unternehmen jedoch eingezäunt wurde.[2]

2007 fanden Lees private und öffentliche Investigationen in einem Ausstellungsraum zusammen. Für seine erste Einzelausstellung «3/4 Vorschläge für eine bessere Lebensart» im Para Site, Hongkong, verwandelte er die Räumlichkeiten dieser Non-Profit-Galerie in ein Café. Textilien hingen an den Wänden (neben Photos, auf denen zu sehen war, wie sie zuvor genutzt worden waren) und bedeckten Tische; die Stoffe waren mit Dessins, aber auch mit vertrauten Wendungen aus Filmen und Popsongs bemalt. Als Kontrast zu den Spuren vergangener gesellschaftli-

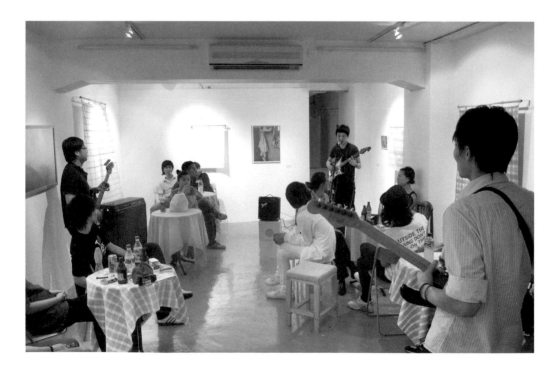

LEE KIT, "3/4 Suggestions for a Better Living," 2007, exhibition view,
Para/site Art Space, Hong Kong / Ausstellungsansicht.

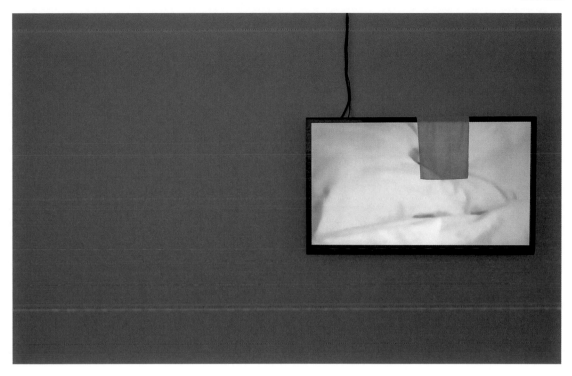

LEE KIT, THERE IS A CUP ON THE PILLOW, 2014, video, readymade /
AUF DEM KISSEN LIEGT EINE TASSE, Video, Readymade.

cher Events belebte Lee den Raum auch in Echtzeit: Freunde und das Personal von Para Site (einschliesslich meiner selbst) trugen schwarze T-Shirts mit der weissen, kursiven Aufschrift *MY FAVORITE WASTE OF TIME* (Mein liebster Zeitvertreib) und servierten den Besuchern Bier zu den sporadisch stattfindenden Gesprächen und musikalischen Auftritten.

Lee war bei diesen geplanten oder improvisierten Anlässen stets präsent, unterhielt sich mit Leuten und trank Bier – er brachte also nicht nur seine bemalten Tischtücher und Vorhänge, Gebrauchsgegenstände seines täglichen Lebens, in den Ausstellungsraum, sondern auch sich selbst. Doch obwohl es in der Ausstellung um Geselligkeit ging und um die Aufforderung ans Publikum, sich zu exponieren und aktiv mitzumachen, bewahrte sich der Künstler inmitten von alledem geschickt seinen privaten Raum: Er war von Freunden umgeben, die ihm als Puffer gegenüber den Besuchern dienten und es ihm

erlaubten, einfach abzuhängen, wie er es sonst auch tat – sein liebster Zeitvertreib.[3)] Neben der gebotenen Privatsphäre und inmitten seiner Orchestrierung eines kollektiven Erlebnisses wandte sich Lee jedoch erneut der immer restriktiveren Politik des öffentlichen Raumes zu. Trotz des gerade neu erlassenen Rauchverbots in Restaurants und Bars war das Rauchen im Ausstellungsraum erlaubt – eine klare Antwort, die auch die Toleranzgrenzen innerhalb des institutionellen Rahmens einem Test unterzog.

In dieser Zeit verlagerte sich Lees Arbeit von öffentlichen Aktionen zu einer intensiveren Auseinandersetzung mit dem Medium Video. Werke wie FILLING UP AN ASHTRAY (Einen Aschenbecher füllen, 2008), in denen der Blick der Kamera unverwandt auf eine Metallschale gerichtet ist, die sich im Lauf einer Stunde allmählich mit Asche füllt, dokumentieren private Performances in seinem Atelier, während eine Serie von «Pscudo-Karaoke»-Video-

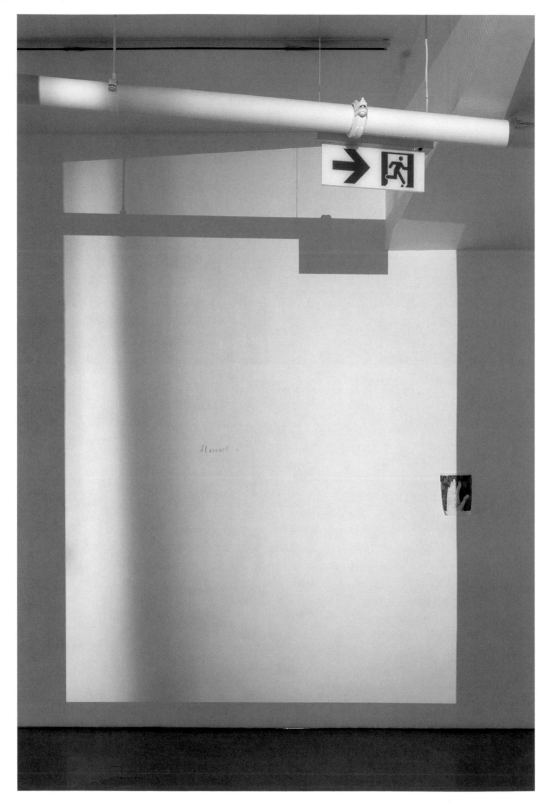

*LEE KIT, FLOWERS, 2015, inkjet ink
and pencil on paper, inkjet ink on wall,
projection / BLUMEN, Inkjet-Tinte und
Bleistift auf Papier, Inkjet-Tinte auf
Wand, Projektion.*

installationen – in denen Lee melancholische amerikanische Popsongs mit eigenen Bildmotiven begleitet – keine Gelegenheit zur aktiven Teilnahme bieten. Diesem Akt des Rückzugs in der Kunst sollte mit dem Umzug nach Taipei 2012 auch einer im Leben des Künstlers folgen. Er wählte das Exil zu einem Zeitpunkt, als eine Reihe politischer Entscheidungen in Hongkong die Autonomie der Stadt auszulöschen und ihre volle Eingliederung in die Volksrepublik China voranzutreiben schien: etwa die Zustimmung zur Hochgeschwindigkeits-Zugsverbindung Guangzhou–Hongkong 2010[4] oder der Versuch zur Einführung des «Moral and National Education»-Lehrplans 2012.[5] Im Vergleich dazu hatte sich das benachbarte, ebenfalls in Konflikte mit der Volksrepublik China verstrickte Taiwan grössere Unabhängigkeit bewahrt. Seit seinem Umzug in die weniger hektische Stadt, fern der hitzigen politischen Debatten in Hongkong, hat Lee die Erkundung seiner eigenen Innenwelt vorangetrieben. Auf rätselhafte Weise kommt dies in THERE'S A CUP ON THE PILLOW (Auf dem Kissen liegt eine Tasse, 2014) zum Ausdruck. Auf einem an der Wand montierten Flachbildschirm zeigt dieses etwas wackelige Video die im Titel genannten Objekte, obschon die Tasse von einem kleinen blauen Handtuch verdeckt wird, das über dem Bildschirm hängt. Dieses Versteckspiel zwischen Enthüllen und Verbergen passt zur anhaltenden Suche des Künstlers nach Privatsphäre und Intimität.

In jüngster Zeit hat Lee begonnen, Installationen zu schaffen, in denen er gemalte Bilder mit Projektionen kombiniert, häufig von Innenräumen. Für eine Gruppenausstellung, die ich letztes Jahr im Spring Workshop in Hongkong organisiert habe, schuf Lee eine ortsspezifische Arbeit. FLOWERS (Blumen, 2015) umfasst drei Ebenen: Eine Projektion zeigt ein Fenster, das von der Altwohnung des Künstlers in Taipei aus zu sehen ist, und zwar so vergrössert, dass es die gesamte Wand ausfüllt; an derselben Wand hängt das Bild einer Hand in Inkjet und Bleistift; ausserdem wurde das von Hand geschriebene Wort «FLOWERS» direkt auf die Wand kopiert. Zusätzlich interagiert die Arbeit mit den Rohrleitungen an der Decke des Ausstellungsraumes, deren Schatten neben denen der Besucher auf das unscharfe Bild fallen. An einem der Rohre hängt ein Notausgangsschild mit einem kleinen fliehenden Männchen neben einem grünen nach rechts weisenden Pfeil. Handelt es sich um ein Porträt des Künstlers, der durch das Fenster entweicht oder der Welt entflieht, um sich hinterrücks wieder einzuschleichen? Oder ist es ein dringender Appell an den Betrachter? Die anonyme, an die Wand geklebte Hand befindet sich am Rand des Vierecks aus Licht, zur Hälfte im Dunkeln. Gerade noch auf der Schwelle erwischt, scheint sie uns Adieu zu winken.

(Übersetzung: Suzanne Schmidt)

1) 2008 standen 156 öffentliche Plätze in der Stadt unter der Verwaltung privater Bauherren, also eine Fläche, die grösser ist als der Hong Kong Park. Luke Ching Chin-wai, «Lee Kit's Picnic, Outside Times Square Causeway Bay, Hong Kong, on 5 March, 2008», *Ming Pao Daily*, 9. März 2008; der vollständige, nicht redigierte Text ist online zugänglich unter www.lukeching.blogspot. com/2008/03/blog-post_08.html (abgerufen am 9. Februar 2016). Siehe auch Lam Ka Man, «Visual Arts and Public Space Issue», *Hong Kong Visual Arts Yearbook 2008*, Mai 2009, www. hkvisualartsyearbook.org/2008/publicissues_items.php?post_id=10055 (abgerufen am 9. Februar 2016).
2) Siehe www.peppeppep.wordpress.com/2008/03/17 (abgerufen am 9. Februar 2016).
3) Wie Lee selbst erklärte: «Wenn mich einer fragte, ‹Wo ist der Künstler?›, antwortete ich einfach, ‹Der Künstler ist nicht da.› Ich wollte mich auf diese Art verstecken und der Zweck solcher gesellschaftlicher Anlässe ist es ja, sich zu verstecken... Es gab auch Zeiten, da richtete ich einen Raum ein oder organisierte einen Anlass, nur um dort sitzen und abhängen zu können. Ich war einfach einer der Menschen, die dort sassen, abhingen oder etwas tranken.» Lee Kit, in: *«You (you)» – Lee Kit, Hong Kong*, hrsg. v. Yung Ma, 55. Biennale Venedig, Ausst.-Kat., M+, West Kowloon Cultural District Authority, Honkong 2012, S. 25 (Zitat aus dem Engl. übers.).
4) Der Bau einer Hochgeschwindigkeitsbahnstrecke, die Hongkong mit Kontinentalchina verbindet, gilt allgemein als gigantische Staatsausgabe, die nur einer kleinen wirtschaftlichen Elite von Nutzen sein wird. Diverse Aktivisten haben zudem auf ökologische und strukturelle Probleme des Projekts hingewiesen.
5) Der Lehrplan der *Moral and national education* (moralischen und nationalen Bildung) ersetzt die bisherige moral and civic education (moralische und staatsbürgerliche Erziehung) und wurde kritisiert, weil er die chinesische Regierung verherrlicht und die Demokratie verunglimpft. Nach den heftigen Protesten 2012 wurde seine Einführung vorläufig auf Eis gelegt.

FRANCESCA TAROCCO

Marked
by
Hand

In 2006, while living and working in Fo Tan—a former industrial hub turned artistic community in Hong Kong's New Territories—Lee Kit began scratching the top of his studio table with his fingernails. Over the course of five years, he continued to scratch away at one small spot of the pale-green veneer until he reached the wood frame beneath. A photograph shot from above, which Lee sent to friends and acquaintances in postcard form, shows the artist's hands lying beside the laboriously created hole. His right index finger and thumb remain in the crevice, as if paused in the act of digging, while his left hand rests close by, silently supportive.

SCRATCHING THE TABLE SURFACE (2006–11) is emblematic of the intimate, reflective side of Lee's practice, studio-based work resolutely made by the artist's own hand[1]—from painted cloths that, after use, are washed by hand to a succession of altered everyday objects, such as those in the 2012 installation SOMETHING IN MY HANDS. Sometimes, as in SCRATCHING THE TABLE SURFACE, the presence of the hand is not merely suggested but made visible, viewed at work or at leisure: The video PAINTING SOMEONE'S FINGERNAILS (2007) documents the eponymous action; the painting PEARS: LASTING CARE (2010) is one of numerous paintings in which Lee has re-created the lotion's logo of a pair of hands, one moisturizing the other.

In recent work, figuration has emerged as a central concern. In 2014, faces began to appear in Lee's paintings—although sometimes with blank features, as seen in A LIFE OF SURPRISE and 1. IN SELF-PORTRAIT, from the same year, the artist's head is missing above

FRANCESCA TAROCCO is assistant professor of Chinese religious and visual culture at NYU Shanghai.

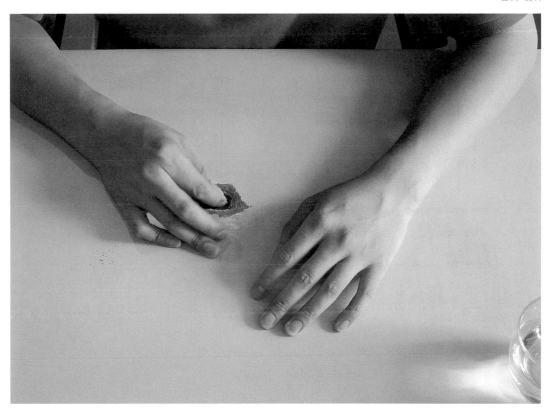

LEE KIT, SCRATCHING THE TABLE SURFACE, 2006–2011, acrylic on plywood, photo document, readymade object, 300 postcards / DIE TISCHPLATTE ANKRATZEN, Acryl auf Sperrholz, Photodokument, Readymade, 300 Postkarten.

the chin, replaced by two thick pink brushstrokes. While these almost-portraits reveal a new focus, imagery of the hand remains ever present. The masculine pair of hands in FUCK YOU (2014), a white-on-white painting on cardboard upon which a purplish blue light is projected, are cut off at the wrist, handsome yet powerless. That work's title is repeated in YOU DON'T KNOW MARY (2014), in which a freeze-frame image of two feet bathed in a bright yellow light—the right foot forever suspended just above the ground, paused in the act of walking toward the viewer—is projected over a vertical piece of cardboard painted black, on which the words FUCK YOU appear twice in a white scrawl. Is this an expression of the anger that seethes within those impotent hands? The disembodied left hand in 0 (ZERO, 2014) might also have something to say as it flashes a thumbs-up sign against the cardboard's uneven black surface; but the top of the thumb has been severed, and its hesitant endorsement is echoed in the tentative, empty oval adjacent, the naught of the title.

On occasion, hands are conspicuous for their absence, after leaving behind their mark in a kind of written stutter, like a chain of expletives: HI; HA, HA; NO; FOR (all 2014). Hand and writing are together again in THE STORY (2015): A white hand appears to be illuminated in the surrounding darkness by a shaft of light that moves diagonally downward from the upper-

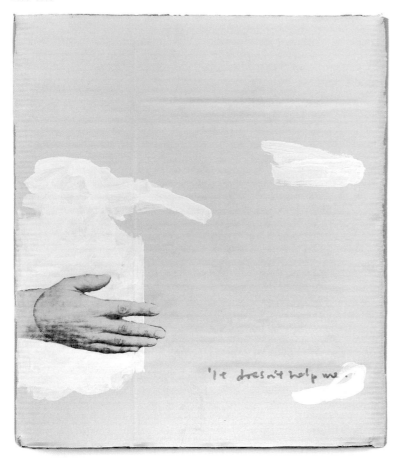

LEE KIT, IT DOESN'T HELP ME, 2014,
acrylic, emulsion paint, inkjet ink, and pencil
on cardboard, 20 ³/₄ x 18 ¹/₈ x 1 ³/₄," /
ES HILFT MIR NICHT, Acryl,
Dispersionsfarbe, Inkjet-Tinte und Bleistift
auf Karton, 53 x 46 x 4,5 cm.

left corner; the story is written below, doubled atop itself as if each letter were shadowed by a doppelgänger. In another painting, a beseeching hand manages to articulate a full sentence, but offers no more support: IT DOESN'T HELP ME (2014). Gathered together, these fragments of bodies, conversations, and internal monologues take on an emotive force—more direct, wry, and violent than Lee's previous work.

A recent diptych, 1, 2 (2015), is calmer and more oblique. A left hand, viewed from the side, is doubled; its white fingers arch slightly over the black background, with the pinky finger elegantly raised. The engaged pose reminds me of the softly shaded hands found in the paintings of Johannes Vermeer, Lee's favorite artist—in particular, those of THE GUITAR PLAYER (c. 1670–72) and WOMAN HOLDING A BALANCE (c. 1662–65).

In a recent interview, Lee explained, "I think hands are the most honest language."[2] The hands that once referred to making and labor now symbolize communication: the failures and shortcomings of meaning; words dulled by daily use; expressions of hopelessness and quiet rage. In excavating experiences of loss and vulnerability, however, Lee asks that we be attentive to their significance.

The two hands in TRAVELING NOT RUNNING (2014) are directed downward into a field of sky blue, index finger extended like the manicule in medieval texts—a pointing hand drawn in the margins to indicate an important section. In "Human Marks," the Hong Kong-born British poet Sarah Howe describes the significance of this symbol, in words that recall Lee's paintings: "Take / that pet of medieval didacts, the *manicule*, or *little hand*: fringe-dweller of / early manuscripts, whose jotted, peripheral fists, sprung with an admonitory digit / lace the tanned margins of our most cankered and flame-buckled books—a fervid / injunction to *look*."[3]

1) In contrast to Lee's public actions, which are discussed in Christina Li's essay, "Claiming Space: Occupation and Withdrawal in the Work of Lee Kit," also in this issue.
2) Lee Kit, quoted in Misa Jeffereis, "In the Studio with Lee Kit," *Untitled (Blog)* (Walker Art Center, Minneapolis), December 22, 2015, http://blogs.walkerart.org/visualarts/2015/12/22/in-the-studio-with-lee-kit/ (accessed February 24, 2016).
3) Sarah Howe, "Human Marks," *Transom 5* (Spring 2013), www.transomjournal.com/issue5/Sarah_Howe/Sarah_Howe_1.html (accessed February 24, 2016).

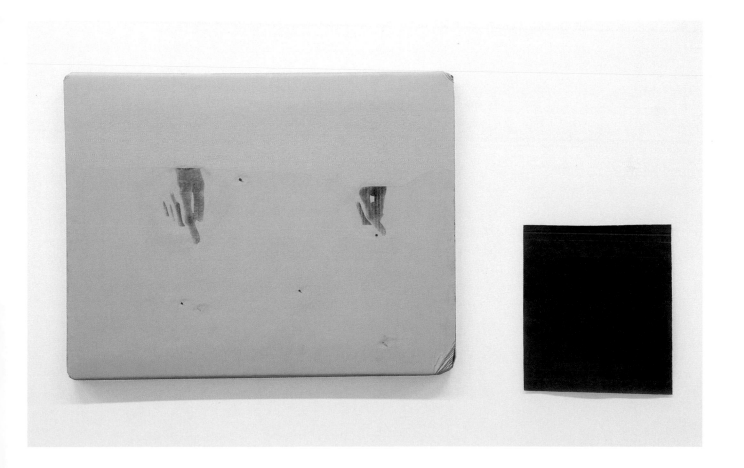

LEE KIT, TRAVELING NOT RUNNING, 2014, acrylic, emulsion paint, and inkjet ink on cardboard, acrylic on paper, 20 ³/₄ x 28 ³/₄ x 1 ¹/₂" / REISEN NICHT RENNEN, Acryl, Dispersionsfarbe und Inkjet-Tinte auf Karton, 52,5 x 73,3 x 4.

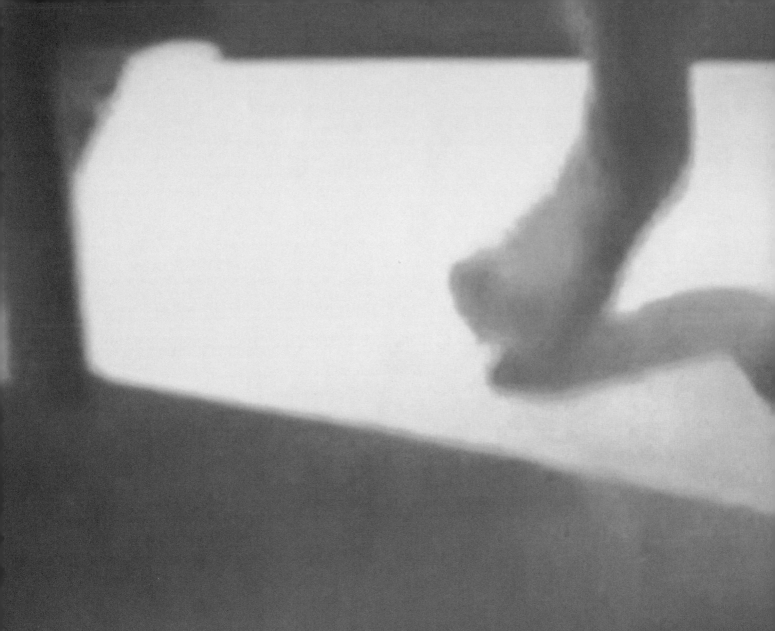

*LEE KIT, YOU DON'T KNOW MARY, 2014, video
projection, cardboard painting, 57 ¹/₂ × 71 ¹/₄," /
DU KENNST MARY NICHT, Videoprojektion,
Malerei auf Karton, 146 × 181 cm.*

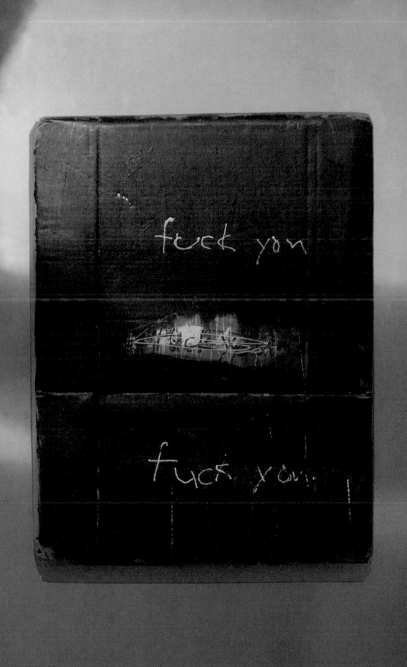

FRANCESCA TAROCCO

Von der

Hand

gekennzeichnet

LEE KIT, 0 (ZERO), 2014, acrylic, inkjet ink, and correction fluid on cardboard, 23 ³/₄ x 28 ¹/₂" / 0 (NULL), Acryl, Inkjet-Tinte und Korrekturflüssigkeit auf Karton, 60,5 x 72,5 cm.

Im Jahr 2006, als Lee Kit in Fotan – einem zur Künstlergemeinschaft umfunktionierten ehemaligen Industriezentrum in den New Territories von Hongkong – lebte und arbeitete, begann er mit den Fingernägeln an der Tischplatte seines Arbeitstisches zu kratzen. Während drei Jahren kratzte er fortwährend an einer kleinen Stelle der blassgrün furnierten Platte, bis das Holz darunter zum Vorschein kam. Ein von oben aufgenommenes Photo, das Lee als Postkarte an Freunde und Bekannte verschickte, zeigt die Hände des Künstlers neben dem in mühseliger Kleinarbeit freigelegten Loch ruhend. Der rechte Zeigefinger und Daumen liegen noch in der Öffnung, als hielten sie nur kurz inne in ihrer Kratzbewegung, während die linke Hand unmittelbar daneben liegt als schweigende Helferin.

SCRATCHING THE TABLE SURFACE (Die Tischplatte ankratzen 2006–2009) ist ein typisches Beispiel für die intime, nachdenkliche Seite von Lees Kunst, im Atelier entstandene, konsequent mit eigener Hand geschaffene Arbeiten[1] – von bemalten Kleidern, die nach Gebrauch von Hand gewaschen werden, bis zu einer Reihe umfunktionierter Alltagsobjekte, wie jene in der Installation SOMETHING IN MY HANDS (Etwas in meinen Händen, 2012). Manchmal ist die Gegenwart der Hand nicht nur angedeutet, sondern wurde gezielt sichtbar

FRANCESCA TAROCCO ist Assistenzprofessorin für chinesische religiöse und visuelle Kultur an der NYU in Shanghai.

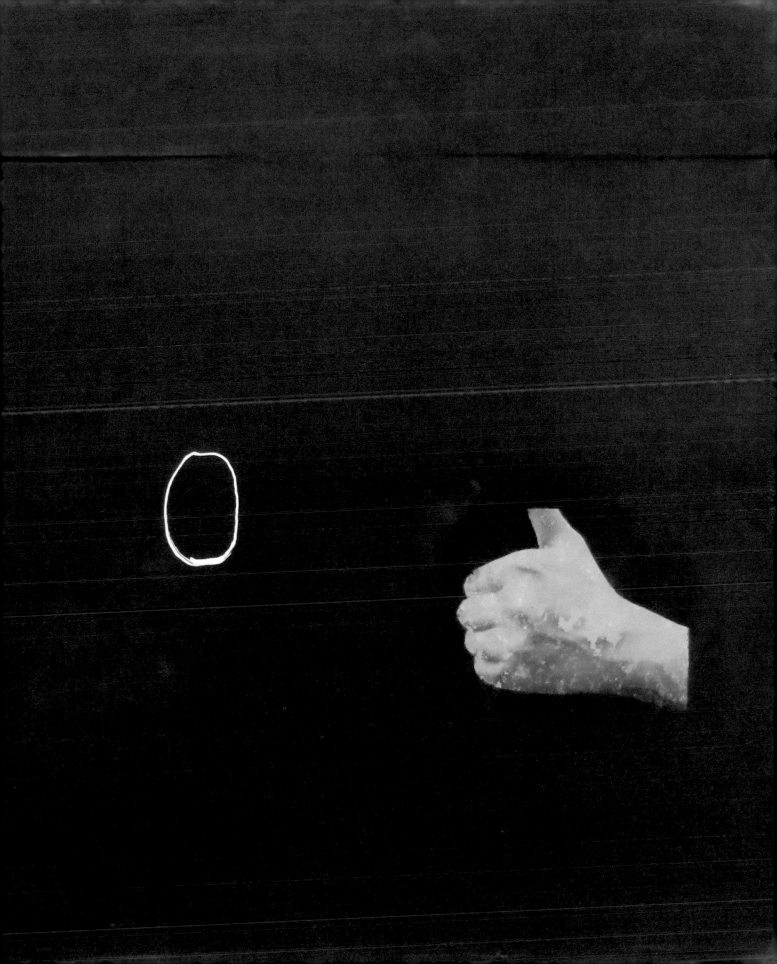

gemacht. Man sieht sie – wie in SCRATCHING THE TABLE SURFACE – bei der Arbeit oder in der Freizeit: Das Video PAINTING SOMEONE'S FINGERNAILS (Jemandes Fingernägel lackieren, 2007) dokumentiert die im Titel genannte Tätigkeit; das Gemälde PEARS: LASTING CARE (Pears: Nachhaltige Pflege, 2010) ist eines von vielen Bildern Lees, die vom Logo der gleichnamigen Handcreme inspiriert sind. Es zeigt, wie eine Hand die andere eincremt.

In seinen neueren Arbeiten hat sich die figürliche Darstellung zu einem zentralen Anliegen entwickelt. Im Jahr 2014 tauchten in Lees Malerei erste Gesichter auf – wenn auch manchmal ohne Gesichtszüge, wie in A LIFE OF SURPRISE (Ein Leben der Überraschung) und 1 (beide 2014). In SELF-PORTRAIT (Selbstporträt) aus dem gleichen Jahr fehlt der Kopf des Künstlers oberhalb des Kinns, stattdessen sind zwei dicke rosa Pinselstriche zu sehen. Obschon diese Beinahe-Porträts eine neue Ausrichtung verraten, bleibt das Bildvokabular der Hand stets präsent. Das männliche Händepaar in FUCK YOU (2014), einer Weiss-in-Weiss-Malerei auf Karton, auf die ein blau-violettes Licht projiziert wird, ist an den Handgelenken abgeschnitten, attraktiv, aber ohnmächtig. Der Titel dieses Werks tritt in YOU DON'T

LEE KIT, HA, HA, 2015, acrylic, emulsion paint, ink and correction fluid on cardboard, 24 ³/₈ x 18 ¹/₈ x 2 ¹/₈" / HA, HA, Acryl, Dispersionsfarbe, Tinte und Korrekturflüssigkeit auf Karton, 62 x 46 x 5,5 cm.

LEE KIT, PEARS, THE LASTING CARE (SERIES: WORKS WITH NO SERIES), 2010, painting, 19 ¹/₄ x 26 ³/₄" / BIRNEN, NACHHALTIGE PFLEGE (SERIE: ARBEITEN OHNE SERIE), Malerei, 49 x 68 cm.

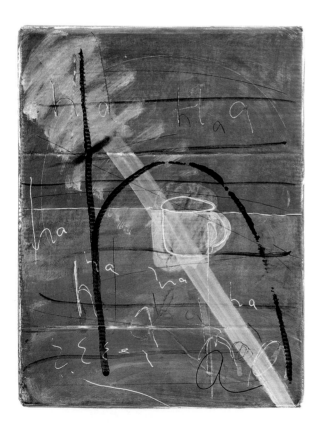
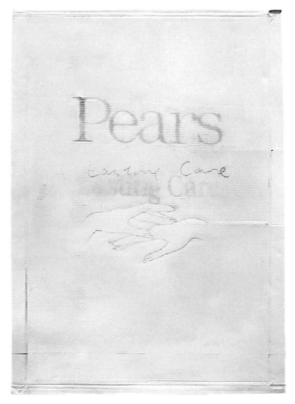

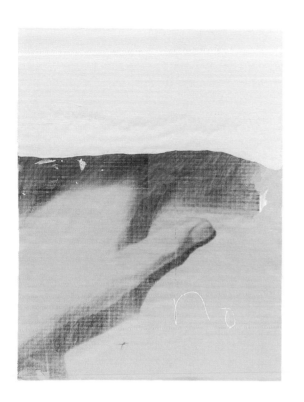

LEE KIT, NO (II), 2014, acrylic, emulsion paint,
inkjet ink, correction fluid, and pencil on cardboard,
23 ³/₄ x 18 ¹/₈" / NEIN (II), Acryl, Emulsionsfarbe,
Injket-Tinte, Korrekturflüssigkeit und Bleistift
auf Karton, 60,5 x 46 cm.

KNOW MARY (Du kennst Mary nicht, 2014) erneut auf: eine Stand-aufnahme von zwei in hellgelbes Licht getauchten Füssen – der rechte Fuss für immer knapp über dem Boden schwebend, mitten im Schritt zum Betrachter hin angehalten – wird auf ein vertikales Stück schwarz bemalten Karton projiziert, auf dem in weisser Kritzelschrift zweimal die Worte FUCK YOU stehen. Ist dies ein Ausdruck der Wut, die in diesen impotenten Händen aufbegehrt? Die körperlose linke Hand in 0 (ZERO) (2014) könnte auch etwas sagen wollen, wenn sie vor der unregelmässigen schwarzen Kartonfläche ein Daumen-hoch-Zeichen aufblitzen lässt; doch die Spitze des Daumens wurde abgetrennt, und das Zögerliche dieser Befürwortung widerspiegelt sich im angrenzenden leeren Oval, der Null des Titels.

Gelegentlich fallen Hände durch ihre Abwesenheit auf, nach-dem sie in einer Art geschriebenem Stottern eine Spur hinterlas-sen haben, wie in der Kette von Füllwörtern: HI; HA, HA; NO; FOR (alle 2014). In THE STORY (Die Geschichte, 2015) haben Hand und Schrift wieder zusam-mengefunden: Eine weisse Hand scheint in der Dunkelheit von einem Lichtstrahl angeleuch-tet zu werden, der sich von der oberen linken Ecke diagonal nach unten bewegt; the story steht darunter, doppelt und leicht verschoben, als würde jeder Buchstabe von einem Doppel-gänger beschattet. In einem anderen Gemälde gelingt es einer flehenden Hand, einen gan-zen Satz zu bilden, was ihr jedoch nicht weiterhilft: IT DOESN'T HELP ME (Es hilft mir nicht, 2014). In Verbindung miteinander gewinnen diese Bruchstücke von Körpern, Gesprächen und inneren Monologen eine emotionale Kraft, die viel direkter, ironischer und gewaltsamer ist als in Lees früheren Werken.

Das neuere Diptychon 1, 2 (2015) ist stiller und weniger direkt. Eine von der Seite be-trachtete, linke Hand wird verdoppelt; ihre weissen Finger krümmen sich leicht vor dem schwarzen Hintergrund, der kleine Finger ist elegant erhoben. Diese Pose erinnert mich an die weich schattierten Hände in den Gemälden Jan Vermeers, Lees Lieblingskünstler – ins-besondere in den Bildern DIE GITARRENSPIELERIN (ca. 1670–1672) und FRAU MIT WAAGE (ca. 1662–65), auch DIE PERLENWÄGERIN genannt.

In einem Interview erklärte Lee kürzlich, er glaube, Hände sprächen die ehrlichste Spra-che.[2] Die Hände, die einst auf das Arbeiten und das Herstellen von Dingen verwiesen, ste-hen heute für Kommunikation: für deren Versagen und Sinndefizite, für die im täglichen Gebrauch abgestumpften Worte, für Ausdrücke einer Hoffnungslosigkeit und stillen Wut. Lees Zu-Tage-Fördern solcher Verlust- und Verletzungserfahrungen fordert uns auf, der Aus-sagekraft der Hände grössere Aufmerksamkeit zu schenken.

Die beiden Hände in TRAVELING NOT RUNNING (Reisen nicht rennen, 2014) zeigen nach unten, quasi in ein Stück blauen Himmel hinein, der Zeigefinger gestreckt wie bei

LEE KIT, FOR, 2014, acrylic, emulsion paint, correction fluid, pencil, and inkjet ink on cardboard, 25 x 18" /
FÜR, Acryl, Dispersionsfarbe, Korrekturflüssigkeit, Bleistift und Inkjet-Tinte auf Karton, 63,5 x 45,7 cm.

den Maniculae mittelalterlicher Handschriften – jenen am Manuskriptrand hingezeichneten auf wichtige Stellen hinweisenden Händchen. Im Gedicht «Human Marks» (Menschliche Kennzeichen) beschreibt die in Hong Kong geborene englische Dichterin Sarah Howe die Bedeutung dieses Symbols in Worten, die an Lees Malerei erinnern: «Schau / nur den Liebling mittelalterlicher Didaktiker an, die *Manicula* oder das *Händchen*: jenen Randbewohner / alter Manuskripte, deren seitlich hingekritzelte Fäuste mit mahnend ausgestrecktem Zeigefinger / die gebräunten Ränder unserer modrigsten und am kunstvollsten beschlagenen Bücher umranken – ein flammender / Appell, *hinzuschauen.*»[3]

(Übersetzung: Suzanne Schmidt)

1) Im Unterschied zu Lees öffentlichen Aktionen, die in einem anderen Beitrag zu diesem *Parkett*-Band erörtert werden, siehe Christina Li, *Platz fordern: Besetzung und Rückzug im Werk von Lee Kit* in dieser Ausgabe
2) Lee Kit, zitiert in Misa Jeffereis, «In the Studio with Lee Kit», *Untitled (Blog)*, Walker Art Center, Minneapolis, 22. Dezember 2015, www.blogs.walkerart.org/visualarts/2015/12/22/in-the-studio-with-lee-kit.
3) Sarah Howe, «Human Marks», *Transom* 5 (Frühjahr 2013), www.transomjournal.com/issue5/Sarah_Howe/ Sarah_Howe_1.html (abgerufen am 30. Januar 2016): «Take / that pet of medieval didacts, the *manicule*, or *little hand*: fringe-dweller of / early manuscripts, whose jotted, peripheral fists, sprung with an admonitory digit / lace the tanned margins of our most cankered and flame-buckled books—a fervid / injunction to *look.*»

LEE KIT, SELF-PORTRAIT, 2014, acrylic, emulsion paint, correction fluid, pencil, and inkjet ink on cardboard, 21 x 18 ¹/₂ˮ; fluorescent light fixture / SELBSTPORTRÄT, Acryl, Dispersionsfarbe, Korrekturflüssigkeit, Bleistift und Inkjet-Tinte auf Karton, 53,3 x 47 cm; fluoreszierende Leuchte.

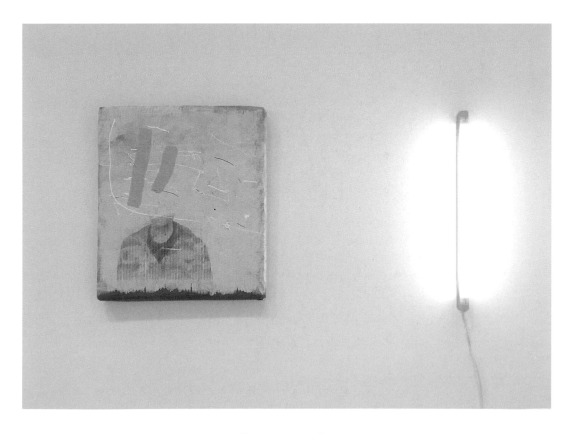

EDITION FOR PARKETT 98

LEE KIT

UPON, 2016

Installation with photograph (archival print,
framed) and towel.
Photograph, 7 $^3/_4$ x 9 $^3/_4$ ", overall dimensions variable.
Ed. 35 / XX, signed and numbered certificate.

Installation mit Photographie (alterungsbeständiger
Print, gerahmt) und Handtuch.
Photographie 20 x 25 cm, Gesamtmasse variabel.
Auflage 35/XX, signiertes und nummeriertes Zertifikat.

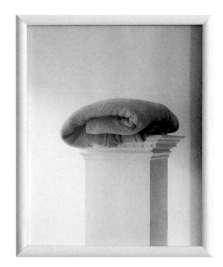

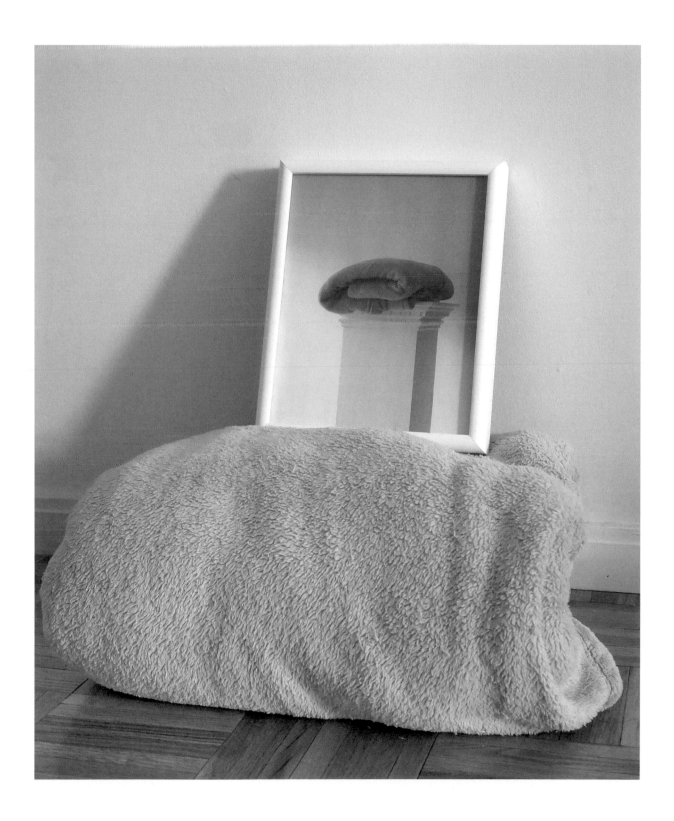

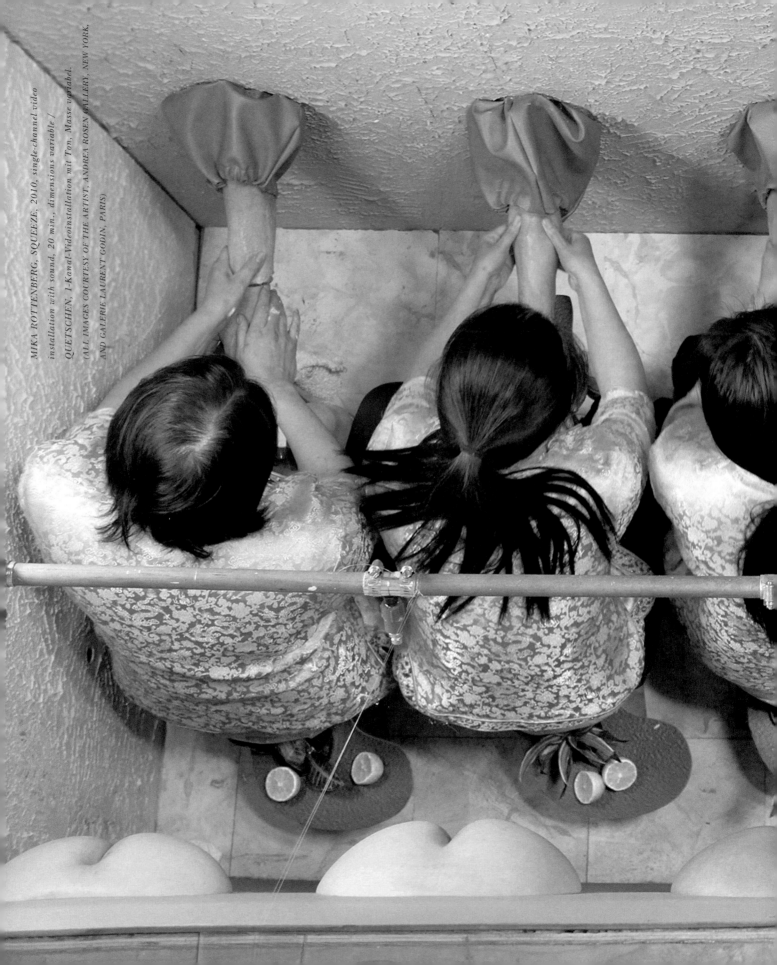

MIKA ROTTENBERG, SQUEEZE, 2010, single-channel video
installation with sound, 20 min., dimensions variable /
QUETSCHEN, 1-Kanal-Videoinstallation mit Ton, Masse variabel.
(ALL IMAGES COURTESY OF THE ARTIST, ANDREA ROSEN GALLERY, NEW YORK,
AND GALERIE LAURENT GODIN, PARIS)

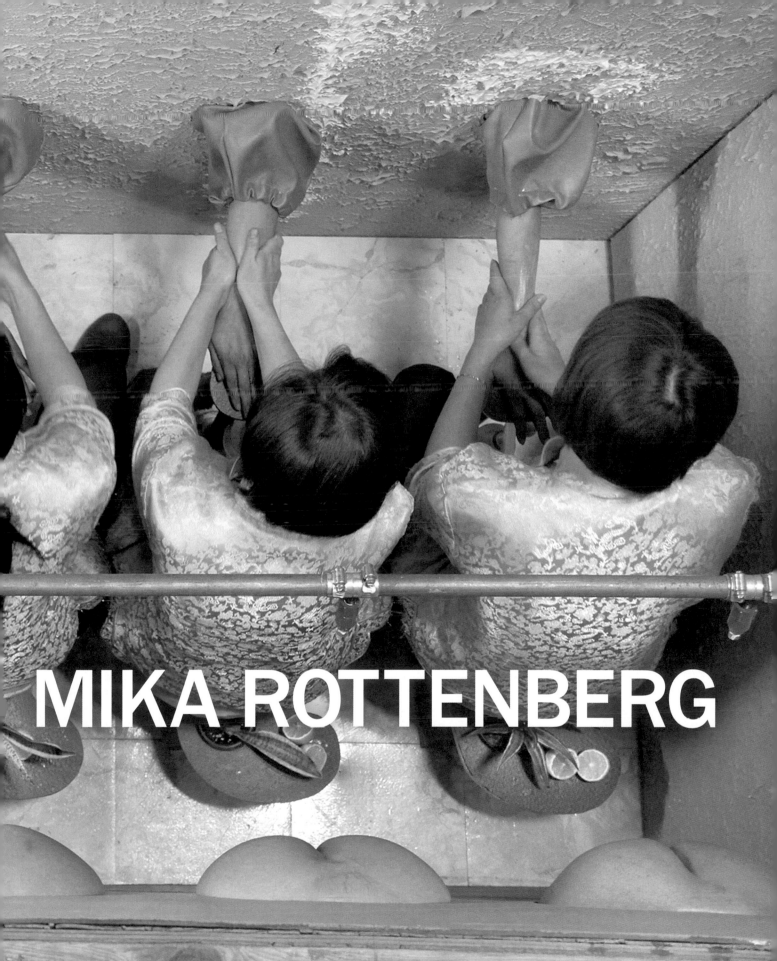

MIKA ROTTENBERG

JONATHAN BELLER

ROTTENBERG PEARLS

I suppose that here too it all depends on what Mika Rottenberg refers to in her own work as the "money shot." Every serious piece of pornography has one. The meaning of the compound word is resonant as it unifies the pursuit of cis-male pleasure and market forces in a ritualized and carefully documented climax. Upon reflection, it suddenly seems that the money shot—in binding together representation, sexuality, and finance—describes an increasing number of ambient images today, not just the graphic trajectory of semen across the screen but that of all would-be iconic visual presentations designed to get consumers to shoot their wad: fashion photography, automobile ads, Instagram hotties, Trump sound bites, art. The idea traverses a complex array of social relations while posing a problem: How to show what you want, avoid the myriad censors, build it to a visceral climax, and cash in?

Indeed, it is arguable that in late capitalist spectacle, the money shot has become a synecdoche for the film/commodity/artwork as a whole. Somehow, in the world of the technical image, where, as Vilém Flusser tells us, every social practice aspires to the image, every image seems to aspire to money. Rottenberg is interested in the modes of production and the channels of distribution for many of the spectacular orgasms of commodity culture, in particular, those of art. Tasteful *and* sexy, I know, but really, consciously or not, these praxis questions are the practical concerns of any producer, be it of pearls, porn, art, or aesthetic theory. Rottenberg's recent work explores the relationship between global economy, feminized labor, the aesthetic, sexuality, and the obscene in contemporary post-Fordist visual culture. As it turns out, in contemporary visual culture, representations designed to evoke pleasure and purchase function on a continuum with the uneven development and exploitation that provide this visuality's conditions of possibility.

Emphatically, we find that what is central for Rottenberg is the role of women—a concern that some might erroneously consider specialized when in actuality every business depends upon the work of women in one way or another. In thematizing the fact, variety, worldwide distribution, unevenness of circumstance, and specialization of labor done by women,

JONATHAN BELLER is professor of Humanities and Media Studies and director of the Graduate Program in Media Studies at Pratt Institute, New York.

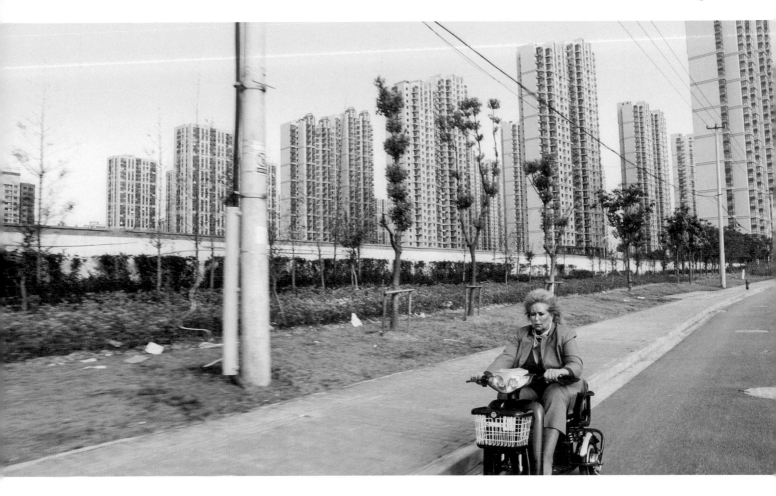

MIKA ROTTENBERG, NONOSEKNOWS, 2015, video with sound and sculptural installation, 22 min., dimensions variable /
KEINENASEWEISS, Video mit Ton und skulpturaler Installation, Masse variabel.

Rottenberg's video and installation work represents what Hsuan L. Hsu has described as "the global art factory."[1] It also raises the complex question of product valorization in financial, political, and aesthetic terms. Rottenberg understands that the art factory is not a stand-alone entity but rather intersects with and depends upon what autonomist Marxism calls "the social factory," in which society is subsumed by capital and everyday activities take on a virtuosic character, as increasingly specialized accommodations by ordinary individuals to the extraordinary protocols of capitalist production. The life-world itself becomes a factory, and the metabolism of the social is reconfigured by capital as labor. In targeting aesthetic production and creating her own money shots from the

relations therein, the artist at once enters into the generic space of the commodification of globalized post-Fordist labor, and endeavors, through her own sensate acts, to poetically redeploy its terms.

With a hyperbolic flair that, like psychoanalysis, finds its truth in exaggeration, Rottenberg's video installations depict rigorously designed and rigorously absurd machines that manufacture impossible products via the unique capacities of mostly women, whose appearances do not fit into the iconic templates offered by those other sense machines known as Hollywood and the advertising industry. New products demand new production regimes demand new sensations and thus new senses; the artist too, if she wants to stave off the falling rate of profit, must

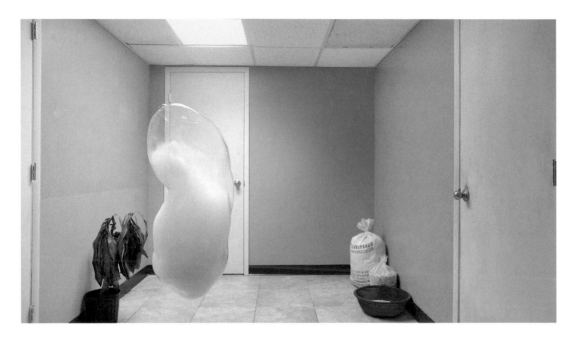

*MIKA ROTTENBERG, NONOSEKNOWS, 2015, video with sound
and sculptural installation, 22 min., dimensions variable /
KEINENASEWEISS, Video mit Ton und skulpturaler Installation, Masse variabel.*

decode and provide. Under the new regime, sense and sensibility no longer function the way they used to (or were thought to), as natural, human faculties relatively autonomous from market forces. Rather, as Rottenberg's work demonstrates on multiple levels, our sense-making faculties are re-structured by markets and intimately incorporated in production networks—they are, in fact, senses of global market forces. No wonder NONOSEKNOWS (2015) seems to follow loosely from "No Nose Knows," an episode of the highly attuned cultural indicator and cutting-edge disseminator of cultural scripts *SpongeBob SquarePants.*

Rottenberg's work self-reflexively embodies the conditions of contemporary *aesthetic* production in its ineluctable relation to capital, gender, globalization, and post-Fordist empire. It is aware of attention economies (the production of value through the extraction of attention) along with a generalized proletarianization of the senses (the putting of the senses to work for capital, as well as their alienation and dispossession from other mental activities). At the start of NONOSEKNOWS, a middle-aged white lady drives an electric cart through deserted streets,

enters a building, and moves through a series of rooms full of magnificent, seemingly sentient, floating bubbles. She goes to her office and, pushing aside a large restaurant dish cart full of haphazardly stacked plates of pasta, vermicelli, udon, and the like, sits at her desk to smell plastic-wrapped potted flowers. She smells them thanks to a breeze generated by a rickety fan connected by a drive belt coming through the floor from a room below, powered by an Asian woman turning a crank while seated at a table with approximately twenty other Asian women, who we slowly realize are inserting micro-slices of foreign oyster bits into small live oysters to force them to grow cultured pearls. With remarkable skill, these women are cutting and splicing oyster with oyster to create future aesthetic appeal; basically, they are editing life in what turns out to be a pearl factory in Zhuji, China.

We figure out that this process is pearl culture, and glean its analogy to video and art-making: Rottenberg's own method is analogous. While upstairs in her modern office the white lady—an imported actor and the only Caucasian in the video—sniffs flowers

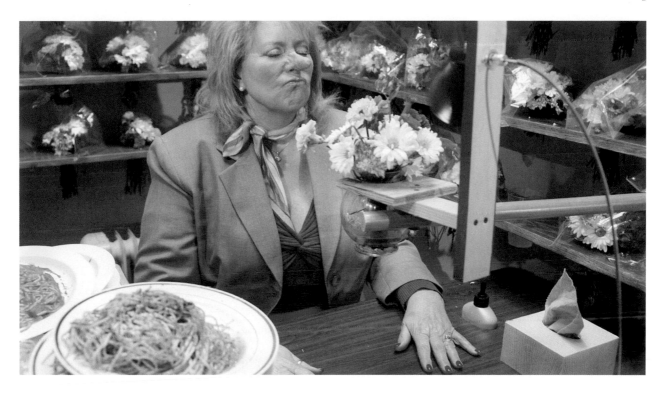

MIKA ROTTENBERG, NONOSEKNOWS, 2015, video with sound and sculptural installation, 22 min., dimensions variable /
KEINENASEWEISS, Video mit Ton und skulpturaler Installation, Masse variabel.

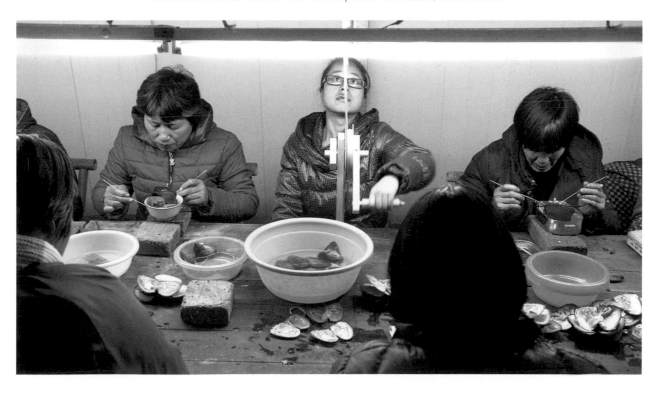

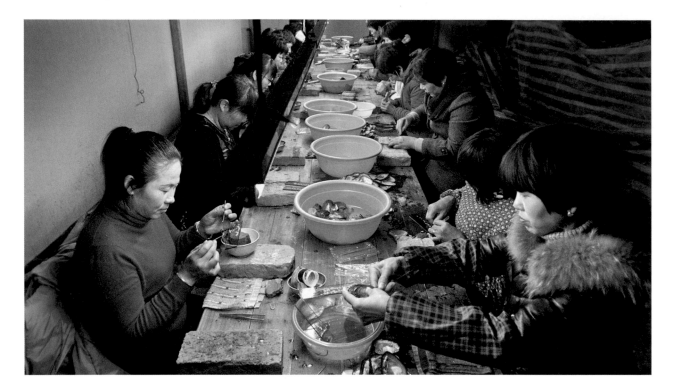

MIKA ROTTENBERG, NONOSEKNOWS, 2015, video with sound and sculptural installation, 22 min., dimensions variable /
KEINENASEWEISS, Video mit Ton und skulpturaler Installation, Masse variabel.

with her steadily growing, highly specialized schnozz, we see also that in a wet kill room somewhere below her, the big oysters are being harvested in a series of (machete) cuts that slash their flesh in half, allowing a working woman in gloves and hat (we never see her face) to use her fingers to hungrily grab the pearls from the muck of gonads. The structure of relations that organizes diverse activities—spanning the gamut of scripted interactions from gonad to pearly aesthetic—is revealed gradually and understood retroactively. As we see another group of about twenty women, each using all ten fingers to sort huge piles of pearls into burlap sacks with incredible dexterity and speed, we realize that those big bags of what we might have thought was rice, previously seen randomly lying around the multiple rooms (or were they offices?) inhabited by those various bubbles, were actually full of pearls.

The documentary footage here of women doing the work of pearl culture is as amazing to those of us who only know pearls from earrings as the footage from another Rottenberg work, SQUEEZE (2010), of lettuce workers in Arizona and of rubber farming in India is to people who only know lettuce from salads or rubber from . . . you get the point. The process of assemblage shown here, revelatory as it is, is also paradigmatic: Cut and splice decontextualized materials with specialized forms of attention in order to capture more attention through the production of commodity-images—what elsewhere I have referred to as the cinematic mode of production. Rottenberg's most recent and perhaps most extraordinary constructions create fantastic scenarios in which various sensual capacities are cut, mixed, ramified, and redeployed in production scenarios that are at once third-world and post-Fordist, crude, and futuristic. Like her previous work, SQUEEZE and NONOSEKNOWS depict Rottenberg's ingenious machines for the making of new types of outlandish and ostensibly useless products, but these are now combined with documentary footage of actually existing labor processes engaged in by women in the global South. In NONOSEKNOWS, the Chinese pearl factory workers are not only shown to underpin the work of the white lady artist in all of her grotesque specialization but are literally incorporated into the product: Their work becomes part of the artwork. This literal incorporation of feminized labor into the artwork makes visible the generalized incorporation of specialized and feminized labor in the rest of commodity culture: from pearls, to beauty products, to nearly every commonplace item.

In a sense, Rottenberg's videos, which have been called surreal, are more realistic than most Realism. SQUEEZE, for example, with all its seemingly surreal watering of isolated tongues and butts, hand massages, lettuce and rubber farming, blush gathering, and machinic chopping of crap, combines its pieces through cutting and splicing to make both a video and a cube—the on-screen "final" product made out of lettuce, rubber, and blusher—that will simply be referred to as "an art object." This art object, sold in seven shares along with the video, is stored in perpetuity in the tax haven of the Cayman Islands. Thus, as commodities produced under conditions of globalization, Rottenberg's own works partake of the same disturbing incorporation and sublation of the labor of global South women as does your iPhone and indeed nearly all commodities today; but they also render that incorporation legible and somehow perverse rather than invisible and unremarkable. At least, Rottenberg pearls are not deracinated and ideologically sanforized, shearing off the history of the production process. Rather, they retain the temporality and signature of their mode of production to the point that the strange imperatives imposed on life and labor by the exigencies of universal commodification are apprehended as at once obscene and amazing. In this, the images are, to use an increasingly unpopular word, dialectical—the product of the entire process is grasped as at once a useless bauble that is part of the flotsam of lurid refinement and rarefied taste of the global bourgeoisie and its art world, and a lucid indicator of the conditions of inequality presupposed and indeed enjoyed by that very same world. In

MIKA ROTTENBERG, NONOSEKNOWS, 2015, video with sound and sculptural installation, 22 min., dimensions variable / KEINENASEWEISS, Video mit Ton und skulpturaler Installation, Masse variabel.

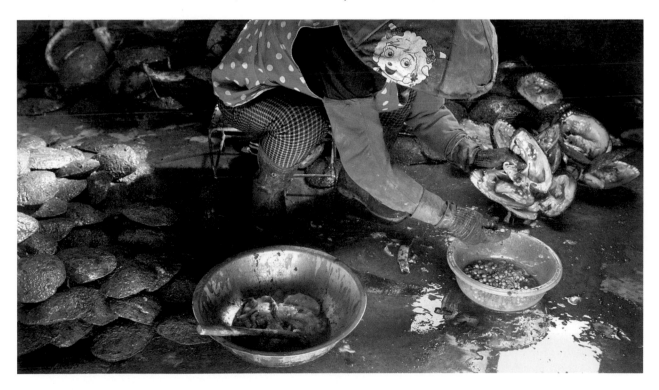

point of fact, the skill of these workers, like the skill of the artist, extends the very idea of what (post) humans, cybernetically intertwined with capitalized technologies, are capable of embodying, enduring, and/or enjoying. Exceeding the dominant ideals governing the normative forms of human beings and humanism, the worker-actors—in their singularity within a world committed to imposing standards, and their seemingly excessive presence within a world committed to effacing the visibility of labor—transmit the kind of fortitude, creativity, everydayness, and dignity with which those facing the conditions of so-called feminized labor (labor that redounds to women or that disempowers workers of any sex/gender conformation) confront the imperatives of the market.

Rottenberg's pearls show us first hand how capitalist production intensifies its processes of alienation. Having separated people from the land and from one another, it now ramifies bodies by isolating, separating, and specializing human capacities and senses and putting them to work. Wagging tongues stick out of holes in sheetrock, butts from walls, feet from buckets of pearls. But strangely, all of these separated faculties require watering with a spray bottle. These little acts of attention and care for fragmented human beings are part of the work necessary for a new distribution of corporeal organization and sense under a production regime that fragments organisms and utilizes their pieces as its own organs. As shown by the massages that take place within the machine of SQUEEZE—offered by Asian workers to the arms of field workers that appear through walls, in work reminiscent of nail salons—the demands of sensual labor (Marx's term for any kind of labor) require sensual care. A remarkable scene occurs when the portals between the visually disconnected spaces of SQUEEZE line up and the women of different worlds can see one another. It is a utopian moment that restitches the ordinarily alienated labor of the multiple forms of work and service to visually construct a kind of community. Here Rottenberg shows that the labor of caring is also part of the labor of labor; her work is also an extension of this care.[2] These are forms of recognition and valorization that to some extent invert the relations of commodification.

Nonetheless, the condition for the emergence of Rottenberg's work is not only third-world labor and non-normative female bodies, organized by the exigencies of work and the production of new needs, but the moneyed, glamorous, well-heeled, and indeed well-pearled world of the rich man's art market. As pearl culture indicates by standing as analogous to art culture through its elaborate process and seemingly sheer uselessness of the product, the entire art market and its world rests atop this sea of invisibilized labor—labor whose form and function, it is imperative to remark, is part of the history not only of hetero-patriarchy but of racism and imperialism. This labor, devalued and erased through patriarchy and racialization, is also the source of much of the world's wealth, including that of art patrons. This is no doubt why, when working on top of all those women of color, the white lady's nose gradually but inexorably grows erect beyond all proportion: To attain representation in the apex of the phallocratic white supremacist capitalist spectacle (aka the art world), and to produce to its taste, it is imperative to go the way of Pinocchio. As even SpongeBob's starfish friend Patrick sensed when he longed for a nose like the rest of the gang, if you want to be acknowledged among the real boys, you have to grow a dick. Or, at least, get a strap-on.

It's noteworthy, then, that the white lady—who arrives at her office after a ride through street after street of empty skyscrapers, completed but lying empty as a result of China's speculative housing bubble—seems to occupy a mid-managerial position. Like the artist, curator, and critic—"smell testers" and specialized sense managers in their own right—her relatively cushy job in the industry run by (here) invisible men is to sniff hothouse flowers and discern some productive knowledge from their scent. She sniffs, her nose grows a few inches, and midway through the twenty-two-minute video comes the first wave of money shots. With huge splatting kerchoos, accompanied by the sound of ringing cash registers, she sneezes plates of noodles. If those climaxes don't satisfy, I suppose we (if you're still with me) can take some satisfaction from the fact that later in the video, when she sticks her nose—now grown to mind-bending dildonic proportions—into a secret glory hole in a wall in her office, all those suspended bubbles pop. These *petites morts* are also money shots—reprises that are at once the aesthetic payoff and the visceral destruction of disembodied abstractions and speculative wagers. The seemingly sentient bubbles were beautiful, delicate, and otherworldly creatures, free-floating next to their bags of pearls, each in its (his?) own private office, but the Rottenberg penetrations burst their nearly immaterial presence and bring their bits of mucus down to earth. No doubt the consequence of the white lady's gender-bending non-conformity also refers to the bursting of the bubble in pearl prices, which, like housing prices in China, have been languishing due to overproduction. But it also, quite poetically, seems to indict the subjectivity that invests in the hegemonic aesthetics of luxury: The patriarchal markets and marketers, with their calculus of infinite expansion, their aestheticized ideas of women and their tastes, along with the invisibility of what has been organized as women's work, have perhaps miscalculated. They have created the conditions for their own destruction and now, at least in this utopian gesture of Rottenberg's work, they're getting fucked for it. That message to cultural managers and connoisseurs accomplished, we again see the catering cart full of sneezed ejaculate—chaotically piled, perfectly formed, artistically shaped plates of exotic noodles from around the world. Are they ready for the garbage . . . or are they for sale? We'll have to see what Mary Boone's pearl necklace has to say about that.

1) Hsuan L. Hsu, "Mika Rottenberg's Productive Bodies," *Mika Rottenberg* (New York and Amsterdam: Gregory R. Miller and Co. and de Appel Arts Centre, 2011), 113.
2) To Rottenberg's great credit—and in a way that would seem redeemable in a non-capitalist system of accounting (should such a system exist) despite her participation in the obscenity of the art market—she shows profound respect for the women with whom she works; she treats them as artists in their own right. In 2008, she created a photo edition with Alona Harpaz, donating the financial profits to build a new weaving center in the Indian village of Chamba.

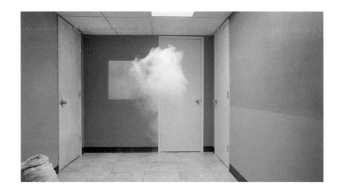

MIKA ROTTENBERG, NONOSEKNOWS, 2015,
video with sound and sculptural installation,
22 min., dimensions variable /
KEINENASEWEISS, Video mit Ton und
skulpturaler Installation, Masse variabel.

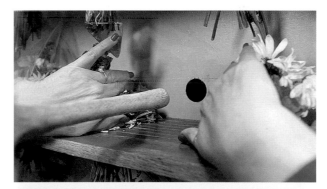

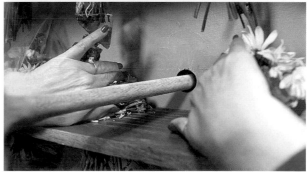

157

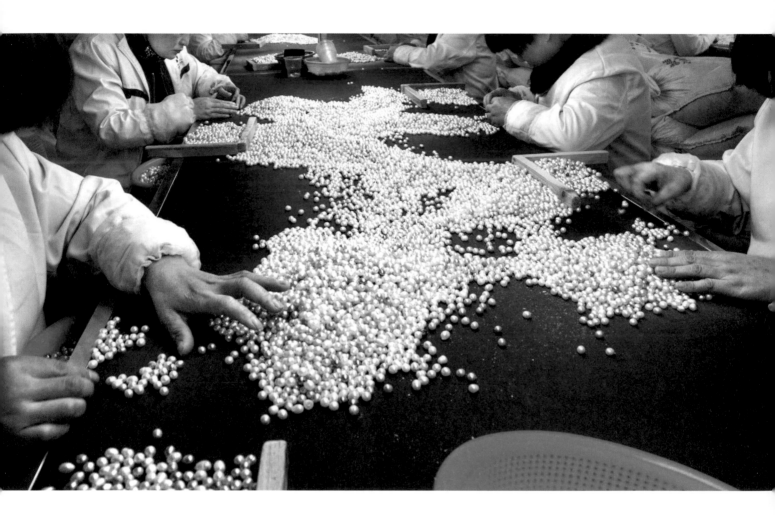

MIKA ROTTENBERG, NONOSEKNOWS, 2015, *video with sound and
sculptural installation, 22 min., dimensions variable /*
KEINENASEWEISS, *Video mit Ton und skulpturaler Installation, Masse variabel.*

JONATHAN BELLER

ROTTENBERG-
PERLEN

Ich vermute, dass auch hier alles steht und fällt mit dem, was Mika Rottenberg in ihrer eigenen Arbeit als «money shot» bezeichnet: dem geilsten Bild. Die Bedeutung dieses zusammengesetzten, ursprünglich aus der Pornoszene stammenden Ausdrucks ist schillernd, denn er bezeichnet einen ritualisierten und akribisch dokumentierten Orgasmus und verknüpft dabei den zissexuell-männlichen Lusttrieb mit den Mechanismen des Marktes. Bei genauerer Überlegung erscheint es plötzlich so, dass der «money shot» – eben weil er Darstellung, Sexualität und Finanzen miteinander verquickt – zunehmend Bilder beschreibt, die uns heute umgeben, nicht nur die graphische Spur des Samenrinnsals auf dem Bildschirm, sondern jene aller angeblich legendären Bildpräsentationen, die den Verbraucher dazu bringen sollen, seine Milch zu verspritzen: Modephotographie, Autowerbung, Instagram-Sternchen, Trump-Sprüche, Kunst. Die Idee durchläuft ein komplexes Feld sozialer Beziehungen, birgt jedoch ein

Problem: Wie kann man zeigen, was man will, sämtliche Zensoren umgehen, es bis zur unwiderstehlichen Spitze treiben und abkassieren?

Man kann mit Fug und Recht behaupten, dass der «money shot», das geilste Bild, im spätkapitalistischen Spektakel zu einer Synekdoche für den Film / das Konsumgut / das Kunstwerk insgesamt geworden ist. Irgendwie scheint in der Welt des technischen Bildes, in der – so Vilém Flusser – jede soziale Praxis zum Bild strebt, jedes Bild nach Geld zu streben. Rottenberg interessiert sich für die Produktionsweisen und Vertriebskanäle zahlreicher spektakulärer Gipfelpunkte der Konsumgüterkultur, insbesondere jene der Kunst. Gediegen *und* sexy, ich weiss, aber eigentlich sind diese praktischen Fragen ein Anliegen jedes Produzenten, egal ob er Perlen, Porno, Kunst oder eine ästhetische Theorie produziert. Rottenbergs neuere Arbeiten untersuchen das Verhältnis zwischen globaler Wirtschaft, Frauenarbeit, Ästhetik, Sexualität und dem Obszönen in der heutigen postfordistischen visuellen Kultur. Wie sich zeigt, gehen in dieser Kultur Darstellungen, die Lust erzeugen und zum Kauf verführen sollen, Hand in Hand mit jener ungleichen Entwicklung und

JONATHAN BELLER ist Professor der Geistes- und Medienwissenschaften und Direktor des Graduiertenprogramms Medienwissenschaften am Pratt Institut, New York.

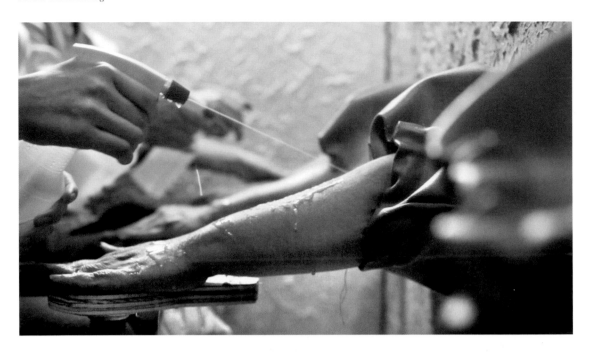

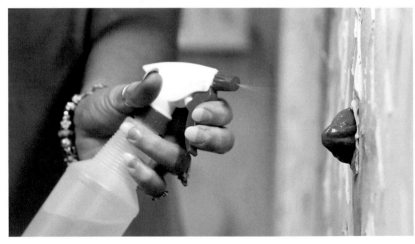

MIKA ROTTENBERG, SQUEEZE, 2010,
single-channel video installation with
sound, 20 min., dimensions variable /
QUETSCHEN, 1-Kanal-Videoinstallation
mit Ton, Masse variabel.

Ausbeutung, die erst die Bedingungen dieser Visualität ermöglicht.

Wir sind überzeugt, dass die Rolle der Frauen für Rottenberg zentral ist – ein Interesse, das manche irrtümlich für speziell halten mögen, wo doch in Wirklichkeit jedes Unternehmen in irgendeiner Weise von Frauenarbeit abhängig ist. Durch die Thematisierung der Realität, der Vielfalt, der weltweiten Verbreitung, der Ungleichheit der Umstände sowie der Spezialisierung der von Frauen verrichteten Arbeit führen Rottenbergs Video- und Installationsarbeiten

vor, was Hsuan L. Hsu als «die globale Kunstfabrik» bezeichnet hat.[1] Ausserdem stellen sie komplexe Fragen nach dem Produktmehrwert unter finanziellen, politischen und ästhetischen Gesichtspunkten. Rottenberg versteht die Kunstfabrik nicht als eigenständiges Unterfangen, sondern als eines, das sich mit dem überschneidet und von dem abhängt, was der autonome Marxismus als «die gesellschaftliche Fabrik» bezeichnet. Hierbei geht die Gesellschaft im Kapital auf und alltägliche Verrichtungen erhalten einen virtuosen Charakter, da gewöhnliche Individuen zunehmend stärker spezialisierte Zugeständnisse an die aussergewöhnlichen Regeln der kapitalistischen Produktion machen. Die Lebenswelt selbst wird zur Fabrik und der gesellschaftliche Stoffwechsel wird durch das Kapital als Arbeit rekonfiguriert. Indem Rottenberg die ästhetische Produktion ins Auge fasst und aufgrund der darin wirksamen Beziehungen ihre eigenen «money shots» fabriziert, betritt die Künstlerin unversehens den allgemeinen Raum der Ökonomisierung der globalisierten postfordistischen Arbeit und sucht durch ihre eigenen sinnlich erfahrbaren Handlungen deren Bedingungen auf poetische Art neu aufzustellen.

Mit einem hyperbolischen Gespür, das – wie die Psychoanalyse – durch Übertreibung zur Wahrheit findet, stellen Rottenbergs Videoinstallationen streng durchgestaltete und konsequent absurde Maschinen dar, die unmögliche Produkte herstellen, und zwar hauptsächlich durch die einzigartigen Fähigkeiten von Frauen, deren Äusseres nicht in jene Kultschablonen passt, die andere Gefühlsmaschinen wie Hollywood und die Werbeindustrie feilbieten. Neue Produkte verlangen neue Produktionsformen verlangen neue Sinneseindrücke und damit neue Sinne: Auch die Künstlerin muss, sofern sie ein Fallen der Profitrate verhindern will, richtig lesen und liefern. In diesem neuen System funktionieren Sinn und Empfindung nicht mehr so wie bisher (oder wie man bisher dachte), nämlich wie vom Markt relativ unabhängige, natürliche, menschliche Fähigkeiten. Vielmehr werden, wie Rottenbergs Werk gleich auf mehreren Ebenen demonstriert, unsere sinnerzeugenden Fähigkeiten von den Märkten umstrukturiert und eng in Produktionsnetze eingebunden – sie sind in Wahrheit Sinneswerkzeuge der globalen Marktkräfte. Kein Wunder, scheint NONOSEKNOWS (KeineNaseWeiss, 2015) eine freie Ableitung aus *No Nose Knows* zu sein, einer Folge des hochsensiblen gesellschaftlichen Indikators und topaktuellen Multiplikators kultureller Skripte: der TV-Serie *SpongeBob Schwammkopf.*

In seiner Selbstreflexion verkörpert Rottenbergs Werk die Bedingungen der heutigen ästhetischen Produktion in ihrem unvermeidlichen Verhältnis zum Kapital, zur geschlechtlichen Identität, zur Globalisierung und zum postfordistischen Empire. Es

weiss um die Aufmerksamkeitsökonomien (die Werterzeugung durch das Gewinnen von Aufmerksamkeit) und auch um die allgemeine Proletarisierung der Sinne (indem man die Sinne für das Kapital arbeiten lässt und sie von anderen geistigen Tätigkeiten entfremdet und abhält). Zu Beginn von NONOSEKNOWS steuert eine weisse Dame mit Knollennase ein elektrisches Fahrzeug durch verlassene Strassen, betritt ein Gebäude und bewegt sich durch eine Reihe von Räumen voller wunderbarer, anscheinend empfindungsfähiger, schwebender Blasen. Um in ihr Büro zu gelangen, schiebt sie einen grossen Restaurant-Speisetransportwagen beiseite, auf dem sich wahllos Pastateller mit Vermicelli, japanischen Udon und so weiter türmen, darauf setzt sie sich an ihren Schreibtisch und riecht an in Plastikfolie gehüllten Blumen. Sie kann den Duft nur dank der Brise riechen, die ein klappriger Ventilator erzeugt, der von einem durch den Boden mit dem darunterliegenden Raum verbundenen Riemen angetrieben wird, welcher dort wiederum von einer wie wahnsinnig strampelnden Asiatin in Gang gehalten wird; Letztere sitzt an einem Tisch mit circa zwanzig weiteren Asiatinnen, die, wie bei näherem Hinsehen deutlich wird, winzige Stückchen fremder Austern in kleine lebende Austern einsetzen, um sie zur Produktion von Perlen anzuregen. Mit bemerkenswertem Geschick schneiden diese Frauen Austern auf und fügen sie wieder zusammen, um ein künftiges ästhetisches Produkt zu erzeugen; wie sich herausstellt, befinden wir uns in einer Perlenfabrik in Zhuji, China, und die Frauen basteln im Grunde an lebenden Kreaturen herum.

Erst allmählich wird klar, dass es hier um Perlenzucht geht, die Analogie zur Video- und Kunstproduktion ist unübersehbar: Rottenbergs eigenes Vorgehen ist analog. Während die Dame – eine ausländische Schauspielerin und die einzige Weisse im Video – in ihrem modernen Büro in der oberen Etage mit ihrem stetig wachsenden, hoch spezialisierten Rüssel an Blumen schnüffelt, sehen wir auch, dass in einem feuchten Todesraum irgendwo unter ihr grosse Austern mit einer Reihe von das Muschelfleisch durchtrennenden (Machete-)Schnitten abgeerntet werden, worauf eine Arbeiterin mit Handschuhen und Hut (ihr Gesicht bekommen wir nie

*MIKA ROTTENBERG, SQUEEZE, 2010, single-channel video
installation with sound, 20 min., dimensions variable /
QUETSCHEN, 1-Kanal-Videoinstallation mit Ton, Masse variabel.*

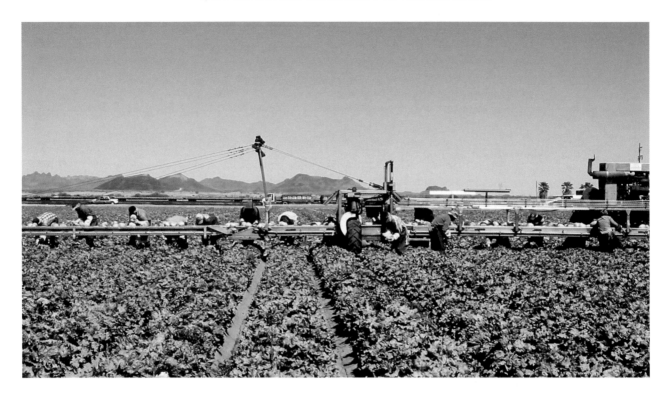

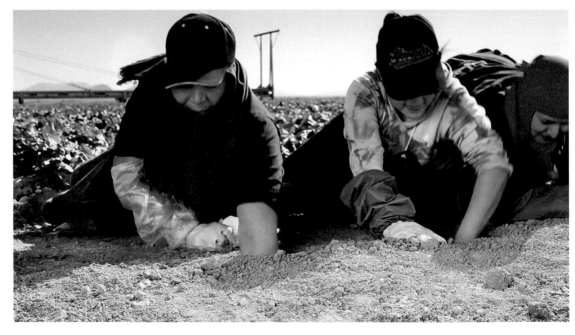

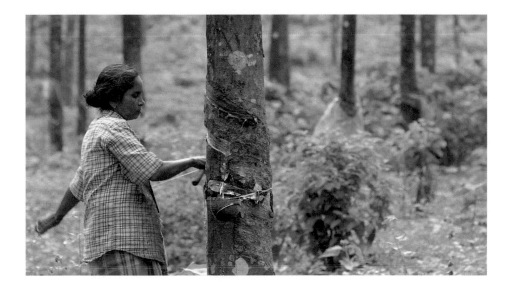

MIKA ROTTENBERG,
SQUEEZE, 2010,
single-channel video
installation with sound,
20 min., dimensions variable /
QUETSCHEN, 1-Kanal-
Videoinstallation mit Ton,
Masse variabel.

zu sehen) mit den Fingern gierig nach den Perlen grabscht und sie aus dem Glibber der Keimdrüsen fischt. Die Beziehungsstruktur, die diese verschiedenen Aktivitäten regelt – und die gesamte Skala der planmässigen Interaktionen von den Keimdrüsen bis zur Ästhetik der glänzenden Perle umfasst –, enthüllt sich Schritt für Schritt und erschliesst sich erst im Rückblick: Erst als wir schliesslich eine weitere Gruppe von rund zwanzig Frauen sehen, die mit allen zehn Fingern unglaublich geschickt und schnell riesige Haufen von Perlen in Leinensäcke sortieren, wird uns klar, dass die grossen Säcke, die wir vorher in den vielen Räumen (oder Büros?) voller schwebender Blasen herumliegen sahen und in denen wir vielleicht Reis vermuteten, in Wirklichkeit mit Perlen gefüllt sind.

Das dokumentarische Filmmaterial über die in der Perlenzucht arbeitenden Frauen wirkt auf uns, die wir Perlen nur als Schmuck kennen, genauso verblüffend wie das Filmmaterial aus SQUEEZE (Quetschen, 2010) – einem weiteren Werk Rottenbergs, das Arbeiterinnen und Arbeiter einer Salatplantage in Arizona und einer Kautschukplantage in Indien zeigt – auf Menschen wirken muss, die Salat nur als Bestandteil ihrer Mahlzeit kennen und Gummi als ..., Sie wissen, was ich meine. Der hier gezeigte *Prozess* des Sammelns ist ebenso aufschlussreich wie beispielhaft: ein Schneiden und Zusammenfügen von

aus ihrem Zusammenhang gelösten Materialien, die an sich schon eine besondere Form von Aufmerksamkeit wecken, zur Herstellung von Bildern von Konsumgütern, die noch grössere Aufmerksamkeit erregen – andernorts habe ich das als filmtypische Produktionsweise bezeichnet. Rottenbergs jüngste und vielleicht ausgefallenste Konstruktionen schaffen phantastische Szenarien, in denen diverse Sinnesfunktionen geschnitten, gemixt, verzweigt und erneut zu Produktionsszenarien zusammengefasst werden, die zugleich drittweltlich und postfordistisch, primitiv und futuristisch wirken. Wie Rottenbergs frühere Arbeiten führen auch SQUEEZE und NONOSEKNOWS ausgeklügelte Maschinen zur Herstellung neuartiger absonderlicher und offensichtlich nutzloser Produkte vor, nur sind sie jetzt mit dokumentarischem Filmmaterial von realer Arbeit durchsetzt, die von Frauen auf der südlichen Erdhalbkugel erbracht wird. In NONOSEKNOWS werden die chinesischen Perlenfabrikarbeiterinnen nicht nur in ihrer untermauernden Funktion für die Arbeit der weissen Künstlerin in ihrer grotesken Spezialisierung gezeigt, sondern sie werden zu einem buchstäblichen Bestandteil des Produkts: Ihre Arbeit wird Teil des Kunstwerks. Diese buchstäbliche Einverleibung der Frauenarbeit ins Kunstwerk macht die allgemeine Einverleibung spezialisierter Frauenarbeit in der übrigen Warenwelt sichtbar: von Perlen über Schönheitsprodukte bis zu fast allen gängigen Gebrauchsgegenständen.

In gewissem Sinn sind Rottenbergs gern als surreal bezeichnete Videos realistischer als fast der gesamte Realismus. SQUEEZE etwa, mit all dem scheinbar surrealen Wasserlassen isolierter Zungen und Hinterteile, den Handmassagen, der Salat- und Kautschukproduktion, der Ansammlung von Rouge-töpfchen und dem maschinellen Schrotthäckseln, verknüpft die einzelnen Teile mittels Schneidens und Zusammenfügens, sodass sowohl ein Video als auch ein Würfel entsteht – der schliesslich als «Endprodukt» auf dem Bildschirm erscheint, aus Salat, Kautschuk und Rouge besteht und schlicht als «ein Kunstobjekt» bezeichnet wird. Dieses Kunstobjekt, das in sieben Teile geteilt, jeweils einzeln zusam-

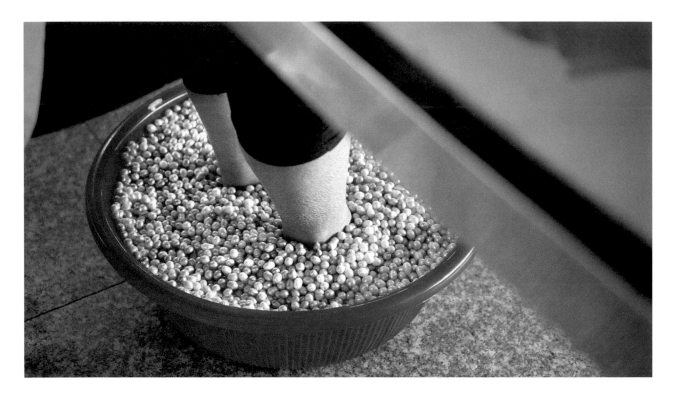

MIKA ROTTENBERG, NONOSEKNOWS, 2015, *video with sound and sculptural installation, 22 min., dimensions variable /*
KEINENASEWEISS, *Video mit Ton und skulpturaler Installation, Masse variabel.*

men mit dem Video verkauft wurde, bleibt auf ewig im Steuerparadies der Cayman Islands gelagert. So wirken Rottenbergs Arbeiten – wie alle Waren, die unter den Bedingungen der heutigen Globalisierung produziert werden – selbst an der verstörenden Einverleibung und Aufhebung der im Süden geleisteten Frauenarbeit mit, genau wie unser iPhone und fast all unsere heutigen Produkte; aber sie machen diese Einverleibung zugleich erkennbar, sodass sie irgendwie pervers wirkt, statt unsichtbar und unbedeutend zu bleiben. Zumindest sind Rottenbergs Perlen nicht entwurzelt und ideologisch sanforisiert, weil sie nicht von der Geschichte ihres Herstellungsprozesses abgeschnitten sind. Vielmehr behalten sie ihre Zeitlichkeit und die Signatur ihrer Herstellungsweise so weit bei, dass die seltsamen Lebens- und Arbeitszwänge, die mit der allumfassenden Kommerzialisierung einhergehen, als ebenso obszön wie verblüffend wahrgenommen werden. In dieser Hinsicht sind die Bilder, um ein zunehmend unpopuläres Wort zu verwenden, dialektisch: Das Produkt des ganzen Prozesses wird als nutzlose Spielerei begriffen, als Teil des Treibgutes der grässlichen Veredelung und des erlesenen Geschmacks der globalen Bourgeoisie und ihrer Kunstwelt und zugleich als deutliches Indiz der ungleichen Lebensbedingungen, die ebendiese Welt voraussetzt, ja sogar geniesst. Tatsächlich erweitert die Gewandtheit dieser Arbeiterinnen, wie auch jene der Künstlerin, die Vorstellung dessen, was (Post-) Humanoide im kybernetischen Verbund bei voller Ausschöpfung der technologischen Mittel zu verkörpern, auszuhalten und/oder zu geniessen imstande sind. Indem sie die vorherrschenden Ideale, die unsere normativen Vorstellungen von menschlichen Wesen und Menschlichkeit bestimmen, sprengen, vermitteln diese Arbeiterinnen-Akteurinnen – durch ihre Einmaligkeit in einer Welt, die so gerne Standards festlegt, und durch ihre unverhältnismässig starke Präsenz in einer Welt, die Arbeit so gern in die Unsichtbarkeit verbannt – eine Art von Kraft, Kreativität, Alltäglichkeit und Würde, mit denen jene, die mit den Bedingungen der sogenannten Frauenarbeit konfrontiert sind (einer Arbeit, die auf Frauen beschränkt ist oder Arbeitende jeglichen Geschlechts entwert), den Zwängen des Marktes entgegentreten.

Rottenbergs Perlen zeigen uns aus erster Hand, wie die kapitalistische Produktion die mit ihr verbundenen Entfremdungsprozesse verschärft: Nachdem sie die Menschen von ihrem Land und voneinander getrennt hat, greift sie nun in den Körper selbst ein, indem sie menschliche Fähigkeiten und Sinne isoliert, separiert, spezialisiert und arbeiten lässt. Zungen züngeln durch Löcher in Gipskartonplatten, Hinterteile ragen aus Wänden, Füsse ragen aus Eimern voller Perlen. Doch seltsamerweise müssen all die unterschiedlichen Funktionen mit Wasser besprüht werden. Diese kleinen Akte der Aufmerksamkeit und Fürsorge für lebendige menschliche Körperteile sind ein notwendiger Teil des Werkes, damit Körper und Sinne neu organisiert werden können im Rahmen eines Produktionssystems, das Organismen zerstückelt und deren Fragmente als eigene Organe nutzt. Wie die Massagen innerhalb der Maschine, die SQUEEZE darstellt, zeigen – asiatische Arbeiterinnen massieren die Arme jener, die auf dem Feld arbeiten und ihre Arme zur Massage durch die Wand strecken, wobei man sich irgendwie an ein Nagelstudio erinnert fühlt –, bedarf die Beanspruchung durch sinnliche Arbeit (und das ist bei Marx jede Arbeit) auch sinnlicher Zuwendung. Eine bemerkenswerte

MIKA ROTTENBERG, NONOSEKNOWS, 2015, video with sound and sculptural installation, 22 min., dimensions variable / KEINENASEWEISS, Video mit Ton und skulpturaler Installation, Masse variabel.

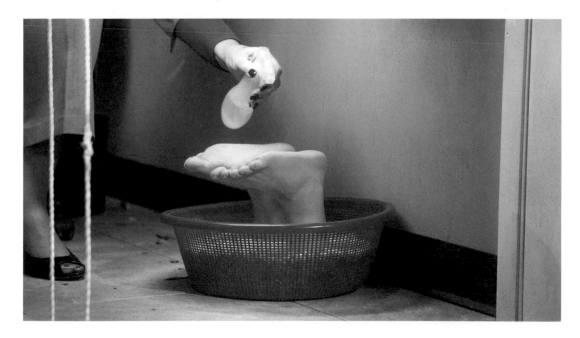

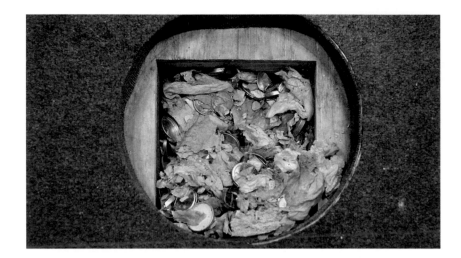

MIKA ROTTENBERG, SQUEEZE, 2010,
single-channel video installation with
sound, 20 min., dimensions variable /
QUETSCHEN, 1-Kanal-Videoinstallation
mit Ton, Masse variabel.

Szene spielt sich ab, sobald die Portale zwischen den visuell getrennten Räumen in einer Reihe stehen und die Frauen aus den verschiedenen Welten einander sehen können. Es ist ein utopischer Moment, der die normalerweise entfremdete Arbeit der vielfältigen Arbeits- und Dienstleistungszweige wieder miteinander verbindet und visuell eine Art Gemeinschaft herstellt. Rottenberg zeigt hier, dass soziale Zuwendung Teil der Arbeit der Arbeitswelt ist; und ihre eigene Arbeit ist eine Erweiterung dieser Zuwendung.[2] Es handelt sich um Formen der Anerkennung und Wertschätzung, die bis zu einem gewissen Grad die Marktverhältnisse auf den Kopf stellen.

Doch der Nährboden für Rottenbergs Werk besteht nicht ausschliesslich aus den Arbeitsbedingungen in Drittweltländern und nicht standardisierten weiblichen Körpern, die von den Arbeitsanforderungen und der Produktion neuer Bedürfnisse bestimmt werden, sondern auch aus der vermögenden, glamourösen, wohlbetuchten und durchaus reich mit Perlen bestückten Kunstmarktwelt der Reichen. Wie die Perlenkultur durch ihre Analogie zur Kunstkultur – aufgrund des raffinierten Produktionsprozesses und der offensichtlich völligen Nutzlosigkeit des Produkts – deutlich zeigt, schwimmt der Kunstmarkt und die gesamte ihm zugehörige Welt auf diesem Meer an unsichtbar gehaltener Arbeit, einer Arbeit, deren Form und Funktion, das muss in aller Deutlichkeit gesagt werden, Teil der Geschichte nicht nur des Hetero-Patriarchats, sondern auch des Rassismus und Imperialismus sind. Diese durch die patriarchalen und rassistischen Verhältnisse entwertete und ausgelöschte Arbeit ist auch die Quelle des Reichtums eines grossen Teils der Welt, auch des Reichtums der Kunstmäzene. Zweifellos ist dies denn auch der Grund dafür, dass die Nase der weissen Dame, die über all diesen farbigen Frauen arbeitet, langsam, aber unaufhaltsam in die Höhe wächst und jedes Mass sprengt: um repräsentativen Charakter für die Gipfelzone des phallokratischen weissen rassistischen kapitalistischen Spektakels (alias Kunstszene) zu erlangen. Denn um deren Geschmack zu treffen, muss man zwingend den Weg von Pinocchio wählen. Das spürte selbst SpongeBobs Seesternfreund Patrick, als er sich eine lange Nase, wie alle andern sie hatten, wünschte: Wenn man zu den echten Jungs zählen will, muss man sich einen Schwanz wachsen lassen. Oder sich zumindest einen umschnallen.

Bemerkenswert ist ferner, dass die weisse Dame – die in ihrem Büro erst nach einer Fahrt durch eine endlose Reihe von Strassen mit leeren Wolkenkratzern ankommt, die zwar fertiggestellt sind, aber infolge der Immobilienblase in China leer stehen – eine Position im mittleren Management innezuhaben scheint. Ähnlich wie bei Künstlern, Kuratoren und Kritikern – die ihrerseits «Gerüche testen» und als spezialisierte Manager der Sinne fungieren – besteht ihre relativ angenehme Aufgabe in der (diesmal) von unsichtbaren Männern geführten Fabrik darin, an Treibhausblüten zu schnüffeln und ihrem Duft irgendeine nützliche Erkenntnis abzugewinnen. Sie schnüffelt, ihre Nase wächst um ein paar Zentimeter, und in der Halfte des 22-Minuten Video folgt die erste Welle der «money shots». Mit gewaltigen, spritzenden Hatschis, untermalt vom Klang klingelnder Registrierkassen, niest sie Pastagerichte auf Teller. Wem diese Orgasmen nicht genügen, dürfte (falls Sie mir noch folgen) doch einige Befriedigung aus der Tatsache ziehen, dass etwas später im Video sämtliche schwebenden Blasen platzen, als die Dame ihre Nase – die mittlerweile irrwitzige dildoartige Ausmasse erreicht hat – in ein verborgenes Schwanzloch in der Bürowand steckt. Diese *petites morts* sind ebenfalls «money shots» – Reprisen, die zugleich das ästhetische Gelingen und die leibhaftige Zerstörung körperloser Abstraktionen und spekulativer Einsätze darstellen. Die anscheinend empfindungsfähigen Blasen waren schöne, grazile Wesen aus dem Jenseits, die, jede in ihrem eigenen Büro, frei über ihren Perlensäcken schwebten, doch die Rottenberg'schen Penetrationen brachten ihre nahezu immaterielle Existenz zum Platzen und liessen ihre schleimigen Komponenten zu Boden platschen. Zweifellos verweist die Konsequenz der geschlechtsübergreifenden Nonkonformität der weissen Dame auch auf die geplatzte Blase der Perlenpreise, die genau wie die chinesischen Immobilienpreise infolge der Überproduktion gefallen sind. Aber sie scheint auch ganz poetisch auf die Subjekte zu verweisen, die in die hegemonische Ästhetik von Luxusgütern investieren: Die patriarchalen Märkte und Händler – mit ihrem unendlichen Wachstumskalkül, ihren ästhetisierten Vorstellungen über Frauen und deren Vorlieben, kombiniert mit der Unsichtbarkeit der Frauenarbeit – haben sich vielleicht verrechnet. Sie haben die Bedingungen für ihre eigene Zerstörung geschaffen und werden nun, zumindest in dieser utopischen Stossrichtung von Rottenbergs Werk, dafür gevögelt. Nachdem diese Botschaft an die Kulturmanager und Kunstkenner angekommen ist, sehen wir erneut den Speisetransportwagen mit Bergen von hingerotztem Ejakulat – chaotisch aufgehäufte, perfekt gestaltete, künstlerisch angerichtete Teller mit exotischen Pastagerichten aus aller Welt. Stehen sie bereit für den Müll ... oder vielleicht zum Verkauf? Bleibt abzuwarten, was Mary Boones Perlenkette dazu meint.

(Übersetzung: Suzanne Schmidt)

1) Hsuan L. Hsu, «Mika Rottenberg's Productive Bodies», *Mika Rottenberg*, Gregory R. Miller & Co. und de Appel Arts Centre, New York und Amsterdam 2011, S. 113.
2) Rottenberg zeigt – auf eine Art, die sich in einem nicht kapitalistischen Buchhaltungssystem einlösen liesse (wenn es ein solches System gäbe), und ihrer Partizipation an den Obszönitäten des Kunstmarktes zum Trotz – höchsten Respekt für die Frauen, mit denen sie zusammenarbeitet, und behandelt sie ihrerseits als eigenständige Künstlerinnen. 2008 schuf sie zusammen mit Alona Harpaz eine Photoedition, aus deren Verkaufserlös der Bau eines neuen Webereizentrums in der indischen Ortschaft Chamba finanziert wurde.

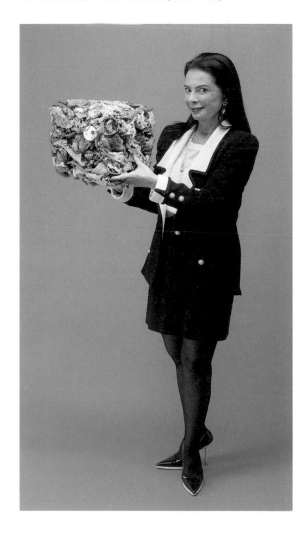

MIKA ROTTENBERG, MARY BOONE WITH CUBE, 2010, C-print, 64 x 36" / MARY BOONE MIT WÜRFEL, C-Print, 162,6 x 91,4 cm.
(IMAGE COURTESY OF MARY BOONE GALLERY, NEW YORK, AND NICOLE KLAGSBRUN GALLERY, NEW YORK)

"Eww, Gross!"

AMELIA JONES

As junior-high-school students in 1970s North Carolina, my girlfriends and I were enamored of the word *gross*, which we used to denigrate anything we found foul, disturbing, or unpleasant—either in a sensorial or emotional way. "Jean is going out with Vance" or "I dropped my lunch on the grass" would precipitate the comment "Eww, gross!" (often accompanied by a screwed-up nose). The world was a challenging place, and gross helped us order it into the palatable versus the disgusting. At the same time, what we viewed as gross was obviously not terribly disturbing to the order of things—it might even indicate something vaguely desirable because it was forbidden. But the melodrama functioned in an odd way as a mode of self-empowerment for girls seeking to be heard in a boys' world—the shrieks and giggles accompanying the statement were part of the effect: Making the boys (or, potentially, other girls) notice as well as repelling them, we created our own world.

Not surprisingly, given this coalitional world-building effect, feminist artists have at various moments adopted strategies akin to this locution, most notably the so-called "bad girl" work of the 1990s, in which anger and humor combine to lambast, critique, and expose the effects of misogyny in the art world and beyond. These works are violent yet funny, both seductive and repellent. Sue Williams's 1992 painting A FUNNY THING HAPPENED ON THE WAY TO THE . . . , which includes cartoonish renderings of rape scenes, and Sarah Lucas's caustic BITCH of 1995, a table from which hang a fish and a T-shirt filled with oranges (which reads as a crude symbolic rendering of a stereotyped version of the female body, smell and all), exemplify this moment.

Mika Rottenberg produces similarly acerbic and funny—although less overtly angry—feminist works, complex video and installation pieces that, for me, evoke an "eww, gross" effect with their bodily excesses, exuberant energy, and cheeky sense of humor (so common among teenaged girls). They produce recognition among like-minded feminist viewers, encouraging a sense of solidarity in the face of the absurdities of the gendered and policed body. But Rottenberg's practice relates not only to the bad-girl attitude of the '90s; it also owes a debt

AMELIA JONES is the Robert A. Day Professor in Art and Design and Vice Dean of Critical Studies at the Roski School of Art and Design, University of Southern California, Los Angeles.

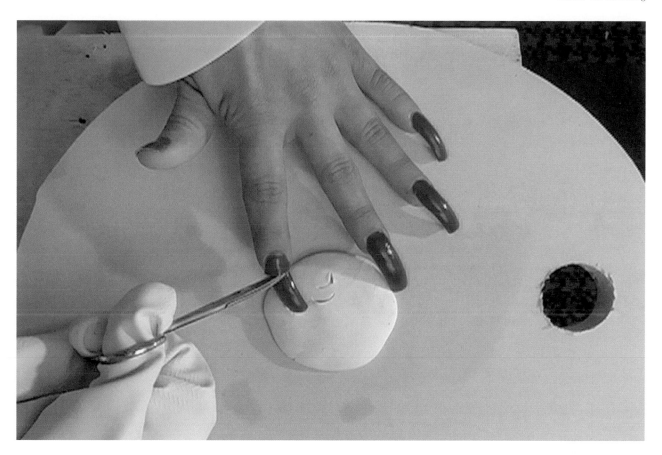

Mika Rottenberg's Late Capitalist Feminism

MIKA ROTTENBERG, MARY'S CHERRIES, 2004,
single channel video installation, 5 min. 50 sec.,
dimensions variable / MARYS KIRSCHEN, 1-Kanal-
Videoinstallation, Masse variabel.

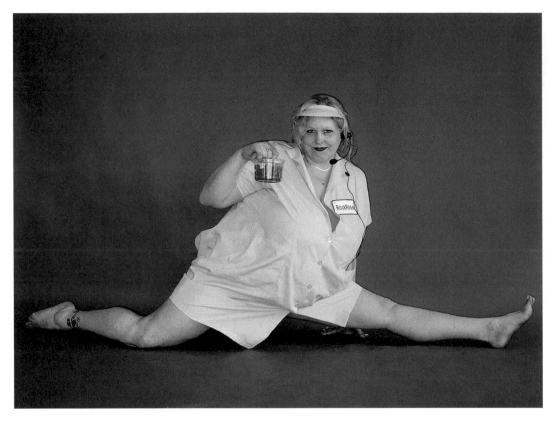

MIKA ROTTENBERG, ROCK ROSE from MARY'S CHERRIES, 2014, C-print /
ROCK ROSE aus MARYS KIRSCHEN, C-Print.

to earlier strategies of feminist art. Her work thus provides an opportunity to rethink these legacies and to explore more contemporary feminist frameworks and tactics in art.[1]

Feminist body art in its early days was largely about making use of the seductive qualities of an "ideal" (slim, white) female body, and feminist video art expanded this by playing with spectatorial expectations and desires. The early videos of Lynda Benglis—such as FEMALE SENSIBILITY (1973), in which two women ostentatiously make out for the video camera—are exemplary of both. Rottenberg's elaborate video installations continue this legacy, but instead feature female bodies that are ethnically diverse and unusual: exceedingly tall, muscular, long-haired, or voluminous. Rottenberg's actors seem to be extreme women for extreme times, and they are often powerful and sensual in their strength; they are not essentialized, like the "womyn" of the separatist phase of the second-wave women's movement. They embrace their excess, and their bodies overflow—into copious sweat, as in TROPICAL BREEZE (2004); long fingernails, in MARY'S CHERRIES (2005); and superabundant hair, in CHEESE (2008). We might laugh, but in solidarity, as twenty-first-century feminists, fully aware of the raucous joys potentially offered by the movements and desires of the female body.

This is not to say that '70s feminist works didn't also play with bodily excess—think of Judy Chicago's MENSTRUATION BATHROOM in the 1972 Womanhouse project in Los Angeles, in which the toilet sat next to a trashcan overflowing with sanitary napkins and tampons painted blood red. Artists celebrated those aspects of female embodiment that society viewed with disgust and that escape the structures of objectification central to both capitalism and patriarchy. In Rottenberg's videos, however, even bodily excess is captured and sold through the mechanisms of late capitalism: Sweat becomes the dampness of wet wipes, fingernail clippings are turned into maraschino cherries, and long tresses are used to make hair tonic. If these transformations seem fantastical, however, note that Rottenberg's actors have themselves monetized their physical attributes: as models, wrestlers, bodybuilders, and "squashers" (fulfilling the desire of people who like to be sat upon by large women).

In the '70s, another chief concern among feminist artists was to make women's labor visible in the social sphere. Mierle Ukeles's "maintenance art" aligned women's work with underpaid labor, as in a 1973 performance where she washed the steps of the Wadsworth Atheneum in Hartford, Connecticut, during opening hours. The previous year, Sandra Orgel performed the task of ironing at WOMANHOUSE, attacking wrinkles with a bored vengeance. As middle-class housewives were largely isolated in their homes at the time, feminist artistic commentaries on female labor focused on spaces literally or symbolically tied to the domestic. Most often a single woman (the artist herself, in the case of Ukeles and Orgel) labored before the audience, enacting the *ennui* of housework or menial labor as art in ways that disrupted both categories.

Echoing women's greater presence in the workforce today, Rottenberg's videos depict interdependent bodies connected via chains of action and reaction across elaborate spaces and Rube Goldberg-esque assembly lines. In TROPICAL BREEZE, for example, a lithe white woman (played by a very flexible dancer, Felicia Ballos) sits on a stationary bicycle inside a truck, pulling out tissues from a box with her foot and sticking them to a pulley with bubble gum, then running them forward to the driver, a muscular black woman (played by Heather Foster, a champion bodybuilder); the driver moistens the tissues with her sweat and then passes them back along the pulley ready to be sold as wet wipes (with the brand name Tropical Breeze). Rottenberg choreographs female bodies into Taylorized movements, underlining the repetitive gestures that result in absurd products.

The famous 1952 "candy factory" episode of the proto-feminist *I Love Lucy* television show comes to mind in relation to Rottenberg's humor, with its element of slapstick, always just restrained enough to prevent it from wreaking havoc. Lucy and Ethel's failure to wrap chocolates on the assembly line fast enough results in them stuffing their mouths with them—in a parody of female self-indulgence and failure to Taylorize. But if Lucy was buffoonish in her performed incompetence as a bourgeois housewife, the real Lucille Ball ran the show behind the scenes. In parallel, Rottenberg's laboring women, despite Sisyphean efforts, are also hugely effective, always successfully moving the production forward, if in tiny or incremental ways. They are affective as well, in their eccentric body types, their strength and agility, their simple extra-ordinariness—which asserts itself as confirmation of women's vast range of potential skills, modes of being, and ways of articulating our agency.

The epically obese woman played by Michelle (aka Trixxter Bombshell) in the 2010 video SQUEEZE is paradigmatic. While other women are shown toiling away, she sits in a state of dignified rest on a creaky rotating disk in a tiny cubicle set into the wall of a grotty, rundown room. Her torpor seems key in some mysterious way to the structures of production; indeed, the artist has explained that the character is giving directions "via telekinesis."[2] We are drawn into a coalitional appreciation of female power that accrues through action (even when it appears as inaction), not exhibitionism, as is so often the case in patriarchal cultures that subordinate women to the image.

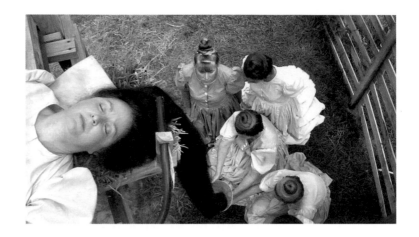

MIKA ROTTENBERG, CHEESE, 2008,
multi-channel video installation with sound,
16 min., dimensions variable /
KÄSE, Mehr-Kanal-Videoinstallation
mit Ton, Masse variabel.

As feminism progressed into the '80s, Marxist feminist critique became central. Barbara Kruger's UNTITLED/YOU ARE SEDUCED BY THE SEX APPEAL OF THE INORGANIC (1981)—a black-and-white photograph of two unmatched gloves (one apparently male, one apparently female) shaking "hands," a scene of displaced intimacy that is disrupted by the brazen text of the title in white over bright red—is a classic work of this genre. Borrowing a line from Walter Benjamin's 1930s critique of commodity fetishism, Kruger's work means business, and it tells you so. Rottenberg takes on the terms of this critique, but expands it through very different means. The humor in the grossness and excesses of her work overrides any sense of serious-ness, and the videos are not dominated by a sense of political motivation, although the issues of labor and gender are ultimately strongly asserted across her oeuvre.

The acceleration and globalization of late capitalism—with the rich getting richer and richer off the backs of the working poor, often women—means that "women's work" is now a very different issue from how it was viewed by '70s feminists. Rottenberg's most recent videos expose the mechanisms of precarious labor across the globe, combining hired performers with actual workers in a mix of invented and real-world situations. In SQUEEZE, both Mexican women picking lettuce in a field in Arizona and Indian women in a rubber-tree plantation reach down into the ground to have their arms massaged by a row of Chinese women—all of these workers read as third-world laborers, anonymized by late capitalism. As their arms cross time and space in the vast network of globalized labor, they also change direction from vertical to horizontal planes of action.

These interconnections and disorientations are also seen in NONOSEKNOWS (2015), which focuses on the sweatshops of women behind the booming Chinese pearl industry. The large white woman who might be in charge of the pearl factory—and who mysteriously sneezes out plates of spaghetti from an ever-extending prosthetic nose—is linked to the Chinese women who plant irritants in oysters in order to stimulate the production of pearls: She periodically uses a spray bottle to mist a pair of feet that poke up from a bucket of pearls on the floor of her office; these feet are shown to belong to a worker sitting in the sweatshop below, which would mean that one of these spaces is upside-down.

The nadir of this activity is a woman sitting alone between a massive heap of mussels and one of cracked shells, taking the live creatures one by one, splitting them open, and squeezing pearls out of the no doubt stinky, rubbery flesh into buckets. The squelching and cracking sounds, the dampness everywhere (the woman wears rubber boots), the squalid cement room—everything conspires to produce a situation that is both radically disgusting and deeply sad. All of this waste of life and effort for piles of fetid garbage and slimy pearls, which will no doubt be used to adorn bourgeois and wealthy women in China and beyond. Here Rottenberg points to the ultimate grossness: the system of global capitalism.

However, by immersing working women in novel versions of their usual spaces and paces of work, narrating their labor through new relationships and spatial disorientations, Rottenberg emphasizes their agency. In her videos, women's bodies are shown to be poignant, funny, and powerful—as if the laboring female body of Carolee Schneemann's intense early works or Ukeles's performances had been passed through the leavening matrix of the bad-girl posture as well as the digestive tract of Paul McCarthy (whose work I consider to be seriously gender-critical and feminist in effect)—"eww, gross" meets the personal is political. We form coalitions over things that revolt and compel us: Girl power can be found in the enjoyment of, while simultaneously being creeped out by, the gross. Through such means we can accept excess as potential pleasure rather than acceding to the limiting positions allotted us by our culture and chafing against the boundaries created to keep us quiet. Maybe we teenage girls were onto something in the '70s.

1) On Rottenberg's relationship to feminism, see her interview with Christopher Bedford, in *Mika Rottenberg: The Production of Luck* (New York: Gregory R. Miller & Co., and Waltham, MA: Rose Art Museum, 2014), 205.
2) Mika Rottenberg, in an interview with Judith Hudson, *Bomb 113* (Fall 2010), www.bombmagazine.org/article/3617/mika-rottenberg (accessed February 10, 2016).

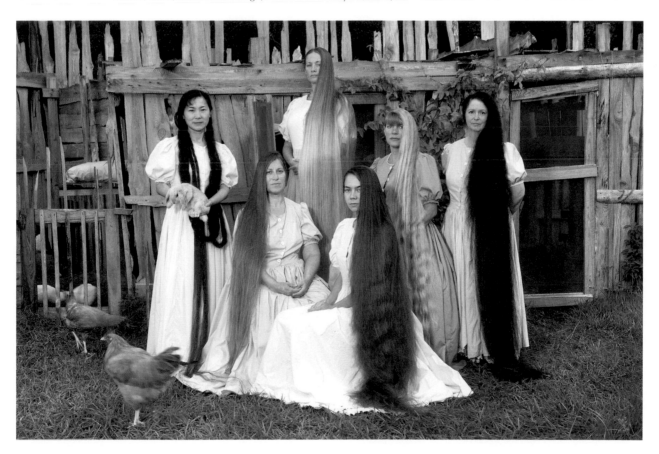

MIKA ROTTENBERG, CHEESE, 2008, multi-channel video installation with sound, 16 min., dimensions variable / KÄSE, Mehr-Kanal-Videoinstallation mit Ton, Masse variabel.

AMELIA JONES

«Igitt, wie eklig!»

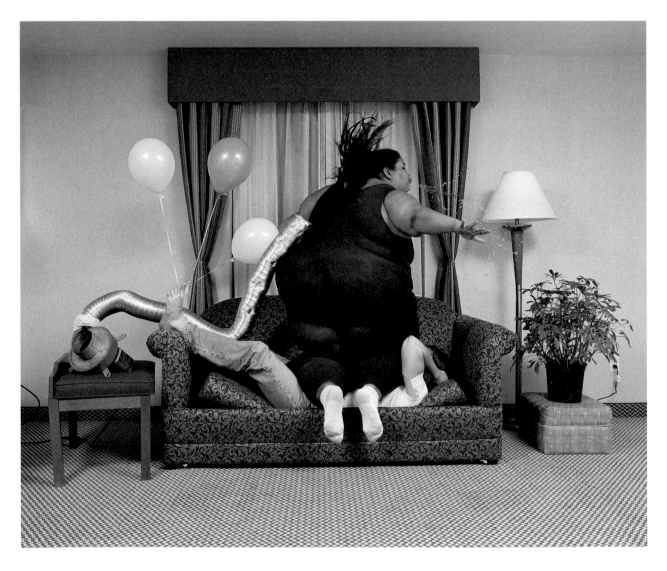

Mika Rottenbergs spätkapitalistischer Feminismus

MIKA ROTTENBERG, 5 SECOND PARTY, 2006, c-print, 50 x 60" /
5-SEKUNDEN-PARTY, C-Print, 127 x 152,4 cm.

Als Mittelschülerinnen im US-Staat North Carolina der 70er-Jahre waren meine Freundinnen und ich fasziniert vom Wort «eklig», mit dem wir alles schlechtmachten, was uns sinnlich oder gefühlsmässig widerwärtig, verstörend oder unangenehm erschien. Sätze wie «Jean geht mit Vance aus» oder «Ich habe mein Mittagessen ins Gras fallen lassen» pflegten den Kommentar «Igitt, eklig!» hervorzurufen, häufig begleitet von einem Naserümpfen. Die Welt war ein Ort voller Herausforderungen und das Wörtchen «eklig» half uns, sie nach Geniessbarem und Widerlichem zu sortieren. Dabei brachte das, was uns «eklig» erschien, die Ordnung der Dinge offensichtlich nicht sonderlich durcheinander – unter Umständen signalisierte es sogar etwas irgendwie Wünschenswertes, war es doch verboten. Das Melodram funktionierte aber auf seltsame Weise als eine Form der Selbstermächtigung für Mädchen, die in einer Welt von Jungs gehört werden wollten. Das die Äusserung begleitende Gekreisch und Gekicher gehörte dazu: Um Jungs (oder potenziell andere Mädchen) auf uns aufmerksam zu machen und sie gleichzeitig abzustossen, schufen wir unsere eigene Welt.

Angesichts dieses bündnishaften Weltenschaffungseffekts überrascht es nicht, dass sich feministische Künstlerinnen zu verschiedenen Zeitpunkten ähnliche Strategien zu eigen gemacht haben, vor allem die sogenannte Bad-Girl-Kunst der 90er-Jahre, bei der sich Entrüstung mit Humor verbindet, um die Auswirkungen von Misogynie in der Welt der Kunst und darüber hinaus anzuprangern, zu kritisieren und aufzudecken. Diese Arbeiten sind brutal und doch witzig, verführerisch wie abstossend. Exemplarisch für jene Zeit sind das 1992 entstandene Gemälde A FUNNY THING HAPPENED ON THE WAY TO THE . . . (Etwas Komisches geschah auf dem Weg zu …) von Sue Williams, das Cartoon-artige Darstellungen von Vergewaltigungsszenen zeigt, und Sarah Lucas' sarkastische Arbeit BITCH aus dem Jahr 1995, die aus einem Tisch besteht, von dem ein Fisch und ein mit Orangen gefülltes T-Shirt herabhängen (was sich als krude symbolische Darstellung einer klischeehaften Version des weiblichen Körpers samt Geruch liest).

Mika Rottenberg schafft ähnlich bissige und witzige – wiewohl weniger offenkundig zornige – feministische Arbeiten, komplexe Videos und Installationen, die mit ihren körperlichen Exzessen, ihrer überbordenden Energie und ihrem frechen Sinn für Humor (der häufig bei Mädchen im Teenageralter anzutreffen ist) für mich einen Igitt-Effekt hervorrufen. Bei gleichgesinnten feministischen Betrachtern erzeugen sie einen Wiedererkennungseffekt und fördern ein Gefühl der Solidariät angesichts der Absurditäten des vergeschlechtlichten und kontrollierten Körpers. Rottenbergs Praxis hat aber nicht nur mit der Bad-Girl-Haltung der 90er-Jahre zu tun, sondern ist auch früheren Strategien feministischer Kunst verpflichtet.

AMELIA JONES ist Robert-A.-Day-Professorin für Kunst und Design und Prodekanin für kritische Studien an der Roski School of Art and Design der University of Southern California in Los Angeles.

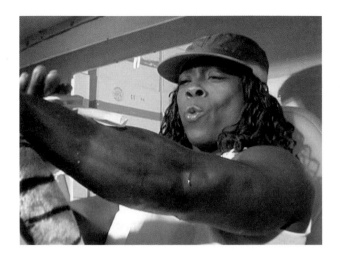 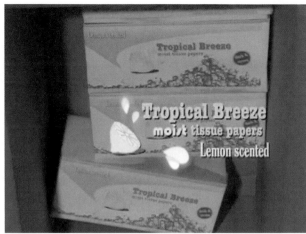

MIKA ROTTENBERG, TROPICAL BREEZE, 2004, single-channel video
installation with sound, 3 min. 45 sec., dimensions variable /
TROPISCHE BRISE, 1-Kanal-Videoinstallation mit Ton, Masse variabel.

Ihr Werk bietet damit eine Gelegenheit, diese Vermächtnisse zu überdenken und zeitgemässere feministische Bezugssysteme und Taktiken in der Kunst zu erkunden.[1]

In ihren Anfängen drehte sich die feministische Körperkunst hauptsächlich darum, die verführerischen Qualitäten eines «idealen» (schlanken, weissen) weiblichen Körpers auszunutzen, und die feministische Videokunst erweiterte diese Praxis, indem sie mit den Erwartungen und Begierden der Betrachter spielte. Die frühen Videos von Lynda Benglis – wie etwa FEMALE SENSIBILITY (Weibliche Sensibilität, 1973), in dem zwei Frauen demonstrativ für die Videokamera miteinander rummachen – stehen exemplarisch für beide. Rottenbergs aufwändige Videoinstallationen reihen sich in diese Tradition ein, zeigen aber stattdessen weibliche Körper, die durch ethnische Vielfalt gekennzeichnet und ungewöhnlich sind: ausserordentlich grossgewachsen, muskulös, langhaarig oder üppig. Rottenbergs Darstellerinnen scheinen extreme Frauen für extreme Zeiten zu sein und sie sind oft kraftvoll und sinnlich in ihrer Stärke; sie sind nicht essentialisiert wie die «womyn» der separatistischen Phase der zweiten Welle der Frauenbewegung. Sie bekennen sich zu ihrem Exzess und ihre Körper quellen über: in jede Menge Schweiss wie in TROPICAL BREEZE (Tropische Brise, 2004), in lange Fingernägel wie in MARY'S CHERRIES (Marys Kirschen, 2005) und in überreichliches Haar in CHEESE (Käse, 2008). Wir lachen vielleicht, aber aus Solidarität, da Feministinnen des 21. Jahrhunderts sich der rauen Freuden, die die Bewegungen und Lüste des weiblichen Körpers bieten können, voll bewusst sind.

Das soll nicht heissen, dass feministische Arbeiten der 90er-Jahre nicht auch mit körperlichem Exzess spielten – man denke nur an Judy Chicagos MENSTRUATION BATHROOM (Menstruationsbadezimmer) im Rahmen des 1972 in Los Angeles realisierten Projekts WOMANHOUSE, wo sich die Toilette neben einem vor Monatsbinden und blutrot gefärbten Tampons überquellenden Abfalleimer befand. Künstlerinnen zelebrierten diese Aspekte weiblicher Verkörperlichung, die einer angewiderten Gesellschaft als etwas galten, was sich den für Kapitalismus wie Patriarchat wesentlichen Strukturen der Verdinglichung entzieht. In den Videos Rottenbergs indes wird sogar körperlicher Exzess durch die Mechanismen des Spätkapitalismus erfasst und verkauft: Schweiss wird zur Feuchtigkeit von Feuchttüchern, aus abgeschnittenen Fingernägeln werden Maraschinokirschen und lange Haarsträhnen dienen zur Herstellung von Haarwasser. Diese Verwandlungen mögen zwar phantastisch erscheinen, man sollte aber bedenken, dass Rottenbergs Darstellerinnen selbst ihre Körpermerkmale zu Geld gemacht haben, nämlich als Modelle, Ringerinnen, Bodybuilderinnen und «Quetscherinnen» (die den Wunsch derer erfüllen, die es mögen, wenn füllige Frauen sich auf sie setzen).

In den 70er-Jahren bestand ein anderes Hauptanliegen in den Kreisen feministischer Künstlerinnen darin, die Arbeit von Frauen im sozialen Bereich sichtbar zu machen. Mierle Ukeles' «Maintenance Art» (Instandhaltungs- oder Pflegekunst) stellte Frauenarbeit in eine Reihe mit unterbezahlter Arbeit, wie 1973 in der Performance, bei der sie während der Öffnungszeiten des Wadsworth Atheneum in Hartford im US-Bundesstaat Connecticut die Vortreppe dieses Kunstmuseums wusch. Im Jahr davor widmete sich Sandra Orgel im WOMAN-HOUSE dem Bügeln, wobei sie mit gelangweilter Wucht Falten attackierte. Da Hausfrauen der Mittelschicht damals zum grössten Teil zu Hause isoliert waren, konzentrierten sich die feministischen künstlerischen Kommentare auf Räume, die buchstäblich oder symbolisch mit dem Häuslichen verbunden waren. Meistens rackerte sich eine einzige Frau (im Fall Ukeles' und Orgels die Künstlerin selbst) vor Publikum ab und inszenierte so die Langeweile der Haushaltsarbeit oder niederer Tätigkeiten in einer Weise als Kunst, die beide Kategorien über den Haufen warf.

Rottenbergs Videos widerspiegeln den heutzutage höheren Anteil von erwerbstätigen Frauen, sie zeigen voneinander abhängige Körper, die durch Handlungs- und Reaktionsketten über kunstreiche Räume und umständlich-absurde Fliessbänder hinweg miteinander verbunden sind. In TROPICAL BREEZE etwa sitzt eine geschmeidige weisse Frau (gespielt von der äusserst biegsamen Tänzerin Felicia Ballos) auf einem Heimtrainer innerhalb eines LKW und zieht mit dem Fuss Papiertaschentücher aus einem Karton, klebt sie mit Kaugummi an einen Flaschenzug und befördert sie dann nach vorne zur Fahrerin, einer muskulösen schwarzen Frau (gespielt von Heather Foster, einem Bodybuilding-Champion). Die Fahrerin befeuchtet die Taschentücher mit ihrem Schweiss und sendet sie dann per Flaschenzug zurück, bereit, um als Feuchttücher (unter dem Markennamen Tropical Breeze) verkauft zu werden. Rottenberg choreographiert weibliche Körper in taylorisierten Bewegungen und hebt damit die repetitiven Bewegungen hervor, die zu absurden Erzeugnissen führen.

Rottenbergs Humor – mit Elementen der Slapstick-Komik, die zurückhaltend genug sind, um zu verhindern, dass das Ganze in Chaos ausartet – erinnert auch an die berühmte «Süsswarenfabrik»-Folge der protofeministischen Fernsehshow *I Love Lucy* aus dem Jahr 1952. Lucy und Ethel sind unfähig, Pralinen am Fliessband schnell genug einzuwickeln, was in dieser Parodie auf weibliche Masslosigkeit und Untauglichkeit zur Effizienzsteigerung dazu führt, dass sie sich die Pralinen in den Mund stopfen. Aber während Lucy in ihrer vorgeführten Unfähigkeit als bürgerliche Hausfrau clownesk war, hatte die echte Lucille Ball hinter den Kulissen das Sagen. Analog dazu sind die sich abrackernden Frauen bei Rottenberg trotz endloser, sisyphusmässiger Anstrengungen ebenfalls ungemein effektiv, indem sie die Produktion erfolgreich vorantreiben, wenn auch nur in ganz kleinen Schritten. Sie sind zudem affektbetont in ihren exzentrischen Körpertypen, ihrer Kraft und Behändigkeit, ihrer schlichten Ausserordentlichkeit – einer Ausserordentlichkeit, die sich als Bekräftigung der enormen Bandbreite potenzieller Fähigkeiten, Seinsweisen und Artikulationsweisen der Handlungskompetenz von Frauen Geltung verschafft.

Die unglaublich korpulente Frau, die Trixxter Bombshell (alias Michelle) in dem 2010 entstandenen Video SQUEEZE (Quetschen, 2010) spielt, ist paradigmatisch. Während andere

Frauen beim Rackern zu sehen sind, sitzt sie in würdevollem Ruhezustand auf einer knirschenden Drehscheibe in einer winzigen Box, die in die Wand eines schäbigen, heruntergekommenen Raums eingelassen ist. Ihre Starre scheint auf irgendeine geheimnisvolle Weise entscheidend für die Produktionsstrukturen zu sein. Tatsächlich hat die Künstlerin erklärt, die Figur gebe «mittels Telekinese» Anweisungen.[2] Wir werden in eine bündnishafte Würdigung weiblicher Macht hineingezogen, die aus Tätigkeit erwächst (auch wenn sie wie Untätigkeit erscheint) und nicht aus Exhibitionismus, wie dies in patriarchalischen Kulturen, die Frauen dem Bild unterordnen, so oft der Fall ist.

Im Zuge der Weiterentwicklung des Feminismus in den 80er-Jahren rückte die marxistische feministische Kritik in den Mittelpunkt. Ein klassisches Werk dieses Genres ist Barbara Krugers UNTITLED/YOU ARE SEDUCED BY THE SEX APPEAL OF THE INORGANIC (Ohne Titel/Ihr lasst euch durch den Sex-Appeal des Anorganischen verführen, 1981), ein Schwarz-Weiss-Photo zweier unpaariger Handschuhe (einer scheint männlich zu sein und einer weiblich), die sich «die Hand geben»: eine Szene der verlagerten Intimität, die durch den dreisten Text des in Weiss auf Knallrot geschriebenen Titels gestört wird. In Anlehnung an einen in den 30er-Jahren im Rahmen seiner Kritik des Warenfetischismus formulierten Satz Walter Benjamins meint Krugers Werk es ernst und sagt euch das auch. Rottenberg greift die Begriffe dieser Kritik auf, erweitert sie aber auf ganz andere Weise. Der Humor in der Ekligkeit und den Exzessen ihres Werkes hebt jeden Eindruck der Ernsthaftigkeit auf und die Videos werden nicht von einem Bewusstsein der politischen Motivation beherrscht, obwohl die Themen von Arbeit und Geschlecht im Endeffekt quer durch ihr Schaffen emphatisch geltend gemacht werden.

Die Folgen der Beschleunigung und Globalisierung des Spätkapitalismus – im Zuge dessen die Reichen auf Kosten der Erwerbsarmen, vielfach Frauen, immer reicher werden – sind auch, dass «Frauenarbeit» sich als Problem heute ganz anders darstellt als für die Feministinnen der 70er-Jahre. Rottenbergs jüngste Videos legen die Mechanismen prekärer Arbeit rund um die Welt bloss, indem sie in einer Mischung aus erfundenen und realen Situationen angeheuerte Darstellerinnen mit tatsächlichen Arbeiterinnen zusammenbringen. In SQUEEZE reichen mexikanische Frauen, die auf einem Acker in Arizona Salat ernten, wie auch indische Frauen auf einer Gummibaum-Plantage herunter in den Boden, um sich von einer Reihe chinesischer Frauen die Arme massieren zu lassen, wobei all diese Arbeiterinnen als durch den Spätkapitalismus anonymisierte Drittweltarbeiterinnen zu verstehen sind. Während ihre Arme im ausgedehnten Netz globalisierter Arbeit Zeit und Raum durchqueren, ändern sie zugleich ihre Richtung von senkrechten in waagerechte Ebenen der Tätigkeit.

Diese Verbindungen und Desorientierungen finden sich auch in der Arbeit NONOSE-KNOWS (KeineNaseWeiss, 2015), in deren Mittelpunkt die die Frauen ausbeutenden Betriebe hinter der boomenden chinesischen Perlenindustrie stehen. Die dicke weisse Frau, die möglicherweise die Perlenfabrik leitet – und die aus einer immer länger werdenden prothetischen Nase auf mysteriöse Weise Spaghetti-Teller niest –, wird mit den chinesischen Frauen in Verbindung gebracht, die Reizmittel in Austern einpflanzen, um die Produktion von Perlen anzuregen. Sie verwendet regelmässig eine Sprayflasche, um ein Paar Füsse zu befeuchten, die aus einem Eimer mit Perlen auf dem Fussboden ihres Büros herausragen. Diese Füsse gehören, wie sich zeigt, einer Arbeiterin, die im Ausbeuterbetrieb darunter sitzt, was bedeutet, dass einer der Räume auf dem Kopf stehen müsste.

Tiefpunkt dieser Aktivität ist eine Frau, die alleine zwischen einem riesigen Haufen Muscheln und einem Haufen geknackter Austernschalen sitzt und die Lebewesen eins nach dem

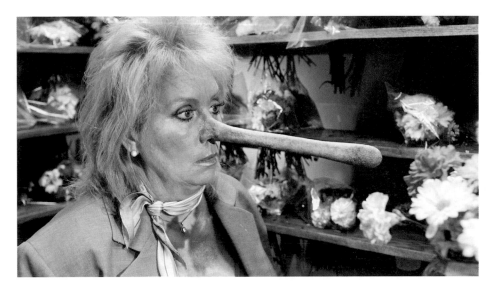

MIKA ROTTENBERG, NONOSEKNOWS, 2015, video with sound and sculptural installation, 22 min., dimensions variable / KEINENASEWEISS, Video mit Ton und skulpturaler Installation, Masse variabel.

anderen in die Hand nimmt, aufbricht und die Perlen aus dem zweifelsohne stinkenden, gummiartigen Fleisch in Kübel auspresst. Die Schmatz- und Knackgeräusche, die Feuchtigkeit allenthalben (die Frau trägt Stiefel), der dreckige Zementraum: Alles trägt dazu bei, eine Situation zu schaffen, die gleichzeitig extrem eklig und zutiefst traurig ist. All diese Verschwendung von Leben und Arbeit für haufenweise übelriechenden Abfall und schleimige Perlen, die ohne Frage bürgerlichen und wohlhabenden Frauen in China und darüber hinaus zur Zierde dienen werden. Hier weist Rottenberg auf die ultimative Ekligkeit hin, nämlich das System des globalen Kapitalismus.

Indem Rottenberg arbeitende Frauen in neue Varianten ihrer üblichen Räume und Arbeitstempi hineinversetzt, wobei ihre Arbeit durch neue Beziehungen und räumliche Desorientierungen dargestellt wird, betont sie die Handlungskompetenz dieser Frauen. In ihren Videos erscheinen die Körper der Frauen ergreifend, komisch und kraftvoll – so, als wäre der arbeitende weibliche Körper von Carolee Schneemanns intensiven frühen Arbeiten oder von Ukeles' Performances durch die auflockernde Matrix der Bad-Girl-Pose wie auch durch den Verdauungstrakt von Paul McCarthy (dessen Werk ich tatsächlich für ernsthaft geschlechterkritisch und feministisch erachte) geführt worden: «Igitt, eklig!» trifft auf «Das Private ist politisch». Wir bilden Koalitionen wegen Sachen, die uns abstossen und nötigen: Girlpower lässt sich im Genuss des Ekligen finden, während es gleichzeitig Angst macht. Durch solche Mittel können wir Exzess als potenziellen Genuss akzeptieren, statt den einschränkenden Positionen zuzustimmen, die uns von unserer Kultur zugewiesen werden, und uns an den Grenzen zu reiben, die inszeniert wurden, um uns ruhig zu halten. Vielleicht waren wir Teenager-Mädchen auf der richtigen Spur in den 70er-Jahren.

(Übersetzung: Bram Opstelten)

1) Zu Rottenbergs Verhältnis zum Feminismus siehe ihr Interview mit Christopher Bedford, in *Mika Rottenberg: The Production of Luck*, Gregory R. Miller & Co., New York, and Rose Art Museum, Waltham, MA, 2014, S. 205.
2) Mika Rottenberg im Gespräch mit Judith Hudson, in *Bomb*, Nr. 113 (Herbst 2010), www.bombmagazine.org/article/3617/mika-rottenberg (letzter Zugriff am 10. Februar 2016).

GERMANO CELANT

Mika Rottenberg's BACHELOR(ETTE)

Mika Rottenberg's installations shift from environment to video and back again. As the artist has explained, "In other mediums like sculpture or painting, it is obvious that a work has specific dimensions and light conditions; I think video should be treated in the same way."[1] The limitation, specificity, and irregularity of her spaces invite viewers to take in her work through not only their eyes but all their senses, an approach to visual narration that is at once biological, cerebral, psychological, environmental, historical, and sociocultural. Rottenberg's imaginary machines put bodies into action, both those of her on-screen characters and her audience, abolishing the distance between them: Our experience of our own corporeality increases our empathy with the video's subjects. This strategy is quite different from that of previous video artists, from Bill Viola to Matthew Barney, Isaac Julien, and Douglas Gordon, who placed the audience in front of their work, keeping the two separate. Rottenberg's logic of presentation is instead in tune with the work of other artists of her generation—such as Nathalie Djurberg and Ragnar Kjartansson—who establish a dialogue between

sculptural environment and moving image in order to turn a mental and visual relationship into a concrete experience.

Rottenberg's videos document employees, predominantly female, both fictive and real, in work situations. Typically, they carry out their duties in solitude and silence, laboring in a chain of individual cramped spaces as they operate convoluted pulleys and sheaves. Some of the characters' actions appear purposeless, of no apparent use apart from the surreal internal logic that informs the narrative. These assembly lines can be organized vertically (e.g, MARY'S CHERRIES, 2004) or horizontally (e.g., TROPICAL BREEZE, 2004). Fueled by human matter, such as red-polished fingernails in MARY'S CHERRIES and sweat in TROPICAL BREEZE, the machinery churns out commercial products: maraschino cherries and lemon-scented wet wipes.

Each video presents a working entity that functions as an autonomous organism, endowed with a life of its own, yet absurd—something like a "bachelor machine," as defined by Michel Carrouges:

The bachelor machine appears first of all as an impossible, useless, incomprehensible, delirious machine. It may not even appear at all, depending on how far it blends into the landscape surrounding it. The bachelor machine may

---

GERMANO CELANT is an Italian art historian, critic, and curator.

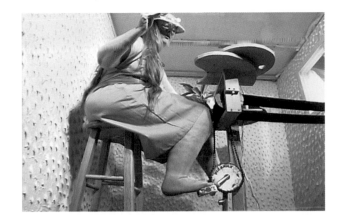

MIKA ROTTENBERG, MARY'S CHERRIES, 2004,
single channel video installation, 5 min. 50 sec.,
dimensions variable / MARYS KIRSCHEN, 1-Kanal-
Videoinstallation, Masse variabel.

MACHINES*

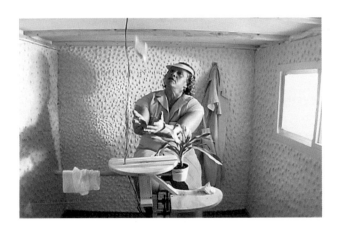

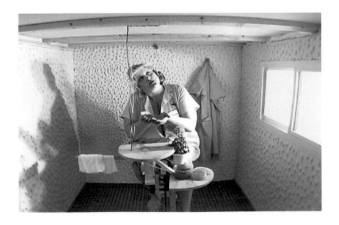

therefore consist of a single peculiar and unknown machine, or of an apparently heteroclite assemblage. . . . The bachelor machine has no reason for existing in itself, as a machine governed by the physical laws of mechanics or by the social laws of utility. It is a semblance of machinery, of the kind seen in dreams, at the theatre, at the cinema or even in cosmonauts' training areas. Governed primarily by the mental laws of subjectivity, the bachelor machine merely adopts certain mechanical forms in order to simulate certain mechanical effects.[2]

Carrouges identifies bachelor machines in the writings of Franz Kafka, Raymond Roussel, Alfred Jarry, and Jules Verne, but he takes the term from Marcel Duchamp and his enigmatic work THE BRIDE STRIPPED BARE BY HER BACHELORS, EVEN (1915–23), also known as THE LARGE GLASS. Made out of a sheet of glass that is traversed by objects and shapes drawn in perspective, so that they appear to be suspended in midair, THE LARGE GLASS places two entities in parallel: the Bride and her Bachelors. As Alain Montesse writes, "Structurally, a bachelor machine looks like a two-storey arrangement, the lower storey being occupied by a reclining man who is the victim of various torments coming from the storey above."[3]

In THE LARGE GLASS, the upper tier belongs to the Bride while the lower panel is the Bachelors'

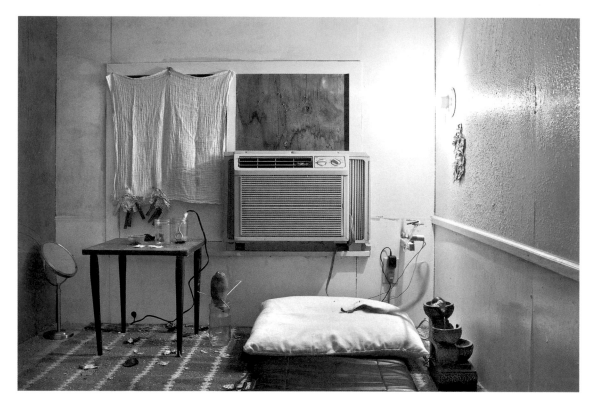

MIKA ROTTENBERG, BOWLS BALLS SOULS HOLES, 2014, video with sound and sculptural installation, 28 min., dimensions variable / SCHALEN BÄLLE SEELEN LÖCHER, Video mit Ton und skulpturaler Installation, Masse variabel.

Domain, made up of nine "Malic Molds." The relationship between the two parts is governed and activated by interacting mechanisms: bars, rods, pistons, cylinders, racks, gears, rollers, levers, rotors, wheels, flywheels, wires, faucets, cranks, and pulleys. Duchamp's intention was to describe a relationship using a system that would not be corporeal and carnal but instead mental and mechanical. While the Bride is a new human being who cannot be defined in either physiological or psychological terms,[4] the Bachelors who occupy the earthbound domain below do not have the same energy and autonomy; they are guided by orders and impulses that they don't understand. They represent a group like the factory or the crowd, destined to receive the secretions and humus that comes from above.

Even from this reductive and basic description, the analogies between Duchamp's bachelor machine and Rottenberg's assemblages are evident. The dimension of transit and interaction between THE LARGE GLASS's two zones regulates and plans the bachelor machine, as in Rottenberg's work. The lower section of THE LARGE GLASS features a chocolate grinder, which produces an edible material; similarly, the lower parts of Rottenberg's machines are a place of production: an image of modern and industrial society. However, Rottenberg explores a circulation that is no longer conceptual and theoretical, abstract and mechanical, and definitely male. Her goal is an interpretation of the machine of living that is not just intellectual and mental but carried out through physical and bodily feeling. Furthermore, of course, her machine is distinctly *female*.

Rottenberg's recent work NONOSEKNOWS (2015), embraces additional modes of subverting and inverting the bachelor machine. While the artist continues to use the terms of THE LARGE GLASS, she extends them to include a vision of the real urban, social, and economic context in which the narrated events take place—a mixture of the real and fantastic that makes the bachelor(ette) machine look more and more like a true expression of society.

The protagonist of NONOSEKNOWS is a woman of imposing physical stature, who suggests the Bride. Arriving at her place of work, she passes through a series of empty spaces with colored walls, animated by large soap bubbles, on her way to a brightly lit office, filled with flowers and dishes of uneaten food. Here her activity consists of sniffing flowers and sneezing, which produces a plate of noodles. On the lower level, corresponding to the world of the Bachelors, dozens of women labor in cold, damp conditions. Filmed at a pearl factory in China, these scenes show three groups of women: The first group places irritants in mussels to produce pearls; next, a single woman shucks a pile of mussels, scooping out their pearls with her fingers and pouring them into a basin; and finally, another group sorts the pearls.

These three spaces and work units represent the meticulous chain of capitalist exploitation—yet, in one of these rooms, a single female worker appears idle; she sleeps with her head on a table, and her feet buried in a bucket of pearls. Her behavior echoes that of the performers Michelle and Sakina, who play similar roles in SQUEEZE (2010) and BOWLS BALLS SOULS HOLES (2014). Moving between wakefulness and slumber, they are aware of their own autonomous power; they are integrated into the system, yet remain in communication with another world. The sweatshop worker might seem to be unconscious, but her feet reappear in the space of the dominant figure

on the upper tier, sticking out of a basket of pearls—now upside down, they represent the possibility of disrupting the system.

In the end, however, the system is not altered, and the Bride remains the mechanism that powers the universe of the Bachelor(ette) workers below. Toward the video's conclusion, the Bride's nose extends to penetrate a hole in the wall behind the flower bouquets. This intervention appears to pop the bubbles in the hallway, which vanish in a puff of smoke. Finally, just before she leaves the office, the Bride sprays water on the feet below her desk, bringing her various functions to a close: control of the passions and force of the Bachelor(ette)s as well as the system of production, and a cooling of their extremities—if not their extremism.

(Translation: Shanti Evans)

* This text is the result of a dramatic editing by Nikki Columbus of a 9,500-word text by Germano Celant that will be published in its totality in the near future.

1) Christopher Bedford, "Interview with Mika Rottenberg," in *Mika Rottenberg: The Production of Luck* (New York: Gregory R. Miller & Co. in association with the Rose Museum, 2014), 221.
2) Michel Carrouges, "Mode d'emploi," in *Les Machines Célibataires* (Paris: Arcanes, 1954). Transl. into English as "Directions for Use," in *Le Macchine Celibi / The Bachelor Machines*, ed. Harald Szeemann (New York: Rizzoli, 1975), 21.
3) Alain Montesse, "Lovely Rita, Meter Maid," in *Le Macchine Celibi / The Bachelor Machines*, op. cit., 110.
4) Arturo Schwarz, *The Complete Works of Marcel Duchamp* (New York: Harry N. Abrams, 1969).

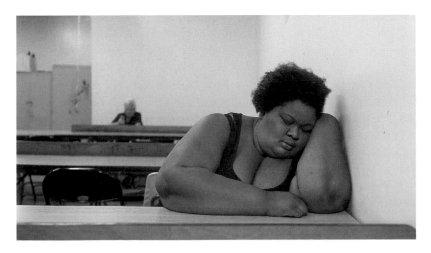

MIKA ROTTENBERG, BOWLS BALLS SOULS HOLES, 2014, video with sound and sculptural installation, 28 min., dimensions variable / SCHALEN BÄLLE SEELEN LÖCHER, Video mit Ton und skulpturaler Installation, Masse variabel.

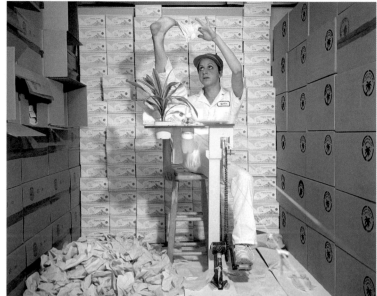
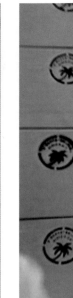

MIKA ROTTENBERG, TROPICAL BREEZE,
2004, single-channel video installation with
sound, 3 min. 45 sec., dimensions variable /
TROPISCHE BRISE, 1-Kanal-Videoinstallation
mit Ton, Masse variabel.

Mika Rottenbergs
JUNGGESELL (INN)

Die Installationen von Mika Rottenberg wechseln von Environment zu Video und wieder zurück. Die Künstlerin erklärt: «In anderen Medien wie Skulptur oder Malerei ist es normal, dass ein Werk bestimmte Abmessungen und Lichtverhältnisse hat. Ich glaube, man sollte es mit Videos genauso halten.»[1] Die Begrenztheit, die Besonderheit und die Unregelmässigkeit ihrer Räume laden den Betrachter ein, das Werk nicht nur mit den Augen, sondern mit allen Sinnen zu erleben – Rottenberg praktiziert eine zugleich biologische, ökologische, psychologische, intellektuelle, historische und soziokulturelle Technik des visuellen Erzählens. Ihre Imaginationsmaschinen setzen Körper in Bewegung, die Körper der Darsteller wie die der Zuschauer, wobei die Distanz zwischen beiden aufgehoben wird. Die Erfahrung der eigenen Physis steigert unser Mitfühlen und Mitleben mit den dargestellten Personen. Rottenbergs Strategie unterscheidet sich deutlich von jener früherer Videokünstler, von Bill Viola über Matthew Barney bis zu Isaac Julien und Douglas Gordon, die dem Publikum einen Platz vor dem Werk zuwies und beide säuberlich getrennt hielt. Dafür finden wir einen ähnlichen Präsentationsmodus bei KünstlerInnen ihrer Generation wie Nathalie Djurberg oder Ragnar Kjartansson, die einen Dialog zwischen skulpturaler Situation und bewegtem Bild in Gang setzen, um eine geistige oder visuelle Auseinandersetzung in ein vitales Erlebnis zu verwandeln.

GERMANO CELANT ist ein italienischer Kunsthistoriker, Kritiker und Kurator.

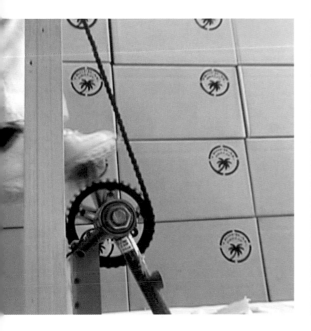
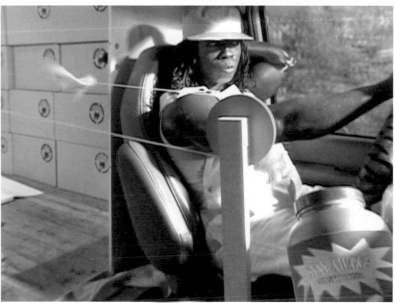

GERMANO CELANT

ENMASCHINEN*

Rottenbergs Videos dokumenticren grösstenteils Frauen in realen und fiktiven Arbeitsverhältnissen. Zumeist führen sie ihre Aufgaben still und alleine in einer Reihe enger Einzelräume aus, in denen sie umständliche mechanische Vorrichtungen aus Flaschenzügen und Seilwinden bedienen. Einigen dieser Handlungen fehlt ein klar ersichtlicher Sinn und Zweck, der über die innere surreale Logik der Erzählung hinausgeht. Die Fliessbänder können vertikal (MARY'S CHERRIES, Marys Kirschen, 2004) oder horizontal (TROPICAL BREEZE, Tropische Brise, 2004) angeordnet sein. Mit menschlichen Substanzen wie rot lackierten Fingernägeln (MARY'S CHERRIES) oder Schweiss (TROPICAL BREEZE) gespeist, bringen die Apparaturen gängige Konsumartikel hervor: Maraschinokirschen und Erfrischungstücher mit Zitronenduft.

Jedes Video zeigt eine Produktionseinheit, die wie ein autonomer Organismus funktioniert und von einem eigenen, wenn auch absurden Leben beseelt ist – nach Art einer «Junggesellenmaschine» gemäss der Definition von Michel Carrouges:

Im Gegensatz zu wirklichen Maschinen und sogar im Gegensatz zu imaginären, aber rationellen und nützlichen Maschinen ... erscheint die Junggesellenmaschine als unmöglich, unnütz, unverständlich, wahnsinnig. Manchmal ist sie überhaupt nicht auszumachen. Nämlich dann, wenn sie eins ist mit der sie umgebenden Landschaft. Die Junggesellenmaschine kann also aus einer einzigen, seltsamen, merkwürdigen und unbekannten Maschine oder aus einem anscheinend sinnlosen Gefüge bestehen ... Die Junggesellenmaschine ist nicht zweckgebunden wie eine von den physikalischen Gesetzen der Mechanik und den gesellschaftlichen

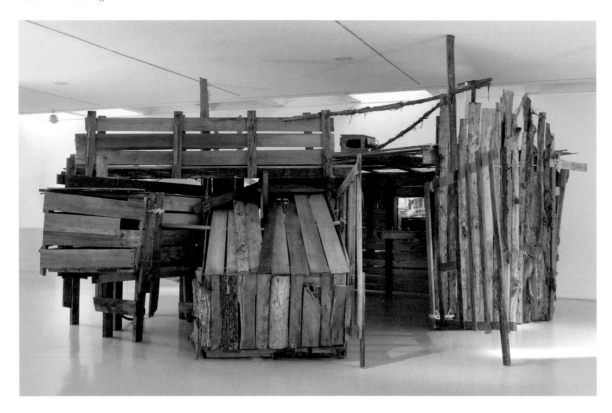

MIKA ROTTENBERG, CHEESE, 2008, installation views, Herzliya Museum of Contemporary Art Herzliya, 2013 / KÄSE, Installationsansichten. (PHOTOS: YIGAL PARDO)

MIKA ROTTENBERG, NONOSEKNOWS, 2015, installation view, Venice Biennale, 2015 / KEINENASEWEISS, Installationsansicht.

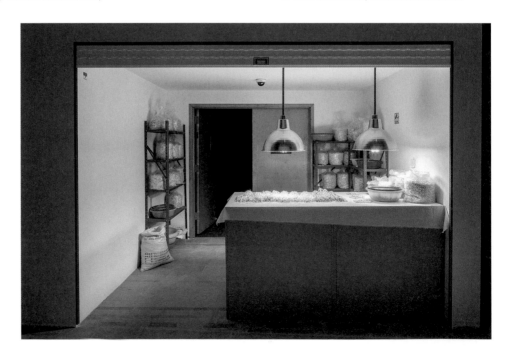

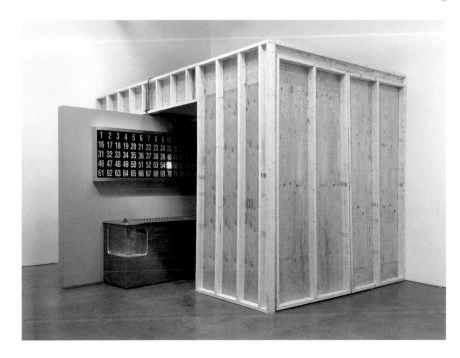

MIKA ROTTENBERG, BOWLS BALLS
SOULS HOLES, 2014, installation view,
Andrea Rosen Gallery, New York /
SCHALEN BÄLLE SEELEN LÖCHER,
Installationsansicht.

Gesetzen des Nutzens abhängige Maschine. Die Junggesellenmaschine ist ein Trugbild, dem man im Traum begegnet, im Theater, im Kino oder auf dem Übungsgelände der Kosmonauten. Die vor allem den geistigen Gesetzen der Subjektivität unterliegende Junggesellenmaschine eignet sich bestimmte mechanische Muster zur Vortäuschung bestimmter mechanischer Effekte an.[2]

Carrouges weist Junggesellenmaschinen in den Schriften von Franz Kafka, Raymond Roussel, Alfred Jarry und Jules Verne nach. Der Begriff selbst entstammt Marcel Duchamps vieldeutigem Hauptwerk LA MARIÉE MISE À NU PAR SES CÉLIBATAIRES, MÊME (Die Braut, von ihren Junggesellen entkleidet, sogar, 1915–1923), kurz DAS GROSSE GLAS genannt. Eine Glasplatte ist mit perspektivisch dargestellten Objekten und Formen versehen, die in der Luft zu schweben scheinen. Insgesamt stehen sich im GROSSEN GLAS zwei Wesenheiten gegenüber: die Braut und die Junggesellen. Alain Montesse schrieb: «Eine Junggesellenmaschine ist in ihrer Struktur zweistöckig, das Geschehen spielt sich auf zwei Ebenen ab. Die untere wird von einem liegenden Menschen eingenommen. Er ist das Opfer verschiedenartiger Qualen, die ihm von oben her zugefügt werden.»[3]

Im GROSSEN GLAS wird die obere Etage von der Braut bewohnt, während die untere den Jungge-

sellen gehört, verkörpert durch neun «moules mâlics» (männliche Gussformen). Die Kommunikation zwischen den beiden Bereichen bewerkstelligt eine Reihe ineinandergreifender Mechanismen: Rahmen, Stangen, Rohre, Kolben, Zylinder, Räder, Zahnräder, Laufräder, Schwungräder, Flaschenzüge, Rollen, Hebel, Kurbeln, Drähte und Wasserhähne. Duchamp wollte ein Beziehungssystem beschreiben, das nicht nur auf körperlicher und fleischlicher, sondern auch auf geistiger und mechanischer Ebene operiert. Die Braut repräsentiert ein menschliches Wesen neuer Art, das sich weder mit physiologischen noch mit psychologischen Begriffen fassen lässt.[4] Die Junggesellen im erdverbundenen Untergeschoss erlangen nicht dasselbe Energie- und Autonomieniveau. Sie sind Regel- und Triebkräften unterworfen, die sie nicht verstehen, und empfangen als Vertreter der arbeitenden Masse Ausscheidungs- und Zersetzungsprodukte von oben.

Bereits diese stark vereinfachte Darstellung macht deutlich, dass zwischen Duchamps Junggesellenmaschine und Rottenbergs Assemblagen unübersehbare Gemeinsamkeiten bestehen. Wie bei Rottenberg wird die Junggesellenmaschine des GROSSEN GLASES durch die Dimension des Austauschs und der Wechselwirkung zwischen ihren zwei Zonen reguliert und kontrolliert. Im unteren Teil befindet sich eine Schokoladenmühle, die Essbares erzeugt. Die untere Region von Rottenbergs Maschinen ist gleichfalls Ort der Produktion: ein Abbild der modernen Industriegesellschaft. Allerdings untersucht Rottenberg Kreisläufe, die nicht länger konzeptuell und theoretisch, abstrakt und mechanisch und schon gar nicht männlich sind. Ihr Bild der Maschine des Lebens soll mehr sein als ein konzeptuelles und intellektuelles Konstrukt. Es artikuliert sich mittels physischer, körperlicher Empfindungen und besitzt vor allem einen dezidiert *weiblichen* Charakter.

Rottenbergs Werke jüngeren Datums, BOWLS BALLS SOULS HOLES (Schalen, Bälle, Seelen, Löcher, 2014) und NONOSEKNOWS (KeineNaseWeiss, 2015), suchen nach neuen subversiven Möglichkeiten, die Junggesellenmaschine auf den Kopf zu stellen. Das Vokabular des GROSSEN GLASES, von dem Rottenberg nach wie vor Gebrauch macht, wird auf die Vision des realen urbanen, sozialen und ökonomischen Milieus ausgedehnt, in dem die geschilderten Ereignisse stattfinden – einer Mischung aus Wirklichkeit und Phantasie, vor deren Hintergrund die Junggesell(inn)enmaschine mehr und mehr wie ein wahrheitsgetreues Abbild der Gesellschaft wirkt.

Die Hauptrolle in NONOSEKNOWS spielt eine Frau von beeindruckender körperlicher Erscheinung, wohl eine Personifikation der Braut. Nach ihrer Ankunft am Arbeitsplatz durchquert sie eine Flucht leerer Räume mit farbigen Wänden, in denen riesige Seifenblasen wabern. Das hell erleuchtete Büro der Braut ist vollgeräumt mit Blumen und Esstellern. Ihre Arbeit besteht darin, an den Blumen zu riechen und zu niesen, wobei sie Teller mit Nudeln ausscheidet. In der unteren, feuchtkalten Etage, der Sphäre der Junggesellinnen, gehen Dutzende Frauen ihrer Beschäftigung nach. Die in einer chinesischen Perlenfabrik gedrehten Szenen zeigen drei Arbeitsschritte: Zuerst setzt eine Gruppe von Frauen Kerne in die Muscheln ein, um die sich Perlen bilden; als Nächstes löst eine Frau das Fleisch aus einem Haufen von Muscheln, entnimmt die Perlen und wirft sie in einen Behälter; abschliessend werden die Perlen von einer weiteren Gruppe sortiert.

Die drei Räume und Arbeitsschritte verdeutlichen die nahtlose Kette der kapitalistischen Ausbeutung.

Nur eine Arbeiterin scheint von der allgemeinen Betriebsamkeit unberührt. Sie schläft mit dem Kopf auf dem Tisch und ihre Füsse stecken in einem Kübel voll Perlen. Ihr Verhalten erinnert an die Darstellerinnen Michelle und Sakina, die in SQUEEZE (Presse, 2010) und BOWLS BALLS SOULS HOLES eine ähnliche Rolle spielen. Im Wechsel zwischen Wachsein und Schlaf wissen sie um ihre innere Kraft. Sie sind Teil des Systems und stehen trotzdem in Verbindung zu einer anderen Welt. Die Füsse der schlafenden Sweatshop-Arbeiterin ragen auf der darüberliegenden Chefinnenetage aus einem mit Perlen gefüllten Kübel – ihre inverse Position markiert die Möglichkeit, das System zu sabotieren.

Doch das System bleibt intakt und die Braut behält ihre Dominanz über die unter ihr liegende Welt der Junggesellinnen. Im letzten Teil des Videos bohrt die stark verlängerte Braut-Nase ein Loch in die Wand hinter den Blumenbuketts. Dadurch zerplatzen die Seifenblasen im Gang zu Rauchwolken. Kurz bevor sie ihr Büro verlässt, sprüht die Braut Wasser auf die Füsse unter dem Tisch. Der Kreis der vielseitigen Funktionen der Braut – ihre Kontrolle über die Leidenschaften und Kräfte der Junggesellinnen sowie über das gesamte Produktionssystem – schliesst sich mit dieser Kühlung der Extremitäten der Arbeiterschaft, wenn nicht gar ihres Extremismus.

(Übersetzung: Bernhard Geyer)

* Nikki Columbus stellte den vorliegenden Aufsatz aus einem längeren Text von Germano Celant zusammen, der zu einem späteren Zeitpunkt ungekürzt veröffentlicht wird.

1) Christopher Bedford, «Interview with Mika Rottenberg», in *Mika Rottenberg: The Production of Luck*, Gregory R. Miller & Co. mit dem Rose Art Museum at Brandeis University, New York 2014, S. 221.
2) Michel Carrouges, «Mode d'emploi», in *Les machines célibataires*, Arcanes, Paris: 1954; dt. «Gebrauchsanweisung. Was ist eine Junggesellenmaschine?», in *Junggesellenmaschinen, Reihe: Ästhetik und Naturwissenschaften / Medienkultur*, hrsg. von Hans Ulrich Reck und Harald Szeemann, Springer, New York 1999, S. 74–75.
3) Alain Montesse, «Lovely Rita, Meter Maid», in *Junggesellenmaschinen*, S. 172–173.
4) Arturo Schwarz, *The Complete Works of Marcel Duchamp*, Harry N. Abrams, New York 1969.

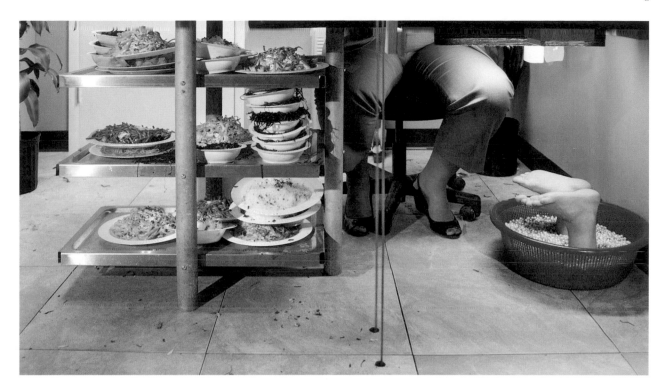

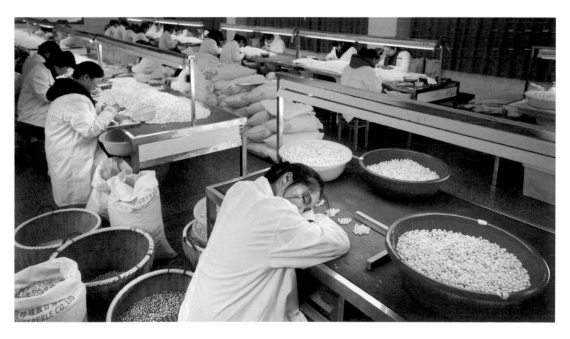

*MIKA ROTTENBERG, NONOSEKNOWS, 2015, video with sound
and sculptural installation, 22 min., dimensions variable /
KEINENASEWEISS, Video mit Ton und skulpturaler Installation, Masse variabel.*

189

EDITION FOR PARKETT 98

MIKA ROTTENBERG

BUBBLE 1 – BUBBLE 6

Single channel video in six versions, with sound,
approx. 15–40 sec. Loop.
Custom-made purse in oyster design
(plastic, silk lining, zipper / 4 ³/₄ x 2 ³/₈ x ¹/₂"),
with pearlescent capsule inside containing memory stick.
Video to be presented on video monitor.
Each video version Ed. 6/2APs signed and numbered certificate.

1-Kanal-Video in sechs Versionen, Ton,
ca. 15–40 Sek., Loop.
Täschchen in Austern-Design
(Plastik, Seidenfutter, Reisverschluss / 12 x 6 x 1 cm),
perlmutterbeschichtete Kapsel mit Speicherstick.
Video zu betrachten auf Videomonitor.
Jede Video-Version Auflage 6/2 E.A.,
signiertes und nummeriertes Zertifikat.

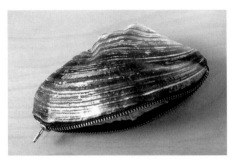

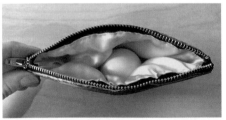

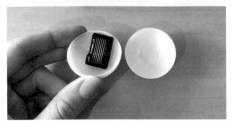

Purse in oyster design with pearlescent capsule
containing memory stick for the video. /

Täschchen in Austern-Design, perlmutterbeschichtete Kapsel,
Speicherstick mit Video.

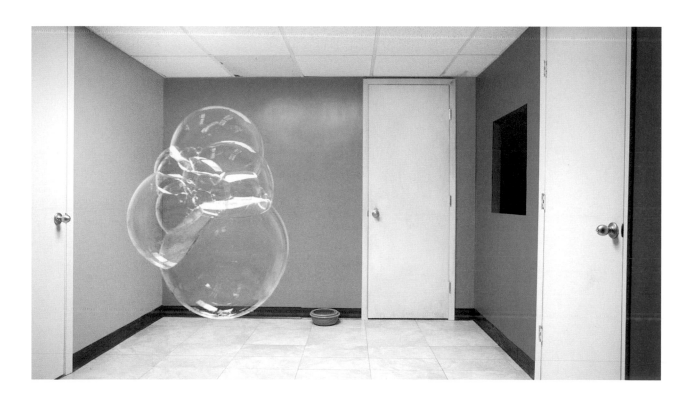

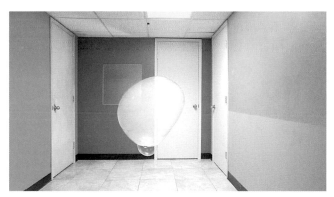

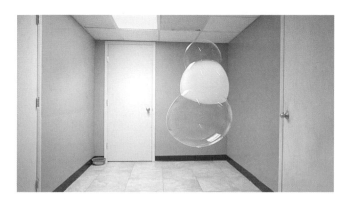

Stills from the video versions "Bubble 1 – Bubble 6",
each version Ed. 6/2APs. /

Stills aus den Videos, Versionen «Bubble 1 – Bubble 6»,
Auflage je 6/2 E.A.

Insert for Parkett 98

From Element to Application

A project by Iman Issa

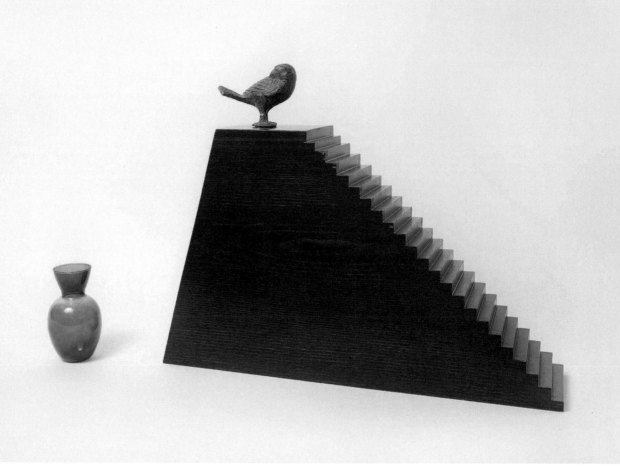

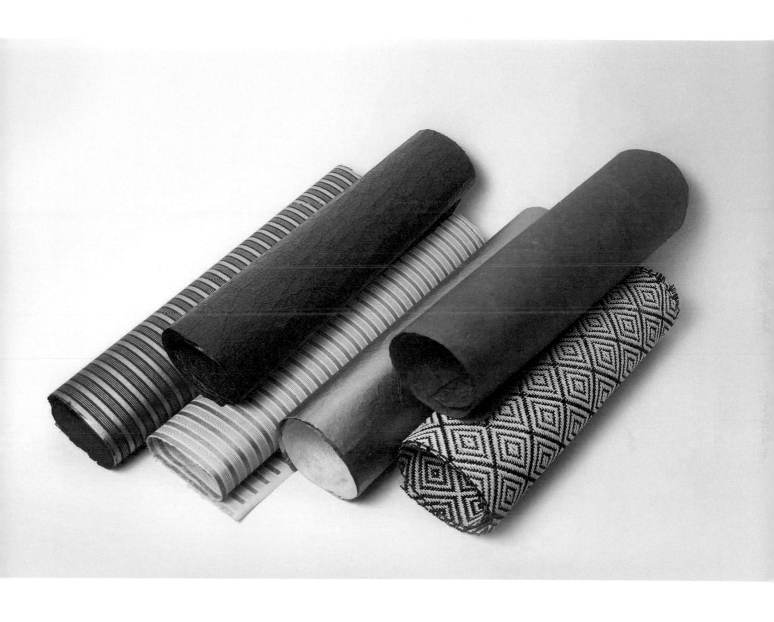

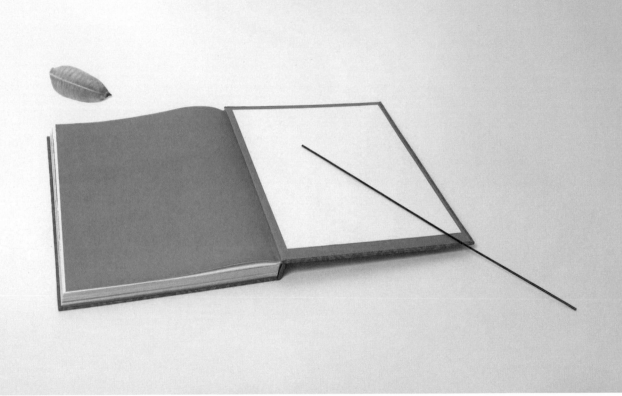

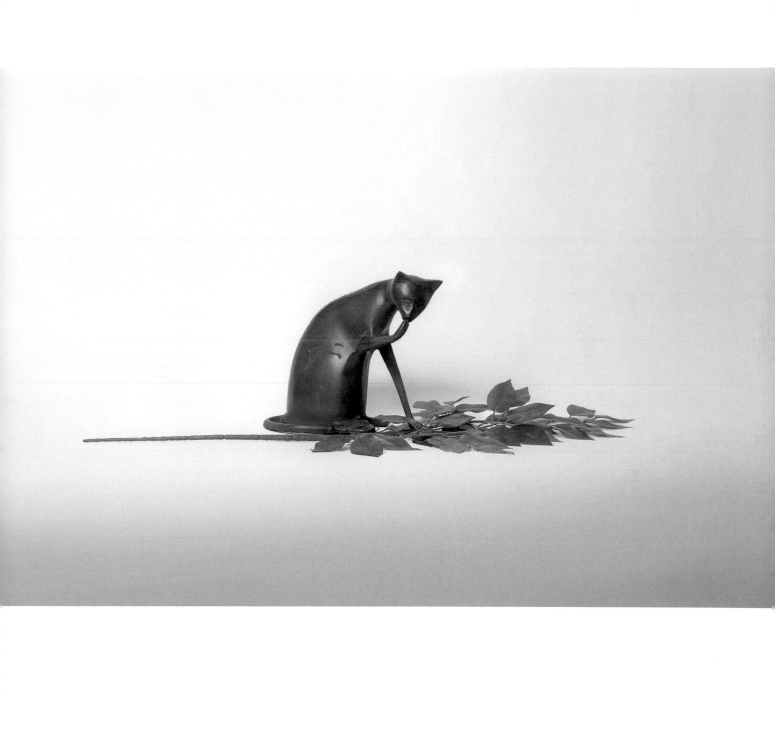

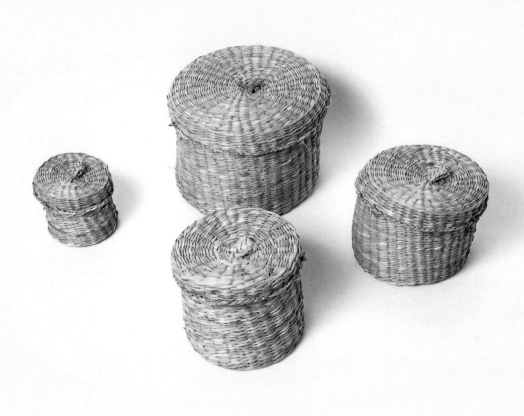

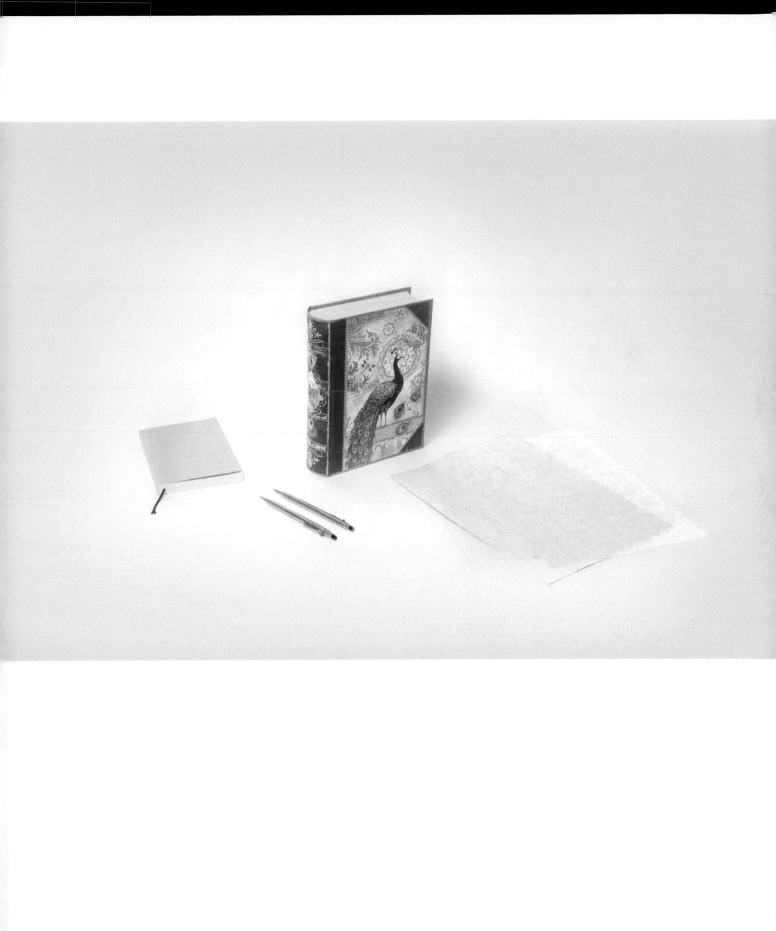

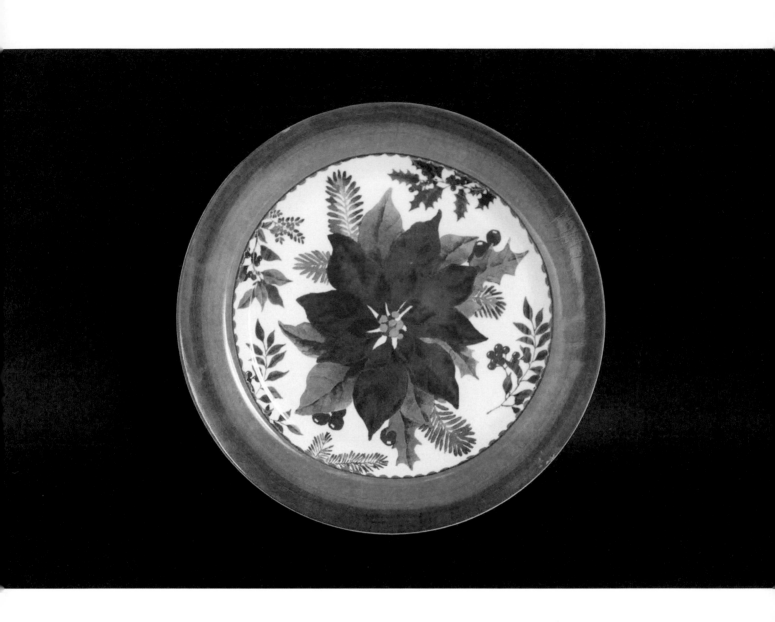

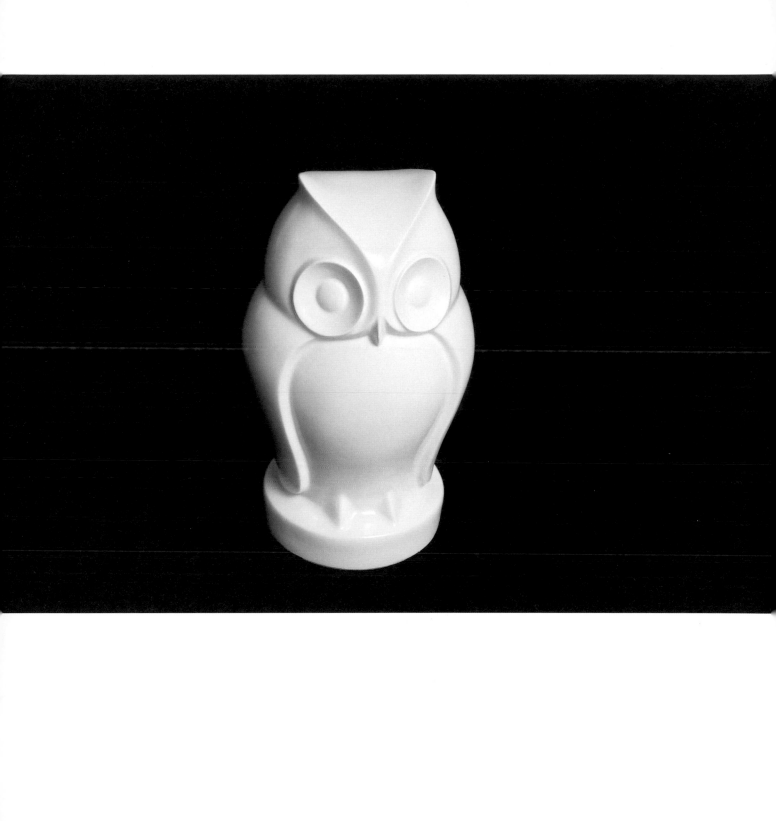

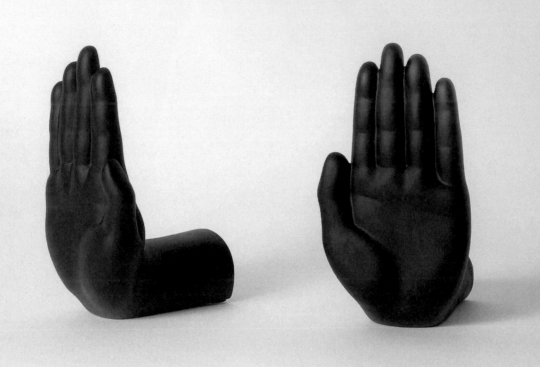

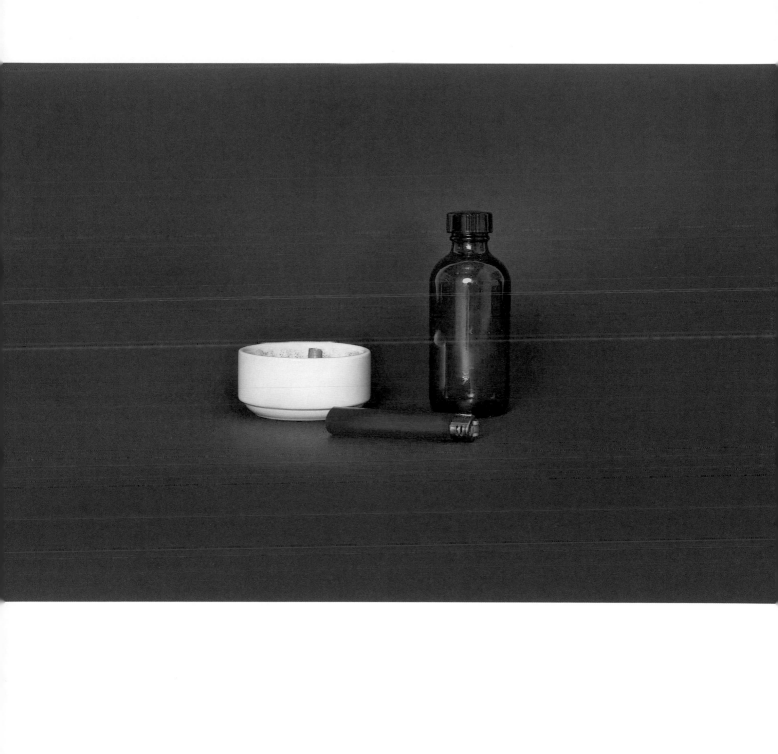

Acknowledgments

The preceding images, although all original and produced by the artist, are indebted to encounters with objects and displays at numerous museums, including:

The World Art History Museum

The Natural History Museum

The Folk Art Museum

The Museum of National Science

The Military Museum

The Regional Museum

The Museum of Regional Art

The Museum of Ceramics

The Agricultural Museum

The Railway Museum

The Museum of Archaeology

The Museum of Antiquities

The Minority Arts Museum

The War Museum

The Geological Museum

Museum of Religion

Museum of Religious Art

The International Museum of Culture

The National Museum of Arts and Culture

The Cultural Heritage Museum

The Police Museum

Museum of the City

The Museum of Portraiture

The Photography Museum

The Museum of International Photography

The Museum of Press Photography

IMAN ISSA, INSERT FOR PARKETT 98, 2016

CLAIRE LEHMANN

Fuck Seth Price:
How the Sausage Gets Made

*The making of contemporary art,
like the making of sausages,
is not a pretty sight.*
—after Otto von Bismarck

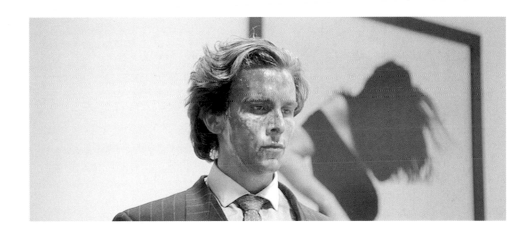

Mary Harron,
American Psycho, 2000,
Patrick Bateman (Christian Bale).

The artist is in trouble. The trouble is not that his studio practice has stalled, although it has, but that's a relatively trifling matter. Instead of making art, the unnamed protagonist wanders across the city, messes around on computers, hangs out in hotel lobbies. A simple case of anomie, it would seem, except that he also kills, blinds, beats, and abducts a few people along the way. These acts of violence happen without any conscious bloodlust: The artist is trapped in a "fugue state," in which he observes the brutal events unfolding with total detachment. His mind, however, is preoccupied with thoughts on the state of contemporary art and culture—thoughts that remain blissfully undisturbed by additional characters or dialogue. Such is the wispy plot of *Fuck Seth Price* (Leopard

CLAIRE LEHMANN is an artist and writer living in New York.

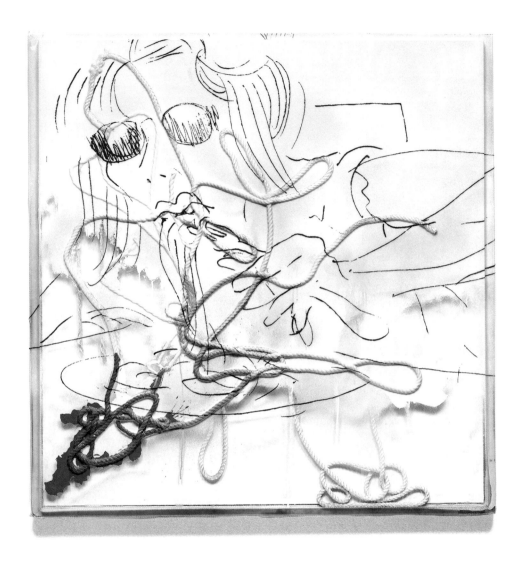

SETH PRICE, NOODLES, 2011, UV-cured inkjet, acrylic paint, enamel on PETG, vacuum-formed over rope, 46 ¹/₂ x 45 ¹/₄" /
NUDELN, UV-gehärteter Inkjet, Acrylfarbe, Email auf PET, vakuumverformt über Seil, 118,1 x 115 cm.

Press, 2015), a novel by Seth Price, the real-life artist and occasional essayist.

The novel begins as an inverted *Künstlerroman* in which the mature artist, looking back ruefully, laments his formation in free indirect style. He has become rich, but disenchanted. Mentally inventorying the past "to figure out exactly where things had gone wrong," he recalls a revelation that came to him in an Italian restaurant in the early 2000s, when the shifting cultural status of Italian food suggested to him something profound about the mobility of signifiers. In midcentury America, he recognized, "Italian food meant Italian-American food," a no-fuss family-dinner option; in the 1980s, awareness of authentic Italian cuisine grew in the professional culinary world, and red-sauce preparations fell decisively out of fashion. But in the new millennium, chefs had come to understand that "spaghetti and meatballs was what people had wanted all along, and why shouldn't they have it?" Thus, these canny cooks "upcycled" the old recipes, and—ta-da—*bucatini con le polpette* appeared on high-end restaurant tables with prices to match. Extending the analogy, the artist understood that he could enact a "spaghetti-and-meatballs recuperation" of abstract painting. "Spaghetti" in this schema equals attractive, living-room-ready paintings, which artists long to make and collectors long to buy, while "upcycling" e udied means of production that could revivify Greenbergian painting's corpse. Our artist-turned-automaton is, in other words, a literal zombie formalist.[1]

In the present moment of the novel, however, the protagonist has tired of contemporary art's "post-problem" status, in which "the market was the only indicator of quality," such that "it was no longer necessary to deem a piece interesting, provocative, weird, or complex"; no, "it was enough to say, 'That painting is *awesome*,' just as you'd say, 'This spaghetti is *awesome*.'" More specifically, though, he's tired of his own ability to succeed within this world, in which overtly contrived paintings reign. In place of art, he has become interested in writing—returning to it after finding early success with "some oddball critical essays that circulated in art-world contexts"—and the bulk of the narrative consists of his disquisitions on the role of art and artists in the digital age, lengthy rambles that consistently return to a fundamental anxiety: "When some part of our attention and experience played out in a timeless, spaceless dataplasm,

when we ourselves were living examples of a magic disavowal that granted power over our bodies to unseen and immaterial forces, what function was left for art?"

In the course of answering this question, the protagonist muses over artistic career trajectories, fandom, cynicism, literature in the Information Age, consumer comforts, economic irrationality, the histories of computing and film, technology and the divine, the nature of true freedom, architecture, the artist-audience relationship, World War II, the persistent suffering of bodies, the "digital regime," and the essence of art and artists. The vexed terrain of how we might profitably view art, for example, is nourished with a gentle shower of analogical options: art as hothouse flower, as subatomic particle, as liberation, as magic, as faith. On the behavior of artists, our zombie (a former artist now enslaved by an unknown entity) identifies what he considers to be the four motivations—the unspoken masters—animating successful contemporary artists: freedom, craft, money, and scene. The "freedom" artist wants to set the terms of his artistic inquiry, and above all, not be beholden to anyone or anything; the "craft" artist is driven to "make cool stuff," filling a vast studio with a thicket of assistants and tools; the "money" artists are obsessed with the machinations of the market, eventually "resembl[ing] the collectors they hung out with"; while the "scene" artist is primarily stimulated by the art world's never-ending party, occasionally attaining the status of "bad boy" or "downtown

figure." Price's character counts Duchamp and himself as adherents of freedom, Rauschenberg as emblematic of craft, and Warhol of money; on specific scene artists, he passes over in tactful silence. *Who is your master?* Never explicitly voiced, this question subtly pervades the novel.

In sum, much of *Fuck Seth Price* traces the politics of cultural work under late-stage capitalism, and although the workplace in question is the white cube rather than the cubicle, similarities between the two are frequently marshaled as provocative examples. Price compares a young freelance software programmer to an emerging artist—both end up having IPOs of sorts, the former when his code is purchased and integrated by a major tech corporation, and the latter when his cunningly engineered art-product bubbles successfully onto the marketplace, supported by 1-percenter flippers. These subjects imagine themselves to be free; but, we are to understand, they have been working all along for masters they cannot see. They are similarly creators of "post-problem" products, circulating within a culture marooned on a historical plateau—one quite similar, as the protagonist points out, to Francis Fukuyama's conception of Western liberal democracy as Hegelian endpoint. What does this moment look like? As Fukuyama wrote in "The End of History," his famed 1989 essay, "We might summarize the content of the universal homogenous state as liberal democracy in the political sphere combined with easy access to VCRs."

"**I have to return some videotapes**," Patrick Bateman says repeatedly in Bret Easton Ellis's 1991 satire *American Psycho*, a torching send-up of the amorality of Manhattan's ultramoneyed class, whose central character has been zombified by the depredations of excess capital and its attendant boredom. Bateman—Wall Street trader, dandy, serial killer—dines at a parade of arch restaurants (where he enjoys upcycled delights *avant la lettre*, including "meat loaf with chèvre and quail-stock sauce," hexagonal pot pie, and ninety-dollar pizza) when he's not wandering vacantly through the city streets, analyzing the merits of recent albums and the imperatives of white-collar dress, or perpetrating ever more baroque acts of torture and murder. Bateman occasionally reflects with perplexity on his psychological state: "I was simply imitating reality, a rough resemblance of a human being, with only a dim corner of my mind functioning. Something horrible was happening and yet I couldn't figure out why." In *Fuck Seth Price*, the fictional artist has his own trajectory of wealth and *ennui*, his own episodes of violence born of unclear origins. What *Fuck Seth Price* mirrors in its apparent evocation of American Psycho is that book's flavor of alienation in an age of liberal democracy when money and "surface, surface, surface" are all that matter.

Indeed, art with a conspicuously gilded patina finds itself in Price's sights. *Fuck Seth Price* includes accounts of two of America's biggest-name artists, Richard Serra and Jeff Koons; they are also timely targets, given the novel's composition in 2014, the year of Koons's mega-retrospective at New York's Whitney Museum of American Art and the completion of Serra's mammoth but inaccessible *East-West/West-East* in the Qatari desert. In a passage about a viewer's typical experience of a Koons sculpture, Price writes, "In the cold evasions of these lustrous surfaces you could expect seduction and manipulation, with undercurrents of aggression, and little tugs at the parts of you in charge of eating and fucking and shitting"—a precisely wrought sentence suggesting that Koons's art is most notable for its sphincter-constricting effects. The steel monoliths of Serra's "building-size commissions for Qatar's ruling family" are described as "Euclidean solids riding the breast of the desert," as though nursing directly from a contemptible source. Although the allegations facing Qatar's Al-Thanis—of supporting terrorism and tolerating abusive labor practices—go unmentioned, the attuned reader will understand the implication: Some artists are unable, or unwilling, to identify their problematic masters.

This focus on the compromised positions of other artists begs the question: What of Seth Price's own practice? The marketing copy for *Fuck Seth Price* describes it as a "hybrid of fiction, essay, and memoir," and for readers familiar with Price's oeuvre, the book's sole account of the protagonist's artwork, which follows his spaghetti-fueled revelation about abstract painting, will ring familiar: a painting featuring a "Foxconn worker's accidental Coke spills on Nigerian mud cloth, scanned and randomly manipulated in Photoshop, printed on Belgian linen stretched over a vacuum-formed frame." This medley of tactics echoes Price's own: the political timeliness of the jihadi beheadings in HOSTAGE VIDEO STILL WITH TIME STAMP (2005); the computer-aided manipulations of DIGITAL VIDEO EFFECT: "SPILLS" (2004); and the charged material provenance of his vacuum-formed "Paintings" (2006–). Later in the book, the fictional artist mentions appropriating bank logos, printing on Mylar, and computer-routing objects "according to the shapes of web-derived JPEGs"—all references to various series in Price's own output. Similarly, Price has penned a number of "critical essays that circulated in art-world contexts," has been lauded by art critics and desired by collectors, and in 2013, he too stopped making work, shutting down his studio for nearly a year to focus on writing.

Fuck Seth Price is the artist's first publication to be classified as a novel. The explicit genre designation is notable, especially as there are thematic overlaps with and outright repetitions of passages from many of Price's earlier essays and artists' books—a scheme of daisy-chaining familiar sentences from one text to the next that Price has long employed. Curiously, the novel recalls a section in "Dispersion" (2002–), Price's first widely circulated text, in which he cites the question: "Could there be someone capable of writing a science-fiction thriller based on the intention of presenting an alternative interpretation of modernist art that is readable by a non specialist audience? Would they care?"[2] Substitute "contemporary" for "modernist," and *Fuck Seth Price* appears to be the artist's reply to this provocation. In keeping with this mass-market approach, Price did not release his novel as a free digital download, as he has with many of his prior texts;[3] it seems he intended the pages of his book to thicken and curl from time logged at the beach.

Artists' novels have historically employed a wide range of narrative techniques (satire, surrealism, *cadavre exquise*, epistolary form, transcription, parafiction), but Price adopts a mode that has been faddish, of late, in the literary world: autofiction, or the quasi-fictionalization of true events from the author's own life—although here, the fictionalizing brackets seem to enclose the author's own *thoughts*. As Price has stated, "with an essay you assume the writer is saying what they really think," while *Fuck Seth Price*, he says, is full of "stuff I think and stuff I don't think, all mixed up."[4] Price seems to have adopted the construct of autofiction so as to write an essay—at times uncomfortably honest, potentially inflammatory, possibly cynical—under the guise of plausible deniability, allowing the elastic fabric of the novel to cloak his intentions.

In implicating Price's real-life practice, *Fuck Seth Price* brings to mind two other contemporary artists' novels: Richard Prince's *Why I Go to the Movies Alone* (1983) and Bjarne Melgaard's *A New Novel* (2012). In Prince's book, which

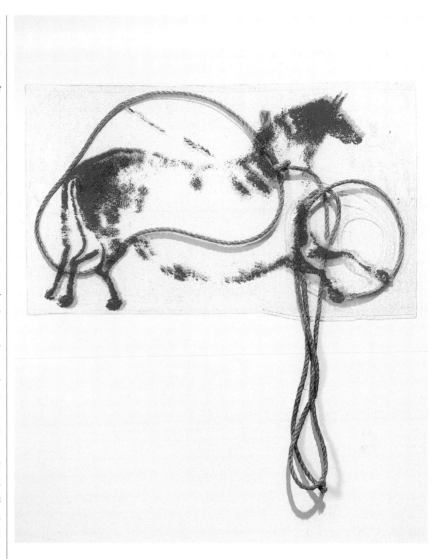

SETH PRICE, DECADENT PIECE, 2006, *fluorescent green, red signage ink on PETG, vacuum-formed over rope lariat, grommet, dimensions variable /* DEKADENTES STÜCK, *fluoreszierendes Grün, rote Beschilderungstinte auf PET, vakuum-verformt über Lasso, Schlinge, Masse variabel.*

strings together several impressionistic episodes, a major character works for the "Tear Sheets" department of a magazine, just as Prince himself did. The artist's interest in appropriation also receives a new spin: Thinking about an alluring woman, Prince's fictional counterpart states that he "had to have her on paper, a material with a flat and seamless surface"; he dreams of a sort of physical possession of her image because "satisfaction, at least in part, seemed to come about by ingesting, perhaps 'perceiving,' the fiction her photograph imagined." Melgaard's *A New Novel* also contains lifelike echoes. The nar-

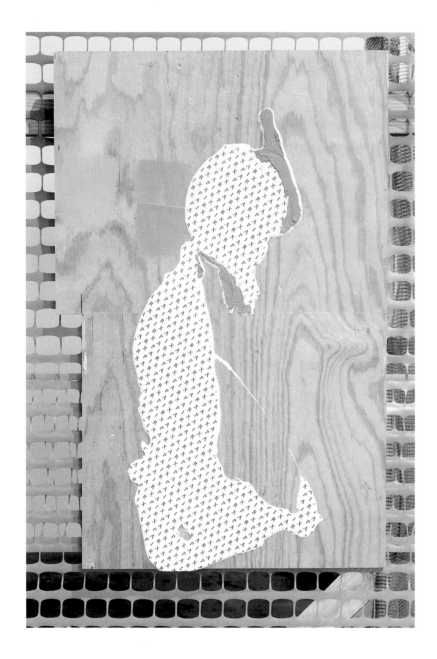

SETH PRICE, SPILL TEST, 2015,
screen print, acrylic paint,
pigmented acrylic polymer on wood,
40 x 36 x ³/₄" /
SPRITZ-TEST, Siebdruck, Acrylfarbe,
pigmentiertes Acylpolymer auf Holz,
101,6 x 91,4 x 1,9 cm.
(PHOTO: RON AMSTUTZ)

rator is a gay painter in New York, obsessed with BDSM and haunted by disturbing memories of past sexual encounters. Attributes of the fictional artist—who "usually only has sex with black men" and enjoys erotic asphyxiation, anal fisting, rape fantasies, and scenarios of extreme violence—will be recognizable to anyone who has been immersed in a Melgaard exhibition, where paintings, videos, and sculptures often feature all of the above. The question of just how autobiographical Melgaard's hardcore subject matter may be continually ghosts it, and *A New Novel* redoubles this effect.

These books, along with *Fuck Seth Price*, test a reader's adherence to the fiction in these autofictions—whether to read such novels as explicating or deepening the subjectivities that the authors' artworks suggest in visual form. The authors and their characters become stereoscopic, their adjacent identities occasionally fusing into a portrait of greater depth, then diverging again. But unlike Prince's and Melgaard's novels, which extend the concerns of their artwork, Price's seems to undercut his. The book reads like an artist grappling with a crisis of faith, as Price subtly implies that his own work has been cannily engineered, the result of the calculated mining of untapped cultural veins; it suggests that he's a shrewd manipulator—or that he fears he is. We can assume the violence in the novel is fictional, but what about the self-doubt?

"This printer is fucked up, so it looks so *awesome*,"[5] Price commented in reference to an image in his early 2016 show at the Los Angeles gallery 356 S. Mission Rd.—his first major exhibition of new work since his year-long hiatus, featuring a staggering forty-eight recent pieces. The checklist includes 2-D works adorned with logotypes; sculptures fashioned from "print-waste from commercial imaging facility" as well as PVC waste pipes; and massive, back-lit images of magnified human skin, shot with a hi-tech camera and digitally composited. If one takes not only the content but also the circumstances of the composition of *Fuck Seth Price* as indicative of an actual crisis in Price's own artistic practice, it seems safe to say that this predicament is over; Price has exorcised his anger about the state of the art world and reentered it. So is the novel all sound, no real fury?

Price reflected, in a recent essay, on certain artists who are "just *daring* you to believe their shtick."[6] Does *Fuck Seth Price* suggest Seth Price's oeuvre is shtick or its opposite? Is the book an exercise in proleptic criticism—the potent vaccination of self-satire that inoculates against further critique—or genuine gloom: *fuck* "Seth Price," this career, this successful whirring of *matériel*, capital, and personnel? Price's writing has always done a lot of theoretical buttressing, propping up his often hermetic, perplexing objects with sturdy intellectual supports, which are sometimes more arresting than the objects themselves. As one writer puts it, "Price has emerged as the single most erudite interpreter of his own work."[7] Yet this erudition doesn't always shine a flattering light on Price, oddly, because it reveals the extent to which Price strives to suffuse his art with cleverness. That Price's brand of cool is a painfully studied sort is on full display in *Fuck Seth Price*.

But a great deal of evidence of Price's abiding belief in art is also sprinkled throughout the book. As Price's analogue contends toward the end of the novel, in a fit of romanticism, "Art was actually a kind of magic, he thought. Giving substance to the ineffable was an occult act. . . . The magic effected by all good artists was the act of making something from nothing, a something from nothing that was powerful enough to change lives and thinking." Or when he parses art's insubordination: "Artists simply need to make things . . . and they often continued to make

things even when it proved economically burdensome"—making *making* itself "potentially radical." We can assume this sentiment is one that Price himself finds valiant, as it echoes throughout his writing elsewhere. In a 2003 video script, he wrote that only artists "understand what it means to imagine something and then go and make it happen by themselves. To create something, not just to consume something"; in at least two other written works, he repeats, "I'm like a person who makes things."[8] And even if we suspect Price of having it both ways with this novel, he transforms an apparent hypocrisy into a central tenet:

These new artworks aroused accusations of cynicism, and he admitted that he was inviting that conversation. . . . The question was, what if you found such compromised behavior complex and compelling? What if you believed that exploring the world of perceived or actual cynicism was a powerful way to understand our contemporary moment? . . . If his paintings were provocative, it was because they drew out acute and omnipresent cultural toxins: anxieties about cynicism and selling out, feelings that had everything to do with how fucked-up it was to live under neoliberal free-market capitalism. He found this exhilarating; he believed *in it.*

Fuck Seth Price doesn't transfix because it's clever—which it is—but because it's vulnerable. So much of Price's previous writing reads as discourse perfectly pitched for some kind of "right" audience, as critically serious, suitably obscurantist, elite. Yet this novel is a frank document of Price's own ambiguous berth in a sea of bullshit:

Price owns up to how rotten the whole enterprise of art can feel, even while confessing that he is unable, or unwilling, to quit. What does it mean to admit that you feel lashed to the oars, but that you would still swim desperately alongside the ship if you weren't?

Price may write with a certain dismay at art's state of affairs, but in returning to his practice, he affirms his own artistic commitment—despite the existential terror of artmaking, which Price has deftly characterized thus: "There's a question to which no artwork has an answer, to which every artwork is susceptible, which is, so what?"[9] Perhaps a sign of his intentions can be seen in a sketch he fashioned as the novel's frontispiece—a simple line drawing of a pair of cartoonish, leaflike hands, their networks of veins visible, reaching out from the pages of an open book. Price

is a nimble operator of cliché, so in that spirit I offer some possible bromides to meet his *so what*: It may be that Price feels stuck in the same old story, and these hands are raised in a cry for help. Or, the option I prefer: the unexpected, affecting possibility that Price wants his work to reach out and touch someone.

1) Although never explicitly invoked in the novel, the phrase "zombie formalism" was coined by the artist and critic Walter Robinson in mid-2014 in an essay published on Artspace.com. The term quickly gained currency, and shortly thereafter, critic Jerry Saltz offered this definition in *New York* magazine: "It feels 'cerebral' and looks hip in ways that flatter collectors even as it offers no insight into anything at all. It's all done in haggard shades of pale, deployed in uninventive arrangements that ape digital media, or something homespun or dilapidated. Replete with self-conscious comments on art, recycling, sustainability, appropriation, processes of abstraction, or

nature, all this painting employs a similar vocabulary of smudges, stains, spray paint, flecks, spills, splotches, almost-monochromatic fields, silk-screening, or stenciling."
2) Mark Klienberg as quoted in Seth Price, "Dispersion," 2002– , www.distributedhistory.com/Dispersion2016.pdf.
3) *Fuck Seth Price* is digitally available in an archive of Price's writing collected on an unlinked-to subpage of sethpricestudio.com, but it is seemingly impervious to Google searches for "fuck seth price pdf."
4) Seth Price in conversation with Charline von Heyl, Whitney Museum of American Art, New York, November 20, 2015.
5) "Seth Price and Laura Owens in Conversation," 356 Mission Tumblr, www.356mission.tumblr.com/post/138501268495, emphasis mine.
6) Seth Price, "Lecture on the Extra Part," *Texte zur Kunst*, September 2015, 136.
7) Chris Wiley, "Short Circuit," in *Seth Price: 2000 Words* (Athens: Deste Foundation for Contemporary Art, 2014), 8.
8) Seth Price, "Sports," 2003, www.distributedhistory.com/Sports.pdf; Seth Price, "Redistribution (video transcript)," in *Price, Seth* (Zurich: JRP/Ringier, 2010), 77; Seth Price, *How to Disappear in America*, (New York: Leopard Press, 2008), 5.
9) Seth Price, "Redistribution (video transcript)," 101.

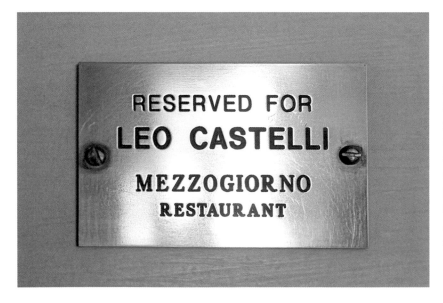

DEVON DIKEOU, RESERVED FOR LEO CASTELLI: SINCE CÉZANNE (After Clive Bell), 2008, color photograph, 28 x 18", plaque at Mezzogiorno, an Italian restaurant in SoHo, reserving a table in perpetuity for art dealer Leo Castelli / Farbphotographie, 71,1 x 45,7 cm, Plakette im italienischen Restaurant Mezzogiorno, Dauerreservation für den Kunsthändler Leo Castelli.

CLAIRE LEHMANN

Kunstwerke sind wie Würste,
man sollte besser nicht dabei sein,
wenn sie gemacht werden.
—nach Otto von Bismarck

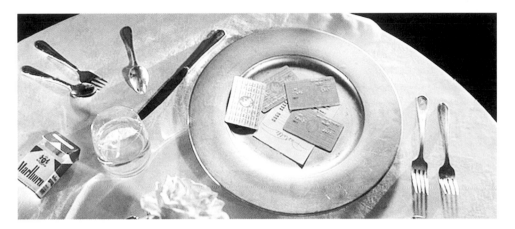

Mary Harron, American Psycho, *2000.*

Fuck Seth Price: Wie die Wurst gemacht wird

Der Künstler sitzt in der Klemme. Und zwar nicht, weil ihm im Atelier nichts mehr einfällt, obwohl ja, das auch, aber das ist noch das kleinere Übel. Anstatt Kunst zu machen, streunt unser namenlos bleibender Held kreuz und quer durch die Stadt, spielt mit Computern, lümmelt in Hotellobbys. Ein klarer Fall

CLAIRE LEHMANN ist eine Künstlerin und Autorin, sie lebt in New York.

von Anomie, ist man versucht zu diagnostizieren, wenn da nicht der Umstand wäre, dass er unterwegs ein paar Leute ermordet, blendet, verprügelt, entführt. Diese Gräueltaten passieren einfach so, ohne besondere blutrünstige Absichten. Der Künstler leidet unter Poriomanie, unter dem Zwang, ziellos herumzuirren. Die Gewaltexzesse nimmt er nur am Rande wahr. Seine Gedanken sind anderswo, sie

befassen sich mit dem Zustand der zeitgenössischen Kunst und Kultur und bleiben unberührt von den Begegnungen und Gesprächen mit anderen Personen. So lässt sich das Handlungsgespinst des Romans *Fuck Seth Price* (2015) zusammenfassen, geschrieben von Seth Price, Künstler und gelegentlich auch Schriftsteller.

Die Handlung beginnt als umgekehrter Künstlerroman. Der reife

Künstler blickt reumütig in die Vergangenheit zurück und beschreibt frei und assoziativ, wie alles begann. Reich ist er geworden, doch nicht glücklich. Im Geiste geht er seinen Lebens- und Schaffensweg nach, um den Punkt zu bestimmen, «wo alles begann schiefzulaufen». Price erinnert sich an ein Aha-Erlebnis, das er kurz nach 2000 in einem italienischen Restaurant hatte. Als er über den Statuswandel der mediterranen Küche nachdachte, erschien ihm die Mobilität von Signifikanten plötzlich in einem neuen Licht. In der amerikanischen Kultur der 1950er-Jahre war «italienisch essen gleichbedeutend mit italienisch-amerikanisch essen», ein schlichtes Mahl für die ganze Familie. In den 1980er-Jahren besann sich die professionelle Gastronomie mehr und mehr auf die Wurzeln der authentischen italienischen Kochkunst und die simplen Tomatensaucen-Rezepte kamen aus der Mode. Nach der Jahrhundertwende wiederum gelangten die Chefs zu der Einsicht, dass die Leute «eigentlich immer nur Spaghetti mit Fleischklösschen wollten, und warum sollen sie die nicht kriegen?». Die schlauen Köche peppten die alten Rezepte auf und schwupps, im Handumdrehen wurden den Gästen von Luxusrestaurants *bucatini con le polpette* serviert – zu saftigen Preisen. Man muss von diesem Trend lernen, dachte Price, und eine «Spaghetti-mit-Fleischklösschen-Renaissance» der abstrakten Malerei einläuten. Die «Spaghetti» sind in diesem Fall ansprechende, wohnzimmerverträgliche Gemälde, die Künstler gerne malen und

Sammler gerne kaufen, und das «Aufpeppen» erfolgt mittels würziger Kunsttheorien und einer meisterlichen Zubereitung, die den Kadaver der Greenberg'schen Malerei zu neuem Leben erweckt. Unser zum Automaten mutierter Künstler ist also ein sogenannter Zombie-Formalist.[1]

An dieser Stelle des Romans hat es unser Held reichlich satt, vom «Post-Problem-Zustand» der zeitgenössischen Kunst zu hören, in dem «der Markt allein entscheidet, was gut ist und was nicht», sodass «es nicht länger notwendig ist, ein Werk für interessant, provokativ, aussergewöhnlich oder komplex zu halten». Stattdessen «reicht es zu sagen, ‹Das Bild war *spitze*›, genau wie man sagen würde, ‹Die Spaghetti waren *spitze*›». Was er im Grunde aber am meisten satthat, ist sein Talent, in einer Welt Erfolg zu haben, in der sich nichts besser verkauft als total manierierte Malerei. Anstelle der Kunst beginnt er sich für die Schriftstellerei zu interessieren. Eigentlich nicht zum ersten Mal, denn er veröffentlichte bereits früher «ein paar schräge kritische Aufsätze, die in Kunstkreisen herumgereicht wurden». Der Hauptteil der Handlung ist weitschweifigen Grübeleien über die Rolle der Kunst und des Künstlers im Digitalzeitalter gewidmet, die wiederholt zu einer düsteren Zukunftsvision zurückkehren: «Wenn sich irgendein Fragment unserer Aufmerksamkeit und Erfahrung in einem zeitlosen, raumlosen Datenplasma ausagiert und wenn wir selbst lebendige Exempel eines magischen Verzichts geworden sind, der die Macht über

unsere Körper unsichtbaren und immateriellen Kräften überlässt – welche Funktion wird die Kunst dann überhaupt noch haben?»

Die Suche nach einer Antwort führt den Ich-Erzähler durch Exkurse zu Themen wie Künstlerkarrieren, Fans, Zynismus, Literatur im Informationszeitalter, Konsumgenüsse, Irrationalität der Wirtschaft, Geschichte des Films und der Digitaltechnik, Technologie und Gott, das Wesen wahrer Freiheit, Architektur, Zweiter Weltkrieg, die Beziehung zwischen Künstler und Publikum, die unablässigen Leiden des Körpers, das «digitale Regime» sowie die Essenz von Kunst und Künstler. Die Vexierfrage, wie Kunst zum persönlichen Gewinn zu rezipieren sei, löst einen Schwall analoger Möglichkeiten aus: Kunst als Treibhauspflanze, als subatomares Teilchen, als Befreiung, als Magie, als Glaube. Was die Verhaltensweisen von Künstlern betrifft, nennt unser Zombie (ein Ex-Künstler, gegenwärtig von unbekannt versklavt) vier Anreize – vier wahre Marionettenmeister –, die erfolgreiche zeitgenössische Künstler motivieren: Freiheit, Handwerk, Geld und Szene. Freiheitsorientierte Künstler wollen selbst bestimmen, welchen Weg ihre Recherche nimmt, und von niemandem abhängig sein; handwerksorientierte Künstler wollen «tolle Sachen» machen, in einem Atelier, das voll ausstaffiert ist mit Assistenten und Ausrüstung; geldorientierte Künstler sind hypnotisiert von den Machenschaften des Markts und es dauert nicht lange, bis «sie selbst so aussehen wie die Sammler, mit denen sie verkehren»; und szeneorientierte Künstler stürzen sich Hals über Kopf in die Marathonpartys der Kunstwelt, wo sie gerne die Rolle des Insiders oder des Enfant terrible spielen. Price nennt sich selbst mit Duchamp als Anhänger der Freiheit, Rauschenberg als typischen Handwerker und Warhol als Verehrer des Mammons. Was die Szenekünstler betrifft, hüllt er sich in taktvolles Schweigen. *Wer ist dein Marionettenmeister?* Diese unausgesprochene Frage begleitet den gesamten Roman.

Kurz gesagt, weite Strecken von *Fuck Seth Price* untersuchen die Politik der Kulturarbeit im Spätkapitalismus. Obwohl der fragliche Arbeitsplatz ein White Cube und kein Zellenbüro ist, werden deren Ähnlichkeiten mehrmals provokant taxiert. Price vergleicht einen jungen freiberuflichen Software-Programmierer mit einem Nachwuchskünstler. Beide erleben Erfolgsmomente: der eine, wenn sein Code von einem Technologiekonzern gekauft und verwendet wird, der andere, wenn sein strategisch platziertes Kunstfabrikat auf dem Markt einschlägt und von superreichen Käufern aufgeschnappt wird. Diese Leute meinen, sie seien frei. Aber sie wissen nicht, was der Roman weiss, nämlich dass sie zur Pfeife eines unsichtbaren Meisters tanzen. Sie erzeugen «Post-Problem-Produkte» für den Vertrieb in einer Kultur, die auf einem historischen Plateau stagniert – das nach Einschätzung des Romanhelden viele Gemeinsamkeiten aufweist mit Francis Fukuyamas Wertung der westlichen liberalen Demokratie als hegelianischer Endpunkt.

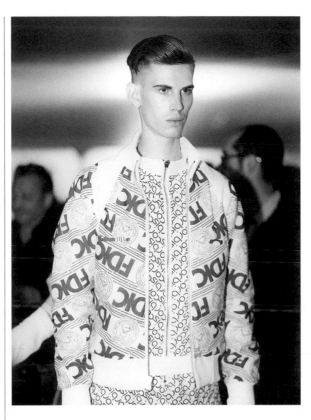

Wie sieht dieser Endpunkt aus? Fukuyama charakterisierte ihn 1989 in seinem berühmten Artikel *Das Ende der Geschichte?* so: «Der universale homogene Staat entspricht im Prinzip einer liberalen Demokratie plus Videorecorder für alle.»

«Ich muss noch ein paar Videos zurückbringen», sagt Patrick Bateman mehrmals in Bret Easton Ellis' Roman *American Psycho* (1991), einer beissenden Satire auf die Unmoral der wohlhabenden New Yorker Oberschicht, deren Held von seinem Reichtum und der unvermeidlich damit verbundenen Langeweile zum Zombie korrumpiert wird. Bateman – Börsenmakler, Dandy, Serienmörder – frequentiert die feinsten Gastrotempel (wo er aufgepeppte Köstlichkei-

ten geniesst, ehe sie noch in Mode kommen, darunter «Fleischkäse mit Chèvre und Wachteljus», sechseckige Pastete und Pizza für neunzig Dollar), wenn er nicht verloren durch die Strassen wandert, die Qualitäten neuer CDs oder die Ge- und Verbote des Geschäftsanzugs analysiert oder immer groteskere Folter- und Mordtaten begeht. Ab und zu wirft Bateman einen verwunderten Blick in sein Innenleben: «Ich imitierte einfach die Wirklichkeit, die grobe Karikatur eines menschlichen Wesens, und nur ein düsterer Winkel meines Hirns blieb in Betrieb. Etwas Schreckliches ging vor sich, doch ohne dass ich begreifen konnte, warum ...» Der fiktive Künstler in *Fuck Seth Price* führt dieselbe von Wohlstand und Überdruss gezeich-

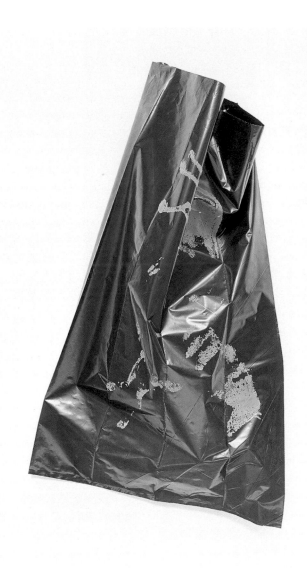

SETH PRICE, NAILED TO THE WALL (HEAD DOWN), 2005,
signage ink on contractor's garbage bag, 62 x 38" /
AN DIE WAND GENAGELT (KOPFÜBER),
Beschilderungstinte auf Gewerbe-Müllsack, 157,5 x 95,5 cm.

nete Existenz und auch er neigt zu Gewaltausbrüchen ohne sichtbare Ursache. *Fuck Seth Price* vermittelt mit seinen Anlehnungen an *American Psycho* das Gefühl der Entfremdung im goldenen Zeitalter der liberalen Demokratie, in der nichts anderes zählt als Geld und «Oberfläche, Oberfläche, Oberfläche».

Auf Kunst mit einer verdächtig güldenen Patina hat es Price besonders abgesehen. *Fuck Seth Price* enthält zwei Passagen über die beiden amerikanischen Kunststars Richard Serra und Jeff Koons. Der Zeitpunkt war gut gewählt, denn im Entstehungsjahr des Romans 2014 hatte Koons eine Mega-Retrospektive im New Yorker Whitney Museum of American Art und Serra vollendete sein Mammutprojekt EAST-WEST/WEST-EAST (Ost-West/West-Ost) in der fernen Wüste von Katar. Price versetzt sich in die Eindrücke eines Durchschnittsbetrachters vor einer Skulptur von Koons: «Man erwartet, dass man von den kalten Ausflüchten der glänzenden Oberflächen verführt und manipuliert wird und dass sich darunter Aggressionen verbergen, kleine Irritationen jener Partien, die fürs Essen, Ficken und Scheissen zuständig sind.» Ein genau kalibrierter Satz, der nahelegt, dass die Koon'schen Werke vor allem durch ihre Fähigkeit bestechen, eine Schliessmuskelverengung herbeizuführen. Die Stahlmonolithen von Serras «Monumentalauftrag für das Königshaus von Katar» erscheinen ihm als «euklidische Festkörper, die auf dem Busen der Wüste reiten», als würden sie an einer verrufenen Quelle saugen. Dass die Herrscherfamilie Al Thani beschuldigt wird, Terrorgruppen zu unterstützen und ausländische Arbeiter in Katar auszubeuten, bleibt unerwähnt. Dem hellhörigen Leser wird trotzdem nicht entgehen, was hier angedeutet wird: Manche Künstler können oder wollen nicht offen zugeben, bei welch fragwürdigen Meistern sie im Dienst stehen.

Das Augenmerk, das Seth Price auf die Schwachstellen fremder Kunstpraktiken richtet, zwingt uns zu fragen: Was hat es mit seiner eigenen auf sich? Der Werbetext für *Fuck Seth Price* bezeichnet das Buch als «Mischung aus Erzählung, Essay und Memoiren». Die einzige detaillierte Darstellung eines Kunstwerks des Romanhelden – sie folgt unmittelbar auf die Spaghetti-Erleuchtung – wird für Kenner des Price'schen Œuvres vertraut klingen. Das Gemälde zeigt «Cola-Spritzer eines Foxconn-Arbeiters auf einem nigerianischen Bogolan-Stoff, eingescannt, wahllos mit Photoshop bearbeitet, auf belgisches Leinen gedruckt und auf einen vakuumgeformten Rahmen gespannt». Dieses Potpourri von Kunsttaktiken erinnert verdächtig an die Vorgehensweise des Buchautors selbst: die politische Aktualität

der dschihadistischen Enthauptungen in HOSTAGE VIDEO STILL WITH TIME STAMP (Geiselvideo mit Zeitangabe, 2005); die digitalen Verfremdungen von DIGITAL VIDEO EFFECT: «SPILLS» (Digitaler Videoeffekt: «Flecken», 2004); sowie die assoziationsgeladene materielle Herkunft der vakuumgeformten «Gemälde» (2006–). An späterer Stelle erwähnt der fiktive Künstler, dass er Firmenzeichen von Banken auf Mylar druckt und Objekte «je nach der Form heruntergeladener JPEGs» durch Rechner schickt – Verweise auf tatsächlich realisierte Werkserien. Wie die Romanfigur verfasste Price «kritische Aufsätze, die in Kunstkreisen herumgereicht wurden», erfreut sich

grosser Beliebtheit bei Kritikern und Sammlern und sperrte sein Atelier zu (2013, für fast ein Jahr), um sich auf die Schriftstellerei zu konzentrieren.

Fuck Seth Price ist der erste Roman des Künstlers. Die klare Genre-Zuordnung fällt auf, besonders wenn man bedenkt, dass es thematische Überschneidungen, ja sogar komplett wiederholte Passagen aus früheren Aufsätzen und Künstlerbüchern gibt – Price liebt es seit Langem, bekannte Sätze in nachfolgenden Texten zu recyceln. Der Roman übernimmt Auszüge aus seinem ersten, populären Text «Dispersion» (2003). Darin stellt Price die Frage: «Gibt es jemanden, der imstande wäre, einen

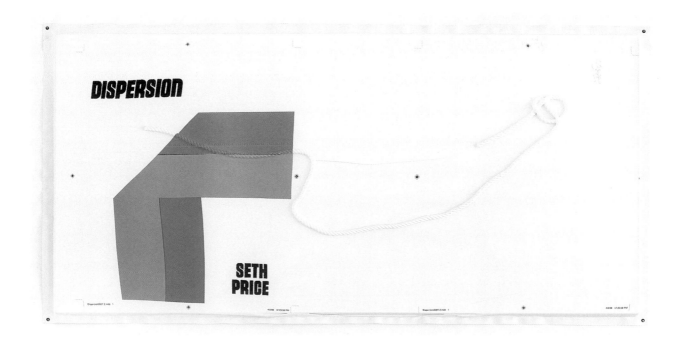

SETH PRICE, ESSAY WITH KNOTS, 2008, detail, screen print on high-impact polystyrene, ropes, in 9 parts, each 48 x 96" /
ESSAY MIT KNOTEN, Detail, Siebdruck auf hochschlagfestem Polystyrol, Seile, in 9 Teilen, je 122 x 243,8 cm.

217

Science-Fiction-Thriller zu schreiben, der eine alternative, auch für Laien verständliche Deutung der modernen Kunst liefert? Gibt es Leser, die so etwas interessieren würde?"[2] Man muss nur «modern» durch «zeitgenössisch» ersetzen und schon wird klar, dass *Fuck Seth Price* diese provokante Frage zu beantworten sucht. Passend zur ehrgeizigen Public-Relations-Strategie ist der Roman nicht als kostenloser Download erhältlich, wie es bei früheren Texten üblich war.[3] Anscheinend wollte Price, dass die Seiten durch intensive Strandlektüre eine wellige und salzige Stofflichkeit gewinnen.

Romane von bildenden Künstlern setzen traditionell eine breite Vielfalt von Erzähltechniken ein (Satire, Surrealismus, Cadavre exquis, Briefform, Transkription, Parafiktion). Price entschied sich für einen beliebten Modus der neueren Literatur: Autofiktion, die Quasi-Fiktionalisierung wahrer Begebnisse aus dem Leben des Autors, eine Definition, die im vorliegenden Fall auch die *Gedanken* des Autors einschliesst. Während man «bei einem Aufsatz annimmt, dass der Autor wirklich meint, was er sagt», ist *Fuck Seth Price*, wie Price versichert, voll von «Zeug, das wirklich so gemeint ist, und anderes auch wieder nicht, alles durcheinandergemischt».[4] Offenbar übernahm Price das Konstrukt der Autofiktion, um unter dem Alibi der glaubhaften Abstreitbarkeit und unter dem Deckmantel eines elastischen Romangespinsts, das seine wahren Absichten verbirgt, eine verstörend ehrliche, potenziell anstössige und möglicherweise zynische Stellungnahme abzugeben.

Auch zwei andere zeitgenössische Künstler haben ihre reale Kunstpraxis in selbstverfasste Romane eingebracht: Richard Prince in *Why I Go to the Movies Alone* (1983) und Bjarne Melgaard in *A New Novel* (2012). Prince verknüpft mehrere impressionistische Episoden, deren Hauptfigur (wie Prince vormals selbst) für die Photoabteilung einer Zeitschrift arbeitet. Der Aneignungsdrang des Künstlers findet neue Betätigungsfelder. Er müsse, bekennt der Romanheld, eine von ihm verehrte Frau «auf Papier haben, auf einem flachen und glatten Material». Er träumt davon, ihr Abbild zu besitzen, denn es scheint ihm «zumindest teilweise Befriedigung zu verschaffen, wenn er die Phantasie, die ihre Photographie vermittelte, in sich aufnahm oder vielleicht ‹wahrnahm›». Auch Melgaards *A New Novel* enthält

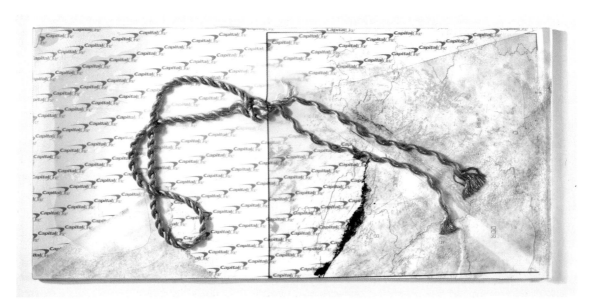

autobiographische Anklänge: Der Erzähler ist ein schwuler Maler in New York, der in die BDSM-Szene eintaucht und von traumatischen sexuellen Erinnerungen verfolgt wird. Das Charakterbild des fiktiven Künstlers – der «meist nur Sex mit schwarzen Männern» und zudem eine Vorliebe für erotische Praktiken wie Atemkontrolle und Fisting, für Vergewaltigungsphantasien und für extreme Gewaltsituationen hat – wird allen Besuchern von Melgaards Ausstellungen vertraut sein, die all die genannten Anliegen in Gemälden, Skulpturen und Videos ausleben. Die Frage, inwieweit der Hardcore-Inhalt tatsächlich aus Melgaards Leben gegriffen ist, schwebt im Raum und geistert auch durch die Seiten von *A New Novel*.

Diese beiden Bücher wie auch *Fuck Seth Price* stellen die Fähigkeit des Lesers auf die Probe, den fiktiven Gehalt in der Autofiktion abzuwägen – ob es möglich wäre, aus dem Roman eine Erklärung oder Vertiefung jener Subjektivitäten herauszulesen, die der Künstler-Autor sonst in visueller Form präsentiert. Die Autoren und ihre Figuren nehmen eine stereoskopische Dimension an, ihre einander umkreisenden Identitäten verschmelzen kurz zu einem tiefer gefassten Porträt, ehe sie wieder auseinanderdriften. Doch im Gegensatz zu Prince und Melgaard, die in ihren Romanen den thematischen Horizont ihrer Kunst ausdehnen, scheint Price seinen eigenen zu sabotieren. Der Leser gewinnt den Eindruck, der Verfasser hätte den Glauben an sich selbst verloren. Price lässt indirekt durchblicken,

dass er seine Arbeiten bewusst auf den Markt zugeschnitten hat, dass sie das Resultat einer kalkulierten Ausbeutung ungenutzter kultureller Strömungen sind und dass er ein gewiefter Strippenzieher ist – oder zumindest fürchtet, einer zu sein. Die im Roman geschilderte Gewalt ist wahrscheinlich frei erfunden. Die Selbstzweifel auch?

«**Der Drucker ist total scheisse, deswegen kommt das so super raus**»,[5] kommentierte Price eine der Arbeiten, die er Anfang 2016 in der Galerie 356 s. Mission Rd. in Los Angeles zeigte – der ersten grossen Ausstellung neuer Werke (49 Stück!) nach fast einjähriger Pause. Die Exponatenliste umfasste Graphiken mit Bildsymbolen, Skulpturen aus «Makulatur eines Bildverarbeitungsdiensts» und PVC-Abflussrohren sowie hinterleuchtete hochauflösende, digital bearbeitete Abbildungen der menschlichen Haut. Wenn man nicht nur den Inhalt von *Fuck Seth Price*, sondern auch die Umstände, unter denen der Roman entstand, als Anzeichen einer akuten schöpferischen Krise wertet, kann man mit gutem Gewissen feststellen, dass die Krise überwunden ist. Price hat seine Wut über die Zustände in der Kunstwelt wieder unter Kontrolle und ist nun anscheinend wieder bereit mitzumachen. Ist der Roman also bloss heisse Luft?

In einem seiner jüngsten Aufsätze meinte Price, es gäbe Künstler, die «*testen* dich, ob du den Mut hast, ihre Masche wirklich ernst zu nehmen».[6] Beweist *Fuck Seth Price*, dass das, was Price macht, eine Masche ist, oder gerade das Gegenteil?

Soll das Buch künftige Kritiken entschärfen, indem es sie selbstironisch vorwegnimmt, oder ist sein Pessimismus echt – *fuck* Seth Price, dieses aus Material, Kapital und Personal zusammengeflickte Karrierevehikel? Price sorgt seit jeher dafür, dass seine oft hermetischen, wunderlichen Objekte durch die selbstverfassten Texte ein solides theoretisches Fundament erhalten, ein intellektuelles Gerüst, das oft mindestens ebenso interessant ist wie die Objekte selbst. Ein Beobachter resümierte: «Price ist zum eloquentesten Interpreten seiner eigenen Werke geworden.»[7] Doch merkwürdigerweise gereicht ihm diese Beredsamkeit nicht immer zum Vorteil, denn sie enthüllt, mit welcher Raffinesse er seine Auftritte orchestriert. Dass die brandheisse Kunstmarke Seth Price das Ergebnis einer gezielten Positionierung ist, wird niemand, der *Fuck Seth Price* gelesen hat, bezweifeln.

Im Buch finden sich allerdings auch ausreichend Hinweise darauf, dass Price den Glauben an die Kunst nicht verloren hat. Gegen Ende der Erzählung gibt sich das Alter Ego des Autors romantischen Anwandlungen hin: «Die Kunst hat wirklich etwas Magisches, dachte er. Das Unfassbare in greifbare Form zu fassen ist nichts weniger als Zauberei... Alle guten Künstler vollbringen ein Zauberstück. Sie machen aus nichts etwas, was stark genug ist, unser Leben und unser Denken zu verändern.» Der Schöpferdrang ist unbezwingbar: «Künstler müssen immer irgendetwas machen... und sie hören selbst dann nicht auf, wenn es finanziell längst nicht mehr tragbar ist» – das

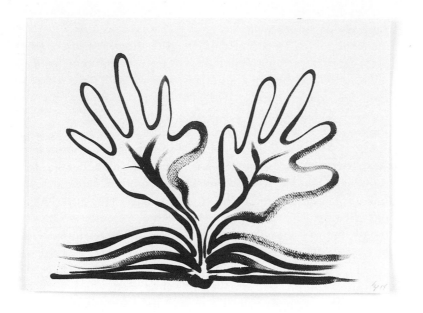

Seth Price, frontispiece for
Fuck Seth Price, 2014,
gouache on paper, 12 x 16" /
Frontispiz für Fuck Seth Price,
Gouache auf Papier, 30,5 x 40,6 cm.
(PHOTO: RON AMSTUTZ)

Machen selbst kann also «potenziell radikal» sein. Wir müssen annehmen, dass dies auf den Autor selbst zutrifft, denn er hat sich in einigen seiner theoretischen Aufsätze ähnlich geäussert. 2003 mutmasste er, dass nur Künstler «verstehen, was es heisst, sich etwas auszudenken und dann ganz allein in die Tat umzusetzen. Dinge zu produzieren und nicht nur zu konsumieren.»[8] Auch wenn es so aussieht, als ob Price mit seinem Roman gleichzeitig auf zwei Hochzeiten tanzen wollte, gelingt es ihm dennoch, anrüchigen Verhältnissen ein solides Prinzip abzugewinnen:

Manche fanden die neuen Kunstwerke zynisch und er musste sich eingestehen, dass er diese Reaktion provoziert hatte ... Was aber, wenn jemand ein solch fragwürdiges Verhalten interessant und faszinierend findet? Was, wenn jemand die Welt des echten oder vorgetäuschten *Zynismus als Mittel empfindet, den aktuellen historischen Moment besser zu verstehen? ... Wenn seine Gemälde provokant waren, dann genau aus dem Grund, weil sie ein gefährliches, weitverbreitetes kulturelles Gift zutage brachten: die Angst davor, in Zynismus zu verfallen und die eigenen Ideale zu verraten, Gefühle, die angesichts der Zustände in der neoliberalen freien Marktwirtschaft unvermeidlich waren. Er fand das befreiend; er glaubte* daran.

Fuck Seth Price ist ein kluges Buch, aber das ist nicht seine Hauptstärke. Was uns berührt, ist seine Verletzlichkeit. Ein Grossteil der früheren Schriften liest sich als Diskurs, den Price gezielt auf das «richtige» Publikum zugeschnitten hat, als ernsthafte Kritik, elitär und schwer verständlich, wie es das Metier verlangt. Der Roman gewährt uns hingegen einen freien Blick auf den Posten, den Price im trügerischen Morast bezogen hat. Er macht kein Hehl aus der Tristesse, die Artisten im Kunstzirkus befallen kann, auch wenn er selbst nicht fähig oder willens ist, sich von seinem Meister loszusagen. Was hat man von einem Menschen zu halten, der auf der Galeere in Ketten mitrudert und selbst dann noch, wenn man ihn über Bord wirft, nebenher weiterschwimmt?

Price mag die aktuelle Lage der Kunst noch so negativ beurteilen; dadurch dass er ins Atelier zurückkehrte, bekräftigte er sein künstlerisches Engagement – trotz der existenziellen Ängste, die mit der Kunstmacherei verbunden sind und die Price einmal so beschrieb: «Es gibt eine Frage, die jedes Kunstwerk aufwirft und die kein Kunstwerk beantworten kann, und diese Frage lautet: Na und?»[9] Vielleicht lässt die Skizze, die als Titelbild des Romans dient, Rückschlüsse auf die Absichten des Künstlers zu: Aus einem offenen Buch ragen in einfachen Umrissen gezeichnete, blattähnliche Hände mit deutlich sichtbarem Adernetz hervor. Price ist ein Virtuose des Klischees. Daher hoffe ich, Sie werden mir den Versuch verzeihen, das von Price gestellte «Na und?» mit ein paar hausgemachten Plattitüden zu beantworten. Es könnte zum Beispiel sein, dass er das Gefühl hat, ausweglos in seiner Routine festzusitzen, und dass er deshalb flehend die Hände erhebt. Besser gefällt mir aber diese zweite Deutung: die unerwartete, rührende Möglichkeit, dass Seth Price mit seinem Werk andere Menschen erreichen und berühren will.

(Übersetzung: Bernhard Geyer)

1) Das Etikett «Zombie-Formalismus», das im Roman nicht direkt gebraucht wird, stammt aus einem Text, den der Künstler und Kunstkritiker Walter Robinson Mitte 2014 in Artspace.com veröffentlichte. Das Schlagwort verbreitete sich rasch und der Kritiker Jerry Saltz versuchte wenig später in der Zeitschrift *New York* die folgende Definition: Zombie-Formalismus «fühlt sich ‹intellektuell› an und sieht auf eine Art cool aus, die Sammler anspricht, auch wenn sich daraus überhaupt keine tieferen Einsichten ableiten lassen. Alles ist in blasse Pastelltöne getaucht und einfallslos zu einem Look arrangiert, der an digitale Medien erinnert, oder es sieht irgendwie hausgemacht oder abgegriffen aus. Das Ganze wird gespickt mit selbstreferenziellen Kommentaren zu Kunst, Recycling, Nachhaltigkeit, Aneignung und Abstraktions- und Naturprozessen. Jedes dieser Werke wiederholt dasselbe Vokabular von Schmierern, Flecken, Kleksen, Sprühern, Spritzern, Tropfen, fast monochromen Farbfeldern und Siebdruck- und Schablonen-Phrasen.»
2) Mark Klienberg, zitiert nach Seth Price, «Dispersion», 2003.
3) *Fuck Seth Price* ist als E-Book auf der Website des Künstlers sethpricestudio.com erhältlich. Eine Google-Suche nach «fuck seth price pdf» bringt jedoch keine Resultate.
4) Seth Price im Gespräch mit Charline von Heyl, Whitney Museum of American Art, New York, 20. November 2015.
5) «Seth Price and Laura Owens in Conversation», in 356 Mission Tumblr, www.356mission.tumblr.com/post/138501268495, Hervorhebung durch die Autorin.
6) Seth Price, «Lecture on the Extra Part», in *Texte zur Kunst*, September 2015, S. 136.
7) Chris Wiley, «Short Circuit», in *Seth Price: 2000 Words*, DESTE Foundation for Contemporary Art, Athen 2014, S. 8.
8) Seth Price, «Sports», 2003.
9) Seth Price, «Redistribution (video transcript)», in *Price, Seth*, JRP|Ringier, Zürich 2010, S. 101.

[Francis Fukuyama, «The End of History?», in *National Interest*, Sommer 1989. Bret Easton Ellis, *American Psycho*, Kiepenheuer & Witsch, Köln 2006. E-Book. «Ich muss noch ein paar Videos zurückbringen», S. 412, «Fleischkäse mit Chèvre und Wachteljus», S. 122, «Ich imitierte einfach die Wirklichkeit», S. 439, «Oberfläche, Oberfläche, Oberfläche», S. 585]

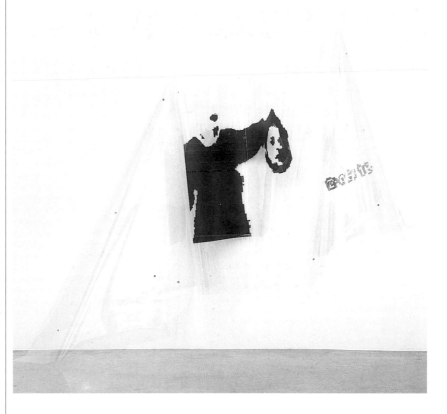

Seth Price, HOSTAGE VIDEO STILL WITH TIME STAMP, (2005–),
freeze-frame from Jihadi video file, screen-printed on archival polyester librarian's
film with signage ink, steel grommets, dimensions variable /
GEISELIVIDEO-STILL MIT ZEITSTEMPEL, Still aus Dschihad-Video,
siebgedruckt auf alterunsbeständiger Bibliotheks-Polyesterfolie, Beschilderungs-
tinte, Stahlösen, Masse variabel.

HOW MANY BUBBLES MUST A WOMAN BURST BEFORE COMING INTO HER OWN?

GEWISSE FRAUENHÄNDE SCHÄLEN DIE PERLEN AUS DEN MUSCHELN,
ANDERE WIEDERUM PFLANZEN IHNEN BLASENWERFENDE VIDEOS EIN.

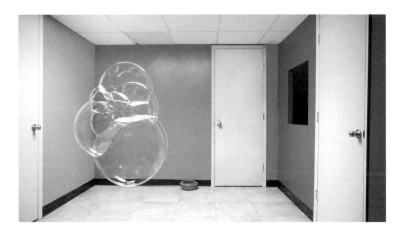

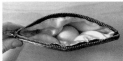 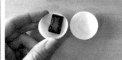

MIKA ROTTENBERG

BUBBLE 1 – BUBBLE 6 (Parkett 98)

Single channel video in six versions, with sound, approx 15–40 sec. loop. Custom-made purse in oyster design (plastic, silk lining, zipper, 4 $^3/_4$ x 2 $^3/_8$ x $^1/_2$"), with pearlescent capsule inside containing memory stick.
Video to be presented on videomonitor. Each video version Ed. 6/2APs signed and numbered certificate.

1-Kanal-Video in sechs Versionen, Ton, ca. 15–40 Sek., Loop. Täschchen in Austern-Design (Plastik, Seidenfutter, Reissverschluss, 12 x 6 x 1 cm), perlmutterbeschichtete Kapsel mit Speicherstick. Video zu betrachten auf Videomonitor. Jede Video-Version Auflage 6/2 E.A., signiertes und nummeriertes Zertifikat.

$ 1900 / € 1700 / CHF 1900

TRACES OF LIFE ON THE SKIN OF
AN AVATAR, AN EXPRESSION OF
EMOTIONS THAT ARE OUR OWN.

LEBENSSPUREN AUF DER HAUT
EINES AVATARS: SEINE EMOTIONEN
SIND DIE UNSEREN.

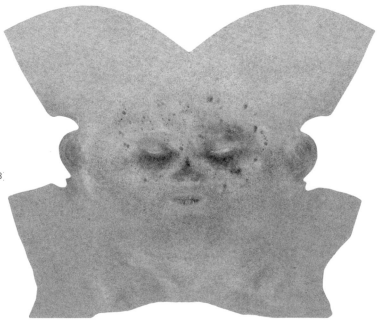

ED ATKINS

SAFE CONDUCT EPIDERMAL, 2016 (Parkett 98)

Archival pigment print on rubber, 23 $^5/_8$ x 20 x $^1/_8$", two grommets, printed by Laumont, New York. Ed. 35/XX, signed and numbered certificate.

Alterungsbeständiger Pigmentdruck auf Gummi, 60 x 51 x 0,1 cm, zwei Ösen, gedruckt von Laumont, New York.
Auflage 35/XX, signiertes und nummeriertes Zertifikat.

$ 1900 / € 1700 / CHF 1900

PRECARIOUS AND THOUGHTFUL:
A FOLDED SIT-IN.

IM LOOP EINER INSTALLATIVEN SKULPTUR:
DAS BILD ALS SOCKEL DES GEDANKENS.

LEE KIT

UPON, 2016 (Parkett 98)

Installation with photograph (archival print,
framed) and towel.
Photograph, 7 $^3/_4$ x 9 $^3/_4$", overall dimensions variable.
Ed. 35/XX, signed and numbered certificate.

Installation mit Photographie (alterungsbeständiger Print,
gerahmt) und Handtuch.
Photographie 20 x 25 cm, Gesamtmasse variabel.
Auflage 35/XX, signiertes und nummeriertes Zertifikat.

$ 1900 / € 1700 / CHF 1900

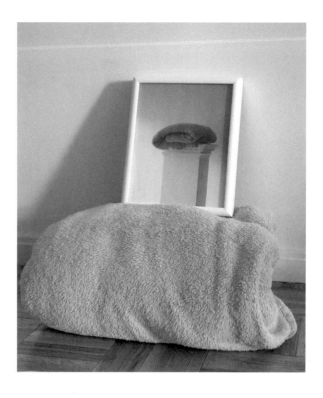

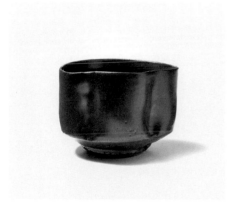 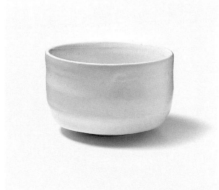

THEASTER GATES

SOUL BOWL, 2016 (Parkett 98)

Stoneware with glaze, two bowls, one in black and one in white, each unique,
diameter 4–5", height 3–3 $^1/_2$", weight ca. 1,2 lbs. each. Packed in box with
Association of Named Negro American Potters (A.N.N.A.P.) Logo.
Ed. 15 / X, signed and numbered certificate.

Tonschalen, glasiert, je eine in Schwarz und Weiss, Einzelstücke,
Durchmesser 10–13 cm, Höhe 7–9 cm, Gewicht ca. je 550 g. Verpackt in Schachtel
mit dem Logo der Association of Named Negro American Potters (A.N.N.A.P.).
Auflage 15 / X, signiertes und nummeriertes Zertifikat.

$ 2800 / € 2500 / CHF 2800

UNTOLD WORLDS FROM LITTLE STICKS DO GROW.

TRANSPORTABLE FARBENLEHRE
ZWISCHEN ORAKEL UND SELBSTBEFRAGUNG.

ABRAHAM CRUZVILLEGAS

AUTOCONCLUSIÓN, 2015 (Parkett 97)

Wooden briefcase, with 34 bamboo wood sticks in 34 different colors,
with a separate 7-color silkscreen inserted in the briefcase,
briefcase interior lined with canvas, briefcase custom made from larch wood and MDF by Stiftung St. Jakob, 13 $1/8$ x 21 x 1 $3/4$", 7,2 lb,
silkscreen printed by Atelier für Siebdruck, Lorenz Boegli
on Bütten 250 g/m^2 paper, 12 x 19 $1/2$".
Ed. 35/XX, signed and numbered certificate.

Holzkoffer, mit 34 Stäbchen aus Bambusholz in 34 Farben,
mit einem separaten Siebdruck in 7 Farben dem Koffer beiliegend,
Kofferdeckel innen mit Leinwand bezogen, Koffer handgemacht aus Lärchenholz
und MDF von Stiftung St. Jakob, 33,5 x 53,5 x 4,5 cm, 3,5 kg,
Siebdruck von Atelier für Siebdruck, Lorenz Boegli
auf Bütten 250 g/m^2, 30,5 x 50 cm.
Auflage 35/XX, signiertes und nummeriertes Zertifikat.

$ 3300 / € 2900 / CHF 3300

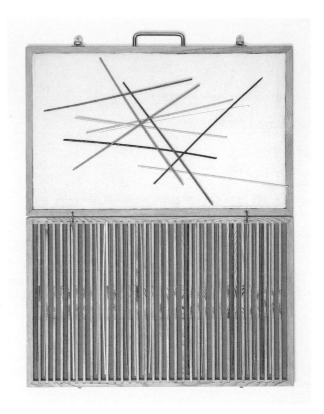

WISTFUL REMINDER OF THE
GRAND PIANO THAT ONCE WAS.
(ON SILKSCREEN)

MODIFIZIERTE SITZGELEGENHEIT
ZU EINEM ABWESENDEN INSTRUMENT.
(AUF SIEBDRUCK)

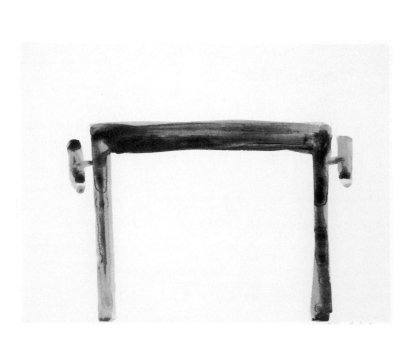

ANDREA BÜTTNER

**PIANO STOOL / KLAVIERSTUHL
(Silkscreen), 2015** (Parkett 97)

Silkscreen in 4 colors,
on 160 g/m^2 Fabriano Design 5,
24 x 25 $1/8$",
printed by Atelier für Siebdruck, Lorenz Boegli.
Ed. 25/XX, signed and numbered.

Siebdruck in 4 Farben,
auf 160 g/m^2 Fabriano Design 5,
47,5 x 62,5 cm,
gedruckt von Atelier für Siebdruck, Lorenz Boegli.
Auflage 25/XX, signiert und nummeriert.

$ 1800 / € 1600 / CHF 1800

DIGITAL FRAGMENTATION:
A UTOPIAN PLEA TO SUBVERT THE EXERCISE OF POWER?

AUCH UBER JÜNGERE UTOPIEN LEGT SICH
EINE UNSTILLBARE RUINENLUST.

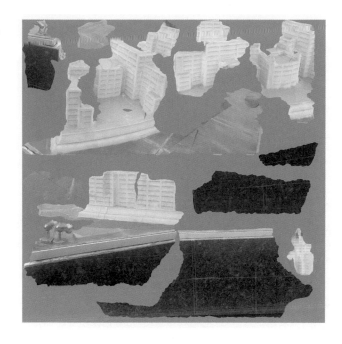

HITO STEYERL

GOSPROM, 2015 (Parkett 97)

Silkscreen in 7 colors, on Invercote G 380 g/m^2,
27 ^{1}/$_2$ x 27 ^{1}/$_2$", printed by Atelier für Siebdruck, Lorenz Boegli.
Ed. 35/XX, signed and numbered.

Siebdruck in 7 Farben, auf Invercote G 380 g/m^2, 70 x 70 cm,
gedruckt von Atelier für Siebdruck, Lorenz Boegli.
Auflage 35/XX, signiert und nummeriert.

$ 1800 / € 1600 / CHF 1800

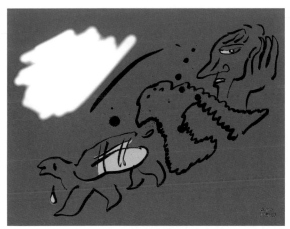

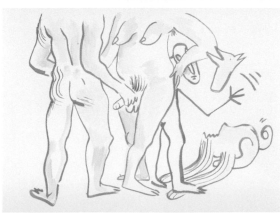

CAMILLE HENROT

EXTINCTION ON THE TABLE, 2015 (Parkett 97)

Two UV prints on both sides of one sheet of white nitrile rubber,
(the work can be installed either flat or loosely and carefully
folded on the wall, a table or the floor), with two grommets.
Printed by Laumont, New York, 22 x 30 x ^{1}/$_8$", ca. 6 lb,
Ed. 35/XX, signed and numbered.

Zwei UV-Drucke auf beiden Seiten eines weissen Nitrilkautschuk-
Bogens, (das Werk kann entweder flach oder sorgfältig gerollt
installiert werden, an einer Wand, auf einem Tisch oder
am Boden), mit zwei Ösen, gedruckt bei Laumont, New York,
55 x 75 x 0,35 cm, ca. 3 kg,
Auflage 35/XX, signiert und nummeriert.

$ 2800 / € 2500 / CHF 2800

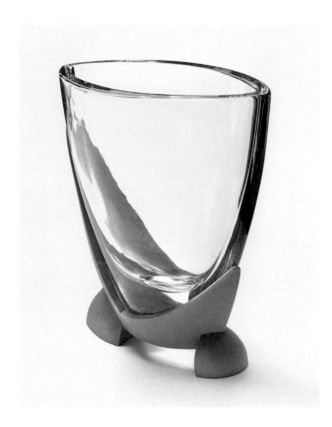

MARC CAMILLE CHAIMOWICZ

LOXOS, VASE, 1989/2015 (Parkett 96)

Crystal glass on aluminum base,
6 ³/₄ x 5 ¹/₂ x 3",
produced by Kunstbetrieb AG.
Ed. 35 / XX, signed and numbered certificate.

Kristallglas in Aluminiumfassung,
17 x 14 x 7,8 cm,
produziert von Kunstbetrieb AG.
Auflage 35 / XX, signiertes und
nummeriertes Zertifikat.

$ 2900 / € 2700 / CHF 2800

JOHN WATERS

«TRAGEDY», 2015 (Parkett 96)

Acrylic, synthetic hair,
painted silicon, urethane,
approx. 18 x 18 x 5",
produced by Alterian Inc.
Ed. 25 / XX,
signed and numbered certificate.

Acryl, künstliches Haar,
bemaltes Silikon, Urethan,
ca. 46 x 46 x 12,5 cm,
produziert von Alterian Inc.
Auflage 25 / XX,
signiertes und nummeriertes Zertifikat.

$ 6600 / € 6000 / CHF 6300

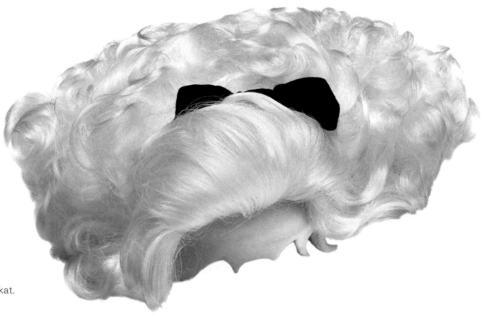

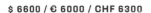

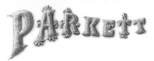

The PARKETT Series is created in collaboration with artists, who contribute an original work available exclusively to the subscribers in the form of a signed limited SPECIAL EDITION. The available works are also reproduced in each PARKETT issue.

Each SPECIAL EDITION is available by order from any one of our offices in New York or Zurich. Just fill in the details below and send this card to the office nearest you. Once your order has been processed, you will be issued with an invoice and your personal edition number. Upon receipt of payment, you will receive the SPECIAL EDITION. (Please note that supply is subject to availability. PARKETT does not assume responsibility for any delays in production of SPECIAL EDITIONS. Postage and VAT not included.)

☐ As a subscriber to PARKETT, I would like to order the following Special Edition(s), signed and numbered by the artist.

PARKETT No.	ARTIST	NAME:
PARKETT No.	ARTIST	ADDRESS:
PARKETT No.	ARTIST	CITY:
PARKETT No.	ARTIST	STATE/ZIP:
PARKETT No.	ARTIST	COUNTRY:
PARKETT No.	ARTIST	PHONE:

☐ I have indicated my way of payment on the reverse side of this form.

Send this form to the PARKETT office nearest you:

PARKETT PUBLISHERS 145 AV. OF THE AMERICAS NEW YORK, NY 10013 PHONE (212) 673-2660 FAX (212) 271-0704

PARKETT VERLAG QUELLENSTRASSE 27 CH-8031 ZÜRICH TELEFON +41-44-271 81 40 FAX +41-44-272 43 01

Visit our website: www.parkettart.com

PARKETT

Die PARKETT-Buchreihe entsteht in Zusammenarbeit mit Künstlern, die eigens für die Abonnenten einen Originalbeitrag in Form einer limitierten und signierten EDITION gestalten. Diese Editionen sind auch in der Zeitschrift abgebildet und können mit dieser Bestellkarte in jedem unserer Büros in Zürich oder New York bestellt werden. Sie erhalten dann Ihre persönliche Editionsnummer und eine Rechnung. Sobald wir Ihre Zahlung erhalten haben, schicken wir Ihnen Ihre Edition(en). Lieferung solange Vorrat. PARKETT übernimmt keine Verantwortung für allfällige Verzögerungen bei der Herstellung der Vorzugsausgaben. Versandkosten und MwSt nicht inbegriffen.

☐ Ich bin PARKETT-Abonnent(in) und bestelle folgende EDITION(EN), nummeriert und vom Künstler signiert:

PARKETT Nr.	KÜNSTLER/IN	NAME:
PARKETT Nr.	KÜNSTLER/IN	STRASSE:
PARKETT Nr.	KÜNSTLER/IN	PLZ/STADT:
PARKETT Nr.	KÜNSTLER/IN	LAND:
PARKETT Nr.	KÜNSTLER/IN	TEL.:

☐ Meine Zahlungsweise habe ich auf der Rückseite angegeben.

Senden Sie die Bestellkarte an das PARKETT-Büro in Ihrer Nähe:

PARKETT VERLAG QUELLENSTRASSE 27 CH-8031 ZÜRICH TELEFON +41-44-271 81 40 FAX +41-44-272 43 01

PARKETT PUBLISHERS 145 AV. OF THE AMERICAS NEW YORK, NY 10013 PHONE (212) 673-2660 FAX (212) 271-0704

Besuchen Sie unsere Website: www.parkettart.com

PARKETT

SUBSCRIBE, COMPLETE OR SEND A GIFT SUBSCRIPTION TO THE BEST BOOK SERIES ON CONTEMPORARY ARTISTS – WWW.PARKETTART.COM

☐ I wish to subscribe to the PARKETT Series, starting with issue no. _____

☐ I wish to send a gift subscription, starting with issue no. _____ (a gift card in my name will be sent to the recipient):

  ☐ for 1 year (2 issues) at US $ 78 (USA/Canada), € 72 (Europe), € 82 (Rest of the World)

  ☐ for 2 years (4 issues) at US $ 148 (USA/Canada), € 128 (Europe), € 164 (Rest of the World)

  ☐ for 3 years (6 issues) at US $ 205 (USA/Canada), € 185 (Europe), € 238 (Rest of the World)

  ☐ for 1 year (2 issues) at the special student discount (US $ 69 for USA/Canada, € 63 for Europe). A copy of my student ID is enclosed. Postage included. All prices subject to change.

☐ I wish to complete my PARKETT library and order the following issue(s): No. _____

  at € 30 each, postage not included.   As of No. 88: € 39.–, $ 45.00
  Within the USA & Canada $ 32, add postage: $ 5 (USA), $ 10 (Canada).
  Sold out: No. 1–13, 16–20, 22–27, 29–33, 35–41, 45.

☐ I wish to order the Set of all 55 available Parkett volumes at US $ 1,250 (USA/Canada), € 990 (Europe, rest of world), plus postage.

☐ I wish to order _____ copies of "200 Art Works – 25 Years", catalogue raisonné of Parketts' editions. 518 p., with text, 200 color repr., US $ 45.00 (USA/Canada), € 35.– (Europe, rest of world), plus postage.

☐ I wish to order _____ copies of "Sigmar Polke – Windows for the Zurich Grossmünster, € 45.–/$ 65.00, (excl. postage)

☐ I wish to order _____ copies of the CD-Rom "Parkett Inserts – 25 Years" featuring all 75 INSERT page book projects made by artists for Parkett. This CD presents for the first time a comprehensive survey of all book pages INSERT projects both in a browsing or a slide-show mode by double pages. € 32.– (USA/Canada US $ 39.00), plus postage.

NAME: _____

ADDRESS: _____

CITY: _____

STATE/ZIP/COUNTRY: _____

TEL.: _____ FAX: _____

E-MAIL: _____

GIFT RECIPIENT: _____

ADDRESS: _____

CITY: _____

STATE/ZIP: _____

COUNTRY: _____

☐ Charge my Visa Card ☐ Mastercard ☐ AMEX

Card No. |_|_|_|_|_|_|_|_|_|_|_|_|_|_|_| Expiration date _____

☐ Payment enclosed (US check or money order) ☐ Bill me

DATE _____

SIGNATURE _____

Send this form to the PARKETT office nearest you:

PARKETT PUBLISHERS 145 AV. OF THE AMERICAS NEW YORK, NY 10013 PHONE (212) 673-2660 FAX (212) 271-0704
PARKETT VERLAG QUELLENSTRASSE 27 CH-8031 ZÜRICH TELEFON +41-44-271 81 40 FAX +41-44-272 43 01
Visit our website: www.parkettart.com

PARKETT

ABONNIEREN, VERVOLLSTÄNDIGEN ODER VERSCHENKEN SIE DIE UMFASSENDSTE BUCHREIHE ÜBER GEGENWARTSKÜNSTLER – WWW.PARKETTART.COM

☐ Ich abonniere die PARKETT-Reihe ab Nr. _____

☐ Ich verschenke ein PARKETT-Abonnement ab Nr. _____ (Der/die Beschenkte erhält eine Geschenkkarte in meinem Namen)

  ☐ für 1 Jahr (2 Bände) zu: € 72 (Europa), CHF 95.– (Schweiz),

  ☐ für 2 Jahre (4 Bände) zu: € 128 (Europa), CHF 168.– (Schweiz),

  ☐ für 3 Jahre (6 Bände) zu: € 185 (Europa), CHF 248.– (Schweiz),

  ☐ für 1 Jahr (2 Bände) zum Studenten-Sonderpreis (Europa: € 63 /Schweiz: CHF 85.–). Eine Kopie meines gültigen Studentenausweises lege ich bei. Preise einschliesslich Versandkosten. Preisänderungen vorbehalten.

☐ Ich möchte meine PARKETT-Bibliothek vervollständigen und bestelle die folgenden noch erhältliche(n) Ausgabe(n): Nr. _____

  zu je € 30 / CHF 45.–, zzgl. Versandkosten (vergriffen: Nr. 1–13, 16–20, 22–27, 29–33, 35–41, 45). Ab Nr. 88: € 39.–, CHF 55.–

☐ Ich bestelle den Set aller 55 erhältlichen Parkett-Bände zu € 990 (Europa), CHF 1400.– (Schweiz), zzgl. Versandkosten.

☐ Ich bestelle _____ Ex. «200 Artworks – 25 Years», Werkkatalog aller Parkett-Künstler-Editionen. 518 S. mit Text, 200 Farbabb. € 35.– (Schweiz CHF 49.–), zzgl. Versand.

☐ Ich bestelle _____ Ex. «Sigmar Polke's Fenster für das Zürcher Grossmünster» € 45.–/CHF 68.–, zzgl. Versandkosten.

☐ Ich bestelle _____ Ex. der CD-Rom «Parkett Inserts – 25 Years» mit allen 75 von Künstlern für Parkett gestalteten Inserts. Die CD-Rom gibt erstmals einen vollständigen Überblick über alle Inserts-Buchseiten-Projekte, sie können doppelseitenweise oder als Dia-Schau betrachtet werden. € 32.– (Schweiz CHF 45.–), zzgl. Versand.

NAME: _____

STRASSE: _____

PLZ/STADT: _____

LAND: _____

TEL.: _____ FAX: _____

E-MAIL: _____

BESCHENKTE(R): _____

STRASSE: _____

PLZ/STADT: _____

LAND: _____

☐ Ich zahle mit Visa ☐ Eurocard/Mastercard ☐ AMEX

Karten Nr. |_|_|_|_|_|_|_|_|_|_|_|_|_|_|_| Gültig bis _____

☐ Mein Scheck über CHF/€ _____ liegt bei.

☐ Bitte senden Sie mir eine Rechnung.

DATUM _____

UNTERSCHRIFT _____

Senden Sie die Bestellkarte an das PARKETT-Büro in Ihrer Nähe:

PARKETT VERLAG QUELLENSTRASSE 27 CH-8031 ZÜRICH TELEFON +41-44-271 81 40 FAX +41-44-272 43 01
PARKETT PUBLISHERS 145 AV. OF THE AMERICAS NEW YORK, NY 10013 PHONE (212) 673-2660 FAX (212) 271-0704
Besuchen Sie unsere Website: www.parkettart.com

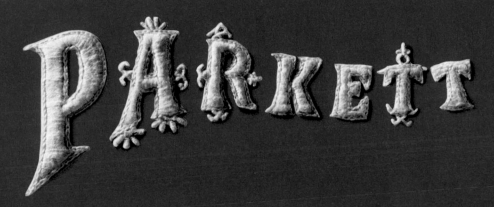

98

Volumes

250

Artists Collaborations

1400

Texts

8000

Color Illustrations

The Collection of All Books

Vol. 1 – 98, 1984 – 2016

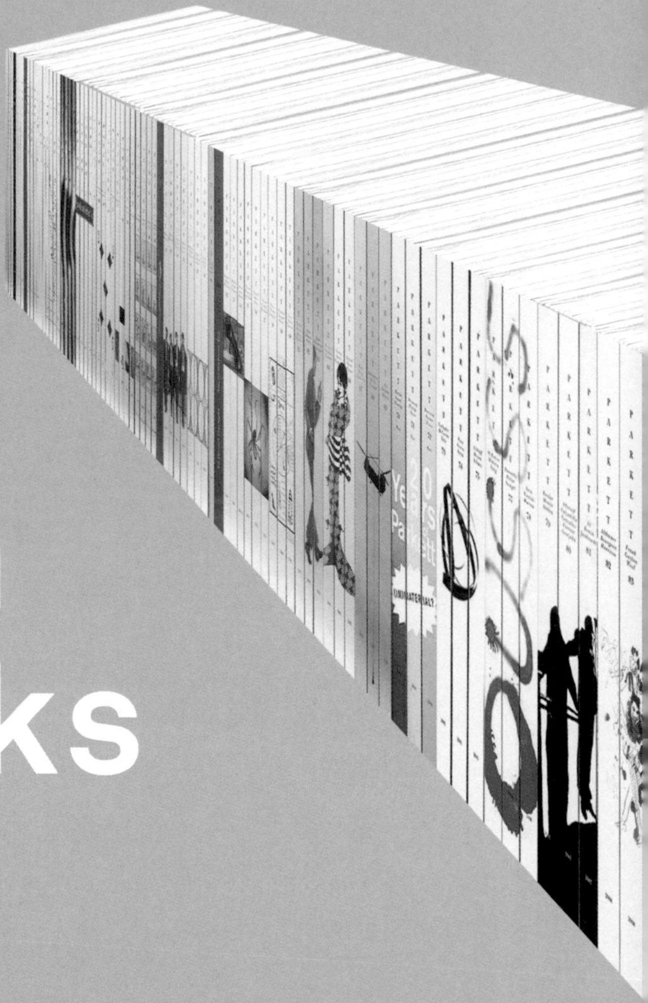

- **Single Volumes**
- **Subscription (1, 2 or 3 years / 2, 4 or 6 Vol.)**
- **Set of all 60 available Volumes**
- **Complete Collection of all Volumes**

More info: **www.parkettart.com/collection-of-all-books**

We gladly assist you in finding missing, out-of-print volumes and completing your collection of Parkett Books.

Please contact us in Zurich or New York.

Parkett Verlag
Quellenstrasse 27
8005 Zurich
+41-44-271 8140

Bozena Civic, Zurich
b.civic@parkettart.com

Parkett Publishers
145 Ave. Of the Americas
New York, NY 10013
+1-212-673 2660

Melissa Burgos, New York
m.burgos@parkettart.com

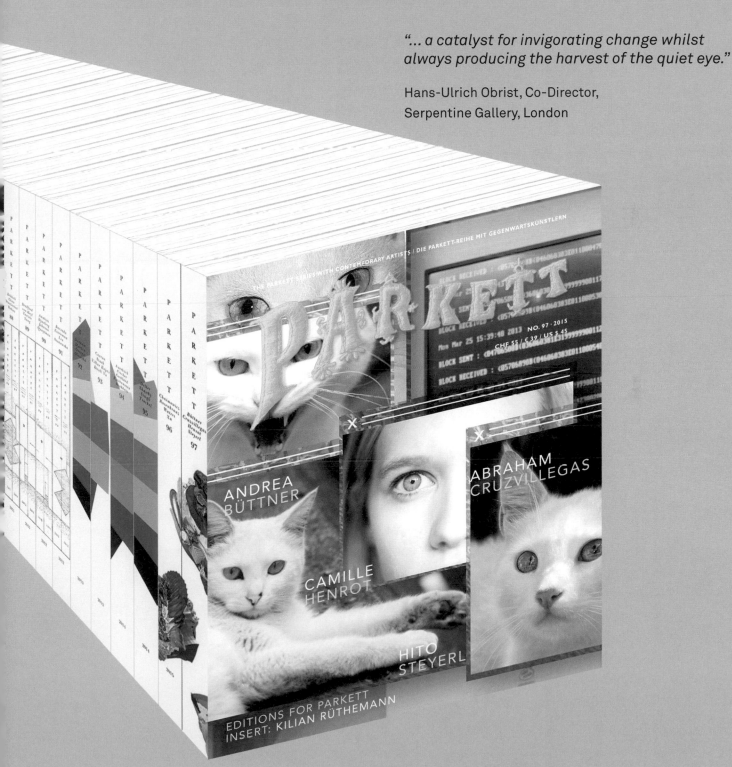

The Collection
of All Books

1984 – 2016

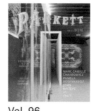
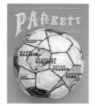
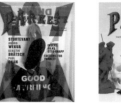
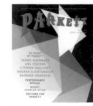

Vol. 97   Vol. 96   Vol. 95   Vol. 94

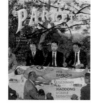
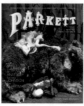
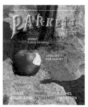
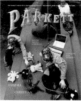
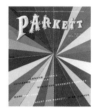

Vol. 93   Vol. 92   Vol. 91   Vol. 90   Vol. 89   Vol. 88   Vol. 87

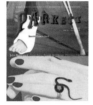
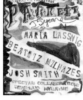
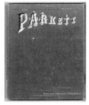
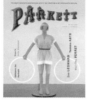
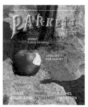
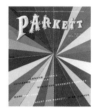
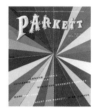

Vol. 86   Vol. 85   Vol. 84   Vol. 83   Vol. 82   Vol. 81   Vol. 80

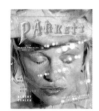
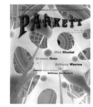
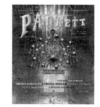
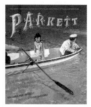
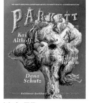
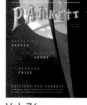
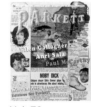

Vol. 79   Vol. 78   Vol. 77   Vol. 76   Vol. 75   Vol. 74   Vol. 73

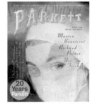
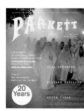
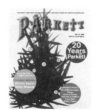
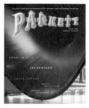
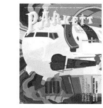
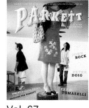
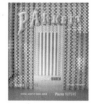

Vol. 72   Vol. 71   Vol. 70   Vol. 69   Vol. 68   Vol. 67   Vol. 66

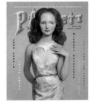
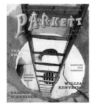
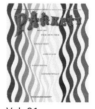
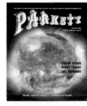
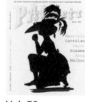

Vol. 65   Vol. 64   Vol. 63   Vol. 62   Vol. 61   Vol. 60   Vol. 59

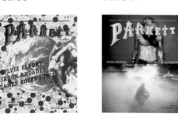
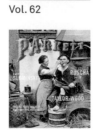
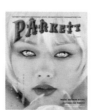
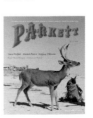
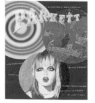

Vol. 58   Vol. 57   Vol. 56   Vol. 55   Vol. 54   Vol. 53   Vol. 52

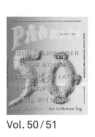
Vol. 50/51

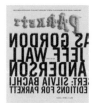
Vol. 49

Vol. 48

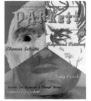
Vol. 47

Vol. 46

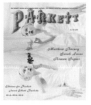
Vol. 45

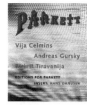
Vol. 44

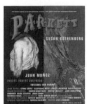
Vol. 43

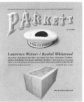
Vol. 42

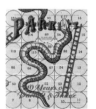
Vol. 40/41

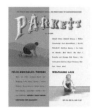
Vol. 39

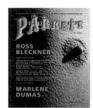
Vol. 38

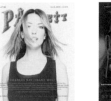
Vol. 37

Vol. 36

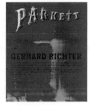
Vol. 35

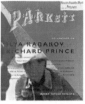
Vol. 34

Vol. 33

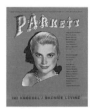
Vol. 32

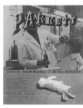
Vol. 31

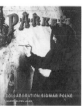
Vol. 30

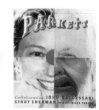
Vol. 29

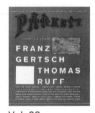
Vol. 28

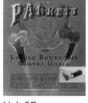
Vol. 27

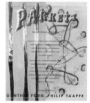
Vol. 26

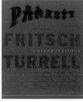
Vol. 25

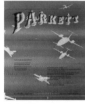
Vol. 24

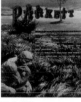
Vol. 23

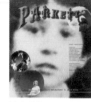
Vol. 22

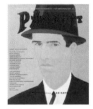
Vol.21

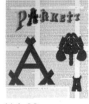
Vol. 20

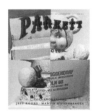
Vol. 19

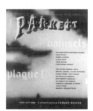
Vol. 18

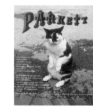
Vol.17

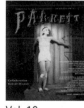
Vol. 16

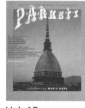
Vol. 15

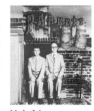
Vol. 14

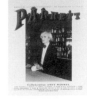
Vol. 13

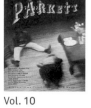
Vol. 12

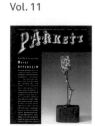
Vol. 11

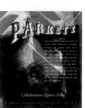
Vol. 10

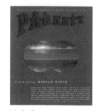
Vol. 9

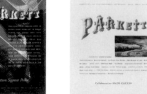
Vol. 8

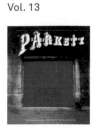
Vol. 7

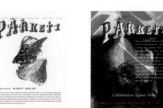
Vol. 6

Vol. 5

Vol. 4

Vol. 3

Vol. 2

Vol. 1

All Artists Alphabetically
Vol. 1–99 (1984–2016)

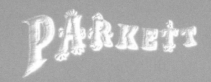

Tomma Abts, 84
Franz Ackermann, 68
Eija-Liisa Ahtila, 68
Ai Weiwei, 81
Doug Aitken, 57
Jennifer Allora /
Guillermo Calzadilla, 80
Paweł Althamer, 82
Kai Althoff, 75
Francis Alÿs, 69
El Anatsui, 90
Laurie Anderson, 49
John Armleder, 50/51
Richard Artschwager, 23, 46
Ed Atkins, 98
Tauba Auerbach, 94
John Baldessari, 29, 86
Stephan Balkenhol, 36
Matthew Barney, 45
Yto Barrada, 91
Georg Baselitz, 11
Vanessa Beecroft, 56
Ross Bleckner, 38
John Bock, 67
Alighiero e Boetti, 24
Christian Boltanski, 22
Monica Bonvicini, 72
Louise Bourgeois, 27, 82
Carol Bove, 86
Mark Bradford, 89
Kerstin Brätsch and
DAS INSTITUT, 88
Olaf Breuning, 71
Glenn Brown, 75
Angela Bulloch, 66
Daniel Buren, 66
Andrea Büttner, 97
Sophie Calle, 36
Valentin Carron, 93
Maurizio Cattelan, 59
Vija Celmins, 44
Marc Camille Chaimowicz, 96
Paul Chan, 88
Francesco Clemente, 9, 40/41
Chuck Close, 60
Abraham Cruzvillegas, 97
Enzo Cucchi, 1
John Currin, 65
Tacita Dean, 62
Jeremy Deller, 95
Thomas Demand, 62
Martin Disler, 3
Nathalie Djurberg, 90
Peter Doig, 67
Trisha Donnelly, 77
Marlene Dumas, 38
Jimmie Durham, 92
Nicole Eisenman, 91
Olafur Eliasson, 64

Tracey Emin, 63
Omer Fast , 99
Cao Fei, 99
Urs Fischer, 72, 94
Eric Fischl, 5
Peter Fischli /
David Weiss, 17, 40/41
Sylvie Fleury, 58
Günther Förg, 26, 40/41
Robert Frank, 83
Tom Friedman, 64
Katharina Fritsch, 25, 87
Bernard Frize, 74
Cyprien Gaillard, 94
Ellen Gallagher, 73
Theaster Gates, 98
Isa Genzken, 69
Franz Gertsch, 28
Adrian Ghenie, 99
Gilbert & George, 14
Liam Gillick, 61
Robert Gober, 27
Nan Goldin, 57
Dominique Gonzalez-
Foerster, 80
Felix Gonzalez-Torres, 39
Douglas Gordon, 49
Dan Graham, 68
Rodney Graham, 64
Katharina Grosse, 74
Mark Grotjahn, 80
Andreas Gursky, 44
Wade Guyton, 83
David Hammons, 31
Rachel Harrison, 82
Camille Henrot, 97
Thomas Hirschhorn, 57
Damien Hirst, 40/41
Carsten Höller, 77
Jenny Holzer, 40/41
Rebecca Horn, 13, 40/41
Roni Horn, 54
Gary Hume, 48
Pierre Huyghe, 66
Christian Jankowski, 81
Rashid Johnson, 90
Ilya Kabakov, 34
Anish Kapoor, 69
Alex Katz, 21, 72
Mike Kelley, 31
Ellsworth Kelly, 56
Annette Kelm, 87
William Kentridge, 63
Jon Kessler, 79
Karen Kilimnik, 52
Martin Kippenberger, 19
Lee Kit, 98
Ragnar Kjartansson, 94
Imi Knoebel, 32

Jeff Koons, 19, 50/51
Jannis Kounellis, 6
Yayoi Kusama, 59
Wolfgang Laib, 39
Maria Lassnig, 85
Zoe Leonard, 84
Sherrie Levine, 32
Liu Xiaodong, 91
Sarah Lucas, 45
Christian Marclay, 70
Brice Marden, 7
Helen Marten, 92
Paul McCarthy, 73
Josiah McElheny, 86
Lucy McKenzie, 76
Julie Mehretu, 76
Mario Merz, 15
Beatriz Milhazes, 85
Marilyn Minter, 79
Tracey Moffatt, 53
Mariko Mori, 54
Malcolm Morley, 52
Sarah Morris, 61
Juan Muñoz, 43
Jean-Luc Mylayne, 50/51, 85
Bruce Nauman, 10
Ernesto Neto, 78
Olaf Nicolai, 78
Cady Noland, 46
Albert Oehlen, 79
Paulina Olowska, 92
Meret Oppenheim, 4
Gabriel Orozco, 48
Damián Ortega, 92
Tony Oursler, 47
Laura Owens, 65
Jorge Pardo, 56
Philippe Parreno, 86
Mai-Thu Perret, 84
Raymond Pettibon, 47
Elizabeth Peyton, 53
Richard Phillips, 71
Sigmar Polke, 2, 30, 40/41
Richard Prince, 34, 72
R.H. Quaytman, 90
Michael Raedecker, 65
Markus Raetz, 8
Charles Ray, 37
Jason Rhoades, 58
Gerhard Richter, 35
Bridget Riley, 61
Pipilotti Rist, 48, 71
Matthew Ritchie, 61
Tim Rollins & K.O.S., 20
Ugo Rondinone, 52
Pamela Rosenkranz, 96
James Rosenquist, 58
Mika Rothenberg, 98
Susan Rothenberg, 43

Thomas Ruff, 28
Edward Ruscha, 18, 55
Anri Sala, 73
Wilhelm Sasnal, 70
Gregor Schneider, 63
Thomas Schütte, 47
Dana Schutz, 75
Richard Serra, 74
Shirana Shahbazi, 94
Wael Shawky, 95
Cindy Sherman, 29
Dayanita Singh, 95
Roman Signer, 45
Andreas Slominski, 55
Josh Smith, 85
Monika Sosnowska, 91
Frances Stark, 93
Hito Steyerl, 97
Rudolf Stingel, 77
Beat Streuli, 54
Thomas Struth, 50/51
Sturtevant, 88
Hiroshi Sugimoto, 46
Philip Taaffe, 26
Sam Taylor-Wood, 55
Diana Thater, 60
Wolfgang Tillmans, 53
Rirkrit Tiravanija, 44
Fred Tomaselli, 67
Rosemarie Trockel, 33, 95
Oscar Tuazon, 89
James Turrell, 25
Luc Tuymans, 60
Keith Tyson, 71
Adrian Villar Rojas, 93
Danh Vo, 93
Cosima von Bonin, 81
Charline von Heyl, 89
Kelley Walker, 87
Kara Walker, 59
Jeff Wall, 22, 49
Andy Warhol, 12
Rebecca Warren, 78
John Waters, 96
Gillian Wearing, 70
Lawrence Weiner, 42
Andro Wekua, 88
John Wesley, 62
Franz West, 37, 70
Rachel Whiteread, 42
Sue Williams, 50/51
Robert Wilson, 16
Christopher Wool, 33, 83
Cerith Wyn Evans, 87
Yang Fudong, 76
Haegue Yang, 89
Lynette Yiadom-Boakye, 99
Xu Zhen, 96

All Volumes & Editions Chronologically
Vol. 1 – 99 (1984 – 2016)

○ = available volumes
◉ = out-of-print volumes
● = available editions

We will gladly assist you in finding out-of-print volumes. Please inquire about the Set of all 55 available volumes. Delivery subject to availability at time of order.

PARKETT IN BOOKSHOPS (Selection)

PARKETT IS AVAILABLE IN 500 LEADING ART BOOKSHOPS AROUND THE WORLD. FOR FURTHER INFORMATION CONTACT:
PARKETT GIBT ES IN 500 FÜHRENDEN KUNSTBUCHHANDLUNGEN AUF DER GANZEN WELT. FÜR WEITERE INFORMATIONEN WENDEN SIE SICH BITTE AN:
PARKETT VERLAG, QUELLENSTRASSE 27, CH-8031 ZÜRICH, TEL. +41-44 271 81 40, FAX 272 43 01, WWW.PARKETTART.COM;
PARKETT, 145, AVENUE OF THE AMERICAS, NEW YORK, N.Y. 10013, PHONE +1 (212) 673-2660, FAX 271-0704, WWW.PARKETTART.COM

NORTH & SOUTH AMERICA, ASIA, AUSTRALIA

DISTRIBUTOR / VERTRIEB
D.A.P. (DISTRIBUTED ART PUBLISHERS)
155 AVENUE OF THE AMERICAS,
2ND FLOOR,
NEW YORK, NY 10013

USA

BEACON, NY
DIA: BEACON
3 BEEKMAN STREET

BERKELEY, CA
BERKELEY ART MUSEUM
2625 DURANT AVENUE

BOSTON, MA
TRIDENT BOOKSELLERS
338 NEWBURY STREET

CAMBRIDGE, MA
MIT PRESS BOOKSTORE
292 MAIN STREET

CHICAGO, IL
MUSEUM OF CONTEMPORARY ART
220 EAST CHICAGO AVENUE

CORAL GABLES, FL
BOOKS & BOOKS
265 ARAGON ROAD

HOUSTON, TX
BRAZOS BOOKSTORE
2421 BISSONNET

LOS ANGELES, CA
MUSEUM OF CONTEMPORARY ART
250, S. GRAND
SKYLIGHT BOOKS
18181 N. VERMONT AVENUE
BOOK SOUP, INC. WEST HOLLYWOOD
8818 SUNSET BOULEVARD
LEAD APRON INC.
8445 MELROSE PLACE

MIAMI, FL
BOOKS & BOOKS
296 ARAGON AVENUE, CORAL GABLES

NEW YORK, NY
MUSEUM OF MODERN ART
11 WEST 53RD STREET
NEW MUSEUM OF CONTEMPORARY
ART STORE
235 BOWERY
ARTBOOK@PS1
22–25 JACKSON AVENUE
PRINTED MATTER
195 10TH AVENUE

GLOBAL NEWS
22 8TH AVENUE
SPOONBILL & SUGARTOWN
218 BEDFORD AVENUE
McNALLY JACKSON
52 PRINCE STREET
ANARTIST
993 AMSTERDAM AVENUE
BROOKLYN MUSEUM OF ART
200 EASTERN PARKWAY
DECADE BOOKS
236 GRAND STREET

OAKLAND, CA
DIESEL, A BOOKSTORE
5433 COLLEGE AVENUE

PHILADELPHIA, PA
AVRIL 50
3406 SANSOM STREET

PORTLAND, OR
POWELL'S BOOKS
1005 W. BURNSIDE
MONOGRAPH BOOKWERKS
5005 NE 27TH AVENUE

SAN FRANCISCO, CA
OWL CAVE BOOKS
855 VALENCIA STREET

ST. LOUIS, MO
LEFT BANK BOOKS
399 NORTH EUCLID

SANTA MONICA, CA
ARCANA
8675 WASHINGTON BLVD
HENNESSEY & INGALLS BOOKS
214 WILSHIRE BLVD

WASHINGTON D.C.
NATIONAL GALLERY OF ART
4TH STREET & CONSTITUTION
AVENUE, NW

CANADA / KANADA

MONTREAL
OLIVIERI LIBRAIRIE BOOKSTORE
5210 CHEMIN DE LA CÔTE DES NIEGES

TORONTO
ART METROPOLE
1490 DUNDAS STREET WEST

AUSTRALIA / AUSTRALIEN

MELBOURNE
MAG NATION
88 ELIZABETH STREET

SYDNEY
MAG NATION
155 KING STREET

ASIA / ASIEN

JAPAN
TOKYO
SHIMADA & CO INC. / 601 ODAKYU
MINAMI-AOYAMA MANSIONS

CHINA
BEIJING
TIMEZONE 8 BOOKS & CAFÉ
NO. 4 JIU XIAN QIAO ROAD
ULLENS CENTER FOR
CONTEMPORARY ART
798 ART DISTRICT, NO. 4 JIUXIANQIAO
LU, CHAOYANG DISTRICT

HONGKONG
TOMART LIMITED (KUBRICK)
SHOP H2, YAU MA TEI, KAWLOON

SHANGHAI
TIMEZONE 8 BOOKS & CAFÉ
NO. 50 MOGANSHAN ROAD

CENTRAL & SOUTH AMERICA / MITTEL- & SÜDAMERIKA

MEXICO
MEXICO D.F.
HABITA BOOKS BY A & R PRESS
PRESIDENTE MASARYK # 201,
COL. POLANCO/DEL.
MIGUEL HIDALGO

BRAZIL
SAO PAULO
LIVRARIA DA VILA LTDA
RUA FRADIQUE COUTINHO, 915
VILA MADALENA

GREAT BRITAIN / GROSSBRITANNIEN

DISTRIBUTOR / VERTRIEB
CENTRAL BOOKS
99, WALLIS ROAD
LONDON E9 5LN

BRADFORD
DAILY NEWS
40 GREAT HORTON ROAD
FUSE ART SPACE
5 – 7 RAWSON PLACE

BRISTOL
ARNOLFINI BOOKSHOP
16 NARROW QUAY

LONDON
ARTWORDS BOOKSHOP
65 A RIVINGTON STREET
CAMDEN ARTS CENTRE
ARKWRIGHT ROAD
HAYWARD GALLERY
SOUTH BANK CENTRE
TATE MODERN
BANKSIDE
WATERSTONE BOOKSELLERS
9/13 GARRICK STREET, WC2
WHITE CUBE BOOKSHOP
144 – 152 BERMONDSEY STREET
ZABLUDOWICZ COLLECTION
176 PRINCE OF WALES ROAD

OXFORD
MODERN ART OXFORD
30 PEMBROKE STREET

SCOTLAND / SCHOTTLAND

EDINBURGH
EDINBURGH PRINTMAKERS
23 UNION STREET
FRUITMARKET GALLERY
45 MARKET STREET

GLASGOW
FAT BUDDHA LTD.
73 VINCENT STREET
TRANSMISSION GALLERY
28 KING STREET

IRELAND / IRLAND

CORK
LEWIS GLUCKSMAN GALLERY
UNIVERSITY COLLEGE

DUBLIN
DOUGLAS HYDE GALLERY
TRINITY COLLEGE

GERMANY / DEUTSCHLAND

DISTRIBUTOR / VERTRIEB
GVA VERLAGSSERVICE GÖTTINGEN
PF 2021
D-37010 GÖTTINGEN

BERLIN
BÜCHERBOGEN AM SAVIGNYPLATZ
STADTBAHNBOGEN 593
DO YOU READ ME?!
AUGUSTSTRASSE 28
THEMATISCHE BUCHHANDLUNG
PRO QM
ALMSTADTSTRASSE 48–50
WASMUTH GMBH
PFALZBURGERSTRASSE 43 – 44

BONN
BUCHLADEN 46
KAISERSTRASSE 46

DÜSSELDORF
MÜLLER & BÖHM
BOLKERSTRASSE 53
WALTHER KÖNIG BUCHHANDLUNG
GRABBEPLATZ 4

FRANKFURT
KUNST-BUCH, KUNSTHALLE SCHIRN
RÖMERBERG /
WALTHER KÖNIG BUCHHANDLUNG
DOMSTRASSE 6

HAMBURG
SAUTTER + LACKMANN BUCHHANDLUNG
ADMIRALITÄTSTRASSE 71/72

HANNOVER
MERZ KUNSTBUCHHANDLUNG
KURT-SCHWITTERS-PLATZ 1

KARLSRUHE
HOSER & MENDE
KARLSTRASSE 76

KÖLN
WALTHER KÖNIG BUCHHANDLUNG
EHRENSTRASSE 4

MÜNCHEN
BUCHHANDLUNG WALTHER KÖNIG IM
HAUS DER KUNST
PRINZREGENTENSTRASSE 1
L. WERNER BUCHHANDLUNG
RESIDENZSTRASSE 18

STUTTGART
LIMACHER BUCHHANDLUNG
KÖNIGSTRASSE 28
HOSER & MENDE
WILHELMSTRASSE 12

AUSTRIA / ÖSTERREICH

LINZ
ALEX – EINE BUCHHANDLUNG
HAUPTPLATZ 21

WIEN
DER BUCHFREUND
SONNENFELSGASSE 4
KUNSTHALLE WIEN
MUSEUMSPLATZ 1

SPAIN / SPANIEN

BARCELONA
LAIE – CAIXAFÒRUM
AVDA. FERRER I GUÀRDIA 6–8

BILBAO
GUGGENHEIM MUSEUM
ABANDOIBARRA ET. 2

MADRID
PUBLICACIONES DE ARQUITECTURA
GENERAL RODRIGO 1

FRANCE / FRANKREICH

PARIS
CENTRE POMPIDOU, FLAMMARION 4
26, RUE JACOB
GALERIE NATIONALE DU JEU DE PAUME
1, PLACE DE LA CONCORDE
LIBRAIRIE DU MUSÉE D'ART MODERNE
9, RUE GASTON DE SAINT-PAUL
PALAIS DE TOKYO
13, AVENUE DU PRÉSIDENT WILSON

ITALY / ITALIEN

MILANO
ART BOOK MILANO
VIA VENTURA 5

ROMA
GALLERIA NAZIONALE D'ARTE MODERNA
131, VIA DELLE BELLE ARTI

NORWAY / NORWEGEN

OSLO
TOPEDO KUNSTBOKHANDELEN WERGE-
LANDSVEIEN 17
STENERSEN MUSEUM
TØYENGATA 53

SWEDEN / SCHWEDEN

STOCKHOLM
KONSTIG AB
ASOGATAN 124

NETHERLANDS, BELGIUM AND LUXEMBURG

DISTRIBUTOR / VERTRIEB
IDEA BOOKS
NIEUWE HERENGRACHT 11
NL-1011 RK AMSTERDAM

NETHERLANDS / NIEDERLANDE

AMSTERDAM
ATHENAEUM NIEUWSCENTRUM
SPUI 14–16

EINDHOVEN
MOTTA
GROTE BERG 70

HAARLEM
ATHENAEUM
GED. OUDE GRACHT 70

HENGELO
BROEKHUIS
WEMENSTRAAT 45

BELGIUM / BELGIEN

ANTWERPEN
COPYRIGHT BOOKSHOP
NATIONALSTRAAT 28A

BRUXELLES
PEINTURE FRAICHE
10, RUE DU TABELLON

GENT
COPYRIGHT BOOKSHOP
JACOBIJNENSTRAAT 8

LUXEMBOURG / LUXEMBURG

LUXEMBOURG
CASINO LUXEMBOURG
41, RUE NOTRE-DAME

POLAND / POLEN

WARSAW
MUZEUM SZTUKI NOWOCZESNEJ W
WARSZAWIE / PANSKA 3

SWITZERLAND / SCHWEIZ

DISTRIBUTOR / VERTRIEB
AVA
CENTRALWEG 16
CH-8910 AFFOLTERN A. A.

BASEL
FONDATION BEYELER
BASELSTRASSE 77, RIEHEN
DOMUS HAUS
PFLUGGAESSLEIN 3
KUNSTMUSEUM BUCHHANDLUNG
ST. ALBAN-GRABEN 16
GALERIE STAMPA
SPALENBERG 2
PEP + NO NAME
GÜTERSTRASSE 189

BERN
MÜNSTERGASS BUCHHANDLUNG
MÜNSTERGASSE 33

LAUSANNE
EX NIHILO
6, AV. WILLIAM FRAISSE

LUZERN
ALTER EGO
MARIAHILFGASSE 3

ST. GALLEN
BUCHHANDLUNG LUECHINGER
MAGNIHALDEN 3
ORELL FÜSSLI RÖSSLITOR
MULTERGASSE 1 – 3

ST. MORITZ
WEGA BUCHHANDLUNG
VIA MULIN 4

WINTERTHUR
VOGEL THALIA BÜCHER
MARKTGASSE 41

ZÜRICH
CALLIGRAMME BUCHHANDLUNG
HÄRINGSTRASSE 4
KUNSTGRIFF BUCHHANDLUNG
LIMMATSTRASSE 270
KUNSTHAUS ZÜRICH
HEIMPLATZ 1
ORELL FÜSSLI KRAMHOF
FÜSSLISTRASSE 4
BUCHHANDLUNG SCHULTHESS
ZWINGLIPLATZ 2

SAINT LAURENT

P A R I S

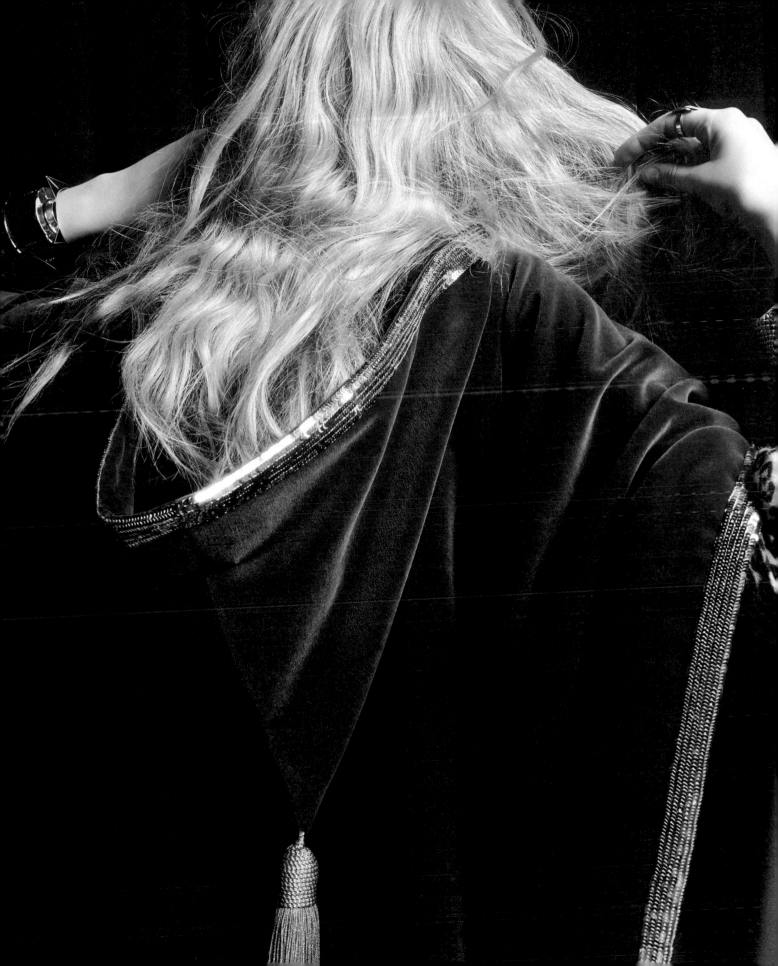

Lee Kit

September 8 - October 22, 2016

JANE LOMBARD GALLERY
518 W 19TH STREET, NEW YORK NY 10011
+1 212.967.8040 JANELOMBARDGALLERY.COM

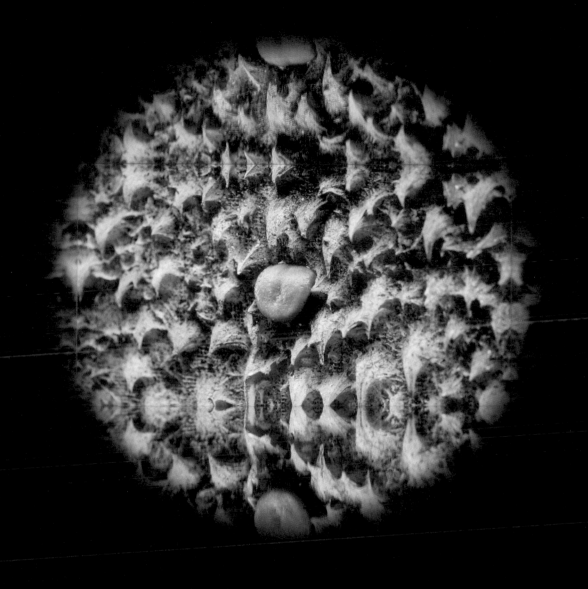

MIKA ROTTENBERG

June 23 – September 11, 2016

PALAIS
DE TOKYO
www.palaisdetokyo.com

MIKA ROTTENBERG IS REPRESENTED
BY ANDREA ROSEN GALLERY, NEW YORK
AND GALERIE LAURENT GODIN, PARIS

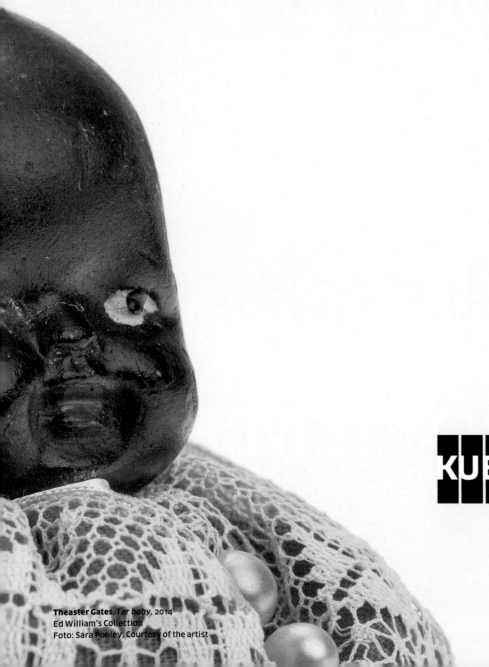

Kunsthaus Bregenz

Theaster Gates

Black Archive

23 | 04 – 26 | 06 | 2016

KUB

Kunsthaus Bregenz
Karl-Tizian-Platz |
6900 Bregenz | Austria
www.kunsthaus-bregenz.at

ELLIOTT HUNDLEY
MAY 13 - JUNE 18, 2016

DANIEL RICHTER
JUNE 25 - AUGUST 13, 2016

ABRAHAM CRUZVILLEGAS
SEPTEMBER 10 - OCTOBER 22, 2016

WOLFGANG TILLMANS
NOVEMBER 5 - DECEMBER 23, 2016

THEASTER GATES
JANUARY 14 - FEBRUARY 18, 2017

REGEN PROJECTS

6750 SANTA MONICA BOULEVARD   LOS ANGELES CA 90038   TEL 1 310 276 5424   FAX 1 310 276 7430   WWW.REGENPROJECTS.COM

MARIAN GOODMAN GALLERY

NEW YORK   24 WEST 57TH STREET NEW YORK NY 10019

Gerhard Richter: Paintings and Drawings
7 MAY – 25 JUNE

PARIS   79 RUE DU TEMPLE 75003 PARIS

Dara Birnbaum: Psalm 29(30)
22 APRIL – 4 JUNE

Matt Saunders: Inondé
22 APRIL – 4 JUNE

LONDON   5–8 LOWER JOHN STREET LONDON W1F 9DY

Ettore Spalletti: Every dawn, is first / Ogni alba, è la prima
28 APRIL – 4 JUNE

WWW.MARIANGOODMAN.COM

Richard Aldrich
Allora & Calzadilla
Ahmed Alsoudani
Kai Althoff
Miroslaw Balka
Matthew Barney
Robert Bechtle
Alighiero Boetti
Claudia Comte
Carroll Dunham
Cecilia Edefalk

Mario Merz
Marisa Merz
Dave Muller
Wangechi Mutu
Jean-Luc Mylayne
Shirin Neshat
Damián Ortega
Philippe Parreno
Elizabeth Peyton
Walter Pichler
Lari Pittman

Gladstone Gallery

Roe Ethridge
Cyprien Gaillard
Gary Hill
Thomas Hirschhorn
Jim Hodges
Huang Yong Ping
Cameron Jamie
Anish Kapoor
Sharon Lockhart
Andrew Lord
Sarah Lucas
Victor Man

Magnus Plessen
R. H. Quaytman
Ugo Rondinone
Gedi Sibony
Walter Swennen
Rosemarie Trockel
Paloma Varga Weisz
Andro Wekua
T. J. Wilcox

Keith Haring Foundation
Jack Smith Archive

24th Street, 21st Street, Brussels
www.gladstonegallery.com

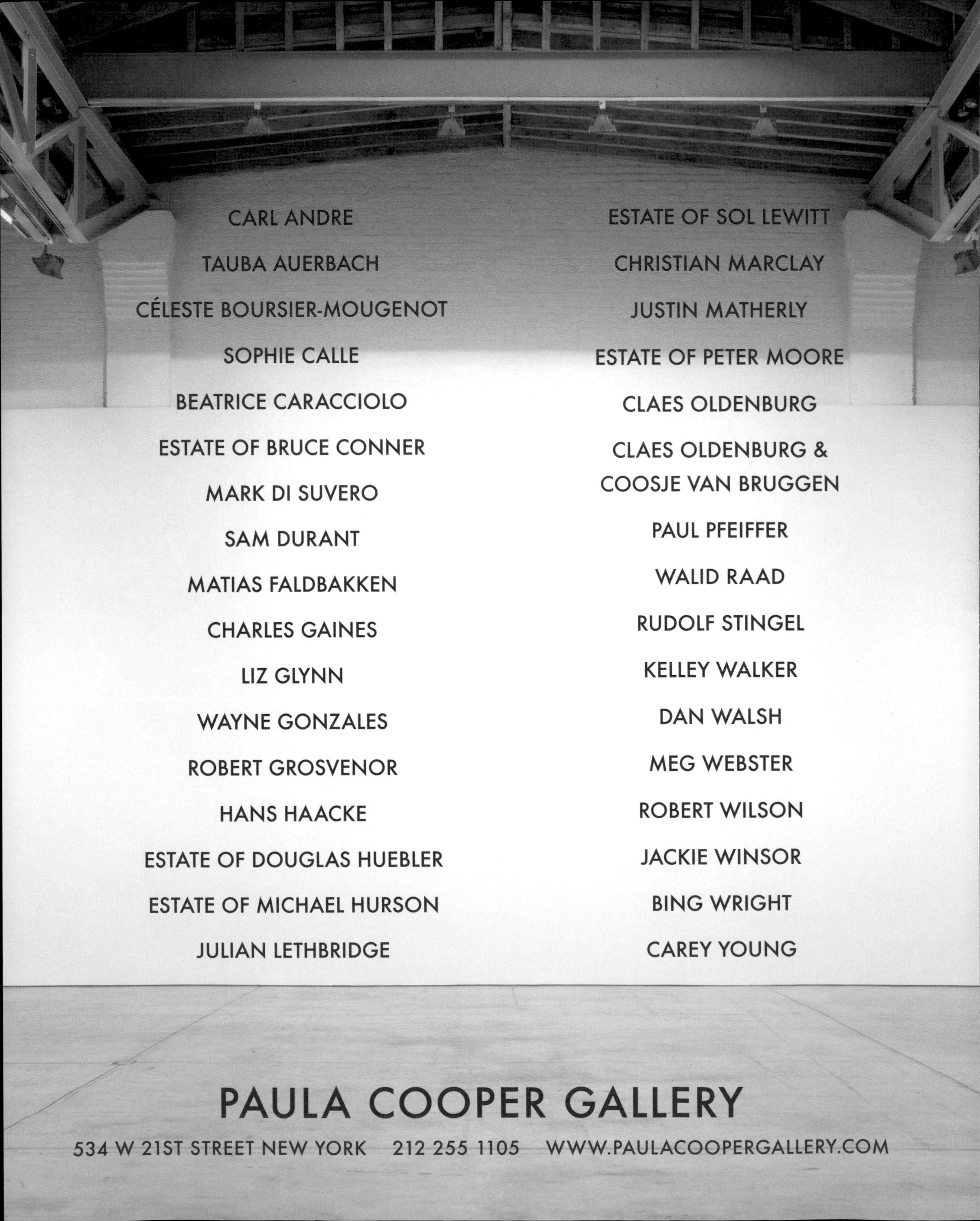

CARL ANDRE

TAUBA AUERBACH

CÉLESTE BOURSIER-MOUGENOT

SOPHIE CALLE

BEATRICE CARACCIOLO

ESTATE OF BRUCE CONNER

MARK DI SUVERO

SAM DURANT

MATIAS FALDBAKKEN

CHARLES GAINES

LIZ GLYNN

WAYNE GONZALES

ROBERT GROSVENOR

HANS HAACKE

ESTATE OF DOUGLAS HUEBLER

ESTATE OF MICHAEL HURSON

JULIAN LETHBRIDGE

ESTATE OF SOL LEWITT

CHRISTIAN MARCLAY

JUSTIN MATHERLY

ESTATE OF PETER MOORE

CLAES OLDENBURG

CLAES OLDENBURG &
COOSJE VAN BRUGGEN

PAUL PFEIFFER

WALID RAAD

RUDOLF STINGEL

KELLEY WALKER

DAN WALSH

MEG WEBSTER

ROBERT WILSON

JACKIE WINSOR

BING WRIGHT

CAREY YOUNG

PAULA COOPER GALLERY

534 W 21ST STREET NEW YORK   212 255 1105   WWW.PAULACOOPERGALLERY.COM

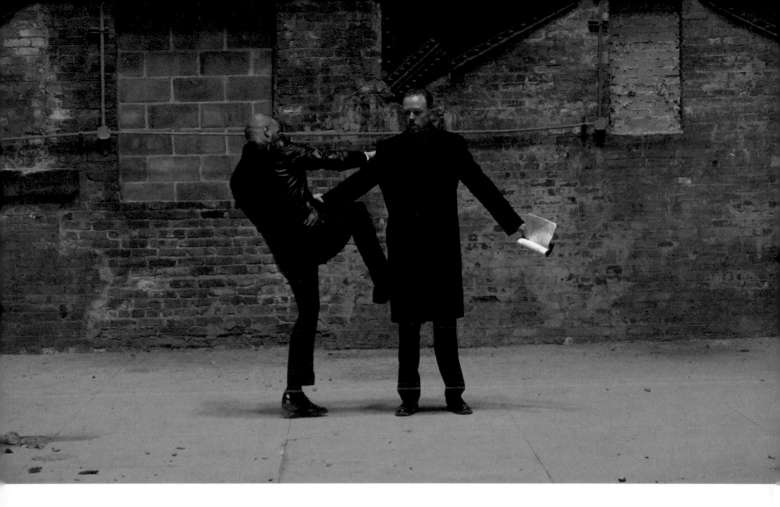

Uri Aran
Two Things About Suffering

01 September – 01 October 2016

Sadie Coles HQ
62 Kingly Street
London W1B 5QN

www.sadiecoles.com

Sadie Coles   HQ

GALERIA ■ HELGA DE ALVEAR

DR. FOURQUET 12, 28012 MADRID. TEL:(34) 91 468 05 06 FAX:(34) 91 467 51 34
e-mail:galeria@helgadealvear.com   www.helgadealvear.com

21 de enero - 16 de abril de 2016
Candida Höfer
The Space, the Detail, the Image

21 de abril - 15 de julio de 2016
Karin Sander
Kitchen Pieces

16-19 de junio de 2016
Art Basel 2016 I Booth P8
Elmgreen & Dragset

CENTRO DE ARTES VISUALES FUNDACIÓN HELGA DE ALVEAR

Jean-Marc Bustamante
Espacios transitorios
22 de enero de 2016 - 29 de enero de 2017

Cáceres, España

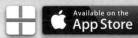 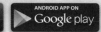

www.fundacionhelgadealvear.es/apps

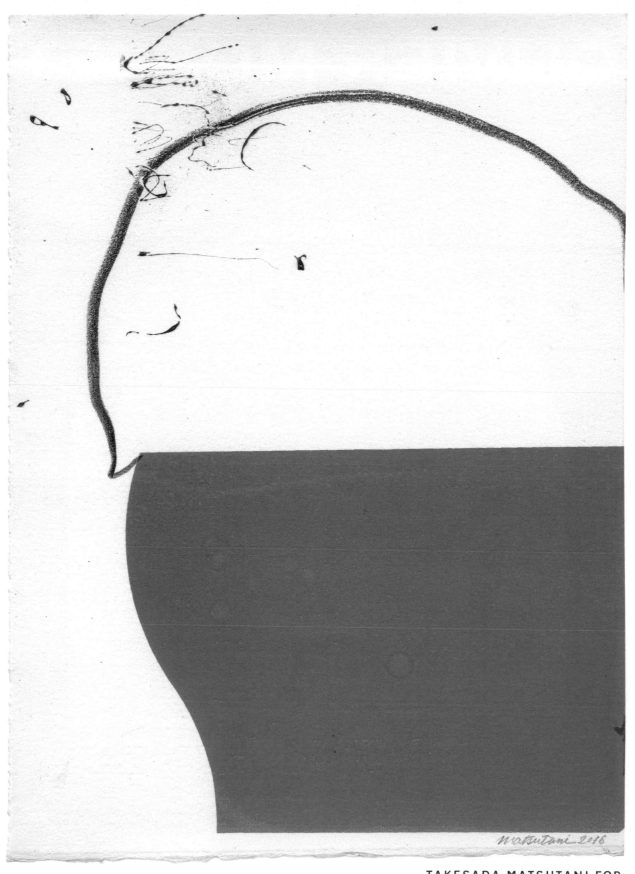

Matsutani 2016

TAKESADA MATSUTANI FOR
HAUSER & WIRTH

OLIVIER MOSSET

JUNE – JULY 2016

Olivier Mosset «Untitled» 2015, acrylic on canvas, 296 x 295.5 cm (116 1/2 x 116 3/8 in.)

GALERIE ANDREA CARATSCH   WALDMANNSTRASSE 8   CH-8001 ZÜRICH
TEL +41-44-272 5000 WWW.GALERIECARATSCH.COM WED–FR 11 AM TO 6 PM

LUCERNE	卢森	BEIJING	北京

Chen Fei
The Day is Yet Long
20.5. – 30.7.2016

陈飞
来日方长
20.5. – 30.7.2016

Shao Fan
Big Rabbit +
14.5. – 17.7.2016

邵帆
大兔子 +
14.5. – 17.7.2016

Christian Schoeler
26.8. – 5.11.2016

Christian Schoeler
26.8. – 5.11.2016

Yang Mushi
3.9. – 16.10.2016

杨牧石
3.9. – 16.10.2016

Hu Qingyan
18.11. 14.1.2017

胡庆雁
18.11. – 14.1.2017

Wang Xingwei
Honor and Disgrace
10.9. – 23.10.2016
Galerie Urs Meile,
Bejing-Lucerne @
Platform China

王兴伟
荣与耻
10.9. – 23.10.2016
麦勒画廊 北京-卢森 @
站台中国

新闻 NEWS

Not Vital
May 21, 2016 – January 2, 2017
Yorkshire Sculpture Park
West Bretton, Wakefield, UK

Yan Xing
June 3 – October 16, 2016
Eli and Edythe Broad Art Museum, Michigan State
University, East Lansing, USA

博览会 ARTFAIRS

Art Basel
June 16 – 19 | 2016
Hall 2.1, S12

Unlimited
Cheng Ran
In Course of the Miraculous

Galerie Urs Meile Beijing
No. 104 Caochangdi, Chaoyang district, 100015 Beijing, China
T +86 (0)10 643 333 93, F +86 (0)10 643 302 03

麦勒画廊 北京
中国北京朝阳区草场地104号, 邮编100015
电话 +86 (0)10 643 333 93, 传真 +86 (0)10 643 302 03

Galerie Urs Meile Lucerne
Rosenberghöhe 4, 6004 Lucerne, Switzerland
T +41 (0)41 420 33 18, F +41 (0)41 420 21 69

麦勒画廊 卢森
瑞士卢森Rosenberghöhe 4号, 邮编6004
电话 +41 (0)41 420 33 18, 传真 +41 (0)41 420 21 69

www.galerieursmeile.com
galerie@galerieursmeile.com

CARTE BLANCHE
by Pamela Rosenkranz
(Aug 2015 – March 2016)

Parkett collaboration artist Pamela Rosenkranz curates a selection of some 50 Parkett Editions and shares an insight into her artistic approach.

«CRUSH»
by Kilian Rüthemann
(Feb – July 2015)

An extraordinary presentation and sen-surround experience of selected Parkett Editions with over ten tons of turquoise-colored, crushed glass on the gallery floor and pedestals made of large glass chunks.

PEOPLE
(Feb – July, 2013)

The show explored the exhibition theme and illustrated with sixty works the innovation and diversity, that artists bring to their Parkett projects in manyfold variations.

CORNUCOPIA
(Aug – Dec 2014)

On the occasion of Parkett's 30 years all editions were presented for the first time together in one room in a special display at the Zurich exhibition space.

ABSTRACT —NATURE
(Sep – Dec 2013)

A playful dialogue among fifty selected Parkett works with unexpected, often enlightening relations.

SMALL IS BEAUTIFUL
(Feb – June 2014)

A never before seen selection of some seventy works from the past thirty years, that all embody one of Parkett's key feature.

IDEAS, VARIATIONS & UNIQUE WORKS
(Oct 2012 – Jan 2013)

Forty groups of works documented the range of imagination and unique-ness that artists bring to their Parkett projects in untold variations.

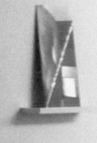

PARKETT SPACE ZURICH

The New Art Dealers Alliance (NADA) is the definitive non-profit arts organization dedi-cated to the cultivation, support, and advancement of... common...

newartdealers.org

Art | Basel
Basel | June | 16–19 | 2016

Galleries | 303 Gallery | **A** | A Gentil Carioca | Miguel Abreu | Acquavella | Air de Paris | Juana de Aizpuru | Alexander and Bonin | Helga de Alvear | Andréhn-Schiptjenko | Applicat-Prazan | The Approach | Art : Concept | Alfonso Artiaco | **B** | von Bartha | Guido W. Baudach | Berinson | Bernier/Eliades | Fondation Beyeler | Daniel Blau | Blondeau | Blum & Poe | Marianne Boesky | Tanya Bonakdar | Bortolami | Isabella Bortolozzi | Borzo | BQ | Gavin Brown | Buchholz | Buchmann | **C** | Cabinet | Gisela Capitain | carlier gebauer | Carzaniga | Pedro Cera | Cheim & Read | Chemould Prescott Road | Mehdi Chouakri | Sadie Coles HQ | Contemporary Fine Arts | Continua | Paula Cooper | Chantal Crousel | **D** | Thomas Dane | Massimo De Carlo | Dvir | **E** | Ecart | Eigen + Art | **F** | Richard L. Feigen | Konrad Fischer | Foksal | Fortes Vilaça | Fraenkel | Peter Freeman | Stephen Friedman | Frith Street | **G** | Gagosian | Galerie 1900-2000 | Galleria dello Scudo | joségarcía | gb agency | Annet Gelink | Gerhardsen Gerner | Gladstone | Gmurzynska | Elvira González | Goodman Gallery | Marian Goodman | Bärbel Grässlin | Richard Gray | Howard Greenberg | Greene Naftali | greengrassi | Karsten Greve | Cristina Guerra | **H** | Michael Haas | Hauser & Wirth | Hazlitt Holland-Hibbert | Herald St | Max Hetzler | Hopkins | Edwynn Houk | Xavier Hufkens | **I** | i8 | Invernizzi | Taka Ishii | **J** | Jablonka | Bernard Jacobson | Alison Jacques | Martin Janda | Catriona Jeffries | Annely Juda | **K** | Casey Kaplan | Georg Kargl | Karma International | kaufmann repetto | Sean Kelly | Kerlin | Anton Kern | Kewenig | Kicken | Peter Kilchmann | König Galerie | David Kordansky | Andrew Kreps | Krinzinger | Nicolas Krupp | Kukje / Tina Kim | kurimanzutto | **L** | Lahumière | Landau | Simon Lee | Lehmann Maupin | Tanya Leighton | Lelong | Dominique Lévy | Gisèle Linder | Lisson | Long March | Luhring Augustine | **M** | Maccarone | Magazzino | Mai 36 | Giò Marconi | Matthew Marks | Marlborough | Hans Mayer | Mayor | Fergus McCaffrey | Greta Meert | Anthony Meier | Urs Meile | kamel mennour | Metro Pictures | Meyer Riegger | Massimo Minini | Victoria Miro | Mitchell-Innes & Nash | Mnuchin | Stuart Shave/Modern Art | The Modern Institute | Jan Mot | Vera Munro | **N** | nächst St. Stephan Rosemarie Schwarzwälder | Nagel Draxler | Richard Nagy | Helly Nahmad | Neu | neugerriemschneider | Franco Noero | David Nolan | Nordenhake | Georg Nothelfer | **O** | Nathalie Obadia | OMR | **P** | Pace | Pace/MacGill | Maureen Paley | Alice Pauli | Perrotin | Petzel | Francesca Pia | PKM | Gregor Podnar | Eva Presenhuber | ProjecteSD | **R** | Almine Rech | Reena Spaulings | Regen Projects | Denise René | Rodeo | Thaddaeus Ropac | Andrea Rosen | **S** | SCAI | Esther Schipper / Johnen | Rüdiger Schöttle | Thomas Schulte | Natalie Seroussi | Sfeir-Semler | Jack Shainman | ShanghART | Sies + Höke | Sikkema Jenkins | Bruce Silverstein | Skarstedt | SKE | Skopia / P.-H. Jaccaud | Sperone Westwater | Sprüth Magers | St. Etienne | Nils Stærk | Stampa | Standard (Oslo) | Starmach | Christian Stein | Stevenson | Luisa Strina | Micheline Szwajcer | **T** | Take Ninagawa | team | Tega | Daniel Templon | Thomas | Tschudi | Tucci Russo | **V** | Van de Weghe | Annemarie Verna | Vilma Gold | Vitamin | **W** | Waddington Custot | Nicolai Wallner | Washburn | Barbara Weiss | Michael Werner | White Cube | Barbara Wien | Jocelyn Wolff | **Z** | Thomas Zander | Zeno X | ZERO... | David Zwirner | **Statements** | 47 Canal | Arratia Beer | Laura Bartlett | Johan Berggren | Bureau | Carroll / Fletcher | Selma Feriani | Foxy Production | Grey Noise | Maisterravalbuena | Mary Mary | Murray Guy | Ramiken Crucible | Micky Schubert | Société | Stereo | Simone Subal | Supportico Lopez | **Feature** | Bergamin & Gomide | Bo Bjerggaard | Campoli Presti | Castelli | Cherry and Martin | Chert | James Cohan | Corbett vs. Dempsey | frank elbaz | Derek Eller | espaivisor | Carl Freedman | James Fuentes | Grimm | Kadel Willborn | Löhrl | Luxembourg & Dayan | Jörg Maaß | Mendes Wood DM | Moran Bondaroff | Plan B | RaebervonStenglin | Lia Rumma | Salon 94 | Sprovieri | Barbara Thumm | Tornabuoni | Van Doren Waxter | Susanne Vielmetter | Waldburger Wouters | Wentrup | Zlotowski | **Edition** | Brooke Alexander | Niels Borch Jensen | Alan Cristea | michèle didier | Fanal | Gemini G.E.L. | Helga Maria Klosterfelde | Sabine Knust | Carolina Nitsch | Pace Prints | Paragon | Polígrafa | STPI | Three Star | Two Palms | ULAE

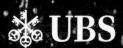

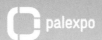

artgenève

SALONS D'ART

artmonte-carlo

call for applications

artgenève: 26 – 29 January 2017

artmonte-carlo: 29 – 30 April 2017

artgeneve.ch

14.–19. JUNI 2016

LISTE

79 Galerien aus 34 Ländern
*neu an der LISTE
Stand: März 2016

VI, VII, Oslo
80M2 Livia Benavides, Lima
Altman Siegel,
San Francisco
Christian Andersen,
Kopenhagen
Antenna Space, Shanghai
Aoyama/Meguro, Tokyo
Arcadia Missa, London
Balice Hertling, Paris
*Bernhard, Zürich
Blank, Kapstadt
BolteLang, Zürich
Carlos/Ishikawa, London
Clearing, New York/Brüssel
Crèvecœur, Paris
Croy Nielsen, Berlin
Ellen de Bruijne, Amsterdam
Dépendance, Brüssel
Document-Art, Buenos Aires
*Bridget Donahue, New York
Essex Street, New York
Agustina Ferreyra, San Juan
Fonti, Neapel
Freedman Fitzpatrick,
Los Angeles

Lars Friedrich, Berlin
Frutta, Rom
Gaudel de Stampa, Paris
Green Art, Dubai
Dan Gunn, Berlin
*Gypsum, Kairo
Bruce Haines, Mayfair,
London
High Art, Paris

Jeanine Hofland, Amsterdam
Hollybush Gardens, London
Hopkinson Mossman,
Auckland
House of Gaga, Mexiko-Stadt
Andreas Huber, Wien
Hunt Kastner, Prag
Instituto de Visión, Bogotá
*Jan Kaps, Köln
*Ellis King, Dublin
Koppe Astner, Glasgow
KOW, Berlin
Kraupa-Tuskany Zeidler,
Berlin
Labor, Mexiko-Stadt
*LambdaLambdaLambda,
Pristina
*Laveronica, Modica
Emanuel Layr, Wien
David Lewis, New York
Limoncello, London
Marcelle Alix, Paris
Jaqueline Martins, São Paulo
Mathew, Berlin/New York
Francesca Minini, Mailand
Monitor, Rom
Mor Charpentier, Paris
Mother's Tankstation, Dublin
*Murias Centeno, Lissabon
Neue Alte Brücke,
Frankfurt a.M.

NoguerasBlanchard,
Madrid/Barcelona
*Nominimo, Guayaquil
Office Baroque, Brüssel
Overduin & Co., Los Angeles
Project Native Informant,
London
Proyectos Ultravioleta,
Guatemala-Stadt
Dawid Radziszewski, Warschau
Raster, Warschau
Real Fine Arts, Brooklyn
Sabot, Cluj-Napoca
Sandy Brown, Berlin
Deborah Schamoni, München
Silberkuppe, Berlin
Gregor Staiger, Zürich
Stigter Van Doesburg,
Amsterdam
Temnikova & Kasela, Tallinn
The Breeder, Athen
*The Sunday Painter, London
*Michael Thibault, Los Angeles
Truth and Consequences, Genf
Federico Vavascori, Mailand

20 JAHRE HAUPT-PARTNER

E. GUTZWILLER & CIE BANQUIERS BASEL

DIENSTAG–
SAMSTAG
13–21 UHR
SONNTAG
13–18 UHR

VERNISSAGE
MONTAG
13. JUNI
17–21 UHR

BURG-
WEG 15
CH-BASEL
WWW.
LISTE.CH

Arch designed by James Stirling. Image selection: Pablo Bronstein. Photography Luke Hayes.

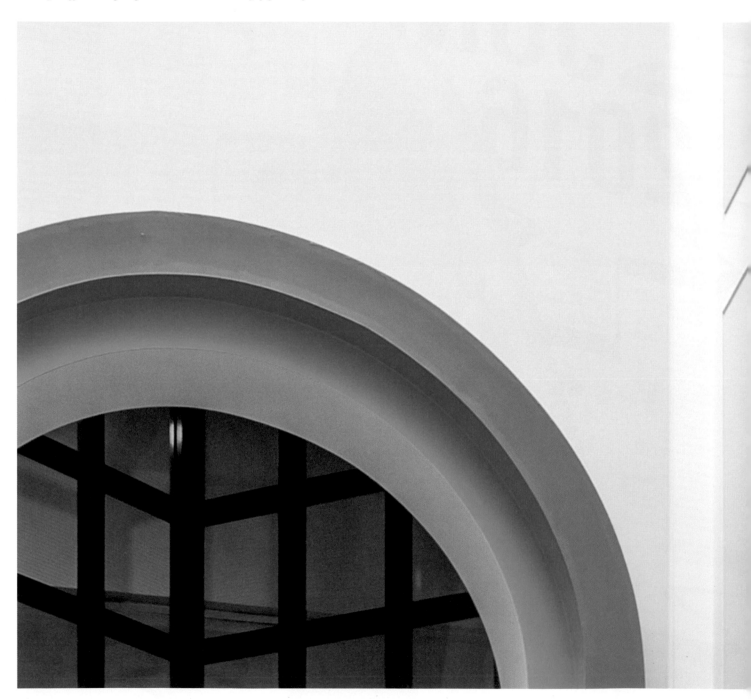

London

**Regent's Park
6–9 October 2016
Preview 5 October**

frieze.com

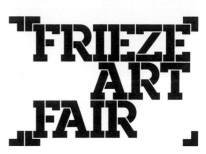

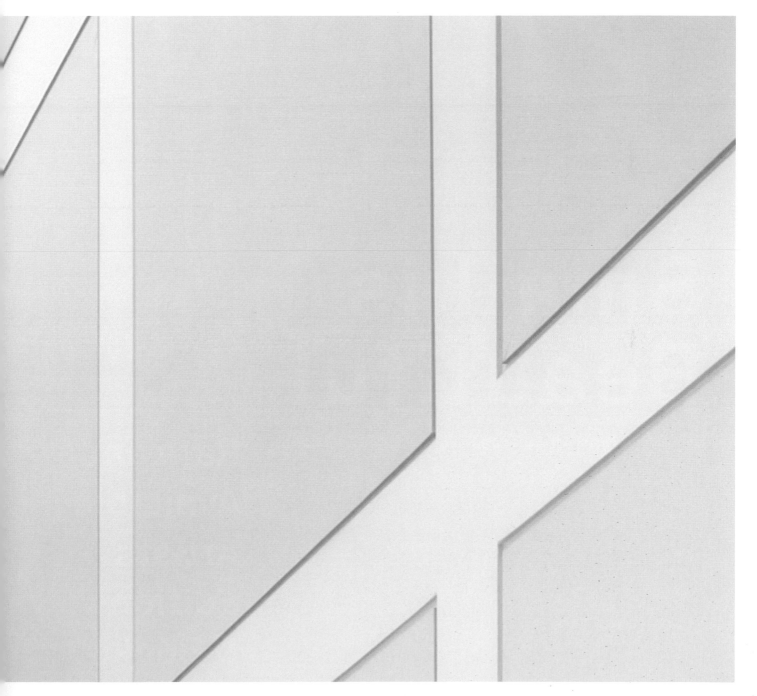

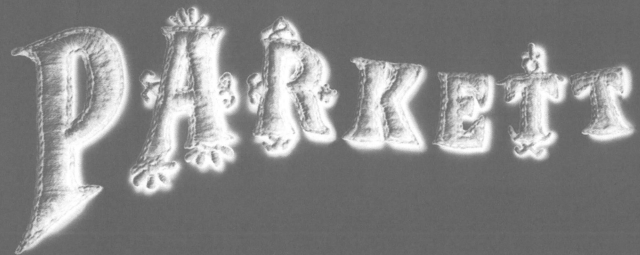

Small is Beautiful

A CABINET-LIKE PRESENTATION
ON VIEW AT PARKETT NEW YORK
BY APPOINTMENT

Parkett New York
145 Ave. Of the Americas New York, NY 10013
+1-212-673 2660

WWW.PARKETTART.COM

SELECTED
WORKS
& BOOKS
FROM
THIRTY
YEARS

**Rare and
Available
Artists'
Editions
& Books**

1984–2016

COLOGNE FINE ART

17. – 20.
November
2016

koelnmesse

Monopol mit Art Basel Sonderheft

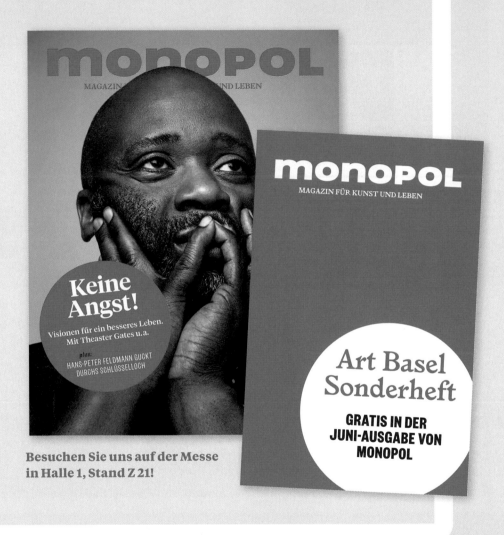

Besuchen Sie uns auf der Messe in Halle 1, Stand Z 21!

Art Basel Sonderheft

GRATIS IN DER JUNI-AUSGABE VON MONOPOL

Mit Ausstellungskalender für die Region, Shopping-Liste – Messe-Highlights im Check, Messeplan und Ausstellerverzeichnis sowie den besten Restaurants, Bars und Hotels.

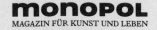

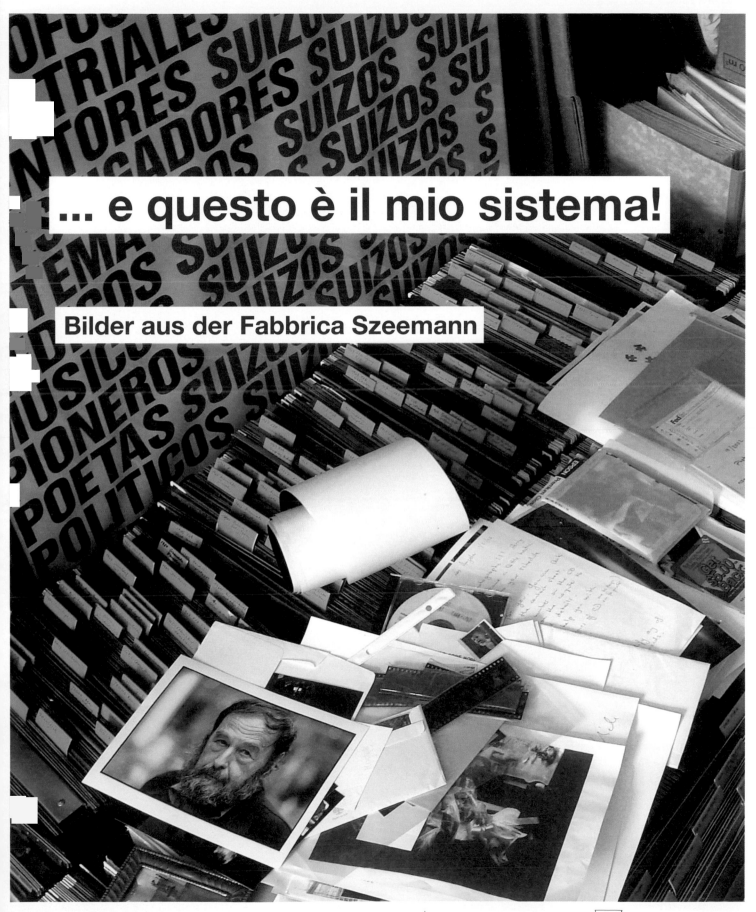

... e questo è il mio sistema!

Bilder aus der Fabbrica Szeemann

Fotos: Aufdi Aufdermauer / Hrsg. Karin Wegmüller   ★ video*company*.ch   Wolfsberg Verlag www.parkettart.com

**Reducing complexity
for a userfriendly experience.**

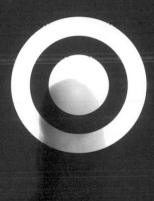

www.eyekon.ch

eyekon digital craft

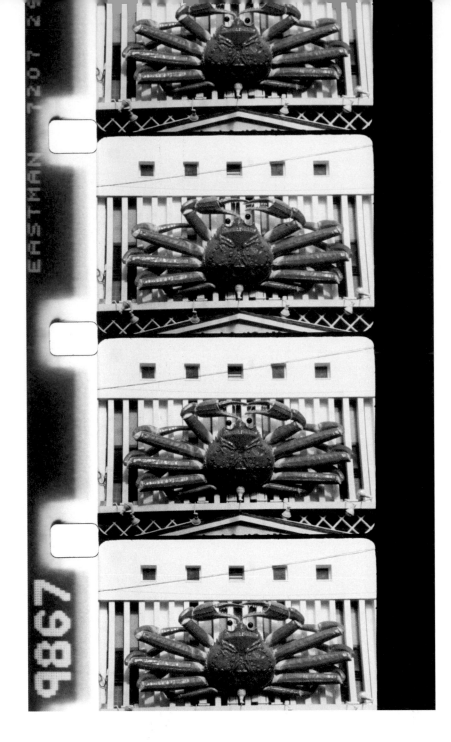

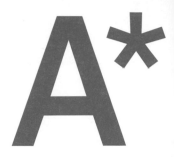

João Maria Gusmão & Pedro Paiva, *Crab*, 2016

*Aargauer Kunsthaus
30.4 – 7.8.2016

Aargauerplatz CH–5001 Aarau
Di – So 10 – 17 Uhr Do 10 – 20 Uhr
www.aargauerkunsthaus.ch

João Maria Gusmão & Pedro Paiva
The Sleeping Eskimo

Marta Riniker-Radich
Manor Kunstpreis 2016

CARAVAN 2/2016: Pauline Beaudemont
Ausstellungsreihe für junge Kunst

FONDATION VINCENT VAN GOGH ARLES

VINCENT VAN GOGH

VAN GOGH IN PROVENCE:
MODERNIZING TRADITION

14.05–11.09.2016

GLENN BROWN

SUFFER WELL

SASKIA OLDE WOLBERS

35ᵀᴱᴿ RUE DU DOCTEUR FANTON, 13200 ARLES
FONDATION-VINCENTVANGOGH-ARLES.ORG

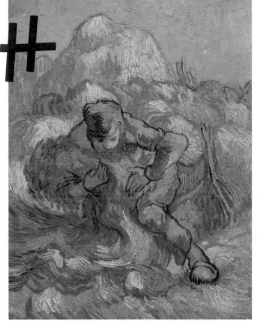

Vincent van Gogh, *The Sheaf-Binder (after Millet)*, Saint-Rémy-de-Provence,
September 1889. Oil on canvas, 44.5 cm × 33.1 cm
Van Gogh Museum, Amsterdam (Vincent van Gogh Foundation)

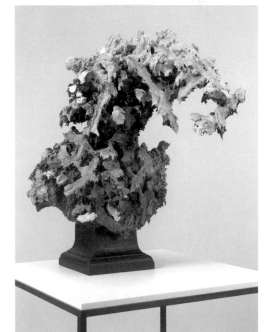

Glenn Brown, *The Hockey Cokey*, 2016
Oil paint and acrylic over steel structure and bronze
88 x 66 x 66 cm. Collection of the artist
Photo : Mike Bruce ©Glenn Brown

PETER FISCHLI DAVID WEISS: HOW TO WORK BETTER

9.JUN–4.SEPT.2016

WALID RAAD

13.OCT.2016–14.JAN.2017

GENERAL IDEA: BROKEN TIME

27.OCT.2016–11.FEB.2017

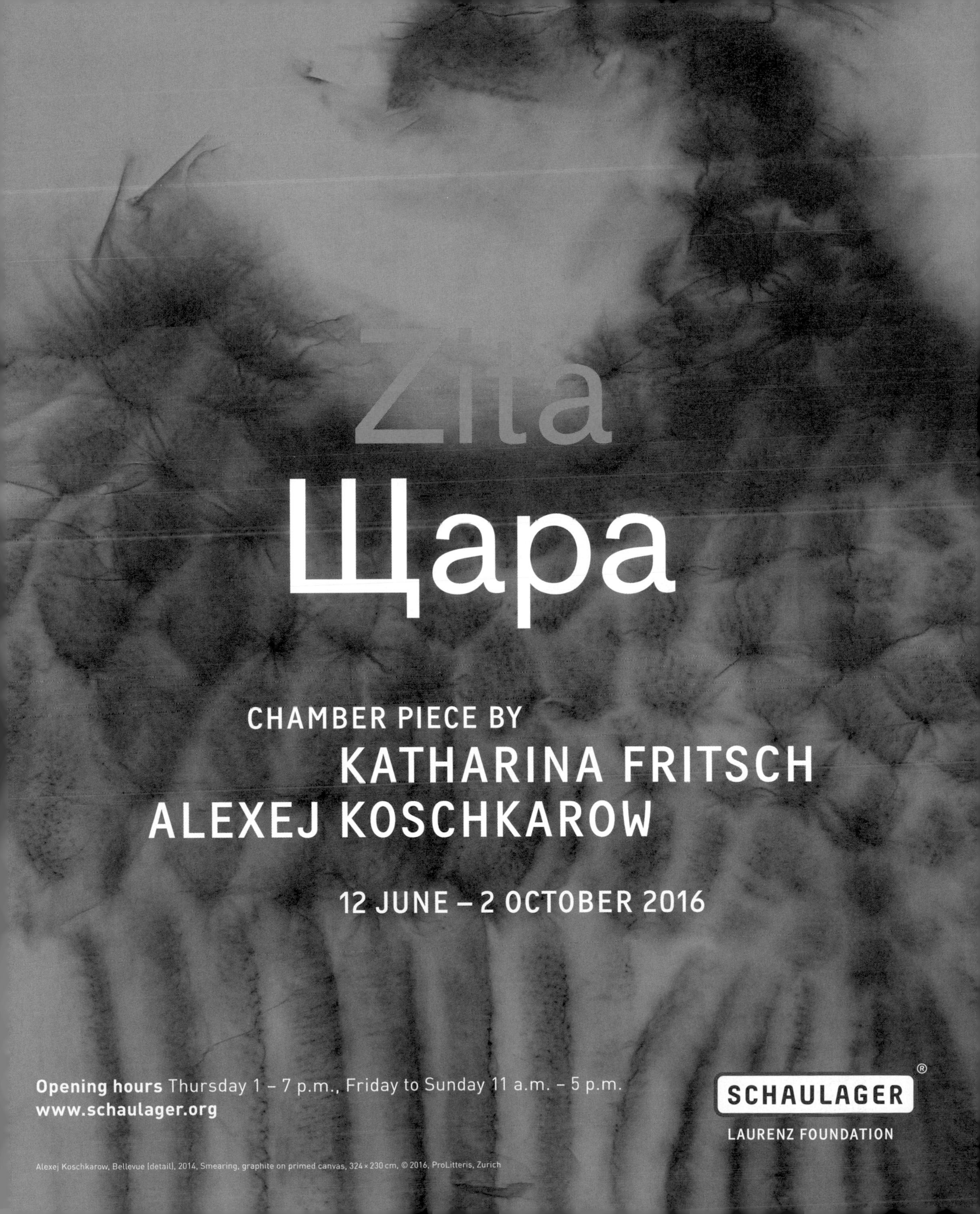

Zita

Щара

CHAMBER PIECE BY
KATHARINA FRITSCH
ALEXEJ KOSCHKAROW

12 JUNE – 2 OCTOBER 2016

Opening hours Thursday 1 – 7 p.m., Friday to Sunday 11 a.m. – 5 p.m.
www.schaulager.org

SCHAULAGER ®

LAURENZ FOUNDATION

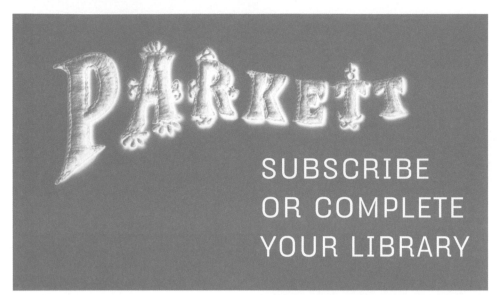

SUBSCRIBE
OR COMPLETE
YOUR LIBRARY

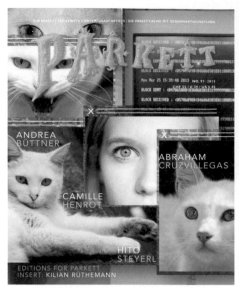

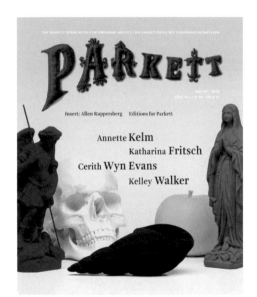

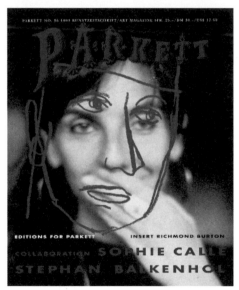

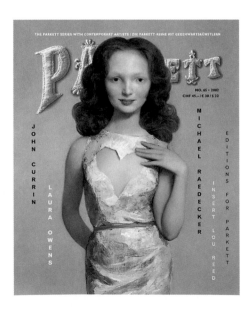

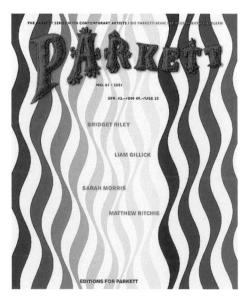

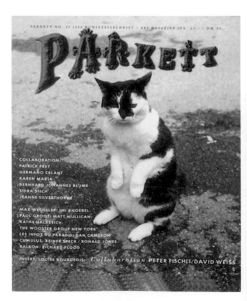

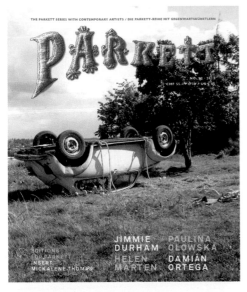

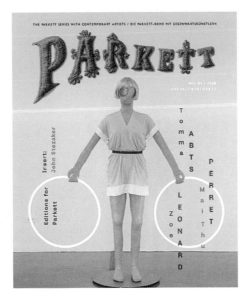

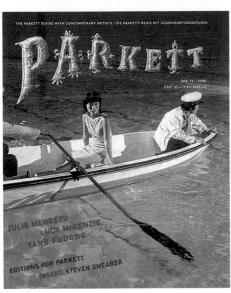

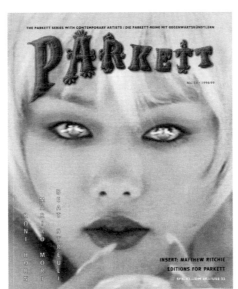

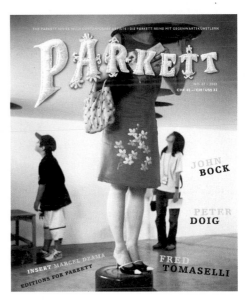

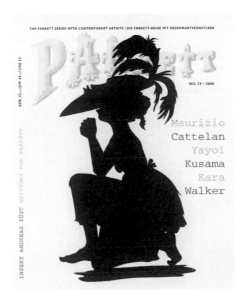

Items to be discussed at a formal meeting

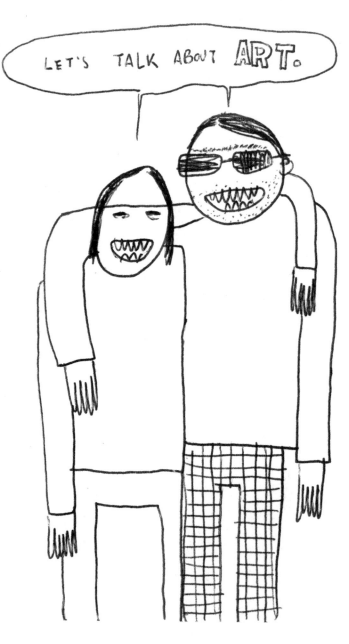

art
agenda

JOHN BALDESSARI

JUNE 11 - AUGUST 6, 2016

ZURICH CONTEMPORARY ART WEEKEND

June 11/12, 2016

ART BASEL - Art Unlimited

Pedro Cabrita Reis, *South Wing*, 2016

MAI 36 GALERIE

RÄMISTRASSE 37   ZÜRICH   +41 (0)44 261 68 80   MAI36.COM

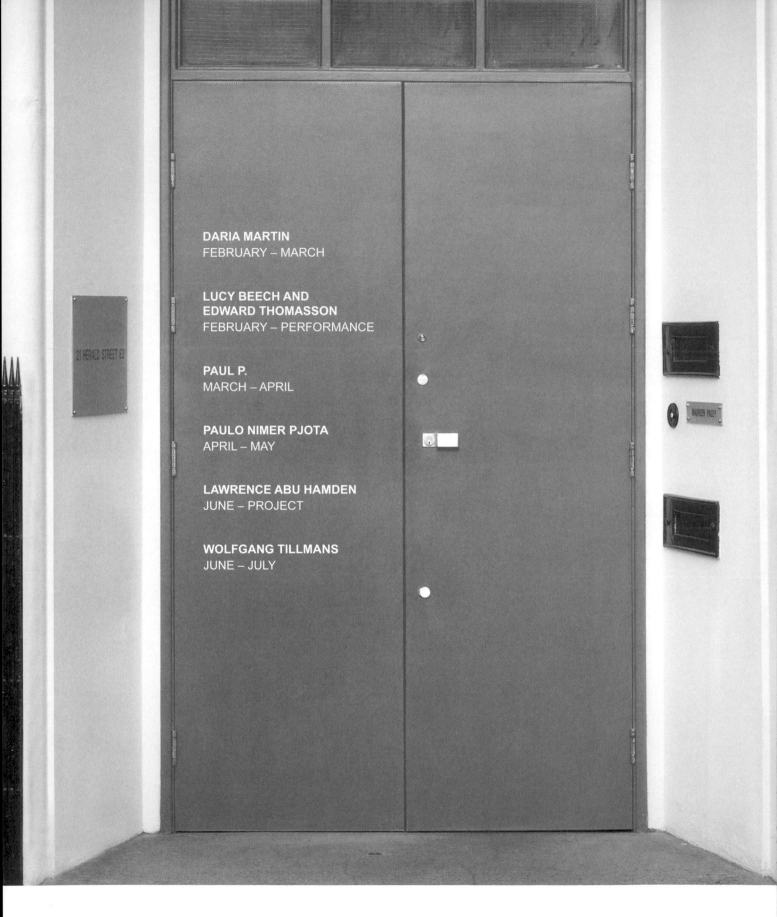

DARIA MARTIN
FEBRUARY – MARCH

LUCY BEECH AND
EDWARD THOMASSON
FEBRUARY – PERFORMANCE

PAUL P.
MARCH – APRIL

PAULO NIMER PJOTA
APRIL – MAY

LAWRENCE ABU HAMDEN
JUNE – PROJECT

WOLFGANG TILLMANS
JUNE – JULY

MAUREEN PALEY. 21 HERALD STREET, LONDON E2 6JT +44 (0)20 7729 4112 INFO@MAUREENPALEY.COM WWW.MAUREENPALEY.COM

JUNE TO JULY, 2016
JOE BRADLEY
MAAG AREAL

SEPTEMBER TO OCTOBER, 2016
JUSTIN MATHERLY
LÖWENBRÄU AREAL

JUNE TO AUGUST, 2016
WALEAD BESHTY
LÖWENBRÄU AREAL

SEPTEMBER TO OCTOBER, 2016
LATIFA ECHAKHCH
LÖWENBRÄU AREAL

JUNE TO AUGUST, 2016
TORBJØRN RØDLAND
LÖWENBRÄU AREAL

NOVEMBER, 2016 TO JANUARY, 2017
DOUGLAS GORDON
MAAG AREAL

SEPTEMBER TO OCTOBER, 2016
MICHAEL WILLIAMS
MAAG AREAL

NOVEMBER, 2016 TO JANUARY, 2017
ADAM PENDLETON
LÖWENBRÄU AREAL

GALERIE EVA PRESENHUBER

MAAG AREAL
ZAHNRADSTR. 21, CH-8005 ZURICH
TEL: +41 (0) 43 444 70 50
OPENING HOURS: TUE-FRI 10-6, SAT 11-5

LÖWENBRÄU AREAL
LIMMATSTR. 270, CH-8005 ZURICH
TEL: +41 (0) 44 515 78 50
OPENING HOURS: TUE-FRI 11-6, SAT 11-5

WWW.PRESENHUBER.COM

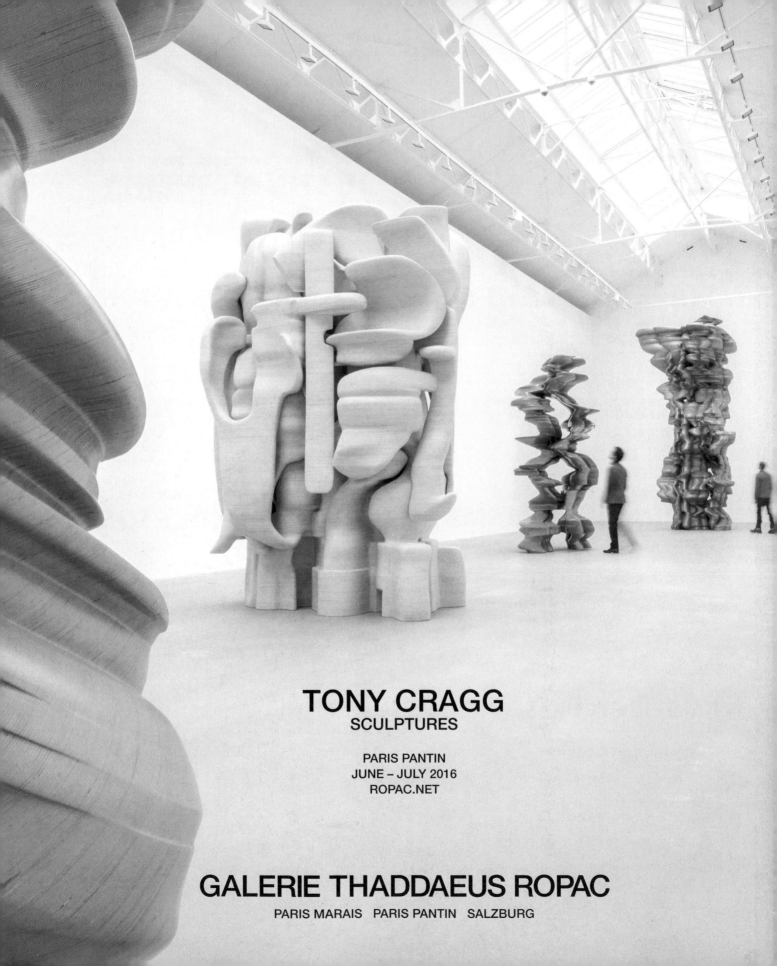

TONY CRAGG

SCULPTURES

PARIS PANTIN
JUNE – JULY 2016
ROPAC.NET

GALERIE THADDAEUS ROPAC

PARIS MARAIS   PARIS PANTIN   SALZBURG